Acknowledgements and dedications

DLAB would like to thank many incredibly awesome people for their support and patronage. There are so many people to thank that they won't all fit on one page, so you'll find many more patrons on the final page—and that's still not everyone. To name everyone who has contributed would take ten pages. The people mentioned here and on the final page are those that backed the print edition of this book, but a massive thank you goes out to all of you. Without your support, this book would not have been possible...

A super special thanks to these nice people/animals . . .

Ash's parents, Chris and Elaine, who helped him fulfil his need to draw ladders and vampires at a very early age, and whose gift of an Amiga introduced him to the world of games. Big brother and esteemed DNF James. Patricia and Frankie. Little sister, Fiona and her big fella Lee. Screwball nephew Mason and recent addition Sienna. And of course Jack, for the thirteen years of awesome he gave to us.

A massive thank you to Elinor's parents, distinguished doctors Pamela, John and to future-doctor Isaac. To the esteemed Molly, Emma and Mr Squish. To all the rats we have known: Hammockman, Straightlineman, Babels (Deutschesfilmorkester Bablesberg), Loki, Rogan, Rich Whoop, Poor Whoop, Pebbles, Marius the Blue, Shambles the Wikky Witch, Odin, Crumbwell, Hector and Loud Mouse.

To people around the world that we took a particular liking to: Scott Haban, David Cumberbeach, Kaz Wright, Rachael Walker, Mark Davidson, Steve Mckinney, Ealasaid A. Haas, Anthony Rigg, Elizabeth Verbraak, Holly Renaud, Greta Dusenbery, Niclas Forsen, Michael and Emma McDonald, Ben Knuchel, Michelle Kelley, Caitlin Stuff, Rick Harmsen, Hannah Ward, Mike Brown, Dorian Iten, Kuzmenkox Alexey, Alan Gust, Jennifer C. Menough, Victoria Chan, Raven Daegmorgan, Jared and Jennifer Simms, Matt Combs, Gianluca G, Julie Nix, Eric Bright, Dennis Fitzgerald, Röbin Kaser, Pendleton Ward, Kate Beaton, Brian Fargo, Ryan North and...

Lewis Whoopler MD · Chris Sauro. Google Inc. · Dylan Sisso, Pixar Studios · Fightmaster General · Jason L Perry · Isis Godfrey-Glynn · Kamal Shaheen · Richard Sweat · Jonathan Martin · Scott McCray · Haley McDonald · Peter Carli · Max Fischer · Kit Ho To · David Clingman · Marjie Myrtle Marmito · Daniel Ley · Rebekah Bernard · Philippe Labouchère · Martin Walker · David A Black · Rafael Dives Perez · Mehfouz Jalal · Pavel Koutny · Gordon Flack · Sean Hernandez · Michel De Ligne · David Luong · Ilan Shredni · Ryan Sukdeo · David Morse · Richard Bullen · Tasha Turner Lennhoff · Diana Godinez · Volodymyr Shulgin · Pixel Academy · Lora Makowski · Alex Padwick · Michael Crane · Austyn Hill · Mary Tindle · Phillip Shoemaker · Darren Cahill · Jim Lee Wei Min · Bjorn Mates · Andrew Watt · Ed Kinsella · Colleen Foley · Daniel Contelmo · Bessie Dai · R.L. McCormick · Barbara Williams · Matthew Sheahan · Kathryn Prentice · Patrick Krum · Michael Machado · Jasmine Choinski · Sherman Tsao · Ellen Scheffers · Ahad Al Saud · Max Wallace · Alan Wisbey

Nicolas Krause · Danny Krog · Rohan Khanna · Laura Marler · Mirco Franz · Rich Palij · James Reed · Matthew Kroen · Tara Morrigan · Jason Hunter · Nol van Meegeren · Patrick Taylor · Allen Taylor · Hannah Driscoll · Eduardo Calenda · Melvin White · Marie Butcher · Paul Lynch · Nicole Mezzasalma · Austin Howe · Bryan Gough · Patricia Rowley · Myles Musser · Rodolphe Duhil · Gabriel Perez · Charles Veile · Stephane Perriard · Benjamin Kristensen · Terry Cooke · Olof Johansson Ström · Mark Mackenzie · Cody Blaschke · Mathew Connelly · Stig Bergan Solholm · Al Meyer · Athena Dyer · Stephen hanrahan · John Hussey · Rob Lugton · Chris Janes · David W Lesko · Michael Tidman · Frank Stanley · Pavel Khlopin · William Dovan · Barbro Maria Westlund-Storm · Francis Le Nguyen · Leslie MacKrell · Cameron Merrick · Micah Rose · Heather Blandford · Doug Hanke · Mike A. Buchanan · Django den Boer · Jeremy Harrison · Laure-Élie Parent · Matt Cody · Rabih Yazbeck · Val Reid · Robert Sjoblom · Marco Rosenberg · Owen Shifflett

Gary Warner · Ann-Sofie Åkerlund · Ben Bruce · Chris Tursi · Julien Gravoulet · Marius Sorli Finnstun · JD Smith · Erika Ruhl · Gerardo Vazquez Jr · Damian Scisci · Kate Fitzpatrick · Paul Arneil · Guan Ming Puah · Alexander Wyatt · Michael Tucker · David Lucardie · Dr. Liviu Constantinescu · Tom Fogarty · Willard Korfhage · Kevin Chan · Daniel Snyder · Christopher Dale · Jeremie Gobeil · Jennifer Day · Jeremy Halvorsen · Arden Clare · Bryce Archer · William Howell · Christopher Pospieszalski · Laurel Kamps · Aron Silverstone · Bart Jones · Alex Williams · Beth Cameron · Truman Simpson · Philip Peterson · Mouin Quiroz · Muhamad Haiz Shamsudin · Miguel Angel Casanova Morales · Hamish Smith · Ramona Brass · Bak Cyril · Beauvais Yang · Vano Chu · Leonard Eshuis · Jacques de Rohan · Carsten Goldbæk Nielsen · David Robert · Victoria Lantz · Jason Lee · Joseph Wilson · Manny Hernandez · Alasdair Mackenzie · Adam Sear · Stephanie Wagner · Alisa Khomyanina · Alan Lee · Stefan Pugliese · Jessi Baughman · Adrian Arias-Palomo · Daniel J. Hutchings · Andrew Martinez

Chris Tierney · Parker Seney · Antti Hallamäki · Alexzandros Lee · Dr K M Franklin · Stephen Tyler · Amy Mack · Justina Iglesia · Stephanie Tran · Ed Sherman · Kuzmenkov Alexey · Edouard Lombard · Tarik Layous · Cesar Antonio · Kevin Lai · David Han · Ciarán Spillane · Jakub Petko · Brian Huizingh · Simon Gerrard · Dr. Gerhard Fertl · Hudson Shires · Madeline Carol Matz · Eduardo Skinner · Sean Gannon · Anuj Amin · Michael Burkhead · Jonathan Withnall · Becky Coker · Justine A Racine · Michael Pleier · Glenn Feunteun · Eric Norlander · Stina Leijonhufvud · Cody Bradford · Carrivale Remi · Steven Bakker · Nicholas Irish · Koen Blanquart · Alexander Kashev · Devin King · Nicholas Deadman · Eleanor Cove · Robert Walter · Paul Whitfield · Matthew Mcfadden · Damian Gordon · Marc Alexander · John Allison · Malgorzata Mider · Helle Thusing · Asher Morgan · Mujammil Khan · Albert Badosa Solé · Justyna Jablonska · James Dale · Gareth Matthews · Tzion Schlossberg · Joe Fusion · Nascom · Michael Nadig · Toby Chang

Paul Cook · Dan Kukucka · Zachary Tan · Andrew Schramm · Richard Davis · Maciej Napieraj · Tim Schurig · Bram Tanamal · Stephen Young · Pete Gutierrez · Justin Lindsey · Rod Fage · Jude Hoffpauir · John Hines · Christopher DeFrisco · Cianan Sims · Carl Christensson · Michael Bishop · Sean Buckley · Greg Cooksey · David Lawson · Carlos Plana Mario · Francis Isidoro · Clinton Rowe · Gopal Metro · Neil Johnson · Emmanuel Aquin · Dan DeLano · Christel Macabeo · Jon Gow · Lila Sadkin · Kristin Olson · Robert Wesley · David Martinez · David Irvine · S Gabbidon · Sam Hirbod · Michael Van Wagener · Antonio F. Pardinas · Mitchell Spivak · Michael Lein · Stefan Hanrath · Chas Euchner · Megan Crewe · Jonathan Arnould · Owen Collier · Francisco Zafra García · Amanda St.Germain · Niall Benzie · Christopher Goff · Adam Ryan · Ruth H Ballard · Gareth Ujvarosy · Julius Ang · Rob Bain · Lewis Allard · Chris Chow · Andrew Kratochvil · Robert Altomare · Alper Atik · Ian McShane · Hope Lewellen

Amit Ginni Patpatia · Margaret Alcock · Taroh Kogure · Cameron Owen · Faisal Naqvi · Atiqah Kamal · Thomas Krech · Fei Leung · Oluf Nissen · Currie Higgs · JD Mion · Ryan Ung · F. John Guerrero · Melinda Smith · Sven Nilsson · Hagar Michaeli · Felix Knischewski · Malte Sussdorff · Vikam Modhwadia · Simon Rossmann · Zsombor Nagy · Helge Gudmundsen · Warner Liu · Michael Twomey · Suzanne Mcendoo · Jeff Wells · Jessop Hunt · Vincent Kueszter · Joe Louie · Cristin Weber · Cristina Spottswood · Alice Maillet · Mike Gonzales · Leo Castillo · Bjørn Sandåker · Elke Habets-Dobben · Erik Bolton · Noah Guyot · Kevin Handa · Robert Vaughan · Adam Bonell · Helton Laurentino Silva · Dana Rae · Melissa Leff · Shawn Kehoe · Chris Chin · Pamela Hichens · Subashini N · Theresa St. Romain · Andrew McHaffie · Jason Truxal · Philipp Dortmann · Ethan Pistella · Stephan Huez · Fernando Otero · Filipe Rita · David Brandt · Timothy Leung · Crystal Chuang · Allison Jones · Adam Robinson · Danny Joseph Patrick Reid

Anna Gold · Ramon Ribas · Simon Nyhus · Elise Catlin · Michal Puto · Becky Felton · Daniel Stampfl · Camilla Saccucci · Alexandra Mariner · Alexander Livingstone · Emilie Garant · Annika Lewin · Mike Nudd · Jessica McGinn · Laura Martin · Dr Maggie Parker · Christiane Nusch · Clive McGrath · Nick Harsum · Tyler Gibson · Daniel Varela de Almeida · Alexis Yang Xinyan · Sarah Howes · Untereiner · Jean-Philippe Poirier · Rainer Angerer · Mikael Stokkebro · Cyan Fullbrook · Wouter Goedkoop · Rachael Binns · Muhtasim Shahriyer · Michele Krause · Karmen Olmo · Annette Berglund · Zero Harker · Mac Senour · James Matuszak · Simon Baldwin · Lindsey Campbell · Jeong-Eun, Park · Marcel Klink · David Ward · Dan Lamphear · Michael Jones · Gary Mcmurray · Mike Rominski · Emilyn Ouch · Fabio Scrocca · Steve Wesley · Britt Hohn · Ian Kobe · Linda Làng · Daniel Rose · Babie Dron · Molon Christelle · Caroline Herdman-Grant · Michelle Brennan · James Warburton · Seamas Dore · Shane Bostick · Noel Arnold

Alex Calara · Shannon McKinnon · Diogo Calado · Peter Gagnon · Daniel Recke Lauritzen · Jeff Skalski · Joe Karame · Liam Rooney · Jose M Bielza · Mikael Hagström · Karl Portman · Alex Panganiban · Jason Gailans · Samantha Chye · Peter Kretschman · Calle Jesus · Cally Lim · Shen Nanzhen · Alesha Unpingco · Nicholas Crawford · Kat Coffey · D. Pitcher · Spontaflex Kurt Wyss · Jonas Rasmussen · Jasmine V · Gareth Butterworth · Felix Thaler · Adrian Harper · Hannah Irons · Philip Hotton · Megan Wiseman · Spike Martin · Catherine Dock · Ken L Tang · Tad Wisenor · Stephen Lee · Grace Bermejo · Kevin Barfield · Paul Bosch · Chris Webster · Laurie Morrison · Toni van den Munckhof · Rebecca Chui · Michael Calabro · Emilia Hald · James Mcle · Donna Downey · Chris Garrett · Olaf willoughby · Jarret Fuchs · Lucy Stanton · Dylan Tevardy-o"Neil · Dr David Whitehead · Joanna Hobbs · Celia Lichtenstein · Charlie Lukman · Josefine Liljerum · Oliver Gaines · Corbin Rogers · Kathy Huang · Javier Alonso Gómez · John Eresman

The world of Drawcraft is a silent, windy place beyond words, alive with feeling. Whether the gale howls love or pain, the stronger the emotion, the truer the motive, the more powerful the magic.

⟁✕✕⬚⬡✎⸰⸲✕✕∨⸱⊙ⱦ⊙⧻⸱∨⬚⊙✕

DRAW
Like a BOSS

A Journey in Drawing Awesomely

ASHLEY EDGE & ELINOR ROOKS

dlab

Key

Listed below are the pins we will encounter as we journey through this book. These provide a quick signal of what we can expect from the text attached to it.

 Boss Key — Super critical info! Look out for Marius the Boss key. He will always endeavour to impart some wise information.

 Tetraforce — When this symbol appears, it means a fundamental principle of the drawing process is being discussed.

 General info — This and that about so-and-so.

 Important stuff — Very useful bits of know-how.

 Equipment — Takes a peek at a piece of equipment.

 NO! — Flat out, don't do it!

 A common problem — Mentions a possible drawback or an obstacle that blocks our path.

 'Big Lok' — This means we have just met one of the colossi. A colossus is a big entity that can either aid us or become an obstacle, blocking the path until they are defeated.

 Demonstration — Gives step-by-step instructions that you can follow along with. There are 43 demonstrations to check out. More about this on the next page.

 Science talk — Looks at the parallels between art and science.

 Closer observation — A more in-depth account of this and that.

 Recommended collectables — Resources and references to consider when constructing your own little atelier (studio).

 Special powers — Learn new abilities!

 History — A little background info.

 Obvious Panda — Obvious Panda apologises for saying something so incredibly obvious. He could, for instance, have been applied to the description of the 'Equipment' pin.

The demonstrations and exercises will have degrees of difficulty ranging from the easiest (Silk Curtain 1) to the hardest (Demon Door 6).

1. Silk Curtain

Ultra easy mode.
This obstacle is a breeze. We can pass it with our eyes closed.

4. Shadow Door

Hard mode.
Be on guard with this one, there could be a trap.

2. Wooden Door

Easy mode.
This task shouldn't pose too much of an obstacle.

5. Arcane Door

Extremely difficult.
Be prepared for a real challenge.

3. Reinforced Wooden Door

Moderate difficulty.
This obstacle is a little harder to crack!

6. Demon Door

Whoa now! Steady on!
Things are hotting up with this Hard-core difficulty level!

This chap to the left isn't a door. This is Guido Bachsmechs, a fearless wanderer. We will follow him as he makes his way through the World of Drawcraft. Along the way, we will encounter many other personalities. Some will aid his quest. Some won't . . .

"Sucking at something is the first step towards being sorta good at something."

— Jake

Introduction

Welcome Adventurer

There are many ways to draw, and over the course of this book, I will present you with the particular methods that I have found to be consistently effective. I hope that this book will help you to better understand and enjoy drawing, because there's no better feeling than when a subject such as this finally 'clicks' into place. The discipline of drawing is rich enough for a lifetime of discovery and delight, and for that reason I will always consider myself a student. However, throughout the following pages, I will put on my teacher's cap and endeavour to pass on what I have learnt so far.

This book aims to offer a comprehensive introduction to the fundamental techniques that underpin classical drawing. I hope to make these techniques as accessible as possible, while also giving you an enriched, rounded appreciation of this art. You will be led, step by step, through exercises which will not only enable you to build your skills but also help you to understand the underlying principles at work. You will also find historical background, scientific explanations, and some musings on the philosophy of drawing. You will encounter characters who embody certain principles, obstacles and approaches, in the hope that they will help to bring these concepts to life, making them more memorable and meaningful.

These pages contain everything you need to learn in order to produce highly realistic drawings, both from observation and from your imagination. However, while I am offering to be your guide and while this book imagines us travelling together, this is, nevertheless, a journey you must make alone. Even if you were to learn under a master artist, working with them in a studio, ultimately it would still be your choices that dictated what kind of artist you became. The most significant choices involve the amount of time and effort you are willing to devote to your practice.

As you progress, you may find that you get stuck, lost or frustrated. Don't worry: getting lost is an essential part of any journey, and you should be prepared for it to happen from time to time. In these moments of difficulty, it can help to think of learning to draw as a quest: this book throws you out into the wilderness of drawing so that you can get productively lost. You will most certainly make mistakes along the way, but this book is set up so that when you fall, you will at least fall forwards and not back.

Welcome to the World of Drawcraft, and more specifically, this mountain! However intimidating it may seem, that's what we're going to climb. Some of the ascent is shrouded in mist. It is our job to move past those misty, mystifying barriers that obscure the path.

Cue Dramatic Adventurer Music!

We join intrepid adventurer Guido Bachsmechs, who is attempting to scale the highest peak of Drawcraft so that mastery over drawing will be his to wield. As you can see, he's fully prepared. Look at that bag! Fully loaded up with all the bits of kit he thinks he needs to scale this mountain. Let's take a peek at what he's lugging around.

From left to right

Toilet roll, paintbrush, pencil, blending stump, colour shaper, mahl stick, lead pointer, stencil, bread, chamois leather, plastic eraser, kneadable eraser, electric eraser, paper, fine tipped mechanical pencil, stick eraser, clutch pencil, graphite powder.

When beginning the ascent of this draughty mountain, people often get a little fixated on which equipment to pack in their inventories. There are so many types of papers, so many fancy pencils and brands to choose from. The essence of this journey is getting back to basics, so for now we'll be setting the subject of equipment aside while we try to understand and come to terms why we and Guido might be setting off on this adventure in the first place. As it happens, this is not the first time he has attempted this journey. Like many of us, he began and abandoned this quest long ago. Let's examine why this might have been.

Why do we lose interest in Drawcraft?

Fatigue is a common reason for giving up drawing, and fatigue can set in for many reasons. We may have been using unhelpful methods, without knowing how to fix our mistakes. We may have come frustratingly 'so near, yet so far.' Maybe we were just written off as totally hopeless. Whatever the reason, fundamentally, we suffer from being unable to make drawings 'look right.' What it ultimately comes down to is that drawing involves so many variables; it's easy to lose control. For that reason, we need an approach that will simplify things and keep us in control of the drawing.

I wasn't an experienced climber at all, but I had all the fanciest gear. I was so excited when I started out, but it was already proving to be far harder than I had imagined. I was getting nowhere, and my confidence was beginning to waver.

You've Been Here Before

Talk about drawing and most adults will tell you they "can't draw." This doesn't really make any sense, though. Drawing isn't something you either can or can't do: instead, drawing ability develops along a continuum, where the infant learning to grip a crayon is at Level 0 and a master draughtsman is Level 10. If you can hold a pencil and make a mark, you must fall somewhere on this spectrum, even if it's just Level 1 or 2. If you can accept that, then it means we're already getting somewhere: if you're on the scale, it means there's a possibility for improvement.

The most important thing to know, as we begin, is that it's always possible to learn. No dog is too old for new tricks. This is thanks to "neural plasticity," which is the brain's ability to form and strengthen connections between neurones at any age. The latest research shows that the human brain never loses its ability to develop these connections, and this process of making neuronal connections is what we experience as learning, improving skills, and forming new habits. Literally, changing our minds. You have begun reading this book so may I be the first to congratulate you on changing your mind.

You've probably begun climbing the Mountain of Drawcraft at some point in your past, but for our purposes, we're going right back to basics, assuming no prior knowledge. First, though, let's take a closer look at some points along the continuum to see where things might have gone wrong for you.

Level 1 — *Natural born scribbler*

Most of us begin our ascent before we learn to walk, when we first play with crayons and other mark-makers. We start with scribbles. Scribbling was so much fun. I have pages I 'coloured' when I was three where the printed outline is totally hidden under purple crayon. Gradually, we gain more control over our mark-making, and forms start to emerge—but these forms are wild, out of control. This is still mark-making for the joy of it, and there's a very slippery, loose relationship between the marks and any meanings assigned to them. I've had a child tell me what they're drawing, only to have them tell me it's something completely different by the time they're done. It's magical to make a mark where there were none before (like on the wall). Can you scribble and enjoy it? Then you have achieved Level 1 in Drawcraft.

Level 2 — *Enjoyer of symbols*

As we develop, we begin to care more about the relationship between our drawings and the world. We want to produce drawings which recognisably reference external objects, real or imagined. Yet how can we reproduce the three-dimensional world in two dimensions, with blunt crayons? We bridge this gap between subject and representation through the use of symbols, which we absorb from the culture around us. Squiggly blue lines are water; the bar of green at the bottom of the page is grass; and a circle with lines coming out is the Sun—or a spider?

Scaling the cliff, I noticed strange scratches covering it. At first they seemed random, natural, but as I climbed they developed into primitive symbols. Ascending to the next ledge, I noticed something. It was a dinosaur, crude but recognisable. This dinosaur marked the highest point I had reached many, many years ago. I was so close to beating my personal best!

At this stage in our development, we are also learning to speak, becoming adept at breaking the world up into words. This linguistic development feeds into our picture-making. We begin to take our visual experience, which is essentially just patterns of colour and shape, and break it down into discrete objects, which we can then reference and tell stories about. This symbolic language allows us to express ourselves quite directly, and at this stage, we are relatively untroubled by the disconnect contained within symbolism: that is, the difference between the sign and that to which it points. We've drawn a tree that looks nothing like the tree outside, but this doesn't bother us yet, so our use of symbols remains free-flowing.

Symbols are fun to play with, but the problem here is that, once we learn the symbolic system, we never forget it. If we want to progress to the next level of drawing and learn to draw from observation, we do have to unlearn it to an extent. This creates a painful, frustrating difficulty. Now, symbolic drawing has its uses. It allows us to communicate many ideas with powerful simplicity, something cartoonists use to great effect. Their very efficiency can be a problem, as we can find ourselves compartmentalising experience too easily, relying on generalisations, assumptions and prejudice. Symbols can interfere with direct observation, and they become a major obstacle to drawing.

Level 3 — Specialisation: Class change to either academic or artist

The jump to Level 3 is a difficult one, so difficult that it can look less like a step and more like a wall. This is the critical point at which we become anxious about making our drawings match our observations. This requires a whole new repertoire of techniques quite distinct from those developed at the symbolic stage. If we don't learn these techniques, we tend to get stuck, and drawing changes from being something fun into being an activity that makes us feel impatient, dissatisfied and inadequate.

For many, this critical stage happens around the ages of ten to twelve. The timing of this crisis isn't random: it coincides with the beginning of a shift from childhood towards adolescence and with changes in schooling, which bring more focus and pressure on 'academically worthy' subjects. Unfortunately, many children have a greatly reduced access to art education around this time (along with musicianship and other artistic pursuits), which only compounds the problem.

As we age, we are pushed towards ever narrower specialisations, so that eventually almost all creative activities and interests fall away or become relegated to hobbies. Most of us lose sight of drawing altogether. Don't worry, though: our creativity may become dormant, but never extinct, the story of drawing isn't over until we can no longer grip a pencil in our hands (or feet or mouths!).

I surmounted the second level, which was a great relief. However, the third level was just too much for me—surely only a giant could reach that platform! I lost my grip and began to slide. As I grappled desperately for a foothold, an awful realisation seized me: I could not scale this monstrous mountain!

The question of 'can you or can't you?'

Sp, when we are asked whether we can draw, it is not a 'yes' or 'no' answer. There are steps we can take towards success and levels to reach that will help us to understand what our strengths are and what obstacles there are yet to overcome. We must walk the straight road before we venture into wilder terrain. On the straight road, you will learn the basics: structure, simplicity and accuracy. It's time to go back to the beginning. In returning the beginning, nothing is lost and there is much to gain.

You Lost All of Your Equipment!

Weighed down by his pack and struggling to scale the sheer rock face, Guido tumbled down off the mountain, plunging into a snowdrift. Happily for our hero, he hadn't actually climbed very high at all, so it was a short fall, and the snow was soft. So soft that, as he struggled to free himself, he had to untangle himself from his huge pack of fancy artist equipment, and the heavy bag sank down, down into the snow, irretrievably lost. It was all gone, apart from two objects stuffed into his pockets . . .

Fortunately, a pencil and some paper is all we need to start this quest. What really matters is that we focus on mastering fundamental drawing techniques and not succumb to distraction of worrying about what tools we need. Mastering the concepts of line, light and form, as well as learning to make your own artistic and technical choices in response to the challenges of drawing, is what matters at the outset.

Art teachers, shoes and good advice

When I was young, I was given some advice, and I totally ignored it. It came from my high school art teacher, who was obsessed with getting the class to draw their own shoes. His whole approach to art seemed to revolve around shoes. Maybe that's why I didn't listen when he finally said something useful, in the form of a shoe analogy: "Athletes competing on the track aren't fast because they have expensive running shoes; they are fast because of all the training they've done."

Unfortunately, the same teacher had also just gotten me hooked on a device known as a blending stump, which I thought was the key to creating great drawings. Beware the excitable young artist who has access to blenders, for they will rush into shading, regardless of whether or not their drawings are structurally sound. This is what has happened with all those weird celebrity pencil portraits you can find online, the ones that are slightly off and a bit creepy. I never drew spooky pop stars, but for years my drawing wobbled along on shaky foundations. Thankfully, along this quest we have some friends to guide us.

'Okay', I thought to myself, 'I give up. I want to go home.' Feeling utterly defeated, I rose to my feet and patted the snow from my coat and trousers.

I had begun to trudge off home when I stumbled against something hard: a chest! I rose to my feet and reached out to open the chest, which, oddly enough, was already unlocked.

You Found a New Companion!

Curious, Guido heaved open the heavy chest and peered inside. There, hopping excitedly up and down, was a little key. Eagerly, he sprang to Guido's shoulder. Somehow—Guido could not understand how this could be possible—he heard the key speak, a wise little voice inside his head. "I am Marius," the voice told him, "Marius the Boss Key, and I will be your guide." Keep your eyes out for Marius, and for the advice he imparts. You will find this in the green text boxes, as below:

"Set yourself to practice drawing, drawing only a little each day, so that you may not come to lose your taste for it, or get tired of it . . . Do not fail, as you go on, to draw something every day, for no matter how little it is, it will be well worthwhile, and will do you the world of good." — Cennino Cennini

Practice

To improve your drawing ability, you need to practice. For all that drawing is ultimately a creative, expressive pursuit, development requires a degree of determination and focus. To maintain your skills, it's also important to keep drawing. Practice and repetition create new neural circuits, like wheels wearing a new pathway. For the same reason, certain basic principles will be repeatedly reinforced throughout this book, to help you learn them.

'Just as iron rusts from disuse; water loses its purity from stagnation, even so does inaction sap the vigour of the mind.'

— Leonardo da Vinci

Please don't feel discouraged by this, though. Don't tell yourself you have to commit to gruelling hour-a-day drawing sessions. Instead, resolve to set aside small sessions of practice. You might begin, for instance, by promising yourself 15 minutes of drawing a day for a month. However busy we are, we can almost always find 15 minutes—and it can be immensely rewarding. For an extra insight, try to keep a log in your sketchbook of every day that you draw. Note how you feel physically, mentally and emotionally before your 15 minutes of drawing, and then how you feel afterwards.

Creative Dojo — Having a space set up so that you can pick up where you left off is a great way to stay in artistic shape. One of the keys to practice is to try to find ways to ensure you are enjoying it simply for its own sake, and sitting down in a relaxing environment always helps.

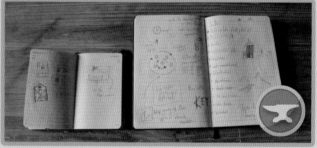

Sketchbooks and art journals are essential for jotting down thoughts and feelings, as well as for developing preliminaries and concepts. The journal can never be underestimated as a tool for personal development. Store what inspires you, even if it doesn't seem like much of an idea—it may come in handy in future. Journals are like a farmer's field, a place to sow ideas that you can later harvest by leafing through them. Look back to see what might be relevant to your next project, or what ideas might set you off in whole new directions. This book you're holding right now, for instance, was born of all the ideas I noted down over the years. Without journals, it would never have been written.

Chances are good that you will notice a consistent improvement in your well-being after your drawing sessions. People who do this are also more likely to stick with their practice. Your daily sessions don't have to produce finished drawings. You might want to try little studies where you tackle particular problems or work to build certain skills. As well as studying technique, make sure you also take time to draw just for pleasure: we need equal measures of practice and enjoyment here. Studying can involve frustration, so we need to take time out to let rip and have fun with drawing. As Leonardo writes in his diary, "The supreme misfortune is when theory outstrips performance." In drawing, enjoy the journey, and the destination takes care of itself.

As I sat down to nurse my sore back, Marius, my key companion, suddenly went bouncing off through the snow. Following him with my eyes, I noticed a large door set into the side of the cliff. I certainly hadn't seen that before. Perhaps it was revealed in the small avalanche created by my fall? A snowstorm was beginning, and it seemed wise to take shelter. Climbing the mountain seemed to be out of the question, so I decided to follow Marius' lead, and explore behind the door.

Just as when he was twelve, the usual way of conquering this mountain has failed Guido once more. What he has found instead of victory is a path that will lead him back to the beginning, allowing him to build his powers of Drawcraft from the ground up.

Let's spin the camera around to get a look at the side of this mountain. Beyond this door (A) is a passage that will deliver Guido to the starting point (B) of his steady climb to the peak. From this direction, he will find reaching the top much easier, as the slope is no longer so extreme. Each one of these steps up the mountain represents a different level in our development. There are sixteen levels in all.

The door was already open and required no key. We entered the dark passage that would take us through the mountain. As I walked all I could think of was my failure to scale the peak. This triggered memories, ghosts from my past that haunted me as I proceeded down the dimly lit passage. Perhaps it wasn't my fault I failed, maybe my training was to blame.

Schooling

Educational Systems

Just as most adults will say they can't draw, most will also claim that they are not creative. Who gave them this idea? Modern education systems are not fundamentally interested in individuality or creativity. Emerging from the Industrial Revolution and European empires, mass education ensured every child learned the same basic skills and was taught the same basic values. Literate, numerate, punctual, and used to following instructions: children from these schools could become useful workers anywhere. With a little more training, they could also become civil servants anywhere in the empire. Similarly, by exporting educational systems across their empires, powers such as Britain and France were able to disseminate imperial values and 'marketable skills' globally. When you hear politicians talk about 'preparing students for the job market' so that the nation can 'compete in the global economy,' it's clear this tradition is alive and well, setting lots of standardised tests.

+2 Rant

> If you cannot presently draw very well, the only thing that has happened is that you haven't been taught a useful method. Art schools, that should know better, often substitute a study of artistic principles for a focus on self-expression, in an attempt to promote a personal style before it has been given time to grow by itself.

I would certainly agree with Ken Robinson when he argues that these old-fashioned models of education actually educate us out of creativity. Creativity is not something you either have or have not got, it is a quality which may be cultivated or discouraged. Our creativity isn't gone, however, just subdued, and with encouragement it can re-emerge. All that is required is that we return to the very beginning of the Drawcraft story, rather than relying on shaky ideas or bad habits that have remained with us since we stopped pursuing advancement in this particular artistic discipline.

 DRAW LIKE A BOSS

I found something strange in the next chamber, a blazing torch that must have been recently lit. I lifted it from a sconce on the wall and peered along the passage. Lining the walls was a procession of carved figures, all identical, marching deep into the shadows. All but one of them had a coat draped over its shoulder. I took one for myself and ditched my own heavy, wet coat.

Of course, there have been strong efforts within modern education to focus more on the development of individual potential, on nurturing creativity, critical thinking and curiosity. The struggle, in many nuanced forms, continues in almost every educational setting. When we wonder why we find drawing difficult—or creative writing—or any kind of playful, original activity, much of the answer can be found in the endless hours we spent at school, learning to sit still and become useful employees. We're here, now, to try to undo some of that process.

+1 Rant

For many people, the education they received becomes something that they must recover from after they leave school and its stifling, outdated curriculum system.

Schools dedicated to art

Even if artists pass through high school unscathed, with their creativity intact, there is still a potential for this to become impacted and misguided. Conformist education also helps to explain a problem with many fine art schools: they emphasise individual expression while offering no technical instruction. When a classmate in my university Fine Arts course asked when we'd learn painting techniques, she was told she should join a hobbyists' club. This extreme rejection of technique is a reaction against the pressures of earlier education. Learning techniques is not, however, an obstacle to creative expression; rather, it will facilitate your discovery of your own unique style.

What Marius told me sort of made sense. I reasoned that perhaps I was creative, but I was still sure I was definitely not talented. Perhaps this snazzy coat would help me at least look like an artist.

Faulty Genetics

"There's no way I can draw," you might argue. "Talent just isn't in my genes!" After all, the great artist Gian Lorenzo Bernini's father was a sculptor, Wolfgang Amadeus Mozart's old man was a composer and music teacher, and Pablo Picasso's daddypops was a professor of Fine Arts. Which means talent is something you're born with, right? Or does it simply mean that these people grew up in an environment that nurtured their creative abilities? What looks like innate giftedness is much more likely to be the result of early exposure, encouragement and guidance.

Talent is something we can make for ourselves. The ingredients are enthusiasm, sound knowledge and consistent practice. Ability to draw is not a mysterious gift that springs from a mystical ether.* It is a skill we develop, over time and with patience. If we begin our adventure believing in a series of discouraging myths, however, we will have failed before we have even begun. We need experience, and to gain that experience, we need a degree of confidence and optimism.

GENETICS MYTH

Ignore snobs. Innate creative ability is a myth, and quite an unhelpful one at that.

+5 Dispel Myth

> "I have no talent. I'm only passionately curious." — Albert Einstein

"Talent is just another name for the love of a thing," as Daniel Pankhurst put it. The basic principles of drawing are simple, and anyone can learn them. If you love drawing, then you will have the motivation to master these first principles, incorporate them into your practice—and then you will be able to go on to create unique, interesting work. If you are able to look at a drawing—your own or someone else's—and know whether it 'looks right' or not, then you are capable of becoming just as discerning as any great artist. Seeing what's wrong is the first step to being able to fix any problems, judge the quality of your work, and develop.

+10 Don't Listen to Marvin

> "In order to be a great artist, you simply have to be a great artist. There's nothing to learn, so you're all wasting your time. Go home." — Marvin Bushmiller

*Michelangelo di Lodovico Buonarroti Simoni (of Sistine Chapel fame) would have you believe otherwise, that he was in fact divinely inspired. His biographer, Giorgio Vasari revealed that the artist actually burned many of his drawings "so that no one should see the labours he endured and the ways he tested his genius, and lest he should appear less than perfect."

No Encouragement

Maybe You Were Made Shy by the Marvins of This World

All this talk about seeing mistakes may be making you nervous. Many people suffer from fear of not being good enough, and this can become an obstacle in any area of life. It can be particularly difficult, though, when it comes to self-expression. Drawing can be very personal, and this can make criticism painful. It takes bravery to share our personal work with others because it leaves us vulnerable.

As we develop, we are like flowers blossoming—and the more we blossom, the more exposed we become. Negative feedback can have the effect of a frost, causing the flower to wither or close. A wintry self-criticism may well set in, leaving the flower reluctant to bloom again.

The chilling effect of criticism is sad, and if this is something you have experienced, I hope to encourage you, to help create a warmer, more encouraging atmosphere. You don't need to share your drawing, now or ever. It can be deeply satisfying to produce artwork just for yourself, in your journals.

HARSH CRITICS

−5 Confidence in your own ability.

There's no way to undo the effect of past discouragement, but we can learn to recognise and resist excessive self-criticism. Towards this end, here are two affirmations to tuck away in your journal.

+4 Confidence

1 "Rest your head and keep your mind cheerful." — Leonardo da Vinci

+4 Confidence

2 Do your best to resist anticipating failure.

You're such a loser.

Who said that? Was that you Marius?

Hearing more voices wasn't a good sign. Thankfully, I reached the end of the dark passage to encounter what must have been the heart of the mountain. I could see a huge cavern, and beneath me I saw a fiery caldera, bubbling with lava. I didn't need the torch to see, but holding it up made me feel reassuringly like an adventurer. Holding my totally redundant torch aloft, I gazed into the cavern. What I saw astounded me . . .

Drawing is Fundamental

John Ruskin once called drawing "dirtying the paper delicately." What importance can this really have? Why should we draw? Why should we take so much trouble and time over things as basic as a pencil and paper?

Drawing is fundamental to every visual art. Learning to draw is a necessary prerequisite to becoming an effective artist, one who can organise and express their thoughts on paper. By embarking on this journey, you are beginning to rediscover your ability to be visually expressive.

Drawing is a challenge. It will take some time to get back in touch with playing in this way again, and it will take lots of practice to master the skills I will be teaching you here. The truth is, drawing never becomes truly effortless. No matter how easy some artists make it look, there is always a degree of challenge involved: this is what makes it worth doing in the first place. With focused practice, you will one day become an artist of refinement and sensitivity. You will be able to express yourself more deeply and to experience the world more sharply. As you produce art, you will also gain truer insight into the works of other artists, appreciating which are great and why. A lost world is here to be explored.

As we embark, remember the power of the stories we learn and tell. We have stories attached to almost every aspect of life, influencing our experiences and actions. Some stories make life richer and more meaningful. Other stories make our lives smaller, poorer and meaner. From prejudices to excessive self-doubt, to myths of talent, these harmful stories can do a lot of damage. The act of drawing, to some extent, breaks through these stories, quietens them for a spell. Instead, it encourages us to focus on seeing, on really seeing what is there. The ability to draw beautifully is secondary to this ability to see. Drawing is a method by which we can connect more fully with the world.

I hope you will find this book thought-provoking, entertaining, challenging and rewarding. I hope it will introduce you to old and new ways of approaching difficult ideas. Drawing isn't easy, but this book will help you find your way and sidestep common obstacles. There's a wonderful magic to conjuring up worlds and life through the strategic application of graphite to paper. Take the instructions in this book, and use them as the beginning for your own journey into this ancient, surprising discipline: only you can determine in which direction your drawing will eventually take you. Explore, experiment, and enjoy.

+4 Okay, already! I'm confident

> "To practice any art, no matter how well or badly, is a way to make your soul grow. So do it." — Kurt Vonnegut

Enjoyment + Focus = Learning

As we've discussed, when we learn new things, we change our brains: the brain remains extremely malleable throughout our lives, able to form new connections between neurones. Similarly, if we avoid practicing bad habits, those connections get weaker and fainter. Neural pathways are a little like actual paths, created through use—and very heavy use can create deep ruts in the path. When we get caught in old, familiar and unhelpful behaviours or thoughts, we really are getting stuck in a neural rut. It takes time to erode old paths and wear new ones, but it's very possible.

+3 No brainer

If we are enjoying the act of learning, then chemicals such as dopamine are released into the brain, and these help in the construction of new networks. Learning something interesting is rewarding, and rewarding chemicals accelerate learning.

When learning is pleasurable, this also helps us to maintain focus. Focused attention is another factor that helps the brain to become more malleable and to form new connections more efficiently. Therefore, it's clear that we should find ways of making practice enjoyable. With drawing, this may involve little changes to your environment or to your subject matter. Keeping it fresh and fun will help you draw better.

Draftsman's Tech Tree

To master advanced techniques, you must first grasp the fundamentals. Drawing is the fundamental skill underlying every branch of the visual fine arts, from painting and printmaking to sculpture and film. Drawing is at the root of visual arts because it deals with value, which is at the root of our visual perception. Visually, our spatial awareness depends mostly on value; colour is actually secondary to our perception of greyscale. So, to drawing we must first turn. Now let's turn the page and have a gander at this Tetraforce tech tree . . .

On a far wall at the opposite end of the inner sanctum was a colossal statue pointing to a perplexing design. Nearby was an inscription made in a language I could not decipher. On another wall were strange circles all arranged in rows. Someone must have already been here, because beneath each circle, the meaning behind it had been decoded and written on the wall. A bit of luck for once!

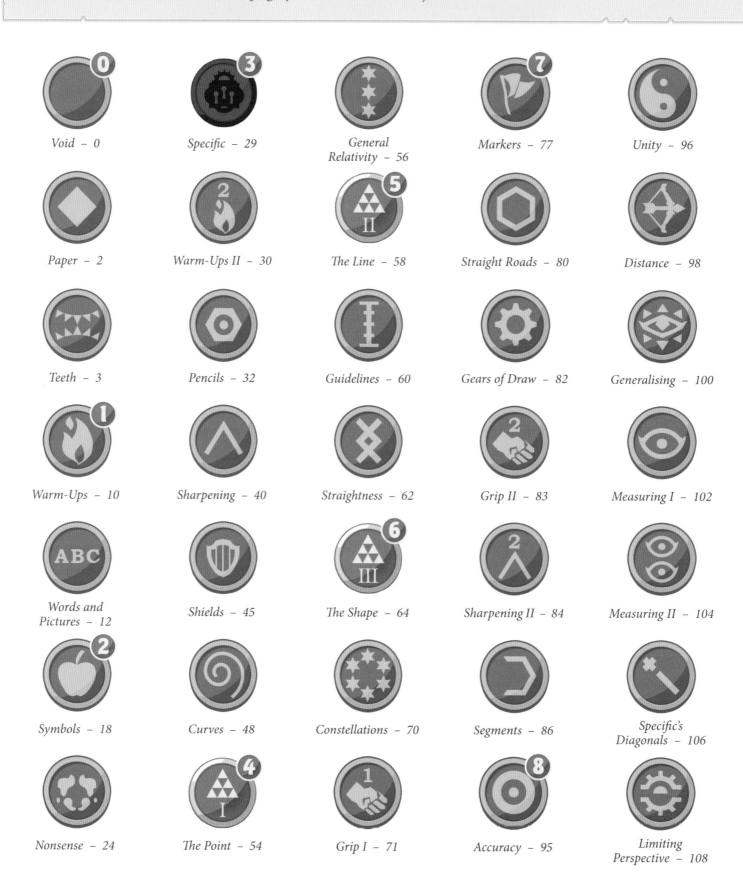

Measuring III – 111

Time – 138

Dark Void – 160

Reflected Light – 180

Musical Tones – 198

Relative Brightness – 242

Ellipses – 114

Checking In – 140

Shadow Anatomy – 164

Tonal Triad – 185

Light – 200

Mastery – 255

2.5D Drawing – 117

Shadow Point – 146

Exploring Hatches – 169

Midtones – 186

Highlight – 214

Copying I – 256

Portraiture – 123

Shadow Line – 148

Open Hatches – 172

Specific II – 189

Blenders – 218

Copying II – 258

Contour – 133

General Shadows – 149

Hatch Direction – 174

3D Elementals – 190

Depth – 227

Copying III – 266

Lost and Found – 134

Shadow Shape – 152

Dark Unity – 176

Planes – 192

Veiling – 228

Copying IV – 268

Grip III – 136

Black Mass – 153

Keying – 178

Spectrum – 197

Erasers – 230

Discovering a Studio – 278

This is not the complete story of drawing, merely the parts I think will intrigue and encourage you to take your drawing further. It is best to proceed in this order rather than skip ahead at any point as doing this may lead to receiving **+10** confusion.

Graphite and Diamond

Before we pick up our pencils, I'd like to introduce you to the history behind this humble yet mighty instrument.

Graphite was first discovered in the 16th century: the seam in the English Lake District, known as the Borrowdale graphite deposit, remains the purest ever discovered. At the time, people believed it was a new kind of black lead, so they called graphite 'plumbagoi,' from the Latin word for lead, 'plumbum.'

In the past, lead was actually used for mark-making by none other than the Romans, who were a little lead-crazy. So crazy, in fact, that they used this toxic metal for making water pipes, makeup and artificial sweetener. A number of people have died in the past from lead poisoning after using a pencil—but not from the 'lead' itself! Rather, the problem was with the lead paint used in coating pencils: when people sucked or chewed them, it could mean game over. Although the misconception lingers on in our language, happily there is no lead in pencils. Graphite is itself completely non-toxic.

+5 Doh!

> The Borrowdale deposit remains the only seam of solid, pure graphite. Initially, local farmers used this phenomenally rare and precious substance... to mark their sheep.

During the 1500's, graphite was so immensely valuable that material mined from the Borrowdale deposit was delivered to London under armed guard. Little guard dudes were left behind to protect the mine, which was only used six weeks a year. While not in use, it was also flooded so that no one from the local villages could help themselves to this precious material. When the graphite finally reached London, it was sent to the Guild of Pencil-Makers, who hand-carved wee wooden cases for each individual pencil.

Now that we've learned about its pedigree, let's examine the atomic structure of graphite to understand what makes it so very special.

As I walked down the dark tunnel, light suddenly exploded everywhere, my torchlight reflecting from a million shiny facets. It appeared to be some sort of abandoned mine!

Nature of graphite

Graphite is made of carbon, and it is one of carbon's naturally occurring forms,* another being diamond. Carbon is an extremely versatile element, as demonstrated by its ability to manifest as both the hardest and one of the softest natural materials. Its flexibility means that carbon is known as the building block of life—and while we don't need to delve into its role in biology, as graphite, it grants us the ability to create our own life forms.

Graphite

In this form, carbon is extremely slippery. This is because the carbon atoms link together to form flat hexagonal sheets resembling chicken wire (A). These thin sheets of hexagons overlap, forming layers that slide across one another. Think about this the next time you glide your pencil over the drawing surface. OK, it probably won't blow your mind, but it's cool to know.

Diamond

Now that graphite is no longer awarded royal guard, diamond and graphite are the prince and pauper of carbon. The difference between soft, slippery graphite and diamond is down to the arrangement of carbon atoms and nothing more. The hardness of diamond is due to the incredible strength of its molecular structure (B), which takes the form of a four-sided pyramid, or tetrahedron. This tetrahedral structure is the reason we are mentioning diamonds at all: the strong pyramid structure is the same formation as the Tetraforce drawing method we will be adopting.

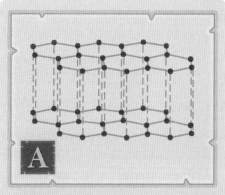

Sheets of this hexagonal pattern are layered one over the other. This atomic structure, of overlapping sheets, is what makes graphite so slippery.

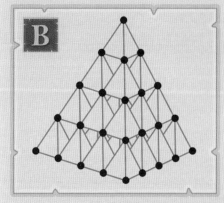

The pyramidal atomic structure is the key to diamonds' strength. Our learning will adopt this same form: the form the Tetraforce is the same as the atomic structure of diamond. In Drawcraft, the two forms of carbon combine: Graphite + the atomic structure of diamond = the Tetraforce.

The Tetraforce

Composed of interlinked connections arranged hierarchically, the Tetraforce represents the steps we will follow in our learning, as we transform graphite from simply being a material on a surface, into becoming a substance that gives the illusion of being something else. The Tetraforce process is what will turn graphite into gold—and absolutely any other material you wish to create, the secret that will allow you to immortalise moments and give your subjects eternal life. In short, the Tetraforce is what will help us get as close to alchemy as anyone ever has.

We will begin by looking at the first four layers of the Tetraforce, which deal purely with line. Later we will uncover five more layers, teaching shadow and light. As we progress through the Tetraforce, we move through dimensions, beginning with dimension zero, at the very top of the pyramid, all the way to that thing most students wish to do: produce a convincing impression of the third dimension.

*+3 Wonder — The third form of carbon bears no connection to our ambition of learning to draw other than that it creates a little bit of wonder. Basically, I can't leave you thinking that diamond is still the hardest known material, so for funs, let's give a nod to a recently discovered third form of carbon: C60 or Buckminsterfullerene. Its atomic structure looks like a football and is so strong it can put a dent in diamond. If the C60 is stretched out it becomes a nanotube, which at the time of writing, is pretty much the strongest structure that could ever be manufactured.

Tetraforce of Line

The Point

The zero-dimension crackles with potential. The first mark is pretty exciting. It only takes a second to make it, but it can become the precursor to hours of work and, finally, to a drawing we can be proud of. During this phase we will consider three points, three stars for us to follow, which will keep us on track.

The Line

In the one-dimensional phase of line, we look at how to begin a drawing using guidelines. These guidelines serve as the backbone of our drawing, and they help us begin in an organised fashion. After that, we will consider the character of line. Simply by selecting the right kind of line, we will have done a lot of the work already. There is one type of line in particular that will unlock much of the power behind the Tetraforce method.

The Shape

The shape, or second dimension, is concerned with networks, the way the object or person is formed. The shape stage is about establishing large, bold shapes that make up the framework from which smaller shapes can grow from later on. During this time, we seek out the most important landmarks, dominant lines and prominent shapes. We seek to capture the fundamental geometries of forms. From these bold shapes, our drawing gains its strength.

The Contour

The basic shape we constructed will eventually become far more nuanced. With the addition of more and more lines, a curvature emerges. The outline becomes more refined and variable in its angles. The outline becomes more sophisticated and eventually comes to resemble the thing we are drawing.

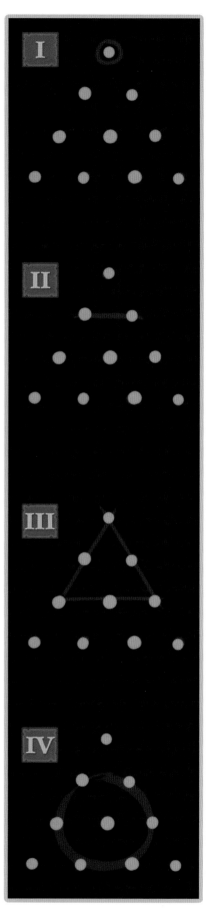

Strange markings aside, where does this door go?

THE GREAT SIFR DOOR

Doorway to Shunyata

Marius led me onwards till we reached an immense door, flanked by two eagle-headed guardians. There was some writing on the base of the door, and as I crept over to take a closer look, my key friend hopped into each of the three locks, turning them until, with a loud clunk, the doors began to shift. As they opened, the mountain itself shuddered, stalactites splintering loose and crashing to the ground around me. There was no time to hesitate! I rushed blindly through the door and out of the mountain and into…

NOTHING AT ALL

Void	Paper	Teeth	Warm-Ups	Words and Pictures	Symbols	Nonsense
0	2	3	10	12	18	24

At first, all I could see around me was white—Marius was nowhere to be seen. It was only when my eyes finally adjusted that I realised I was standing on a very flat, white plain, beneath a white, clouded sky. I could feel snowflakes gently hitting my face and melting on impact. It was so bright—a barren wasteland with no hint of which way to go. As I turned around, I realised that even the door I had just passed through had vanished. I had a sense of terrifying vastness, of empty space stretching out in all directions. The biting wind and swirling snow did not fill me with much hope. In fact, this nothingness filled me with a sense of terror greater than any I had yet experienced.

Bugger All

Zero is nothing at all. Nil, nada, zip. Thus, paradoxically, zero is that within which all things are possible. If we really go back to basics, we approach this curious state in which there is nothing, so there can be everything. By trying to become 'blank slates,' we become like the blank sheet of paper that confronts us every time we begin a drawing.

Blank paper is scary. Humans struggle with the idea of nothingness. When the idea of zero reached medieval Europe from the Middle East, it was feared as heretical. William of Malmesbury called zero 'dangerous Saracen magic.' Many modern Westerners feel a similar chill of dread when contemplating Buddhist ideas of nothingness and the void. Perhaps zero, nothingness and the void seem dangerous because they are so powerful, so dense with potential.

Nothingness is boring. That's not a bad thing: a bored mind can be a very creative one. You can experience this by trying to sit for five minutes without thinking of anything, just clearing your mind completely. If you try this, you will almost certainly find that you cannot do it: random thoughts keep popping into your mind. That's not failure; it's a demonstration of the mind's creativity. Similarly, think of what happens when you sit through a boring meeting or class with paper in front of you: you doodle. You produce random lines and shapes, just for pleasure.

Accessing our doodly state can help us overcome the fear of the empty page. One of the reasons we fear the blank paper is because, in its void, it's impossible to tell whether our first marks will be right or wrong. Later, we'll learn just how empowering that is. For now, though, forget about getting it right. We're Level 0, which means we're getting back to enjoying drawing for its own sake.

When we get back to zero, we create a welcoming void in which surprising things can pop into being. Shapes emerge from the void, random swirls and unexpected energies . . .

We will come to see that everything is made possible by these three aspects. Yes, three. One of them is a little shy, but it's there all the same. The above image shows 'On', 'Off' and 'Nothing' (the background is this image's attempt to express the idea of nothing).

What we're talking about here is a computing rule derived by Willem van der Poel. This rule expresses whether something is allowed or forbidden. This language is endlessly expressive, and it allows computers to operate.

We artists also work with On, Off and Nothing: we use the positive force of the pencil, together with the subtractive power of the eraser. The empty paper that holds it all is Nothing. In short, Nothing has a critical role to play in everything.

The first obstacles to drawing are psychological

The Void has infinite possibility; we can create anything within this space. This realisation can be liberating or paralysing. Our aim on this journey is to embrace it as the former.

Our first task in this freezing tundra is to warm up. We'll do this in two parts. We'll begin by warming up our hand, building momentum that we can carry into our work. The next step is to then warm up our minds, helping us get loose from the apparitions that inhibit our artistic vision. As empty as the paper is and no matter how idle and empty you might think you are, you cannot help but bring some baggage along with you when first starting out.

As we'll see, this baggage comes in the form of the ghosts we bring along with us into the Void, but they can be defeated. These ghosts rise up out of our pasts and our assumptions, and they seriously distort our vision. As we draw, they seek to guide our hands, and if we let them possess our drawings, we will become very confused and probably never make it out of the Void.

As we will learn, one of the best ways to defeat these ghosts is to enter a state of mind that embraces 'no sense': only by leaving behind meaning can we hope to escape this place. Minds emptied of meaning, we are able to see past the ghosts and truly assess our surroundings: we need to look without labelling or judging. It is only by discovering the void within us that we can escape the Void, because it is the void that liberates our vision.

The Void gives no indication of a direction to go in, so once we have warmed up hand and mind, our next step is to get our bearings and take stock of the terrain so that we might traverse it more surefootedly. To help us, we will also seek out a guide. Two will offer their services. One is known as the Specific, and the other is the General. They are poles apart, but we must select one to show the way. They will explain which path is the best to take. Over the course of our journey, we will find it necessary to follow both of these guides: by harnessing their powers, all things are created.

It's pure evil, isn't it? Look at it lying there, staring at us. Our task is to work within this void. Upon this surface, we have the potential to communicate an infinite amount of things. From creating the illusion of all kinds of textures, to evoking an image that expresses humour, sadness or joy—all the way to conjuring a person who seems so alive they might almost move.

By initiating one action, we usually set in motion something else. By placing this rectangular piece of white toned paper down before us, we have already made choices about our drawing. The white tone is our first choice—we could have started with grey or sepia, for instance. Whether you choose white or toned paper will call for different techniques when it comes to applying light and shade to your drawing.

The second choice we made was opting for rectangular paper. This choice will have an impact on composition. What if we'd chosen a square? Because of its four equal sides, the square is an ancient symbol of perfection, like the circle—and that is why we aren't going to choose a square piece of paper. Squares and circles both give a sense of completeness, purity, deadness. The variation of long and short sides which characterises the rectangle lends it a solid, structural quality.

The proportions of the rectangle make it perfect for arranging a composition that has vitality. We should avoid perfect balance in all aspects of drawing. Variety creates interest and liveliness, and, whatever the subject matter, we want our drawing to come to life, right?

Blinding light!

On top of all the challenges of drawing, we immediately start off at a disadvantage: the white paper is blinding. One of the reasons why the white paper is so intimidating is that the surface that we're working on is effectively one giant highlight. This is a problem, because in drawing, the highlights are one of the last things we should concern ourselves with. Confronted with this glaring white, any mark will look wrong. For that reason, we should begin by just setting out a few markers to help us orient ourselves. Before we get into placing markers though, let's investigate this landscape a little more.

This place is weird!

Paper Landscapes

Choices, Choices

Before we even start drawing, there are so many questions to ask and choices to make. "What paper should I use? What sort of table? Or would an easel work better?" Mostly, the answer to all of these questions is, "Base your choices on whatever makes you feel comfortable." There are no wrong answers. However, by experimenting with lots of different materials and set-ups, I have learned some things which you might find useful.

It is advisable to become thoroughly familiar with all your equipment. This enables you to avoid running into major surprises in the middle of a major drawing. As my shoe-obsessed art teacher would say, you wouldn't set off on a thousand-mile hike in shoes you'd never worn, right? We wear them in, and so too with our tools: we get to know them in order to get the best out of them. So, let's begin with paper. The first thing you should consider when choosing drawing paper is its tooth, which is to say, how rough it is. You can feel a paper's tooth by rubbing your hand over its surface.

> The more tooth a paper has, the rougher it feels to the touch. Also, the greater the tooth, the more particles of graphite it can hold. This means that paper with more tooth will let your drawings go darker.

Understanding the basic properties of paper is of paramount importance, because the surface you choose will affect the outcome of your drawing. For instance, not all tones are available to all papers: if you choose a paper which is too smooth when drawing a subject featuring deep shadows, you may not be able to achieve the darkness you want. Different papers also have different levels of tolerance for erasing. Because erasing is a major part of my drawing process, I prefer to use smoother boards—a board is simply a sturdy paper. These can handle a fair amount of abuse from pencils and erasers without having their fibres destroyed. Finally, I need surfaces which are smooth enough to render subtle tonal transitions (a patch that goes from light to dark), so that things that need to be smooth, such as glass or water, can be properly described.

These are a fair number of variables to consider when it comes to deciding which paper will suit your style and chosen theme, so the best thing to do is experiment with a few different types and manufacturers to find out which you prefer. Ultimately that is the only way to know what the limitations of a surface are. One of the first things I try with a new paper is firmly applying a soft pencil grade such as a 4B and then trying to remove it with a variety of erasers. For instance, I found that watercolour paper doesn't hold up well to the eraser; the paper quickly becomes damaged, and it is therefore not a good choice for me because of my extensive eraser use.

The weight of the paper is another thing to consider. The weight of the paper is the grammage (GSM), determined at the pulping stage of the paper. Basically, the weight indicates the thickness of the paper. Personally, I try not to work on anything less than 200g/m².

Teeth

White in Tooth and Draw

The feedback you get from different drawing surfaces is quite obvious: you can feel the tooth of the paper as your pencil moves across its surface. A heavily toothed paper will wear your pencils down much quicker than a smoother surface. More importantly, a paper with a heavy tooth will make realism very difficult, if not impossible, since tonal progressions will never be perfectly smooth.

However, you can flatten out areas on toothy papers, if your drawing just needs a small area of smoothness. Do this by laying another sheet of paper over your drawing surface, then rubbing the area with the round end of a pencil. Becoming familiar with your surface can give you a lot of confidence, especially when it comes to knowing how easy or difficult it is to erase.

Tooth is not to be confused with texture; however, you could have a highly textured paper with very little tooth, for instance.

Knowing how dark you can go on a particular paper will inform you as to how truncated your range of values might be. Neither charcoal nor graphite can make a pure black, so no matter what paper we choose, the full range is never truly accessible to us.

Realism

For realist drawings, you will most certainly want to go with a smooth paper, such as the one pictured on the far left. The reason for this is that it's much easier to hide your pencil marks effectively on smooth surfaces. A textured paper applies that texture to everything you draw, whereas a smooth surface allows you to mimic any texture you choose. Smooth paper has an almost imperceptible tooth, so it also allows for seamless tonal transitions, permitting you to more accurately mimic the way light works on surfaces and allowing you to create more effective illusions.

Know your limits

Every surface has limits: limited darkness, limited detail or limited tolerance for erasure. As you negotiate these limitations, it's important to consider which paper will be most appropriate to your subject matter and technique. By experimenting, you will be able to make informed decisions.

In images (A, B), you can get a sense of just how great a difference in darks there is between smooth and textured paper. Because I have found that Bristol board provides a good combination of characteristics for realist drawing, this is the one I use for the kind of drawings I like to make. Let's now take a look at some of the different finishes of Bristol board available.

A 9B Derwent pencil applied firstly to the textured paper (A) and then to the Bristol board (B). You can't quite see it in this image, but the wash on the Bristol board is much smoother, even in this quick application. The textured paper, on the other hand, absorbs much more graphite, achieving a darker tone. Within that tone, however, the grain remained persistently visible.

The smooth Bristol board doesn't take in as much graphite, leaving it to break up and sit on the surface as little crumbs. Personally, I prefer to trade a slightly lighter value for a more even tone.

Bristol Board

All of the drawings in this book (except the Pebble demonstration on page 207) were produced on plate finish Bristol board, as this is my preferred working surface. It offers a polished and highly durable surface which accommodates a wide variety of different mediums, including airbrush, charcoal, coloured pencils and marker pens. It is, in short, a very versatile working surface.

Not all Bristol boards are alike, however, as they will differ slightly between manufacturers. I use an acid-free* 200g/m² (or 110 lbs) Canson board, although there may well be a better board out there that I haven't yet tried. It's good to keep an open mind about materials and equipment and not become set in our ways. You can practice on any sort of paper, but eventually, the goal should be to find a happy marriage between your surface, medium and particular subject matter. For me, the happy union is one of smooth white Bristol board with Staedtler pencils.

The Plate Finish

There isn't one perfect paper that we can choose, but there are papers more geared towards certain types of drawing. Bristol board with a plate finish provides extremely high resolution: this smooth board surface allows your drawings to be incredibly detailed. Since I enjoy making detailed images, the plate finish is the one I go with more often than not. If you require a bit of texture and richer black tones, you may want to go for the vellum Bristol board instead.

*Be sure to opt for acid-free paper. Note that 'pH neutral' doesn't denote that a paper is acid-free. If a paper says 'acid-free' then it means that nothing has been added later after the paper was made to make it acidic whereas a paper that is pH neutral may well have been treated to a bit of acid. A paper can absorb acidity from our hands, different types of drawing medium, the tape that we attach the paper to the table and even the table surface itself.

The Vellum Finish

Bristol board with a vellum finish has a bit more tooth to it, meaning that you can produce deeper blacks in your drawings. Unfortunately, if you want to achieve a very smooth result, you will have to push a lot harder with your smoothing tools. Textures are, however, easier to build up on this rougher surface: as the pencil point skips along the raised points of the tooth, it leaves a graphite trail containing white spaces. This introduces a variety which can become useful in some images that require ultra-fine textural effects.

If you have trouble deciding

A good way of deciding which paper to choose is to consider the main texture in your image. For a portrait of a person or animal, you might take into account the need to create smooth human skin or finely rendered fur, meaning a plate finish would be your best bet. For rougher textures such as rocks and sand, however, a vellum finish might be worth trying. If the texture of the subject is not important to you then the choice of which paper to go for may be dictated by whether you want an impressionistic appearance or a highly defined and realistic one. A heavily textured paper being best for the former and smooth for the latter.

Preparing the surface

Generally, my preparation of the working surface involves a few things which have now become habitual. When I get a new pad of Bristol board, I usually tear out the first page and begin work on the second. The reason for this is that the first page will usually have been damaged by rubbing against the cardboard cover. This spare page can become a useful place for experimentation.

The second thing I do is get a ruler and create a one-centimetre margin around each side of the paper I am about to work on. This sets the paper up in my mind as a surface that's ready to go. This is mostly for practical reasons. A margin supplies a space where I can overrun, without drawing onto the table. Later, it will also make it easier to mount the drawing behind a card frame.

A margin defines the working area, so pencil strokes can go beyond it while remaining on the paper. Without a margin, our strokes might end up on the table itself.

As I knelt to inspect the ground, it suddenly reared up in front of me and became altogether too bitey for my liking. Maybe this was Jack? The one that supposedly ate the Boss Key? The sooner I got out of here, the better really.

A Surface to Place Your Paper

So, you've got yourself some paper. Now, where do you put it? When choosing a work surface, the main factors to consider are the smoothness and firmness of the worktop. Any bumps or indentations on the desk surface will show through in your drawing. Paying attention to your working surface is an important way of staying in control and preventing unintended effects. Sometimes, of course, you may wish to use rubbings as a way to generate quick textures, but more often we want to avoid such effects.

Another important aspect of staying in control is making sure that, whatever surface you choose, your paper does not slide around. You should prevent this by affixing it to the desk with either Blu-Tack or masking tape.

Masking tape may leave a sticky residue, so make sure to apply it only within the areas marked out as your margins. You may also wish to invest in some artists' tape. This is easily removable and will usually come away without damaging your paper.

A pencil that passes over a paper that is placed directly on a wooden table will allow the wood grain show through. Unless we are drawing garden fences, this effect is often inappropriate.

Surface hardness

The pencil will react with your paper in different ways depending on the hardness of the worktop surface. You can place the drawing sheet directly onto a hard surface, or you can pad your paper by placing a couple of sheets underneath it, creating a degree of softness and 'give'. This can, however, reduce your control and produce some inconsistent effects. Personally, I prefer the consistency that comes from working directly on a hard, smooth worktop.

Trapped graphite

Remember the trick of smoothing down a paper's tooth by rubbing it? As we work, we are actually doing exactly this. A paper's tooth is not impervious to wear or damage, and eventually, our pencils will flatten the tooth. This has a couple of effects. First, it can cause that unsightly, shiny graphite glare on areas heavily covered with graphite. Second, when the teeth are pushed down, graphite particles can become trapped under them. Trying to erase these areas will leave a slight blemish.

The flattening of the paper's tooth is one very good reason for working lightly: a light touch causes minimal damage and leaves as little graphite embedded into the paper as possible. If we go in heavily from the start, we're likely to regret it sooner or later. We never know which areas might later need to be clean and white such as required for highlights and such.

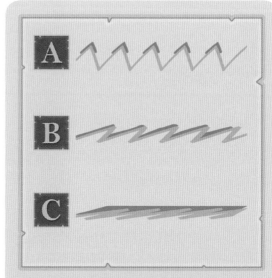

With a light wash from the pencil, the graphite will sit on top of the paper's tooth (A). The more we work over the top of this, the more the tooth will begin to lie down (B). Eventually the paper tooth will become flattened (C), trapping some of the graphite material, making it difficult if not impossible to remove later on.

Distortion

One very troublesome aspect of drawing on a flat, horizontal surface is that it can result in distortion. The larger the drawing, the greater the potential for distortion. From your seated position, everything might look correct, but unless you check your drawing from other angles, the resulting distortions will mean that your picture will only look correct when viewed from this low angle.

We can see a dramatic example of this kind of distortion in Hans Holbein's painting, *The Ambassadors*. This painting features an extremely distorted skull, which only appears correctly proportioned when viewed from one low side angle (A). This effect is known as anamorphosis.

Although Holbein definitely intended this effect (B),* distortion is usually an unwelcome accident. I once attempted a full-length life-sized self-portrait while working on a flat desk. By the time I thought to look at it upright, the work was no longer salvageable.

Even if you do not work on an upright easel, it is still essential that you check your work from several angles. Be sure to hang it on a vertical surface and view it straight on.

A detail from *The Ambassadors*, painted in 1533 by Hans Holbein. Ultimately, our aim is to enable viewers to see and appreciate our work face on rather than solely from the angle where you positioned your chair as you drew.

Places to Work

1

Easel

All artists should own an easel because certain approaches to drawing call for being able to work on a vertical axis—procedures like 'sight-size' (which we will discuss later) are impossible without one. A good easel will last you a lifetime, so be sure to buy reputable brand. Make sure it's sturdy and has a nice little shelf that can hold pieces of equipment. The easel's upright position and stability are very helpful in projects such as life drawing; an easel affords you a clear view and great control while reducing distortion.

The upright easel also reduces any tension in your drawing technique: the position allows the artist to use their whole arm, while a horizontal desk encourages a tighter 'writing' style. The writing style is too tight for the beginning stages of the drawing, although it is useful for the latter stages of refinement, such as subtle contour and value progressions. The upright position of the easel also allows you to walk away from your work, an essential method of checking. Your arm can get tired while working with an easel, however, because there's nowhere to rest your elbow. At this point, either take a break or switch it up and move over to a table.

*Perhaps this skull is there to serve as a memento mori, a reminder that no matter how much opulence surrounds you, death is always present. By distorting the skull, Holbein shows us two dimensions: the conventional portrait of the two people surrounded by objects representing the living, and the skull representing the dimension we can't see, the land of the dead. Neither being properly viewed at the same time. We don't need to walk round the right-hand side of the picture in order to view it properly: it is, in fact, possible to view the skull through a drinking glass, which acts as a lens. Was the purpose, therefore, for medieval goths to raise a toast to death? Probably.

Table

Drawing at a table should be a nice, relaxed set-up where you can work, rest your arms and have your equipment close by your paper. As we've seen, working flat on a table can result in distorted drawings, so you should only use a table in conjunction with other, more upright surfaces. Another issue with tables is that the temptation to place cups of tea on them is often overwhelming, which has caused me a few disasters in the past. Working at a table can also make it difficult to keep your eye on the whole picture: you sit at a fixed distance from the paper, but in the process of drawing, it is essential that we are able to walk away and view it from a distance. If you are going to use graphite powder, you should apply it while your work is laid flat on a table because on an easel, a lot of the medium just falls off as waste.

Typical adjustable draftsman's table.

Angled Desk

The angled desk presents a happy medium. It can be adjusted to be completely upright, for when you wish to walk away from the work to check it; or it can become a flat desk where you can work and rest your elbows. The angled desk is great for long drawing sessions. Every now and again I alternate how I view the surface, moving from vertical easel to horizontal table surface. Working from different perspectives helps me to avoid getting stuck in one viewpoint and permits me to see the work anew as I change viewing styles.

As I move into more detailed work, I change my grip on the pencil to a more focused writing-style, but when working at an upright easel I find it uncomfortable to hold the pencil in this way. The solution for this, I find, is to use a slightly tilted board because this offers the best of both worlds. When working at the angled desk, you may consider a different chair than you might normally use for say, when using the computer. I often use a kneeling chair like the one pictured to the right, which I find really quite comfortable and not at all hard on either my knees or back.*

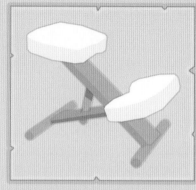

A kneeling chair may help your posture when working at the angled desk or easel. Your rump rests on the higher cushion, your knees on the lower, and your legs tuck underneath.

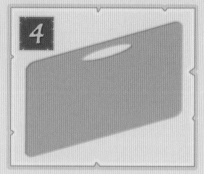

Basic portable drawing workstation.

Drawing Board

A drawing board of about 19" x 25," made from either plywood or masonite, is a useful bit of kit to have when drawing from life. You can purchase these at art stores, and they often come with clips already attached, which is handy. The ideal properties of such a board are that it is flat and sanded smooth, with a firm surface that won't bend as you work. There is a hole on one side for your hand so that you can grip it while standing. A board can also be rested against a chair or used in conjunction with an Artist's Donkey stool, which is effectively a bench that you straddle like a horse while sketching.

 *Coming from someone with sciatica and a slipped disc, this is quite a recommendation!

Posture

Spinal Trap!

Time to think about posture. Yup, a bit boring, but if we're going to be getting down to some serious drawing, we should make sure those hours spent at the desk don't do us an injury.*

1 Your head should be straight and not tilted either up or down.

2 Shoulders should be relaxed.

3 Your back should be straight as a pole with only a slight natural curve.

4 The gap between your calf and the chair leg should be about four fingers deep.

5 Your knees should be a little lower than your hips.

6 Wrists should be relaxed on the table and not bent.

7 Working surface should be positioned slightly below eye level.

8 Arms of the chair should be close to the table so your arms can rest and remain on the same level as the table.

9 Feet are completely flat on the floor or are on a footrest.

10 Table is ideally positioned at a height at about 24" - 32".

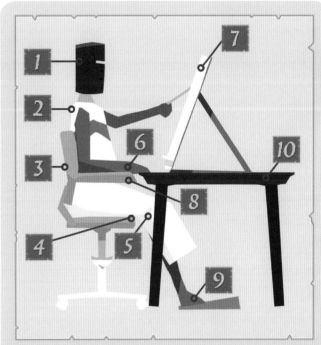

Posture — The ideal seated setup for working at an angled desk apparatus.

The wintry chill of this place did not abate. I needed to warm up somehow. Realising the ground I stood on was made of paper, I decided to build a fire and try a few things. Without a guide, I didn't really know the best ways to warm up yet. Not only were my methods inefficient, one of them was actually cursed . . .

Warm-Ups

You Levelled Up to Scribbler!

The warm-up is simply a way of getting into a state of mind where our hand and eye coordination are brought into closer harmony, ready to perform at an optimum level. All kinds of disciplines hold the warm-up in high regard—running, dancing, singing—and the reason behind this is that warming up makes you alert and prepares your body and mind for the task ahead.

In a scribble warm-up, hold your pencil near the end and move your whole arm. Draw circles clockwise and anticlockwise. Draw vertical and horizontal lines, make patches of hatching, and build up momentum. This energy will carry through into your actual drawing. While we're in the endless Void, we might as well make the most of infinity: drawing a nice figure-eight over and over again is a great way to put the hand in gear, ready for a session of drawing. Do these scribbles for about thirty seconds.

A quick session of scribbling is a great precursor to beginning a drawing. Better to warm up on some scrap paper rather than on your actual drawing.

Shadow Warm-up : Ringu Style*

1 Draw around and around about a hundred times till you make a black circle.

2 Then, around this black void of despair, trace a wider circle, moving around and around and around.

3 To completely enter the trance-like state, make another orbit around and around and around.

4 Add some lines emanating from the centre to complete your Evil Well—I mean, 'warm-up'.

Loosen up

Scribbling gets your muscles warmed up, and this next exercise will warm up your stroke, making it freer. A free, loose stroke will enable you to draw more boldly, while remaining open to change and avoiding the problems associated with tight little studies. It also gets us used to moving our pencils in all directions, taking us beyond the habitual motions our hands make while drawing.

10 DRAW LIKE A BOSS

*+3 CURSED — On doing this, did you feel energised and warmed up? Or you just get a nasty sense of doom? Unfortunately, if you completed this exercise, you have now been hexed and will see something very awful in the mirror tonight. Sorry about that.

Walk the Line Method

As Paul Klee said, drawing is like 'taking a line for a walk'. When you go for a walk, you shouldn't be staring at your feet—look where you're going, enjoy the scenery, and don't get so caught up in focusing on how to walk that you trip over yourself! In this next exercise, we will be practicing just this.

The idea here is simple: don't look down, and don't pick up your pencil. Instead, keep your eyes fixed on the object you're drawing. We almost have to feel our way through the drawing in order to get any representational accuracy. Unable to take cues from the paper, we are left to look even harder at the object, so that our concentration is intensified.

Artists will use this technique to pin down a first impression of something and capture the sensation of the thing, focusing on gesture or essence without involving the rational mind, which can block our ability to see.

This focus breaks us out of the habit of drawing what we expect to be there rather than what we actually see. There is no erasing allowed, so you can use any mark-making tool you wish. Look down at the paper surface and place your pencil at the top left or right, whichever feels most comfortable. Then, look around you and choose something to draw. Your subject can be anything: a sleeping dog, a combine harvester—anything that is around.

As you draw, you may find yourself experiencing your subject as a landscape you are exploring, following its ridges and contours with your pencil. The movement of your eye and the movement of your pencil become united. Don't worry if your lines start to overlap and criss-cross. Take as much time as you wish on this, keeping your eye scanning and the pencil moving. When you are satisfied you have exhausted all possibilities with one subject, move onto another object, letting the line wander a little further along the page where it can continue to record the movement of your eyes, never allowing the pencil to leave the page. Once you feel your hand sufficiently relaxed you are then ready to begin drawing.

Draw from the Well

Most of what we imagine is recombined from what we've already seen, a 'well' of inspiration. We can deepen the well simply by viewing new images: visiting galleries and museums, scrolling through the internet, or talking with others and sharing creative ideas. I find that the act of research is an essential part of warming up when beginning a drawing from imagination.

The reason why research is critical to original and imaginative drawings is that all of this imagery and artwork you're exposed is then combined with your own personality to become something entirely new. The trouble is, we're also creatures of habit. Without research, you may find that the drawings you do from imagination tend to fall into certain predictable, routine patterns. This is a sign that you need to refresh your well by engaging more deeply with unfamiliar imagery. Explore new things: this is the best way to generate original work.

Corpus Callosum Bridge

So that's the physical warm-up over with——now we must look to the psychological pitfalls we encounter when drawing. As well as learning practical methods for circumventing these difficulties, it's also helpful if we take some time to consider how our minds work. Over the next few pages, we are going to learn about the brain and how it moves between different behaviours. Next, we'll delve deeper into the primal human love of symbols, and we'll understand the kind of obstacles these symbolic systems can present in drawing.

Neuroscientists are mapping, in ever more detail, the different regions of the brain associated with specific functions. Our grey matter comprises a multitude of areas dealing with memory, computation, colour perception, emotion, and endless other functions.

This grey matter is divided into two hemispheres: the right and left brain, which we are probably all familiar with. These hemispheres are joined by a dense bundle of nerve fibres, the white matter known as the corpus callosum bridge (A). This bridge connects the two hemispheres, allowing them to communicate with one another. In the rather basic language of 'right vs. left brain', this means we can generate creative ideas and then test their logical viability.

Where the problems begin

By understanding that various mental functions are located in different areas of the brain, we can begin to understand why it's so difficult to switch rapidly between different activities and ways of thinking. It's a little like trying to do something in the kitchen and living room at the same time, or like changing gears too quickly in a stick-shift car.

Most of us are much more accustomed to verbal than visual thinking, so verbal processes are likely to intrude when we try to draw. The more we practice, however, the easier it will become to enter a wordless, visual state: as neural networks build and build, the transition becomes almost effortless.

It isn't actually true that the brain's abilities are divided between the right and left cerebral hemispheres. This is an oversimplified, almost metaphorical understanding of the different functions within the human brain.

The myth of the right vs. left brain originated in the observation that certain functions, such as speech, tended to activate one hemisphere more than the other. Newer understandings of neuroplasticity reveal that the brain is far more malleable than 'right vs. left' suggests. For instance, if one hemisphere is damaged, or even removed, at an early age, then the other side can assume, in part or even in full, the functions of the section that was removed. It's always good to remember this adaptability when we're learning new skills.

Old brain — Mounted on the brain stem is the so-called 'R-complex' or 'Reptilian brain' (B), which evolved hundreds of millions of years ago. This region of the brain is where you'll find aggression, self-preservation, ritual, social hierarchies and territoriality. Basically, all the primitive aspects of human behaviour. Movies with gratuitous violence try to appeal to this part of you. Politicians and advertisers also use tricks to activate and manipulate this primitive part of the brain. Because our reptilian brains function largely outside of conscious control, we may not realise just how often and how strongly our behaviour is driven by this part of ourselves.

I Multitasking

Juggling Ideas

We truly feel the cognitive burden when we try to engage two separate areas of the brain at the same time—it's like rubbing your tummy while patting your head. Try counting while juggling, or playing the piano while doing the eight times table. What you'll probably find if you attempt these exercises is that one activity will fall into the rhythm of the other: you will count in time with your juggling and recite multiplication tables to the rhythm of your piano music.

When we are drawing we don't necessarily use one part of our brain but rather many parts of it. What we actually do is flip between different parts of our brains very quickly. One benefit of practicing a skill is that it eventually becomes much easier to slip into that mindset: if you draw frequently, it will become very easy to sit down and start drawing.

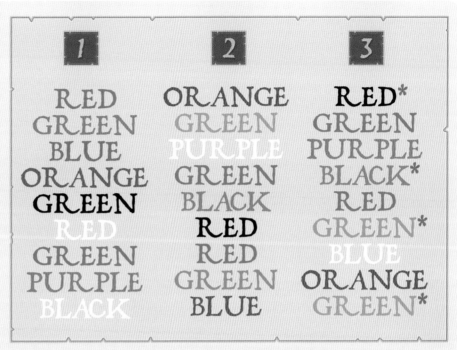

1	2	3
RED	ORANGE	RED*
GREEN	GREEN	GREEN
BLUE	PURPLE	PURPLE
ORANGE	GREEN	BLACK*
GREEN	BLACK	RED
RED	RED	GREEN*
GREEN	RED	BLUE
PURPLE	GREEN	ORANGE
BLACK	BLUE	GREEN*

If we try something new, then there are no networks in place to make the process more fluid. Learning something new is hard because you are setting up new networks: your brain is actually changing shape, but the more you practice, the stronger the new networks will become.

Silk curtain (ultra easy mode)

Read the words in the first column out loud, ignoring what colour the ink is. You should be able to fly through this pretty quickly.

Wooden door (easy mode)

Now move over to the second column. This time say what colour the word is, ignoring the word itself. You will probably find yourself moving significantly slower this time.

Shadow door (hard mode)

In the third column, if the word has an asterisk beside it, read the word. Otherwise, say the colour. This exercise requires us to multitask, flipping between the visual and verbal sections of your brain. If you stumbled during this exercise, you have encountered some of the brain's natural limitations. We can only consciously focus on one thing at a time. When we draw, we need to practice remaining fully immersed in the visual parts of our brain, avoiding the verbal. As we've seen above, interference from the wrong part of our brains can cause us to hesitate and falter.

The Paper Scrunch

For this exercise, as with 'Walk the Line', we will only be looking at the subject (a piece of scrunched up paper) and not at the paper we are drawing on. If we don't look at what we're drawing, we're not going to be judgemental about it. If we can't see what we're doing, then we also won't be able to predict where the pencil goes next. Not looking at our work makes it easier to be spontaneous.

This sort of study is a step towards deactivating our habitually verbal and logical modes of thinking. By playing with a nonsense form and pure vision, we produce a 'don't give a care' style, which is less a record of the object itself than of the paths your eye took while scanning its contours. This is about drawing for the enjoyment of looking at an object, perceiving its edges without attributing meaning; in effect, returning to child mode.

1 Scrunch up some paper and set it on the table in front of you. Set a timer for three minutes. This exercise draws upon meditation techniques, allowing time to drop away as you enter deep concentration, and the timer helps you to come back. Buddhist monks burn sticks of incense during meditation for the same purpose.

2 Close one eye to limit your view to two dimensions. Examine the crumpled ball of paper in front of you. You will be focusing on the intricate folds and ripples of this object.

3 Make sure you are comfortable. Look at your drawing surface and place your pencil down where you wish to begin. Keep your hand on the paper with your pencil poised. Now, look up to your subject.

No peeking! — As you are working you will probably be tempted to look at the drawing— but don't do this. If you do, it will end the study as it will initiate self-criticism and doubt.

How the drawing looks at the end doesn't matter much. The important thing here is taking the time to observe the subject without judging the marks you make.

4 Draw what you see, as meticulously as you can. Bit by bit, move your hand as you move your eye along the edge of the subject. Go slowly. This is a descriptive exercise that tracks the contours of the object as seen by your eyes.

5 You should be trying to copy the detail of the paper's folds, moving slowly but not hesitantly. Let yourself draw spontaneously.

6 Avoid simply focusing purely on the perimeter; record the complexity within the object too. This is a pure union of seeing and recording from that visual experience. Don't allow yourself to look away from the scrunch except to blink. Try to keep your pencil moving at the same speed as your eyes: every movement of your eye should guide the motion of your pencil, without any hesitation or delay.

I did that?

When I did this exercise, I produced marks that were unfamiliar. The results surprised me; I was working in a very unusual way. Not looking at my paper allowed my strokes to become much less inhibited—my pencil was dancing with no one watching! This shows just how much our judgement, assumptions, expectations and use of symbol systems can influence the drawing process. We'll explore this in more detail later.

We have warmed up, reconnected with observing an object closely, and bypassed symbolic and judgemental thinking. Yay! Nevertheless, this is obviously not a way to create a proper, realistic representation. For that, we are going to need to look at the drawing surface as well as the subject, and make adjustments by comparing the two.

In this image, you can see the result of my normal drawing process. This sketch shows the early stages of my working, as I lay down a general impression. This is the product of looking at both my subject and at my drawing surface. It's generally advisable to spend far more time looking at your subject than at your paper.

The image at the bottom is an example of a finished contour drawing. This is produced by working over the lightly drawn sketch (B). It's slightly blockier in its appearance than the subject actually was. The contour doesn't contain as many specific variations as the actual scrunch; instead, you can make out intervals where I have produced simplified line segments. This is the way that I often work, adding a little extra straightness to the contour. This is because a blockier contour creates a greater sense of structure and mass.

Thus, my drawing is an idealised or stylised version of my observations, and this is fine. The important thing is to make sure that any deviations from your observations are the result of choice rather than an error.

Drawing conclusions

Drawing blind is another way of getting into creative gear. It can also be a profound exercise because the point of looking at something is to come to know it and to see it in a whole new way. Trust your hand, trust your eye, trust your object, and let your judgement sit this one out.

This should not be the last time you do this exercise. Taking the time to do warm-ups such as this before embarking on a new drawing from observation can be greatly beneficial.

Has this enabled you to draw? No. Give up.

SHADOW YOU

Offense - Undermines you with negative chatter.

Your Own Worst Enemy

Uh, now, don't panic, but unfortunately, that last warm-up has had an unintended consequence. You've accidentally summoned the entity known as Shadow You. Shadow You has some pretty unhelpful comments to share about your last drawing, and about your ability to learn to draw, and actually just about you in general.

No matter what we do in life, our minds contain the potential for generating this adversary—Shadow You isn't just your inner critic, he's the self that emerges when we're stressed, that suddenly has you thinking and acting really differently from normal. Sometimes, with a lot of work, we can make use of his input, but he's usually an uncomfortable, confusing or even destructive presence.

In this instance, Shadow You has sprung up from the left hemisphere realm of language—and Shadow You applies words harshly, eagerly pointing out mistakes, telling you that you can't draw and that drawing is dumb anyway. Your visual side doesn't have the words to answer back. It doesn't help that Shadow You gets much bigger whenever you try to learn something new and challenging. The best strategy is to recognise Shadow You without taking its criticisms seriously: soon, this will shrink it down to size.

Standing up for yourself

The habit of being hyper-critical and self-effacing is a very typical one for people learning something new like drawing, and it really is nothing to worry about, because it's one of the easiest bosses to stomp on. Recognise that our verbal faculties don't simply shut up when we draw—instead, our self-talk can become a stream of discouragement. Happily, we can defeat this by recognising that it's normal and has no connection with reality: just because our Shadow tells us we're rubbish doesn't make it true. Watch out for typically shady statements, such as:

1. *That looks nothing like it's supposed to.*

2. *Why can I never draw people right?*

3. *I will never be able to do this.*

4. *What's the point anyway . . .*

Why are you following me? You know I don't actually know where I'm heading?

That's precisely WHY I'm behind you. Idiot.

Think happy thoughts

One of the most important thing to remember when learning anything is that, instead of indulging your inner bully, you should try to guide your thoughts towards more constructive ways of thinking. Cultivate a positive inner dialogue while drawing. Rather than passing judgements, ask questions, be curious. We want drawing to become second nature, and we can only do this with enquiry and encouragement. It won't happen all at once, but we can nurture our growth with questions like these:

1   *Is that the right shape in relation to this shape?*

2   *Is the distance between that and this correct?*

3   *Hey, that looks kinda like a heart shape. I should draw it in a similar manner.*

Internal monologue II

Another way of harnessing your verbal mind to help you stay in touch with your intentions is to repeat a word that describes the effect you're currently trying to achieve. Don't name the object you're drawing; instead, find a word for the quality of its lines. Drawing uneven rocks, you might repeat "jagged, jagged, sharper . . ." With drapery, you might repeat words like "soft" or "sinuous." Switch your inner monologue from distracting labels into a helpful description, from nouns to adjectives or adverbs. (Do remain aware of your surroundings, however: don't sit in a busy cafe drawing your scone knife and muttering "sharp, sharp, stabby . . .")

Unfortunately, using words to disarm Shadow You has spawned another demon: The Symbol!

I looked up from my tamed Shadow and found myself gazing into the piercing yet vacuous gaze of a demon, his form both grotesque yet hideously familiar. The mere sight of him made me feel like a tiny child. His gaze made me queasy. He sang a garbled incantation, and it transformed me into something awful beyond description . . .

You Levelled Up to Symbolist!

One thing that unites children around the world is the ability to conjure symbols. These can be delightful depictions of a child's feelings, or they can be truly nightmarish entities that haunt their parents' sleepless nights. Why do children communicate in this way? Well, cut them some slack, their motor functions are not yet fully functional, which means they just can't help summoning creatures like the one we see in the image to the right. He is built from symbols that do not originate from direct observation but rather from ideas that children have. This is why children draw people with humongous heads and massive arms and hands: these are the most important parts of the body for the child, and their scale matches their priority.

The problem is, we don't outgrow symbols. Instead, we become enmeshed in increasingly dense, sophisticated symbolic systems. We become so fluent in these symbols that we forget there is any way to experience the world except through the divisions and meanings imposed by these systems.

SYMBOL

Offense - Substitutes reality for a delusion. But really, why do all children draw him?

"The average human looks without seeing, listens without hearing, touches without feeling, eats without tasting, moves without physical awareness, smells without awareness of odour and fragrance and talks without thinking."

— Leonardo da Vinci

What are these monsters?!

Symbols can be words, pictures, gestures, sounds or clothing: any signifier which points to a significance beyond itself or towards an abstracted concept. Symbols tend towards simplification and certainty: we 'know' what someone is like from how they dress, or we 'know' what someone means when they speak. This feeling of certainty is a problem as we try to become more curious about what we are seeing. There is an adaptive and necessary purpose to symbolic thinking: it prevents us from being overwhelmed by the impossible density of sensory information available and the infinite variables present in the world.

I feel ill.

To constantly see the world raw and fresh would be overwhelming. As photographer Manuel Bromberg said, "The obvious contains more than your senses can bear." Our minds, kindly, protect us and enable us to function by using symbols and habit to eliminate most sensory data from our conscious awareness. Symbols are firmly embedded and readily available whenever we encounter familiar objects or experiences.

So many of the processes that constitute our existence take place far from conscious awareness and control: breathing, digesting, healing—and often, all too easily, potentially conscious behaviours like moving, seeing, hearing and thinking become subsumed into this automatic flow. For convenience, we surrender awareness. The cost of this, however, is the richness of experience and the ability to be present. Documentarian Albert Maysles said, "Tyranny is the deliberate removal of nuance"—and symbolic systems have a tyrannical way of doing just that. When symbolic systems dominate, they bleach experience, reduce and simplify our lives.

You pick up an apple to eat it. You can do this without really thinking. You might check for bruises or wormholes, but you do this so rapidly you're hardly aware of it at all. Before you know it, the apple's gone, and you never really saw what shape it was, what colour. The details of familiar objects are not considered to be very important, so the brain would rather you eat the apple and move on efficiently to the next experience, which it will also label, categorise and assess for potential usefulness or threat.

A symbolic life is one that runs on autopilot

Take a deep breath. Hold it a moment. Now slowly let it go. Repeat this exercise three more times. Close your eyes and focus all of your attention on your breath. Where do you feel your breath? In your nose, on the back of your throat, or perhaps primarily in your chest? Before you read this paragraph, when was the last time you noticed yourself breathing? Why ask such strange questions? Well, looking is somewhat similar to breathing: we do it constantly, and we depend upon it, but we only very occasionally actually pay close attention to it. We have occasional moments, often ones of surprise, in which we truly 'see', but too often, we allow our senses to run on autopilot.

'Learning to see' has become almost cliché when we talk about learning to draw, but if you think about it for a second, it's a very odd phrase. Learning to see, however, is an attempt to dissolve our symbolic systems, push aside the survival mode for a time and question what we are experiencing. If we surrender attention and awareness, we allow our mind to slip into a somnolent state thick with assumptions and preconceptions. In this default state of awareness, 'Artistic-Vision Mode' is definitely off and 'Survival Mode' is on. We're not awake to the luminosity of the clouds or the reflected light on a wall, we're just trying to catch the train or do the shopping while making sure we don't bump into anything. Symbols are a practical shortcut, a way of saving energy, and a way to produce stilted, inaccurate drawings.

'A' is for . . .

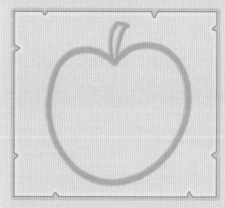

Symbols are simply basic representations of something, a shortcut that allows us to rapidly understand what is going on. We can call to mind countless symbols and draw them without much trouble at all. Apple, Sun, House, Dog, Rainbow: they're all there, stored ever since childhood, but for the most part they are quite useless for helping us to see what is really there.

The shapes and sizes of the objects that surround us are varied and complex; even two identical objects can be different depending on their orientation to us. Trying to capture the world on paper while peering through the lens of symbolism will always inhibit our goal or capturing what is unique about our subject.

The drawings to the right were produced by the six-year-old artist Mason Bradley. Of course, they bear very little resemblance to the outside world, and that is because they are a product of an intellectual exercise and reflect the child's thought process. For example, the man on the right is a depiction of me.* I have never worn a hat like this. In fact, Mason has never seen me wear any hat at all. However, he seems to have an idea that men wear bowler hats—a notion that was dated when his grandfather was a boy. Nevertheless, he's given me a hat. These are extremely generalised and simplified linear descriptions, referring more to abstract concepts than to any concrete, particular or observable reality.

Although you have probably moved on somewhat from Mason's level, if you sit down now and try to draw a face from imagination, you'll probably produce something that doesn't really look very much like a real face. Instead, it will be a collection of 'face symbols.' Simplicity is great for drawing, but it's important to simplify appropriately. Our drawings should not be simplified according to the symbolic conceptions we carry in our minds. Not only is the human nose not a small circle, it's also not an 'L' or 'U' shape with clearly defined sides. The eye does not always look like an oval with a black dot in the middle with wispy, black, spider-leg eyelashes.

The thing is, though, that even when we try to draw carefully from observation, the mere act of drawing outlines involves a degree of abstraction and symbolic representation following predefined cultural norms.

Line is an abstraction; it belongs to the symbolic. However, it is also a wonderfully versatile, sensitive tool, which we can wield with discretion and intelligence.

When we draw from observation, we necessarily simplify and abstract our visual experiences, but we must do it by selecting the most essential and unique elements of the subject, so that the drawing is manageable, while also capturing the essence of our subject. In this way, abstraction and simplification become a way of taking charge, becoming actively involved in

This is my border collie, Jack (A), and this is Jack as drawn by my six-year-old nephew Mason (B). Yep, (B) is pretty scary, but also informative. Notice how he's translated Jack's black and white patches into spots—he may also have an idea from illustrations that 'dogs have spots,' regardless of whether or not this particular dog does. Mason has also given us a kind of Cubist approach to the problem of foreshortening: he's drawn Jack's muzzle in profile, but he's also drawn a nose directly under the eyes, as if seen from the front. All the legs are on a single plane, and they're drawn to conform to the symbol for a human leg, as you can tell by looking at the people he's drawn. This is a drawing pieced together entirely from his symbolic vocabulary, owing very little to observation. The symbolic elements are mostly represented in profile, as this is the easiest, most characteristic view.

*I can also not explain the skull and crossbones on my torso. Does he know something I don't?

perception. One of the wonderful gifts of evading symbols is the chance to freshly encounter pattern and 'non-sense.' Don't let symbols explain away the world. As we break down our habitual labelling of the world, we may also glimpse its fundamental interconnectedness, the way one object relates to and merges into another, the way outlines shift and vanish in certain lights. To draw is to reclaim our vision.

Basic orientations

The image (A) on the right is something like the image of 'hand' that we have recorded in our minds. When we encounter something like image (B), with its foreshortening, our brains tend not to really 'see' that, but instead to translate it into the more easily 'readable' image (A). If we try to draw image (B), our brains will interpret the image as 'wrong' or nonsensical, because it differs so vastly from our concept of 'hand.' This helps us to appreciate the severe limitations on the usefulness of the symbolic in drawing.

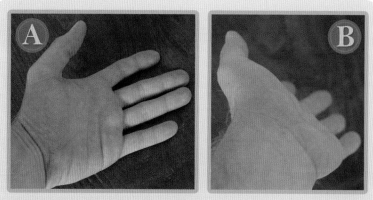

The brain has a hard time remembering what objects look like from various angles—it's too much information to record. Instead, we tend to remember objects seen from the most common and easily identifiable angles. Drawing something from an unusual angle, then, becomes a major challenge to our symbolic concept of that thing.

In favour or symbols

We've done a lot of symbol-bashing now, and as much as we need to try to avoid letting them guide our observational drawing, they aren't all bad. After all, they provided all of us with our entry into drawing in the first place. Symbols can allow for wonderfully direct communication, especially when they're deployed playfully. Cartoons are a great example of the creative use of symbolic drawing.

Having fun with symbols can help children, and adults, to have fun with drawing. Getting into realism too soon can be very frustrating. When I was a kid, I never really cared about realism: I preferred cartoons, and this meant I was never disappointed with my efforts. Instead, I just had fun making pictures. Children should be encouraged in cartooning, taught techniques to help them expand and develop within this symbolic realm, rather than being pushed towards realism too soon.

Symbols stay with us, so why not make use of them? I will forever enjoy little doodles and silly sketches that rely on this system of abbreviated communication. After all, how often can we say that a realistic drawing makes us laugh?

This kind of drawing facilitates self-expression, storytelling, quick results and enjoyment. There is plenty of time to pursue realism later. There is also no need to ever abandon this playful use of the symbolic: drawing cartoons remains one of my favourite forms of play. As much as symbols can harm any attempt at realism, it's a great way to capture experiences and find new ways of laughing at life.

Eye of the Beholder

Windows to the Soul

We previously looked at 'perception' in terms of the way in which something is understood, or interpreted and converted into a symbol. Now, I want to discuss perception in terms of the way in which we are made aware of something through the senses. For the visual artist, the most important sense is that of sight. You should take comfort in the fact that as humans, we all have the same visual faculties as any great artist of the past. We suffer the same limitations as Leonardo da Vinci, who, incidentally, took great interest in learning how the eye worked.

The basic mechanics of sight are that light enters the eye and is refracted (bent) by the cornea, as it passes through the pupil. The light then passes through the lens, which completes the refraction and focuses the light onto the retina. The retina converts the light into electric impulses that are transmitted through the optic nerve to the brain, where these impulses are interpreted as an image.

BEHOLDER

Once again, you harbour your own worst enemies, in your eyes.

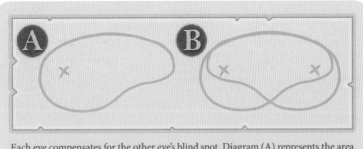

Each eye compensates for the other eye's blind spot. Diagram (A) represents the area of vision of our left eye with our right eye closed. Diagram (B) shows our vision with both eyes open, revealing the areas of overlap and compensation.

The Void within us

You are probably already aware that each eye has a blind spot. Usually, each eye compensates for the other's blind spot, as you can see in diagram (B). If you close one eye, then you get the situation shown in diagram (A), where the second eye is no longer covering the first eye's blind spot. But if we close one eye, we don't suddenly get a black hole in our vision.

The reason for this is that our brain fills in that gap in our vision, using information from the areas around it. The hole so neatly that we're not even aware of it. Now, this little blind spot doesn't have much of an impact on our drawing, even though we often draw with only one eye open. No, the problem isn't our actual, physiological blind spot. What's worrying is what this reveals about our brains and its adaptive tricks.

Seeing the Void — Look at the letter 'R' and close your left eye. Then move your head closer and closer to the letter 'R'. At a certain distance, the letter 'L' will disappear, to be replaced by the general area surrounding of the letter 'L'. The same applies if you look at the 'L' while closing your right eye and moving your head closer to it until you have placed the blind spot over the letter 'R'. This simple demonstration reveals the positions of our blind spots. Now, if our brains fill in our blind spots with information from the general surrounding areas, how else is it modifying our perceptions?

Sensory adaptation

Whenever the brain takes in the same information for a long period of time, it basically stops processing it. This process of familiarity leading to a lack of awareness is known as 'sensory adaptation,' and we can understand it using several examples. If a noise continues in a constant, steady way for long enough, we stop really hearing it—this often happens with ticking clocks or fans, but it can even happen with annoying sounds like car alarms. Sometimes I've been relieved that an alarm has finally stopped only to realise that, no, it was just sensory adaptation.

It's not that we aren't actually hearing the sounds anymore; we just filter out the noise we can 'take for granted.' Likewise, if I place my hand on your shoulder, you'll feel it at first. After a while, though, you will stop noticing. If I start moving my hand, though, you will probably say "Ugh, stop touching me! Also, did you fart?" Don't worry, soon you won't be able to detect that either! Sensory adaptation applies to all senses. It's slightly different with vision, because our eyes constantly flicker very slightly (movements known as 'microsaccades'), meaning our vision is constantly 'refreshed'. This keeps our vision active and prevents sensory adaptation from 'blacking out' our vision.

This refreshing doesn't work as efficiently for our peripheral vision, however. This is why, if you stare at something, you will find yourself experiencing 'tunnel vision': your microsaccades refresh your focal area, but because they don't work on the peripheries, your peripheral vision goes blank, and you seem to go selectively blind.

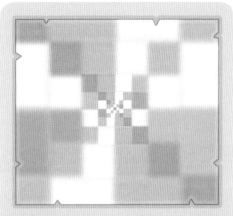

The highest resolution can be found in the centre of your focus. The further away from the centre the fuzzier the image becomes. A lot of drawing focuses on 'seeing the whole' and vision that is only partially focused does make this is a tricky thing to achieve. Fear not, we have a myriad of ways we can go about seeing the whole later on.

Getting warmer, getting colder

Previously, we used the colour exercise to evoke our personal limitations with regards to multitasking. We then tried a little pure observation to reconnect with highly focused observation. I want to slam these two things together now and have you try evoking sensory adaptation.

Find the white dot in the centre of the image to the right, between the terracotta and purple blocks. Now stare at this dot for 30 seconds. After this time has passed, quickly move your gaze down to the white spot between the two Guidos. You should notice that both images take on a different hue: the one on the left seems colder and the right looks warmer. The reason is sensory adaptation: staring at the two colours caused your eyes to adapt and accept them as the norm. They become a temporary norm against which your eyes adjust. Thus, in contrast to the 'normal' terracotta, the blue of the image below it looks much bluer, while it seems yellowish when compared to the purple 'norm'.

Just as we gradually stop seeing things that feel familiar and secure, we can also gradually become blind to our own drawings if we work on them long enough. After spending hours looking at the paper, we become blind to its successes and mistakes. This is one reason why it's important to take breaks while working.

Neuroscientist Beau Lotto demonstrates that as you focus your gaze upon a fixed point for a given amount of time, your brain is learning, adapting to a new normal.

What's in a Name?

Behold, one of the most important things in art: nonsense! Seems a little early to be dealing with such powers, but the implications of symbols are profound and should therefore be addressed as early as possible. If we can harness nonsense to our advantage, then we will have a great tool at our disposal for swatting away the pesky habit of drawing from what we know rather than what we see.

Constant labellers

Humans are animals that love meaning and generally abhor things when they don't make sense. We search for meaning even in places where there is none—think about the way we find familiar objects in the random shapes of clouds. We want to understand, and if we can't, then we feel off balance. We not only want everything to make sense, we also want names for everything. We love names, they make us feel secure.* Unfamiliar things are renamed according to more familiar objects (for example, the German for 'capybara' is 'water pig').

Reality is just stuff and nonsense that we apply meaning to. Take this atom here for instance. An atom is nothing like this: an atom is a fuzzy quantum cloud. Nevertheless, this symbol represents atoms and conveys information about their structures, even without our ever having seen an atom.

This is a good example of how symbols can simultaneously communicate information effectively, while also leading to some serious misrepresentations. After years of looking at images like this, for example, it's hard not to think of electrons as being like teeny, tiny planets, rather than the actual reality of an atom, which is much stranger and harder to define.

Even if we can't figure out a useful function for something, we at least give it a name. The naming of babies has deep significance across cultures, and infants recognise their names from at least four months. This naming becomes part of the means by which we are identified, called out, instructed—and disciplined. Our names help to make us subjects and objects within society.

Right along with the impulse to name comes the urge to separate and categorise. We teach children to name colours, shapes and common objects: the child calling out the names it knows is coming to control the world. Yet this sense of control through separation and identification becomes an obstacle to all art and elevated experience, not just drawing.

The goal of the artist at the start is to see the whole object, but when we first encounter an object, our first impulse is to offer up verbal descriptions of its various parts. One reason why drawing from observation is difficult, then, because direct observation is impossible. We have no direct, unfiltered access to external reality. Perception is filtered through myriad mental processes. Light itself is fundamentally uncertain and tricksy: it is simultaneously particle and wave, with a quantum indeterminacy. We can take some comfort from this fundamental uncertainty bundled into the very nature of sight: when we're uncertain of precisely where something should go in our drawing, we're just participating in the great slipperiness of light, vision and perception.

We have spent most of our lives thinking in terms of a world separated out into categories and little boxes. We're going to now follow a path of least resistance and borrow from this strategy of putting the world into boxes, making it work for us in drawing. Yet rather than using boxes to assign meaning, we are going to impose them on an image to help de-construct meaning.

      *We even have a name for the need to find meaning in meaningless patterns, 'Apophenia'.

Path of Least Resistance

It can be unhelpful to see the world as a collection of separate things: our goal is to see the 'whole', in which everything is interrelated. In order to move towards this holistic vision, however, we're going to break things into down. By superimposing a grid onto an image, we break it into parts.

From being a single image, it becomes a series of boxes, each containing meaningless lines. The grid makes it easier to copy an image not simply because it gives us guidelines, but also because of the abstraction it imposes, which makes it easier to look at things without naming them.

As you move from (A) to (C), the grid gets larger. It becomes progressively less effective at helping to gauge relative positions. Nevertheless, you should find this exercise quite simple, akin to riding a bike with stabilisers. Like the pure observation exercise, this method is not the way to draw, merely a place to begin playing with abstraction. Level 2 is indeed basic, but abstraction is a critical aspect in drawing. We're almost ready to Level Up.

The parts

Using tricks such as the grid to help us focus on parts isn't just an exercise for beginners. Some experienced artists achieve a similar isolating, effect by using a rolled up tube of paper or by peering through binoculars. Isolating part of an image abstracts it, and although it's a bit cumbersome to be grabbing a roll of paper every now and again, tricks like this can help an artist to focus more clearly.

Isolating parts in this way can also help you to compare the relative sizes of things: you can check how different parts of an object fit within your tubular viewfinder, and this helps you to check and challenge your assumptions about scale and relationships.

Tip — It can be useful to add numbers down the sides so that you quickly see the coordinates of how each square corresponds to the one on the other page.

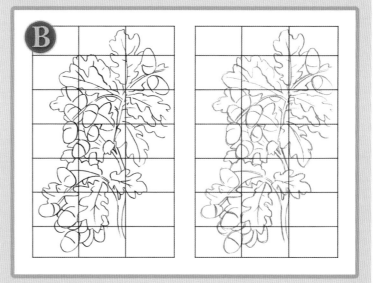

Overriding the Symbol

Have you ever read a picture book with a child? They like to read images by pointing to objects and naming them: 'Doggy! Car! Dinosaur!' Our verbal systems never really grow out of this. You may have experienced going to a photography exhibition only to find yourself skimming past the photos very quickly, with an inner monologue that sounds something like this: "Tree. Mountain. Capybara. Tree. Rocks." This is a clear instance of our labelling getting in the way of actually seeing: even though we know this isn't how art works, it's all too easy to subconsciously believe that, if we have identified the subject, we have actually seen the image.

A level of abstraction, then, helps us to see images by forcing us to observe them more closely. As we draw, we are seeking to view the world washed clean of meaning. Upside down drawing is one way of accessing this nonsense-vision: like the gridding method, it interrupts normal patterns of recognition.

NONSENSE

Seeing the object as just a shape make things far easier.
+10 Artistic Seeing

If we look at things in a way that defeats what we are expecting to see, we will, necessarily, see something unexpected. This way of seeing will eventually become a state of mind that we can initiate without gimmicks such as grids or drawing upside down.

A Complex Picture

Alan Watts tells us, "When you get free from certain fixed concepts of the way the world is, you find it is far more subtle, and far more miraculous than you thought it was." Turning an image upside down will allow us to see it freshly. With the image inverted, we also stand a better chance of copying it accurately, since the words that describe the thing aren't so readily at hand. This sort of exercise works wonders when drawing human faces—when doing a portrait, I often turn the image upside down to check how well things are going. Unlike the gridding technique for defeating symbols, the upside down drawing method is something I commonly employ. I should add, though, that gridding may be a method you retain in your own practice, and this is not something to be ashamed of. After all, Leonardo da Vinci, Albrecht Dürer, Johannes Vermeer and Vincent van Gogh all used grids a fair bit.

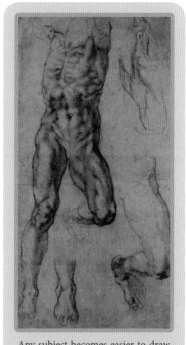

Any subject becomes easier to draw if it is made unfamiliar.

Upside down

For this exercise, you'll need a flat picture that has clearly defined line-work. It can be anything, so long as it is easy to make out the lines. For this demo, I am using the Michelangelo drawing shown to the right, but I have traced it to make its line-work more distinct. Once you've got your image, turn it upside down. So far, so good.

Setup

Get some A4 paper the same size as your original. Place them side by side, with your blank paper on the same side as your drawing hand, so that you can see your model easily. Affix your pieces of paper to the table, so they don't move around.

When you have everything nicely lined up and secured on your drawing surface, take an A3 sheet of paper and use it to cover both your reference and your working paper. Move this cover sheet up or down just slightly, so that it reveals a little bit of your reference image at a time.

Looking at this little sliver of revealed reference, try to copy this section onto your working surface. Now move your cover sheet a little further, and continue to copy.

You will probably find that this exercise gets more difficult as you go on: once a certain amount of the reference is revealed, your mind will tend to leap back into meaning-mode. It's easiest to focus on simple copying while the lines are still abstract, before it becomes too obvious what it is these lines represent.

You Levelled Up!

Level III

Powerful self-expression comes about through mastering this abstract quality in drawing. Draw upon the abstract nature of the world and not what you think you know about it, because nonsense is key to unlocking sight. Art occurs when you are able to see beauty in the meaningless, the extraordinary in the ordinary. It's very important that we revere the abstract and make sure it isn't drowned out by 'objects'. What is familiar is comforting, but if we surround ourselves entirely with familiarity, stagnation will be the result.

The exercise complete, I held my shiny triangle aloft with pride. What a reward! I had come so far! Suddenly, a nearby vase began to shudder and quake. Uh-oh. It seemed that I had accidentally summoned a colossus. The creature shook its great antlers, caught sight of me—and grinned.

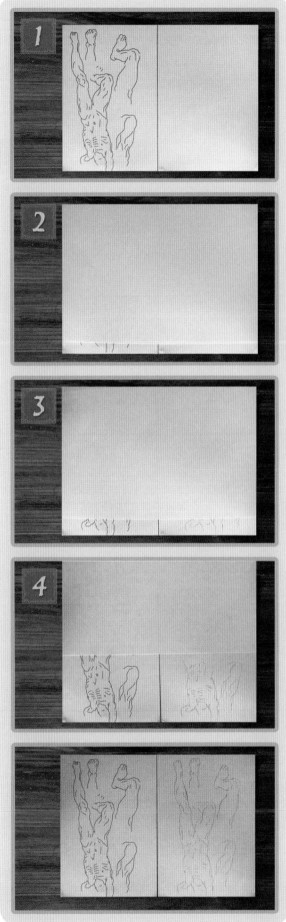

THE SPECIFIC

The Specific	Warm-Ups II	Pencils	Sharpening	Shields	Curves
29	30	32	40	45	48

As my pixellating hands finished the drawing, I saw a strange creature, feet poised on the rim of a vase. She greeted me with a grin. "I am the colossus known as the Specific, and I hereby restore to you your details!" I looked down at my arms and saw that the curse of low resolution had been lifted. I was grateful, but sceptical. The Specific had begun standing on tiptoes with her chest puffed out, trying to look big. "You're a colossus? You're tiny! I mean, you're bigger than me bit still, hardly colossal."

She laughed and leapt from the vase, turning a pirouette. "Here's the deal: I'll help you restock your inventory, and then you can battle the demon known as Sebum. If you defeat Sebum, I'll be your guide."

The Specific

You Found a New Companion!

In a very non-committal sort of way, the Specific has decided to help you. Already she seems a little distracted and possibly about to leave you alone. Although the Void is about overcoming psychological problems, the Specific is not a representation of one side of the brain over the other. Her character reflects certain aspects of drawing, some of which are quite beneficial—and others which are not.

In drawing, we have opposing forces: straight and curved, rough and smooth, exact and ambiguous, intricate detail and empty space. And in order to draw well, we need to learn to control these forces and put them to use, without allowing them to become too extreme. We need to use both ends of the polarity, achieving a balance.

For example, a picture made mostly of curves will be soft and gentle. This isn't a bad thing really, but all pictures need the strength provided by some straightness. If things are left to be purely curvaceous, then the picture will lack variety of line and always be weaker for it. Too much straightness, however, swings the pendulum the other way, and, if taken too far, can become rigid, spiky and aggressive.

Generality doesn't consider nuance. It's concerned with establishing an orderly structure. If you have a picture that is overstuffed with detail, the eye won't necessarily know where to land. The point will be lost or diluted, and the image may just end up being confusing. On the other hand, if we don't add some specificity and character to the picture, it may become generic or meaningless.

By meeting the Specific we have met one of the two colossi that will guide our picture-making. So far, things have been quite theoretical and abstract, and the Specific is excited to help us get stuck into some drawing. She also has a few shiny tools to share.

At these very early stages, however, what we're really seeking is generality, a way to logically structure our vague impressions. Which is why meeting the Specific so soon may be trouble…

We find ourselves considering these two fundamental opposites once again. Instead of thinking of 'on' and 'off', this time, we are thinking in terms of different types of line. The basic types of line we'll be investigating are curves (A), and straight lines (B). One will lead us out of the Void. The other is a Boss, an extremely unhelpful kind of line that won't guide us at all.

If the Specific were a classically decorated pillar, she would be the most elaborately ornate one there is: the 'Corinthian'. If she were cake, she'd be Black Forest gateau, rich in detail and fussiness.

She's full on, exciting, and loud. She's always dancing about, always joking and talking quickly. She's nice, sure, but she's also kind of exhausting.

Vague? General? Logic? Nahhh! Let's do a tiny drawing!

To achieve anything big you have start small.

Also, I'm double jointed. You will fail if you try to do this.

Small Studies

There are many benefits to playing with a few preliminary studies before committing yourself to a major drawing. Thumbnail sketches allow you to loosen up, put yourself in the right frame of mind, and go ahead and get some of those inevitable mistakes out of the way.

Mistakes in thumbnail studies help us to identify some of the major trouble spots and misleading assumptions we may encounter in the image we're trying to recreate. Thumbnails allow us to experiment, mess up, and figure things out. These small studies don't guarantee that you won't make mistakes in your main work, but they'll certainly help you avoid some major problems.

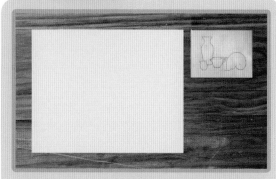

Planning gives you confidence and lets you embrace controlled accidents, unhindered by worry. In this image, I have my large surface area of paper ready beside a small thumbnail sketch that I am happy with. This will serve as a reference.

> Within the thumbnail study, you can bring problem areas out into the open from the get-go. As with making pancakes, your first attempt is often the worst one. You can usually recognise this first attempt by its tight, fussy appearance.

It is far easier to make a successful small drawing than it is a large one. Try drawing a very large circle. Now try drawing a much smaller one. Which one looks more like a circle? Which one has much more obvious errors? Remember: the larger the line, the larger the margin for error. This is why it makes sense to make a small plan before committing to your large work.

For example

When doing thumbnails as preparation for a larger work, do your sketch on paper which is proportional to the paper you'll be using for your full-scale drawing.

For example, if you're going to be doing a drawing on A3 paper, you can make yourself some nice thumbnail slips by dividing another A3 sheet into eighths.

Slips of paper proportionally reduced and ready for thumbnail studies.

Preliminaries

Small studies are also very useful for experimenting with composition, because they are relatively quick and easy. Below, you will see a demonstration of two slightly different approaches to the thumbnail.

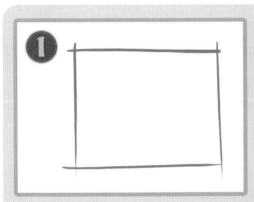 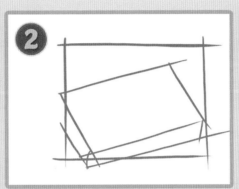 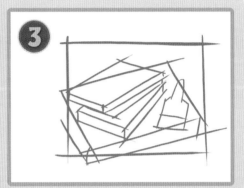

This first series of images starts off with a rectangular frame of a definite proportion already marked out (1). In the next two panels, I have placed the elements of the objects I am drawing within the frame.

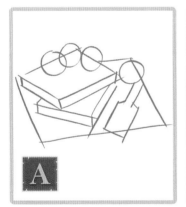  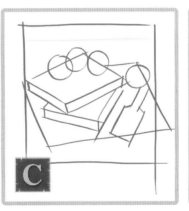 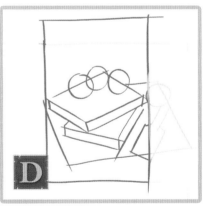

A, B, C, D Panels

Next, I drew a thumbnail without first marking out a frame (A). Once I had laid out these basic shapes, I drew a frame around them as you can see in (B). Drawing without a frame gave me a greater feeling of freedom. In (C) I tried allowing a little more space by adapting the frame, while in (D) I experimented with a totally different orientation. This approach helps me think about how to allocate space, an essential consideration when constructing a composition. Both approaches to the thumbnail are equally valid. Whether you begin with a frame or add it later on, I find that the thumbnail is the best way of warming up before commencing a new piece of work.

Pencils

Monsieur Conté

We can't talk about the truly fascinating history of pencils without giving a mention to the great eighteenth-century French alchemist wizard Nicolas-Jacques Conté. He was notable for two reasons: first, he loved to fly around in hot air balloons, and second, in 1795, he invented the modern pencil. In 1795, France had been at war for several years, and it had become difficult to get hold of graphite. This shortage was caused by the use of graphite to lubricate the insides of cannons (utilising the molecular slipperiness of graphite, which we discussed earlier). Faced with this graphite shortage, Conté cut his graphite powder with clay, which acts as a binding agent. He then fired this mixture in a kiln. Pencil manufacturers have been using this admixture of clay and graphite ever since.

The proportion of clay to graphite determines what grade the pencil is. The harder grades contain a lot more clay, and the softer grades have less. Since graphite is more expensive than clay, cheaper pencils will not only contain proportionally less graphite, the graphite/clay mixture won't be as finely processed, giving the pencil a scratchy, uneven quality. Because pure graphite is quite a crumbly material, the softer the grade, the more likely it is that the point will snap during use or whilst being sharpened—the Derwent 9B is particularly prone to this. The harder pencils are used for the lighter areas; the closer to the highlight, the harder the pencil I use.

There are three types of pencils: wood-encased pencils, mechanical pencils and solid sticks of graphite. Our toolbox could be further extended with the addition of charcoal and carbon, but as I work predominantly with graphite, these last two are beyond the scope of this book. It's also worth noting that these other media do not interact especially well with graphite.

> The darkness of graphite does not change. It is the same value from 9H all the way to 9B. The difference comes from the amount of clay added. The more clay, the lighter the pencil grade.

Pencils come in a variety of grades, usually ranging from the very hard 9H to the very soft 9B, with the slightly anomalous F thrown in between the H and HB grade (the letter was selected arbitrarily). Different manufacturers offer slightly different ranges. At the time of writing, Koh-I-Noor offers twenty grades from 10H to 8B for its 1500 series; Derwent produces twenty grades from 9H to 9B for its graphic pencils and Staedtler produces sixteen from 6H to 8B for its Mars Lumograph pencils. Caran d'Ache Technograph 777 offers a range from 4H to 6B. The Tombow Mono 100 offers a range between 4H and 6B and is considered by many to be the highest possible quality pencil for drawing. The grades are not necessarily consistent between manufacturers. Pencils with the same grade but different manufacturers may have different hardnesses, producing different tones.

I wonder where Marius went. This doesn't feel like the right place to start.

Wood-Encased Pencils

With the wood-encased pencil,* it is possible to fashion the kind of point you need, whether needle sharp, blunt or chiselled. As we have just seen, there are a variety of wood-encased pencils to consider, and all have a useful application. The trouble with this tool is that it surrenders its sharp point easily, and working with a rounded nib creates a fuzzy line. In essence, the drawing loses resolution if the sharpness of the nib is not maintained. I prefer the wood-encased pencils over the clutch when it comes to the block-in. The reason for this being that the wooden pencils are physically lighter and allow me to be more breezy with my mark making which is an incredibly important quality for that stage.

I don't have one particular brand that I use all the time: because the character of particular grades of pencil varies with manufacturer, I find each brand has its own advantages. I like the Tombow Mono-graph, Staedtler and Caran d'Ache ranges of pencils, from 9H all the way to 6B. For the really dark grades of 7B to 9B, I prefer Koh-I-Noor or Derwent, because they seem easier to apply over existing layers of graphite. Although Faber-Castell make some decent clutch pencils, I'm not particularly fond of their wood-encased ones.

Most artist grade pencils will produce a nice consistent line and in time you'll establish a preference of your own. The graphite from the brands I have mentioned tends to have far fewer impurities than other, cheaper pencils. You'll know from using lower quality pencils that, every now and then, they throw up these horrible black grains. These are impurities within the graphite, and they are a constant source of frustration to the artist. These inconsistencies can really throw a spanner in the works; they are very hard to remove and can sometimes damage the paper.

The graphite in these relatively expensive Tombow, Staedtler and Caran d'Ache pencils is no different from that in cheaper pencils. The main difference between them comes from the quality of the filler that is mixed with the graphite to produce various degrees of hardness. It is the poor filler that causes the pencil to give off those nasty, scratchy dots. The pencils of today are synthetically manufactured, which gives a greater consistency, at least within the brand.

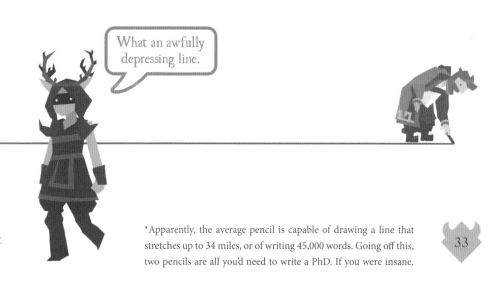

What an awfully depressing line.

*Apparently, the average pencil is capable of drawing a line that stretches up to 34 miles, or of writing 45,000 words. Going off this, two pencils are all you'd need to write a PhD. If you were insane.

The pencil mystery

Prepare yourself for some shocking news: the grades at the end of the Staedtler soft range, the 7B and 8B . . . are not pure graphite. *Something* is added to make them very dark indeed. The reason for this is that pure graphite isn't actually black. By adding this mysterious dark matter substance, these two pencils extend the range of graphite far beyond its natural limits. The unique substance that is added to these grades of pencils remains, to this day, a closely guarded secret.

Which to use and when?

Knowing when to change pencils is like knowing when to change gears on a bike: you begin to get a feel for when you are fighting against the pencil, when you need a lighter touch or more power. If you find you need an extremely gentle touch to get the light misting you want, you should probably slide along the H scale to find a pencil you can apply without having to take so much care.

Similarly, if you find you're having to push down heavily to get the darkness you need, you should probably shift higher up the B grades to find a pencil that will do this more easily. Experiment with changing grades so that you start to get a feel for the capabilities of each pencil.

It is not essential to have every single grade of pencil (much less every grade of every brand), and at first, a vast collection may just be a distraction. It is possible to accomplish a lot with a small range of pencil grades—consider starting out with 2H, F and 2B. You may wish to get a few darker grades to add to these three if you feel that your drawings need a bit more punch. It is also possible to 'mix' these three basic pencils to mimic some other grades.*

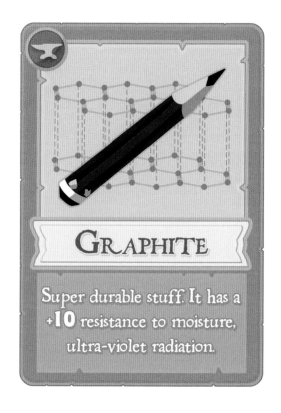

GRAPHITE

Super durable stuff. It has a +10 resistance to moisture, ultra-violet radiation.

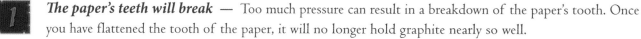

A good general rule of thumb is, if you can't achieve the value you want with medium pressure, change the grade rather than changing your pressure.

While we're on the subject of pressing too hard, there are a couple of other reasons to avoid doing this:

1   ***The paper's teeth will break*** — Too much pressure can result in a breakdown of the paper's tooth. Once you have flattened the tooth of the paper, it will no longer hold graphite nearly so well.

2   ***Burnishing will occur*** — Rubbing graphite continuously and with a lot of pressure polishes it and makes it shine. I find the shine distracting and try to avoid it as best I can. With finished drawings, you can get around this problem by taking a photo and having a print made: this will remove the shininess. Still, this is a troublesome enough issue that it's worth looking at it in a bit more detail.

*For instance, if you wish to create a tone similar to an H, all you'd need is a base of 2H with a wash of F over the top. Likewise, you can create a B value by firmly applying a base of F and passing over it lightly with a 2B. The difference between the F and HB grades is very small, but I tend to prefer the F because of the extra degree of control that F offers... however, this might just be in my head.

Shiny Graphite

Reflective by Nature

So, as we have said, the downside to graphite is its shiny, reflective quality. Although graphite is made of carbon, which is a non-metal, it has a metallic lustre—it even conducts electricity.

The shininess of polished graphite can produce a glare that makes the drawing hard to see from certain angles. This is a particular problem with softer pencils—exactly the ones that you will be using to achieve your darkest values.

Glaring error — Image (A) shows how a patch of hatch appears when viewing the paper straight on. Image (B) was taken at an angle in order to catch the light and reveal the unwanted shiny effect. The patch in (B) appears this way because after many re-workings of the area, the nib of the pencil has polished the area.

Ironically, then, by trying to achieve the deepest darks by repeatedly developing a particular area, you can easily create an unwanted reflective surface instead. Two ways of minimising the impact of the polishing effect are as follows:

Reduce your pressure

Take care not to press down too hard on the paper surface. When you need a dark area, use a 5B or 6B to generate that darkness as opposed to pressing down harder with a lower grade. Even with the 5B and 6B, take care not to press too hard, as this will still create that unwanted glare.

Aim to build up your tone with two or three layers, to avoid burnishing. Try to become adept at choosing the right pencil for the tone you need in a particular area, as this will reduce the number of times you need to rework an area to achieve the darkness you require.

Limit the quantity of graphite

The softer B pencils contain greater amounts of graphite (the culprit in generating all that unwanted glare), whereas the H range contains far more clay in its mixture. Clay doesn't cause shine at all, so a drawing made using only the H range would have far less glare.

Drawings sometimes need the greater impact that comes from the rich darkness of the B grades. By excluding B grades, we would sacrifice the darks' ability to make those lights pop all the more. If you're really set on only using the H range and need a way to include darks without creating shine, then you could always apply the darks by applying graphite powder with a brush. Working with graphite powder can be a little chaotic, however, takes some getting used to.

If the reflectivity of graphite really impedes the effect you're trying to achieve, you could also try experimenting with charcoal and carbon pencils, as these don't reflect any light at all.

Use a fixative

During my time at university, I tried using unconventional fixatives like hairspray to seal my graphite and pastel drawings, but the efficacy of these can be unpredictable, so test them before applying them to your work. There are also several brands* of purpose-made fixatives to choose from, as well as ones specialised for different media, I have used Winsor and Newton's fixative for pastels and found it to be pretty decent.

Pencil Anxiety

Graphite Geekery

So far, all this pencil talk has been a little technical, and, as much as much as I will be obsessing over the finer points of pencils, it's important not to take the details too seriously, especially not at first. People who are new to drawing sometimes believe that they need every pencil, and, while learning, they get hung up on having to know exactly what grade to use, when to use it and for what exact purpose. There isn't one magic grade of pencil which you must use for the block-in stage, for instance. It can be done lightly with any of the middle range of pencils. There are no definite answers here. You'll gradually come to feel what is right for you and your way of working just by using the different grades. Anyway, with that caveat, let's continue with a bit more pencil geekery.

Staedtler 7B VS Derwent 9B

A striking dark value can be a useful thing in drawing, and having confidence in your tools' performance in such an area is important. The extreme darks and the highlights are the things that really set a drawing apart and make it pop, so to speak. With that in mind, I will now explain why I prefer the Derwent 9B over the Staedtler grades that go beyond 7B. I will demonstrate using a big dark blob (A). That dark patch to the right is the result of five layers of hatching with a 5B. We're now going to look at how this patch of hatch reacts with these two pencils.

VS.

Working from left to right, I have hatched over the 5B blob and found that the Staedtler 7B isn't taking hold at all. It is, in fact, skipping over the surface leaving the area still fairly light. In areas which already have graphite applied, the Staedtler 7B does not darken effectively. You can see that, as I draw further to the left, away from the dark 5B hatching, it gets darker. This is because the 7B is starting to do its job–but only in places where there is little to no graphite already applied. This is due to the mystery darkening substance, interacting poorly with graphite.

This next example begins exactly the same, with a prepared ground of 5B patch of hatch that I go over with the Derwent 9B, from left to right. In this case, it is taking hold, actually darkening the area that is covered by graphite. What's more, I am able to continue beyond the area of 5B and create a progression of value that does not involve it suddenly getting darker, as in the first image. The Staedtler 7B is darker than the Derwent 9B, but, for transitioning tones on already laid graphite, it just doesn't cut it.

*There are also workable fixatives that still permit you to work on the picture. Not only do these allow erasing, they also create a synthetic 'toothed' layer that can accept layers of graphite over the top. This means that, even after you've mounted your picture and put it on the wall, if you later notice a mistake, you could go in, erase and continue working. When dry, the fixative also creates a matt finish, reducing graphite glare.

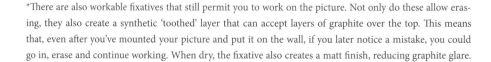

Line Edge

The quality of line you make with the pencil will vary a lot, depending on what sort of pencil you use. The softer grades, that go from B to 9B, will produce a grainy, soft-edged line. Drawing lightly with these softer pencils will produce a line filled with white spaces, because pressing lightly allows the graphite to sit on top of the tooth, rather than being worked into the valleys of the paper's tooth. The amount of white space in the line will vary, depending on how textured your paper is. A highly textured paper will cause large intervals to appear in the line.

The top line is a mark made with a B grade. The bottom line is one made with a H grade. The H is light and leaves behind far fewer crumbly bits of graphite dust.

As you apply more pressure to the B grades, the nib will start to crumble and distribute crumbs of graphite across your drawing surface. The softer the pencil, the more this will occur. The H grades produce a far cleaner and sharper line than the B grades. Getting a nice dark area of tone with a sharp edge will require you to use a combination of B and H grades.

Level II Pencil

Fine-Tipped Mechanical Pencil

Along with H grades, the mechanical pencil is an excellent tool for sharpening up the edges of value blocks made in B grade. This tool can deal with detail better than a wood-encased pencil because its ultra-fine lead yields a very delicate and consistent line.

This is a precision tool, and, therefore, doesn't produce a thick-lined wash. It is a tool for focusing on the teeny tiny details, a definite asset in any artist's toolbox.

The mechanical pencil also doesn't require sharpening, which helps maintain the artist's focus and concentration. Finishing touches are dealt with very accurately with the fine nib of this tool.

Mechanical pencils do not betray a grain: their application is smoother than wood-encased pencils,* which makes them great for passing over washes that contain gaps. The mechanical pencil blends and grinds down those graphite particles, creating a more even patch of tone. I wouldn't recommend it for the blocking in stage or adding large washes of tone, however. Finer nibs like the 0.35 nib likes to break a lot, so go easy on the pressure with these leads. The Tombow Mono-graph mechanical pencil, pictured above, is hands down the best mechanical pencil I have ever used.

*Wooden pencil leads can have a bit of wax or grease added for extra smoothness, whereas, in the case of mechanical pencil leads, this is replaced with oil.

Mechanical pencils are essential in the creation of realistic drawings. I tend to use them in the latter stages of a work, as they are just so darn fine-tipped. The leads range from the incredibly precise 0.35mm to the 0.5mm and 0.7mm—the latter two are still precise, but not ridiculously so. I know of some artists who actually work with nothing else, but I prefer to use them sparingly. For the process of adding definition, I use the mechanical pencil in conjunction with the regular wood-encased and clutch pencils. I can only go very dark with the wood-encased pencils and not with the mechanical pencils.

We don't always want our edges to appear furry. However, a sharp, clearly defined edge can sometimes make a form appear flat, rather than rounded and three-dimensional. A very sharp edge also looks quite unnatural—always better to have an element of softness, even if it is to a tiny degree.

Line edges

The mechanical pencil's primary function, for the way I work, is as an edge modifier. Keeping the edges in check is an essential habit to cultivate. By breaking down the furry edges produced by the wood-encased pencils, we can add a great deal to the overall realism. A sketchy pencil drawing is also a beautiful thing, but, in the case of hyper-realism, it is best to use the mechanical pencil to maintain clear definition.

Level III Pencil

Clutch Pencil

The clutch pencil is a wonderful tool with many advantages over the wood-encased pencil. Like the fine-tipped mechanical pencil, this tool retains a constant length: they don't whittle down to stumps. Because the length doesn't change, we always have the full range of pencil grips at our disposal.

With the clutch it is possible to wash in tones without worrying about little granular inconsistencies getting thrown up, because the graphite sticks are incredibly smooth.

The Staedtler clutch has its own 'lead pointer' sharpening tool, which we will be looking at later on—yeah, exciting, I know, but it is a good thing to have around when using tools like this. You can refine the clutch pencil's lead to a sharp, needle-like point, which works wonders when detailing things.

The Faber-Castell 2H and 2B clutch pencils also fit the Staedtler pointer. The fatter Faber-Castell 4B does not, so I mostly use a sandpaper block to sharpen that one—but again, I'm getting carried away with specifics. We'll look at the finer points of sharpening later.

These are the grades of clutch that I like to have around. I have one for the 2H 2B, 4B and HB leads. I have one for each grade because the alternative is to insert a different lead into a single clutch each time I want to change grade. Besides, the 4B is the only clutch body that can fit its massive leads.

One pet hate for me is constantly reaching for the wrong pencil grade. For the most part I don't have a problem since my Staedtler clutch is blue. This makes the search for the HB easy. The 4B is also recognisable, as it has a thicker barrel. The 2H and 2B, on the other hand, are very similar, so I find that attaching a sticker is a good way to differentiate them.

You know the saying: the awesome is in the details.

I'm pretty sure that's not how the saying goes.

Level IV Pencil

Quantum Clutch Pencil*

I have been saving up for one of these for quite some time now. It is the essential piece of kit for anyone who wishes to take their drawings to the level beyond imagination. This technical wonder was specially designed by a department known as 'Aperture Cryograph', a company that resides in an abandoned uranium mine, directly below the CERN complex in Switzerland. The quantum clutch was created for those artists who work with hyper-realism, and it is one of the few pencils in the world that require an invitation before you can acquire one. That's right: there is actually a waiting list on these. I had to use four types of ID just so I could accept the parcel when the mysterious courier arrived.

> Want to shade the underside of a plant cell's nucleus? No problem. Need more detail on that tricky photon? Booyah! The Quantum clutch pencil enables you to draw with an unparalleled exactitude, making it possible to render the individual atoms of the subject you are drawing.

Eraser

This pencil doesn't just blend, it also bends the fabric of time and space. Simply apply the eraser fitted on the end, and it will generate tiny genetically modified black holes (you can set the radius of the event horizon, so don't worry, it won't erase everything). These are specially designed to eliminate graphite molecules while producing zero damage to the paper's tooth—instead, it actually improves the surface. Oh, you thought black holes didn't have genes? That's why you don't work at Aperture Cryograph.

The undo button

On the underside of the pencil, you'll find this neat little feature, which gives you the ability to travel back in time to a point before you made that daft error, whilst retaining the memory of how you went wrong in the first place. Beware the butterfly effect, though: try not to touch anything but your drawing! It's also worth noting that the Quantum Clutch has an 'auto-shade' function already switched on; you may want to de-activate that, as it does make the process of drawing a little too easy.

QUANTUM CLUTCH

(Artistically devastating).

*Complete and utter nonsense. We're in the Void and a bored brain will yearn to create a stimulus. What follows is the product of a mind that has bored itself silly by giving advice on ways to tell your clutch pencils apart.

Quantum range

The B grades on this pencil are quite extraordinary, going as far as a 4,070,733,805B. Those genetically modified black holes look pale in comparison.

The H grades are equally phenomenal. The light misting created by grades beyond 13H is so fine that it actually makes the areas it passes over haunted (H stands for haunted!). Whether or not you want to be able to hear muted screams of the long-departed rising your paper surface is up to you, and it really depends what you are trying to achieve with your work. The disadvantage to this pencil is that lead gloves need to be worn by the user at all times. This is, of course, to limit the damage to your DNA as you wield this artistically devastating device.

I'm not sure I believe anything you say anymore.

Sharpening

High-Definition Drawing

One way of working is to have your pencil's tip fashioned in such a way that it has one it a fine tip for details and a side edge for mass drawing, roughing out ideas and shading. A sharp tip will delve further into the tooth of the paper, whereas the side of the tip will glide over the tooth, leaving more white spaces in the mark you have made.

It's useful to remember that surface graphite is much easier to remove than graphite that is within the tooth. A sharp pencil will create high-definition drawings, whereas a blunt tip will create a more blurred and unrefined effect.

The sharpness of the pencil enables sharpness of mind. A sharp point focuses our intentions and translates them more faithfully—it is hard to know where a blunt tip will draw when you place it on the surface. We will talk more about the importance of maintaining a sharp mind when we hit the Contour Coast later on.

MASTER OF POINTS

Even the sharpest mind is dullened by a blunt pencil.

To put it bluntly, a round-tipped pencil will lower the resolution to your drawings. Only sharp tips produce high-definition drawings.

1

Metal Pencil Sharpener

Avoid cheap plastic sharpeners: they have a nasty tendency to snap nibs and chew up pencils. A little old fashioned metal sharpener will do just fine with wooden-cased pencils, but I still find them a bit fiddly. Once they get blunt, they'll be snapping nibs all over the place.

For this reason I prefer using the kind of hand-cranked sharpeners you find in schools. To get a bevelled nib after using this sharpener, you will need to scribble the pencil on some scrap paper or sandpaper. We'll get to why you might want that bevelled nib in a second.

This sharpener may not seem very useful, but don't throw it away just yet. It does have a use, not for pencils, but rather for sharpening stick erasers. I like to have both a sharp-tipped eraser and a second, blunt one nearby. I use the blunt one to erase areas that don't require precision, so I don't waste that nice pointed tip on areas that require mass erasing.

2

Pocket Knife

With a pocket knife, you can choose what kind of nib to fashion, from flat chisel to vicious spike, but it is a rather blunt instrument when it comes to crafting the tip. It also has the disadvantage of being slower and using up energy that could be better used in the drawing.

Knives do allow you to expose large amounts of lead. Having a well-exposed side of your lead allows you to create washes while retaining a sharp point, meaning that you can switch back and forth as needed, thus widening the range of your strokes. When carving this type of point, be sure to whittle away enough wooden casing to allow yourself to get the very low angle required to make the most of the exposed graphite.

Sharpening to a long, needle-like point is okay with the harder grades because these are, as you'd expect, in less danger of breaking. With the softer grades, however, there is a greater chance of the nib breaking. With these softer pencils, it is helpful to use a knife rather than sharpeners, because the knife allows you to sharpen in such a way as to retain as much supportive wood casing as possible, as we will now see.

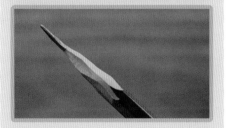

Having the side of the tip available enables you to use a wider range of strokes.

Adding strength to sharpness

When crafting your pencil points, it is better to aim for an angled and ever so slightly dulled tip, rather than an incredibly sharp point. It is counter-intuitive, I know, but a certain lack of sharpness in the nib works wonders for maintaining sharpness over time, because it supplies the nib with a little support. An extremely sharp point will wear away within a few strokes, and it is also very likely to snap off, possibly damaging your paper in the process, and forcing you to return to your pencil sharpener.

Having a chiselled point to your pencil is ideal as it gives you the ability to control your line weight just by using a different part of the tip. A simple turn of the hand can yield an altogether different stroke (A), and if you adopt this particular chiselled tip, you will gradually gain intuitive awareness of the exact shape of the tip and exactly how to turn the pencil to make the kind of pencil stroke you want. As you become increasingly sensitive to your tools, the pencil becomes an extension of your arm, so that it almost seems to have nerves, and the act of drawing comes to feel ever more directly connected to your thought process.

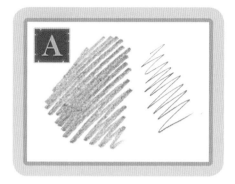

Sandpaper

Sandpaper beats knife on two counts. Firstly, a sandpaper pad can be used to give more precise control over the tip of the pencil. This is especially true when creating a bevelled edge.

Sandpaper allows you to rapidly achieve a sharp tip, permitting you to return to work much sooner. You can also use fine sandpaper to finesse the points made by other means.

The second advantage is the by-product that is generated from this type of sharpening: graphite powder. The fine graphite collected on the sandpaper needn't go to waste; it can be collected in a jar and applied with a paintbrush, to create a smoky atmospheric effect.

Sandpaper can be an awkward thing to handle on its own. It helps to get a cheap sanding block from the hardware shop. You can even glue your sandpaper to this to make a sharpener block.

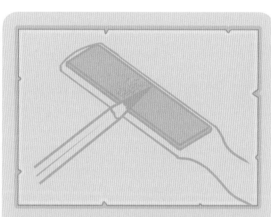

One way of sharpening with sandpaper is to have a sandpaper block. Glide the pencil tip over the surface with a minimal amount of pressure, while rotating it to get a sharp, even tip.

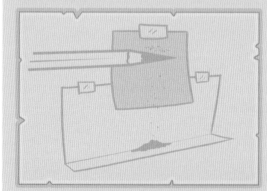

Another way is to have creased paper taped to a nearby wall, with a sheet of sandpaper taped over it. The paper catches the graphite that falls onto it so it can be used later on.

Experience with points

Initially, you will want to visually check the shape of your nibs to make sure they are right for the occasion, but, after you have been drawing for a while, you will find that you are able to judge the shape without even looking, just by the feel of the pencil. A pointed tip will feel very different to a blunt one, and sometimes a blunt tip will give off a truly awful sound as you work.

Level II Sharpeners

Electric Pencil Sharpener

I use a Swordfish electric pencil sharpener and have done for quite a few years now. It wasn't cheap and seemed like an extravagance at first, but it's saved me much effort and allowed my concentration to remain on my work.

The blades still haven't needed replacing, even after five years of use. The only issue is that you have to take out the tray every now and again to dispose of the wood shavings. The not-so-good part about this device is that it makes the collection of graphite powder impossible, what with all the wood shavings being included in the waste pot.*

The electric sharpener makes drawing at home at night a little tricky, because its noisiness may wake everyone up, but it's a wonderfully efficient bit of equipment to have around.

Some more pointers about sharpening . . .

1. Drawing in a precise manner is hard enough without adding to your difficulties: be sure to keep a sharp pencil.

2. The sharpening tool should always be within easy reach.

3. The act of sharpening should not take more than ten seconds to do. The more quickly you are able to return to your drawing, the better. The reason for this is that sharpening is a job outside of drawing. This chore can allow your mind to wander from the task at hand and will allow distraction to creep in. Your pencil might be sharper but your concentration may be a little broken.

4. It's good practice to wipe the pencil tip after sharpening so that any excess shards of graphite clinging to the tip don't end up deposited in the drawing, spoiling your fine lines. These shards are also buggers in that they are easy to smudge.

Are you okay? Only, you've been staring at that blade for an hour now.

 LEVEL 3 — SPECIFIC

*You could of course sieve the shavings, but if you find yourself panning for graphite, you may have just reached an insane a level of obsession. You may be lost to us.

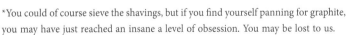

43

Lead Pointer

Clutch pencils benefit greatly from the Staedtler lead pointer tub. This device has two holes on the top, one that produces a blunt tip and another that produces a needle-like point. The tub also works to clean graphite powder off the newly sharpened nib using a fibrous lead-cleaner in the top.

Draftsman's artillery

The filed-down powder of graphite looks a lot like gunpowder, which is appropriate considering the early military uses of graphite. Powdered graphite can be bought in small tubs, or you can collect your own while sharpening your pencil on sandpaper, or your clutch pencil in a lead pointer tub.

You may find that graphite powder bought from the shop isn't quite as dark as you'd like. For this reason, it is a good idea to buy dark matt pencils, such as Ebony sketching pencils*, and sand them into a jar. This can give your drawing the boldness it needs to stand out.

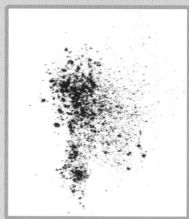

Graphite dust is a wonderful addition to a draftsperson's arsenal because you can almost paint with it. It's comforting to know that whatever you put down in dust can be completely removed by eraser: it remains on the surface of the Bristol board if not worked too heavily into the paper.

Mass drawing

Powdered graphite is particularly useful for filling in large areas, such as the background. Laying in such large areas of shadow with a sharp pencil is extremely time-consuming. By brushing on graphite, we can quickly develop these areas. Be aware that the powdered graphite will work differently on different papers, so try it out on a test sheet first to check its effect.

A dusting of graphite powder has also revealed this crime scene: previously, this surface was rubbed by my hand, contaminating it beyond repair.

Easily smudged

The downsides to graphite powder are that it can be smudged easily, and breathing in the graphite powder for too long can make your throat sore, so be sure to work in well-ventilated conditions. When using powdered graphite, be extra careful in securing your drawing shield (details about shields next on the next page) as this fine powdered material shifts around easily—don't sneeze!

The biggest problem with graphite powder is how messy it is. Not all the powder that is applied to the surface necessarily adheres to the paper. For this reason, use powder only when working on a flat surface. Remove excess by tipping the paper vertically; do not blow or brush the powder as this can cause unwanted marks. There are also devices known as 'blow bulbs,' which will mimic the effect of blowing on the paper, but without the risk of accidental spittle.

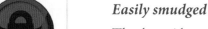　*Be aware, ebony pencils contain carbon. This is what gives these pencils their extra punch.

The Demon 'Sebum'

Greasy Adversary

There are many items of equipment that I use to shield the drawing from my hand; all have their advantages and disadvantages. There are shields I replace very often and others I never have to replace. The main function of these devices is to keep our grubby mitts* from touching the surface of the paper. This is because our hands harbour an enemy: the oil produced by sebaceous glands, which is a fatty, waxy, cellular debris known as sebum.

It may keep our skin handsome, waterproof and safe from salt, but sebum is the scourge of the drawing world. Even if you have just washed your hands, your skin still contains oils that can ruin a drawing. Once oil combines with graphite, the tone will not rub out easily, and attempts to erase will leave the paper slightly off-white. Such damage is easily noticeable in areas that contain flat patches of tone. So grab yourself a shield, and save yourself a lot of unnecessary hassle.

SEBUM

Offense - Grease attack. An easy Boss to deal with if you have a shield in place.

Shields

Mahl Stick

This shield is a long stick that is used as a hand support when we're working on larger pieces at upright easels. It enables the artist to move around the paper efficiently while keeping their hand steady. My homemade mahl stick is comprised of a 30-inch bamboo stick, although you may prefer something sturdier. It has a champagne cork stuck on the end, around which I have wrapped a piece of fabric (a sock), secured tightly with rubber bands.

The mahl stick is also often used by painters, as the padded end can be rested against a canvas without damaging the surface. A mahl stick is particularly useful when you need to keep a steady hand, as when working on areas of detail, or when suffering from coffee jitters.

When making your mahl stick, be sure to use a reasonably smooth stick: you need to be able to move your hand easily along its length, and you definitely don't want to get any splinters.

*Brit-speak for hands.

Acetate Sheet

This transparent sheet is a shield which allows you to keep an eye on the whole picture while also protecting your drawing from the dreaded Sebum.

Drawbacks

Acetate generates static electricity, which will attract particles of graphite. Once these little graphite-strays stick to your acetate, the slightest movement will rub them across the drawing. The static also means that this guard isn't very nice to glide your hand over—or maybe that's just me; it's worth giving it a try to see if it bothers you.

In the past, I have tried wearing latex gloves to avoid contact with the drawing surface, but these had two detrimental effects. Firstly, they allow you to continue to redeposit graphite with the gloves, and secondly, you lose contact with the pencil. I know surgeons manage it just fine, but I found that I need to have direct contact with my tools to allow my hand the most sensitive possible connection with the pencil.

CLEAN!

As they always say: cleanliness is close to Godmode-liness!

Three Bits O' Wood

When arranged as in the picture on the right, these pieces of wood form a bridge-like set up that keeps your hand well away from the paper. Place two equally thick wooden boards or books next to your drawing surface, then lie a sturdy strip of wood across them, upon which you can rest and steady your hand as you work.

Drawbacks

Having your hand at a distance from the drawing surface can be troublesome when it comes to working on details. I prefer to be closer to the surface. If you like this arrangement, however, you can take it further by creating a wooden frame all around the paper (3), allowing you to position your wrist-plank at almost any angle and making every part of the drawing accessible.

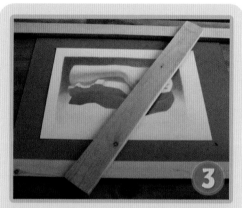

I feel a little disconnected from the work when using this; however, it works very well indeed when trying to finesse more technical work, such as architectural drawings and the like.

Begone! Foul demon!

DRAW LIKE A BOSS

Little Finger

This method has nothing to do with the unpleasant backstabber from *Game of Thrones*. The artist's little finger placed against the surface can be used as a bridge, stabilising the hand as you draw. I find this a little awkward, but give it a try; it may work for you. Also, be sure that your little finger is touching your hand guard and not the drawing surface itself.

Paper Under the Wrist

Often the simplest solutions are the best, and it doesn't get much simpler than this. A piece of paper board under my wrist is the guard I use most often, and it is particularly excellent when concentrating on small sections of a drawing. It is also a safe, clean, handy space for making notes and sketches before committing to a mark that needs to be right the first time.

It is important that you don't allow the hand guard to shift around on the paper, otherwise it will act as a blender, smudging everything as it passes over. I sometimes use things like masking tape, Blu-Tack or bulldog clips to fix the hand guard to the table.

Drawbacks

The downsides to the paper shield are that it does obstruct your view of the picture, and this can cause the drawing to become disjointed: over the course of working on a picture, it is easy to lose touch with the aspects you can't see. To remedy this, get in the habit of peering under the paper at regular intervals, to make sure you're still on track. A stiff piece of Bristol board usually serves as a decent hand guard, but note that while the paper guard should be stiff, it shouldn't be so rigid that it can't be bent back to let you see underneath.

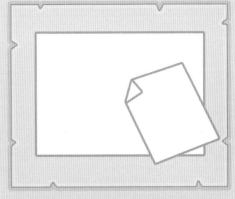

To conclude the Specific's intro to bits of kit

Ideally, you should try to focus on getting a proper understanding of light and form before you worry too much about pencils and papers. There are so many tools and so many different approaches to drawing they can be combined with for us to experiment with when the time comes.

If I am constantly moving the guard around the picture, however, I tend not to fix it to the table. I often dog ear the paper guard so it's easier to pick up when I want to check how everything is looking.

Any mediums you select will have benefits and drawbacks, and there is no single tool that can do everything. There also is no magic combination of tools that will suddenly make you better: it is always the time spent practicing that leads to improvement. While practicing, you will come to know what tools work best for you and for your preferred style of drawing. Experimentation is essential for discovering your personal style. Now, let's get back to examining line, and the different styles of line that are involved in picture making.

Yeehaw! You beat him. I guess I should teach you the way of the curve now then, eh.

Emotional Lines

Curves are everywhere; they are organic, flowing. Trying to copy an exact curve from life is like trying to draw a dancer during the dance. Curved lines can be very beautiful and effective expressions of life and can build to become swirling, exuberant vortices of energy—which is all very nice, but not an ideal starting point for drawing a line. Why is this?

A curved line, no matter how small, contains an incredible amount of information. To draw from life using curves is to draw with extreme specificity, and chances are that most of the curves you draw will actually be the product of guesswork. And yet, laying down curvy contours is what many people think of as 'drawing'. When you draw, do you use tensely curling lines and try really hard, going so far as to stick your tongue out with the intense levels of concentration? I'm afraid it won't help. No amount of focus will make this method work, as we are about to find out. No matter how proficient an artist is, they always approach curves with caution—in drawing, there is such a thing as too much freedom.

The Specific is . . .
Playful
Elaborate, fussy
Tight, closed
Decorative
Finely detailed
Childish
Emotional
Energetic
Exciting
Unpredictable
Attention-seeking
Meddlesome

Enlisting the Specific's help early on can only lead to pandemonium.

Asking the Wrong Questions?

The symbol to the right can help us remember the dangers of the Specific. Question marks signify questions—and we need to ask the right ones—but they also symbolise confusion. The symbol itself, with its curl and its little dot, perfectly represents the two things that get us confused when drawing: curves drawn too soon, and tiny details! Beware both of these, and remember the '**?**', lest ye be led astray.

The trouble with curves is, curved lines don't actually behave like question marks. Curves aren't questions: they're closed statements. Curves are statements of certainty that try to boldly declare every detail and nuance of a thing's shape. Drawing a curve too early is like drawing conclusions too soon, before you've asked the important questions and examined all the angles, leaving yourself no room to change your mind or admit mistakes. It's just asking for trouble . . . but what better way is there to learn than by asking for a little trouble?

Getting Specific

This exercise should help you understand curves and the caution with which we should treat them. To put it simply, curves are a real bugger to draw right off the bat. The contour of a curved form, like this vase, consists of an almost infinite multitude of angles. Describing them accurately is a massive challenge. Let's take a look at what trouble we can get into by attempting to capture the specifics of a shape at the beginning. This is going to get ugly, but it's all for the best. As William Blake so neatly put it "If the fool would persist in his folly he would become wise." So let's persist and attain some wise.

1   *Setting up* — With a ruler, draw a vertical line on your paper that is at least four inches long. Make it dark enough to see clearly.

2   If you are right-handed, draw half a vase on the left-hand side of the line, like the one in the example below. It can be any shape really, just so long as it's nice and curvy.

3   *On the other hand* — If you are left-handed, draw half a vase on the right-hand side. The important thing here is that you should be able to see the first half of the vase as you try to copy it over on the other side.

4   Place your pencil at the top, on the other side. Without lifting your pencil, using one continuous, firm line, try to copy the first half of your vase.

5   Now, raise your fists in the air and declare, to the great art gods, that this method of drawing shall no longer haunt your artistic repertoire.

 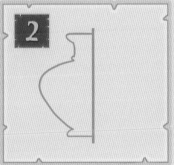  

Compare your first line to your attempted copy. If the two lines match perfectly, congratulations, you are a wizard and no longer need any instruction from anyone about anything ever again. In fact, game over, your life is complete! The rest of us mere mortals will have to make do with learning some patience, humility—and technique.

The Learning Curve

The previous exercise should have given you a sense of how difficult it is to draw a seemingly simple line. This might seem like a discouraging lesson in the impossibility of drawing. Don't worry, though: it's not that drawing is difficult, it's that drawing the wrong way is difficult. After all, you wouldn't learn to drive by taking hairpin curves at high speed on a narrow mountain road.

> A single, curved line, drawn out right, is a complete statement. With no room for changing your mind. Be careful.

If you try to record your observations with a single, curving contour line, that line will be full of hesitation and uncertainty—because you don't know enough about your subject yet. This kind of drawing is close-minded and overly confident, whereas what we need is a little doubt. It's impossible to create the kind of living, expressive work we're aiming towards without asking the necessary questions first.

The Specific, therefore, should be introduced slowly—never take her up on her offers of early assistance, no matter how interesting and exciting they seem. Accepting her invitation turns her into a Boss who blocks our progress. Once she starts to dominate the early stages of our work, our picture begins to tighten up, restricting any flow of development. All those curves become constricting tendrils, strangling our work and preventing movement.

Our pencil marks can communicate passion, playfulness and wit, but they can reveal impatience, tightness and anxiety just as clearly. The Specific lures beginners into drawing painstakingly careful outlines, but you need to resist this temptation and break the habit. Drawing this way produces stilted, inaccurate work, as well as stifling your enjoyment and limiting your growth.

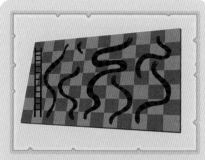

Just as you would avoid hairpin turns when learning to drive, you also want to avoid the curvy snakes of 'Snakes and Ladders'. Asking you to take part in the last exercise was sort of like getting you to crash your car on the circuit then step on a snake.

My motives were entirely benevolent, however. As much as going back to square one might not feel too good, it is heartily recommended, so that you can start from a basis that is pure and reasonable.

The line is a device used to forge simple relationships between the most essential components of an image, to be able to do this, you need to have a general understanding of what you are observing.

SPECIFIC

Allow her to dominate the work and things will quickly spiral out of control.

> So, three things to avoid early on in the drawing: **curves**, **details** and **dark lines**.

The Specific told me she knew the way, that she'd get me doing awesome drawings, that she'd make it all fun, and that I should skip ahead to 'the cool stuff.' All the lovely curves, the intricate details. I followed her, and soon found myself lost, all sense of direction gone, in a state of bewilderment. I was wandering in a bog, mud sucking at my feet, every step sinking me deeper into the mire.

Curves had led me to become entangled in snarls of briars and vines; they were somehow winding round me, coiling ever tighter. Lost, bogged down and confused, I looked up, seeking guidance from my playful friend. Although she was there right in front of me, she was not as I knew her. The sprite had become a giant, and she was not smiling anymore. Her expression was tight, her muscles tense, and it didn't look like she wanted to let me past.

The Specific can get us into lots of trouble with drawing, and she's one of the hardest bosses I've ever faced. I still have difficulty knowing when to invite her in, and once I do, I struggle to control her. Worst of all, she's the companion I turn to when I'm feeling bored or frustrated with a drawing. At those times, the temptation to invoke her is almost irresistible, but if I give in, I know I'll end up frustrated to the point of wanting to give up.

Take heed, adventurer

The longer you hold out before letting the Specific guide you, the better. You have the best chance of working well with her once you've developed a solid sense of the entire composition. It's this firm sense of the whole which keeps her in safe limits, giving her space to dance without allowing her to lead you astray. If you entered this adventure with confidence, I hope that hasn't been shaken. However, doubt is a vital quality in learning. As Voltaire put it 'Doubt is not a pleasant condition, but certainty is absurd'.

Best of three?

Tightness

Quantum Entanglement

If you're making dark marks early in a drawing, it probably means that you're gripping your pencil too tightly. Getting too dark too soon can also be a sign that you are rushing to see results. Nothing in drawing is instantaneous. Proceed slowly, however, with open eyes and a light step, and you'll get there.

Artist's paradox

The irony is that it's easier to spot mistakes when marks are darker, but unfortunately, darkly defined mistakes are also much harder to correct. If you need to remove a heavy line, you're likely to leave at least some blemish or damage on the surface. I can assure you that, in the beginning, it is always far better to imply things than to state them heavily state them–this lets you find your way and fix mistakes.

Pacing yourself

A successful drawing is often the result of hours of sustained concentration. One of the hardest things is maintaining an inner balance between creativity and restraint. It is best to proceed systematically, keeping an even pace and allowing the drawing to develop without forcing it. Work lightly and correct errors as you find them.

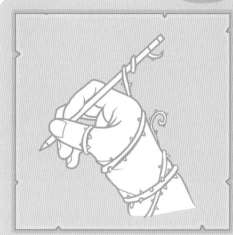

Draftsman's rigor mortis — Watch out for your pencil stroke becoming too dark too early in a drawing. It is essential that you keep your marks light, as this leaves your drawing open and easy to change, meaning you have a greater chance of staying on course.

The particular way that we hold the pencil in the early stages can often be the factor that draws us into becoming ensnared and drawing lines that are too curvaceous. Fear not, we will soon encounter remedies for that also. You'll likely feel strongly drawn to making dark, curvaceous lines, because a bold, carefree line is a beautiful thing.

Resist the urge to 'fix' the mistake by drawing over it more darkly. And once again, do not rush into the details. You can't sprint a marathon, and you wouldn't add icing to an unbaked cake: in the name of all mixed metaphors, do not let your drawings get dark, curvy or detailed too soon!

Try not to make the mistake of going darker when you realise you've made a mistake. It's a natural tendency, but it's like trying to resolve a disagreement by raising your voice: it all ends in an awful shouting match. This is like arguing with the line, shouting over the previous statement. Erase mistakes. Don't try to 'hide' them by darkly drawing over them.

And where have you been?!

 DRAW LIKE A BOSS

THE GENERAL

The Point	General Relativity	The Line	Guidelines	Straightness	The Shape	Constellation	Grip I
54	56	58	60	62	64	70	71

At that moment, another colossus appeared and pulled me from the perilous snares. After all this time, it appeared Marius had gone to get help. The colossus he brought back with him seemed to be some sort of spirit encased in ancient armour. "I'm the General," he said, "and it's a shame we didn't meet earlier. It appears you've fallen in with the wrong crowd. In fact, Guido, although you found the first piece of the Tetraforce, you've completely missed the point." With the summoning of the General, the Tetraforce had begun . . .

> The first piece is not just about sharp pencils. It's about points.

My failures haunted me. The General reassured me that a little failure was important, as it gave me a place from which I could grow. Now he was here to guide me, I shouldn't have any more problems. He invited me to sit with him, look at the stars, and forget all about vases. The Specific jumped in at this point and suggested that, now that the stars were revealed, we could use them to plot a course.

POINT

Level Up! – The Point of it All

Guido scrambled to his feet beside the General. A fresh breeze had cleared the sky, which was now dark and filled with stars. As we follow Guido and the General into this new territory, we are finally going to start getting our bearings. The stars will guide us, allowing us to escape from the weird, childish uncertainty that gripped us in the Void.

As you struggle to master drawing, you may ask yourself "What's the point?" This is the wrong question, adventurer: instead, ask yourself, "Where is the point?" We are about to learn how to use points to help locate objects within a drawing.

Three particular stars

Sailors have something to teach artists: the art of celestial navigation. When finding their way across the void of the sea, sailors orient themselves using fixed, known points in the sky. Artists, too, must make use of known points to keep them from getting lost. Three evenly-spaced stars in the night's sky, known as Orion's belt, are the points of light we should be concerned with. For artists, they take on a different meaning: they represent the first steps in analysing any subject.

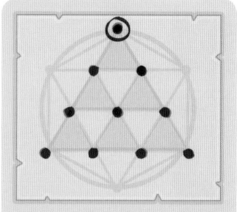

There is no simpler dimension from which we could begin a drawing than the point. The point is like a seed, planted in the Void, full of potential. It only takes a second to make this first mark, but it can become the precursor to hours and even months of work.

There are many ways to begin drawing from observation, but the best that I've found is starting with three evenly spaced points, which are used as the basis for visual analysis.

The logic involved in the type of beginning we're about to consider can mean that your drawings may begin to appear quite mechanical. Don't worry. As we go on, the process becomes increasingly intuitive and emotional, and a likeness begins to emerge, because drawing evolves from an interplay between analysis and intuition.

These three crucial points will help us begin to combine the intellectual rigour of the General with the chaotic energy of the Specific. When the mathematical and mystical come together, remarkable things can happen.* The three points anchor us in this process. To appreciate their importance, let's take a moment to look back towards the Specific by learning what happens if we try to navigate using too many stars at once.

*"Creativity is intelligence having fun," as Albert Einstein once said. As much as we need the General's guidance, we won't be leaving the Specific behind.

Straight to the Point

"If you were still following her," the General said, gesturing at the Specific, "she'd have you trying to chart a course using every star in the sky. That's simply more information than we need. For my first lesson, I want you to chart just a few stars, to learn how to handle a cluster of variables in a controlled setting." Instead of hundreds of points, we'll be using only nine. From this, we'll discover how sensitive we are to seeing subtle differences. By attempting to position nine points correctly, we should get a sense of how difficult it would be to work with a greater number of variables. The General's first lesson is also a dig at the Specific.

1

To begin

Place two pieces of cartridge paper (basic printer paper) adjacent to one another. Take your pencil and draw nine dots at random on the sheet to the left.

2

Move to the paper on the right and try to copy the exact positions of the dots as best you can. There are some questions you can ask to help: how does each dot relate to the edges of the paper? How do they relate to each other? Are they higher? Lower? Directly below or above? The more points you plot, the more difficult this task becomes. This is useful because it illustrates how quickly things get confusing when we are working with lots of variables.

The thing is, any given object will have dozens or hundreds of variables to consider. The key is to focus on the most important points. Try to get a few things right from the start, before you move on to the next level of the Tetraforce, the line.

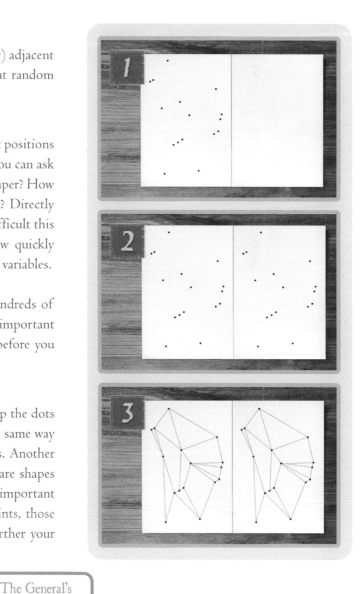

3

In order to check your accuracy, take a ruler and join up the dots on both pieces of paper, making sure that you do it the same way on both. By joining the dots, we are generating shapes. Another thing to realise here is how much easier it is to compare shapes than the positions of scattered dots. This reveals an important trap: if you make mistakes when positioning your points, those mistakes will become more and more obvious, the further your drawing progresses.

> The General's lessons are so dull!

General Relativity

Specific Order

Rational analysis, that's the name of the game here. By using reason to analyse our observations, rather than relying on assumptions, we can truly begin a drawing. We need a tool for noting down our analysis, and for this we use the point. Points are one of the most important organisational devices used in the drawing process: they are the simplest possible description of one thing's position relative to another.

The further we progress up the Tetraforce and through our drawings, the easier it will become to evaluate whether our marks are accurate—but the harder it will be to make changes.

Drawing points, on the other hand, requires very little commitment—it is much easier to rub out a point than a line. Similarly, a straight line is easier to amend than a curve, and a single value is easier to adapt than a fully shaded tonal progression. Using good judgement at the basic levels sets us up for a greater chance of success later on. Get it right when it's simple, and you won't have major revisions waiting for you when it gets complicated.

> The key is knowing where to place the Specific.

There's no way to get these two marks wrong; they are pretty much the closest we can come to establishing some facts in our drawing. The more 'facts' you feel certain of in your drawing, the more confident you'll feel. By placing these points (I use dashes so I can see them better), you are deciding how big your subject will be, and by establishing a sense of scale, you can also better understand the object's placement within the frame.

This setup of three simple points, or dashes, neatly separates the drawing into manageable quarters: top left, top right, bottom left and bottom right.

Highest and lowest point (A)

To get back to the point, reason tells us that an object will always have a highest point and a lowest point (A). These top and bottom points can be marked on the paper with two dots or dashes. The General advises us to always start with the easy things first, and it doesn't get much easier than drawing two dots, does it?

Middle point (B)

It's also pretty obvious that, if a thing has a top and a bottom, it must have a middle point too. Establishing the mid-point is one of the fundamentals of judging proportion. Look at your subject, and use your pencil to gauge its halfway point. After doing this, ask yourself whether this point corresponds to an easily identifiable aspect of your subject,

Wait... so you can be in two places... at the same time?

Sure.

Sure.

such as a human figure's hips or the underside of a person's nose? Mark this midpoint on your paper, and feel secure in the knowledge that you already have a general idea of what is going on in the middle. Top and bottom points are one of those really useful aspects that are so basic they easily get overlooked. These points locate our subject within the paper surface, ensuring that we use the space wisely. They constitute the very beginnings of working out a good composition.

> Don't worry about anything but basic size and placement right now. If you can get the simple things right, then you are on the right track.

Ambiguity (C)

If a subject has a top, bottom and middle, it must also have left and right extremes, right?

The trouble is, these points are not nearly as straightforward: they are uncertain.* However, if you can successfully pin down these two specifics, you will have begun to establish your subject's proportions.

In time we will learn techniques for more accurately positioning these side points, but for now, it's alright to settle for eyeballing them. Even though we're trying to be careful, we don't have to be exact.

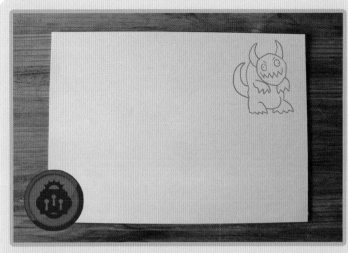

Establishing the top and bottom points of your composition also stops you from summoning a Corner Dweller, a tight little study lurking in the topmost corner of the page. I'm sure you've summoned a few in your time, or seen someone else in art class troubled by these little jerks.

Once we decide where the top and bottom points are, the question arises: where are the sides? This question isn't quite as simple, but we can still go about answering it an orderly manner. The first step, shown here, is to draw a guideline down the centre of my paper, using a ruler and an F grade pencil. Your line should, of course, be much fainter than the one shown here. Also, there's no need to draw huge dark question marks. Oh, and by the way, by drawing a line down the centre you have just Levelled Up!

Landscape variant (D)

It is, of course, completely fine to decide that you want to begin by establishing your side points rather than your top and bottom, making the sides your 'facts'. Which orientation you choose will often depend which is longest on your subject, the height or the width. The important thing is that your first two marks are 'facts' while marks on the other axis are conjecture.

*This is a little like the Heisenberg uncertainty principle, in that if you determine positions on one axis, you cannot be sure of points on the other axis. Certainty will always be counterbalanced by ambiguity. (Shush, science-folks, we know this isn't really quantum mechanics, but we've found this comparison personally helpful).

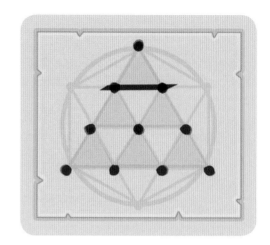

Level Up! — Journeyman!

You're Levelling Up all over the place now! We've now reached Level 5, when we finally get to talk about line in the way we should use it to make images. Before we start drawing lines, however, I'd like you to take a moment to consider just how weird lines are.

We're all familiar with using outlines to represent objects, but look around you: not an outline to be seen! Outlines are a useful convention, as real as the equator or an hour. The line is like something invented so that an equation can work, some kind of particle that is only there in theory and not actually found in nature.

There's an interesting theory that the convention of outlines originated as a way of integrating physical experience into visual representations. When we touch and handle objects, we experience them as solid and stable. Our fingers feel surfaces which are clearly distinguished from the space around them. And although the leather shoe feels different from its rubber sole, experience tells us they're connected, so we're likely to include them both in the outlined shape of a shoe (perhaps using another line to mark the shift in texture). Visual experience isn't nearly this consistent: change the angle or the light, and the visual boundaries between objects can shift and dissolve. Outlines are a way of drawing what we "know" is there, even when that knowledge doesn't quite match up with what we see.

> A line doesn't belong to the subject: it is a shared boundary between 'thing' and the space around it.

A useful symbol

Lines are both a differentiation device and also a measuring tool, designating an object's boundaries or limits, signifying where the object ends and its surroundings or context begin. Lines are very much like words, in that they are devices for breaking up the world, compartmentalising objects. This 'divide and conquer' approach to reality is necessarily artificial, a convenient fiction.

If we can name an object, we feel that we know it, we've 'got a grasp' on it. In exactly the same way, a clearly defined outline can help us feel secure. For artists, lines are a very useful way of organising thoughts and ideas on a surface. Straight lines are the best tool to use for this. In fact, knowing how to use straight lines is the key to good drawings. Just by knowing this, you become a better artist.

Points and straight lines work very well together to build a drawing. This is incredibly important and certainly worth shouting about! Using these tools, we can make bold statements, combining intuition and logic.

Whoop! Another triangle thing!

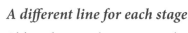

A different line for each stage

Although we are beginning with straight lines, it's worth noting now that we will need different types of lines at different stages of the drawing process. Lines can be either analytical or intuitive, and it's important to learn which type to use and when. In the process of drawing, we can also come to appreciate the inherent beauty of all lines—a realisation that will, in itself, help us to produce beautiful artworks. What we're going to investigate now is another kind of intellectual line: the structural line. Structural lines don't represent visual experience; rather, they are a way of noting what you have discovered about an object. The line we drew between our top and bottom point was a key structural line. Structural lines are the scaffolding of your drawing, holding it together until we reach the point when the scaffolding can be dismantled, and the drawing can stand alone, supporting its own weight.

 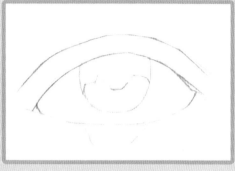 

Block-in Lines   **Contour Lines**   **Hatching Lines**

Later On . . .

Over the course of a drawing, you will probably reconsider most of your lines. Even when lines are correctly placed, the drawing will reach a stage where you need to remove them in order to increase realism. As we've learned, lines are characteristics of drawings, not of actual visual experience. Visible outlines mark an image as 'just' a drawing, not a window to another reality. In the series of images below, outlines are removed and adapted using pencils, erasers and blenders of all kinds. In time, you will learn all about the subtle art of finessing an image in this way.

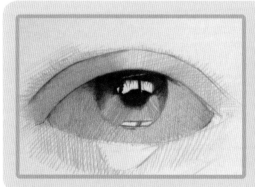 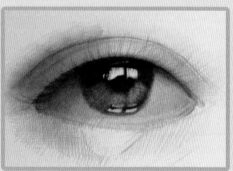 

 Ooh, seeing this drawing come together has done something to you, hasn't it? You may now be feeling a little impatient. Wanting to hurry up and get to the 'fun part'? I've been there; most of us probably have: fists full of blenders, laying down values left and right. It doesn't end well. Remember: master the core principles, and get the structure right first. Don't start arranging knick-knacks in the house before you've actually built it.

Guidelines

You Found the Long Road!

There are two kinds of lines here on the second level of the Tetraforce. First, there are the lines we draw between points to delineate shapes. Second, there are the guidelines we use to help gauge proportions, placement and angles.

We've already discussed the first guideline: the vertical line you draw straight down the middle of the picture (A), or else its horizontal cousin, if you've chosen that variant. Whichever you opt for, these guidelines must be marked out very lightly (in the illustrations to the right, the guides have been darkened to make them more visible).

Each composition will call for different guidelines, according to its most important aspects: using guidelines, you will link points of interest and establish relations between them. You can lay down as many guidelines as you like, to the point of gridding out your entire working area. The further you take the gridding process, the closer you move towards mechanical or technical drawing.

In defence of the General

Guidelines can feel rigid and formulaic, especially when you aren't used to working with them. If you employ too many guides, they can get in the way of direct observation. Don't lean on crutches so heavily that you forget to use your legs. Guidelines are here to support your efforts, aiding your intellect and direct observations.

As you begin, you may feel that the General is a dull, restrictive guide, frustratingly meticulous and logical. He has another side, however, which is much more dynamic. This is revealed in the second kind of guideline, called an 'action line' (C). This is a line which captures the subject's movement or tilt. It is the dominant line of energy running through the object, the most important idea of the drawing.

I find that it is beneficial to discover dominant lines within the model as this will give more clues about the gesture of the model than might be suggested by the outline alone.

Truly the General is as dull as a sack of hair.

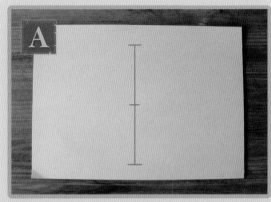

A line dropped down through the three points gives us a direction to go in. This line is an incredibly useful aid, as we will see. However, as much as creating this guideline can aid us in drawing, it is not the only way to begin.

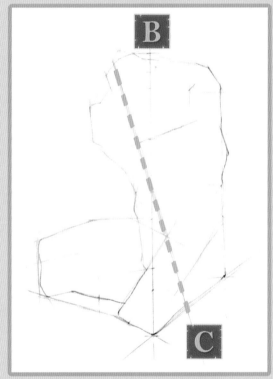

In this drawing of the Belvedere torso, two major guides are in place. There is the vertical one that runs straight down from the area marked (B), and there is an action line emanating diagonally from (C). This action line helps me describe the way this torso is angled in space. This characteristic tilt and twist is also known as the model's 'gesture.'

In studies like this, don't worry about leaving in guidelines. Don't bother removing them to tidy up—only erase them if they prove inaccurate or unhelpful.

You Found the Hookshot

Look at the study of the torso on the previous page. See all those lines that seem to be stretching out further than they need to? Those lines might look show-offy and dramatic. They're not. They're actually a really helpful measuring tool.

Extending lines this way is like using a grappling hook to grab onto other objects. They help you to establish informative relationships between different aspects of your composition.

Ugh, so many curves! This isn't an ideal still life for a beginner. It will be useful, however, to see how such round forms can be converted into straight lines and blocky shapes. We can also see how using extended lines allows us to keep figuring things out, analysing our next step. After all, at the beginning, we don't necessarily know where the lines we make need to stop.

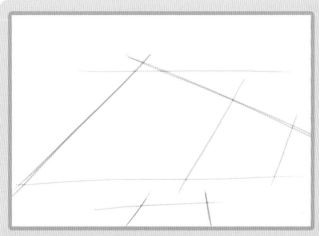
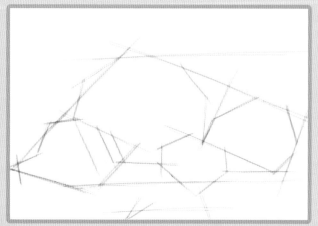

Not a single line in the images above begins with a certain beginning. Clearly, they do begin somewhere, but that starting point is an approximation: at this point it's almost impossible to be sure of any object's placement. These lines are slashes, gestures that attempt to define one side of an object in a general way. As various lines intersect, rough shapes begin to emerge.

These lines represent my best estimates, and although a lot of thought and concentration has gone into figuring them out, I used very little energy in actually marking them. This is good, because I will almost certainly have to correct some of them. When that time comes, I won't be sacrificing much effort. I can happily adjust and readjust these lines to form an ever more accurate representation of the subject.

Let your workings remain

Leaving you guidelines in, as I have done in the previous drawing of the torso, can be a good thing. It gives us a chance to look back later on and see our workings. These contain valuable information.

When we draw from life, the visual experience poses a series of problems. If you think about solving a maths problem, the workings are in some ways more important than the answer. Guidelines show how the drawing developed, and they'll help us to reflect on our own development. The only guidelines you must remove are those which turn out to be inaccurate. Make it a habit to purge all misleading or unhelpful guidelines.

The General is . . .

Serious, Practical

Uninvolved, Plain

Open, Adaptable

Predictable

Abstract, Ambiguous

Essential

Intellectual

Mechanical

Work-oriented

Stable

The General Way

The ancient Romans built straight roads so that they could see the enemy approaching. Likewise, artists drawing from observation construct straight lines so that we can keep a clear view of what is coming up ahead. Our drawing should always be developed from a highly simplified form, a line drawing that treats the subject as an angular two-dimensional shape. We do this so we can work out proportions and angles without having to worry about the million tiny nuances of a complex contour.

Taking a straight road to our destination is far more efficient than following a wandering path that dips and curves with every tussock of grass. That's a great way to get lost in the wilderness.

Straight as an arrow.

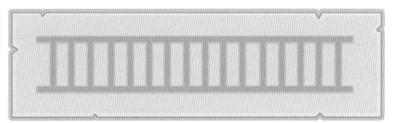

Just as ladders allow us to advance in the game of Snakes and Ladders, adopting them as a style of line enables us to move surefootedly. A straight line is heading towards accuracy. A curved line, snake-like, risks sending us backwards.

Completely straight?

At this point you might be saying, "Well, I can't even draw a straight line!" Neither can I. If I try to draw a straight line very slowly, I end up with a laboured mess like (A).

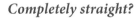
A

Even if you think you're being super slow and careful, the line will look like a lie detector graph and speak volumes about your hesitancy. In short, if you let yourself get tense and worried, you'll mess it up. Instead, be quick and daring, but use a light touch. The line will look a lot better, and if it's not good enough, you can try again without making your marks too dark.

What I mean by a 'straight line' is a line drawn relatively quickly in a general direction, not a painstakingly perfect line drawn with a ruler. Where you see 'straight,' read it as 'straightish' instead.

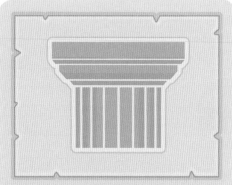

This image shows the top of a Doric pillar which is far plainer than the Corinthian pictured earlier. This pillar has strength and dignity, but for all these good qualities it could easily be accused of being, well, a bit boring.

Classical pillars, however, were never really straight from top to bottom: they always had a slight curve to them. This is an aesthetically pleasing effect we refer to as 'entasis'. The Greeks knew full well that the straight line was boring, and so, to add variety and interest, they added a slight curve to their pillars (entasis also created an illusion of the pillars rising higher than they actually did).

So, to summarise, we're not interested in drawing perfectly straight lines; otherwise, we'd just use a ruler to draw. Our lines should have a slight curve to them, which, luckily for us, is a property inherent to drawing a line anyway, as they are never perfectly straight.

LISTEN! The straight line is unfinished, an open line of enquiry which simply asks, "Could this be the way things are?" Over time, the straight lines' questions are answered through a process of elimination and discernment. A drawing may seem to begin mechanically, but the way it develops is organic.

A Grand Unified Theory

So, for a drawing to come alive and be truly harmonious, it must reconcile the opposites: it must have the qualities of both the straight line and the curve. Nevertheless, we must use only one kind of line to build our scaffolding. And I'm sure if you saw some curvy scaffolding, you would be smart enough not to climb it.

The General is our principle guide on this journey, and the Specific plays a supporting role. To put it another way, the smaller details must be subordinated to the main ideas. Nevertheless, a drawing will feel incomplete unless it has these small sparks of interest and particularity.

By uniting the power of the straight with the exuberance and energy of the curve, we can go on to develop truly harmonious and wonderful drawings.

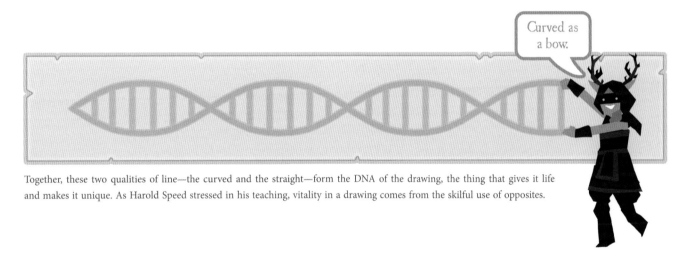

Curved as a bow.

Together, these two qualities of line—the curved and the straight—form the DNA of the drawing, the thing that gives it life and makes it unique. As Harold Speed stressed in his teaching, vitality in a drawing comes from the skilful use of opposites.

Everything has its downsides

The General will enable us to begin our drawings successfully. However, if he dominates too long, the picture will remain vague, cold and impersonal. The General's greatest weakness is a tendency to become generic. At a certain point, it will be necessary to invite the Specific to take the reins. Don't worry, there's no way we'll forget about her—she's always eager to seize control. At this point, however, the only specificity we need is marking out our highest and lowest points, allowing us to get a sense of control and order. Next, we must consider the use of line to generate shape enclosures. Well done adventurer, you just found yourself in the second dimension. Leeeeevel Up time!

SHAPE

Level Up! — Shape Shifter!

The pencil is ideal for drawing lines. It's far less effective, however, at generating large masses. It's difficult to create these general forms with the specific point of the pencil. Some tools are far better suited to generating mass: painters can simply select a large paintbrush and create general shapes with a single motion (A). This is simply impossible with a pencil. Producing large masses in pencil, therefore, requires a different, more cerebral approach.

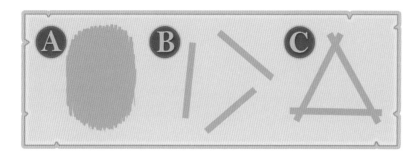

Pencils generate mass by outlining shapes, describing the boundaries of forms. Creating an outline requires that we put lines together, like separate atoms being joined into a molecule (B, C). A shape is basically a structure made up of at least three straight lines, or any number or curves.

When we look at an object or image, the first thing that hits us is shape. We read an object's silhouette much more quickly than we read its inner details. Thus, when drawing, the first thing we want to capture is an object's general shape. When trying to pin down this silhouette, it's helpful to think of your subject as if it were flat. Because we're only drawing from a single viewpoint, it makes sense to think of objects as if they were flat, at least in the early stages of the drawing.

Once we've seen the object as a flat shape, we'll probably realise that it contains a lot of curves. Most shapes are curved to an extent, and, as we've seen, curves are tricky to draw. Straight-edged shapes are far simpler to draw, because they have fewer variables: a single line has a single tilt, unlike the many changing angles of a curve. So, we're going to learn how to translate curved objects into straight-edged ones.

At the third level of the Tetraforce, we can use lines to generate shape enclosures. We're flattening the world into a series of silhouettes, like cardboard cut-outs, or shadows on a wall.

Shapes are fundamental to composition, and good compositions are ones that combine large and small shapes in a way that is balanced. A small shape, for instance, can be balanced with a lot of space, or several larger objects.

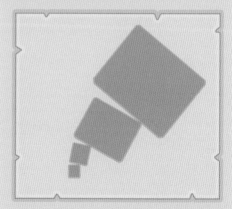

Always give priority to larger shapes! Smaller shapes must remain subordinate to larger shapes and to the whole. Otherwise, we get lost in detail again, and it will be hard to maintain compositional balance, much less accuracy and control.

I hope there aren't many more of these triangle things!

Line and Shape Overview

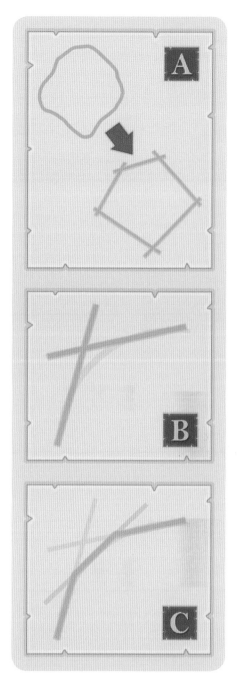

Constellation (Where polygons begin)

How do we go about breaking down a complex, curved shape? We begin by going ultra basic. For this we use the constellation, a shape that sums up a form very simply: it notes its position, the location of its extremities, its most dominant angles and its general gesture.

The constellation distils micro-modulations of line into strong, directional marks, which are easily interpreted and adjusted. The first step to highly refined and complex visual studies is this extreme simplification.

Because this shape is so simple, it is easy to measure the distances between its lines and check the accuracy of its angles. These qualities make it an essential starting point for strong drawing. The constellation is basic, but it contains the fundamentals.

Block-in (How lines develop)

Stage one of the block-in is completed once we've produced a constellation that accurately encapsulates the basic structure of our subject. After this, we can begin to subdivide its lines. We must make these adjustments slowly, building methodically upon the broad, simple foundation of the constellation.

Gradually, your constellation will reduce in simplicity, as we add more and more information. Place the lines of your block-in with confidence but not certainty: stay open to the idea that they may need to be changed and corrected. The block-in stage is an intellectual process of exploration and adjustment. Your work at this stage will look rough and unfinished, but this is just as it should be.

Intermediate block-in (How lines continue to be developed)

Drawing is a process of revision. As we refine and develop our block-in, as more and more measurements reinforce one another, we will eventually begin to approach a likeness. Mistakes and miscalculations are inevitable. The key is to remedy them as best we can before we begin adding value.

Walking on the Long Road was much easier, though I had to agree with the Specific that it was a little dull. It must've been the middle of the night when we made camp. Resting by the fire, we began to talk. My companions, it seemed, were as curious about me as I was about them.

Small Talk

"Let's get to know each other," the Specific said, clapping her hands. "First things first, Guido: I want to know all about your dog! Draw me a picture." Before I could say anything—like, for instance, that I don't actually have a dog—she'd thrust pencil and paper at me, looking so excited I couldn't bear to disappoint her. Feeling foolish, I tried to draw a dog . . .

Draw a random squiggle, like the dog-like shape to the right. Try to copy this shape. As you know, this is quite difficult, and the more intricate and curvy your original, the trickier this gets.

As with the Vase of Folly exercise, you won't be able to achieve a 100% copy. Don't worry the point of doing this is to give you something to compare with your next drawing . . .

Getting Personal

The General shook his head. "That doesn't matter. Tell us the essentials, Guido." He gestured towards the stars. "What is your sign? Show me your constellation." I never paid much attention to that kind of thing, but it's crazy how earnest an invisible spirit can look. I couldn't let the big guy down. Time to make up a constellation!

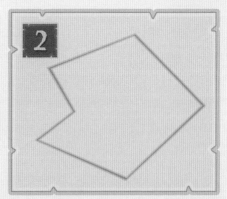

This time draw a shape, any shape, consisting of only five or six straight lines. Now try to copy it. You should find this much simpler.

Here we are only dealing with a few angles and lengths, and this is a much more manageable set of variables.

Use the hookshot mentioned on page 61 to overshoot the lines. Don't try to make them end right where you think they might, as shown in image (?)

A Farm Viewed From Above

The world is a constantly shifting kaleidoscope, a myriad of patterns that come at us all at once. So, to help with this information overload, I want you to think of the visual experience as a big cake, a lavishly decorated one with a cherry on top. Now, what I want you to do on being offered this cake is to refuse it, and only take the cherry.

This is an act of selection: you're taking a part of the cake but not all of it—in fact 99% of the cake has been rejected. For now, this is the spirit we're going to adopt in drawing. Before we can draw something, we first need to select what parts we want, and then build from the ground up. For this, we need basic geometric shapes: these are going to be our building blocks, the forms we're looking for in nature. Soon, we're going to practice using these simple shapes to build up natural forms.

Before we attempt to convert our experience of the world into basic shape patterns, I want you to prepare by simply copying random straight-edged shapes. I'd like you to literally stick down shapes on a surface, and then try to draw them as accurately as you can. Let's take a look at the two ways that you can go about this.

We have had a go at copying the lines of a shape; now I want you to get used to copying masses, big blocks of tone. For this exercise, you need several highly contrasting shades of paper, scissors, and glue—and, of course, your usual pencil and paper.

Cut out some blocky shapes, using only straight lines. Make sure you get a variety of sizes. Stick your shapes to a sheet of paper, arranging them to make large masses so they look like an aerial view of a countryside. Hey look, you've created an abstract composition!

Now take a blank piece of paper, the same size as the one you used for your collage. Your goal is to draw a copy of your collage, replicating its shapes as accurately as possible. Once you feel comfortable with your ability to reproduce two-dimensional shapes, you are ready to try copying shapes from the third-dimension.

Gridded Still Life

This exercise launches us into drawing from three-dimensional objects, using a simple still life. We're not doing a fully rendered still life, just a few small studies. Small studies are great practice, and the results can be rather charming.

This is a level up from copying two-dimensional shapes, but don't panic! Because we're drawing straight-edged objects, the composition is still actually just a collection of shapes, exactly like the ones you copied in the last exercise. The only difference is that we'll be translating from three dimensions.

I've set up my easel facing the subject, with a frame made of cardboard attached to the side. This frame serves as a viewfinder, isolating the subject from its surroundings and thus making it easier to focus. This set-up can make still lifes a lot less daunting.

The black-framed viewfinder is attached to the side of my easel. When using this set-up, be sure to place the viewfinder on the opposite side to your drawing hand. This saves you forever looking across your arm to see the subject.

Screening off the surroundings also helps give the negative space* of our background a shape. This gives us another means of judging the accuracy of our drawing. The frame also helps in working out different compositions, because we can easily move objects around within the frame.

For this exercise, it is a good idea to select objects with basic, straight edges such as books.

Before you begin copying the still life, place your viewfinder against your drawing surface and trace the open space of the viewfinder onto your paper. This will assist your judgement of how to place objects within the scene.

You can further reduce the difficulty of this of copying a still life by gridding up your viewfinder. First, measure out regular intervals along the back of your card and mark them with a pencil.

Next, using these position guides, tape threads to the back, stretched taut, to form a grid. Finally, mark out a proportional grid on your paper. As in our previous gridded exercises, these guidelines will help you gauge your accuracy, and can help you build confidence in your observational skills. The confidence we build here is essential for the next exercise, in which we will make the leap to drawing from life without any device to assist us.

*Hey! What happened to not assuming prior knowledge? Okay, not to worry if you haven't heard of negative space. We'll be covering this in full when we reach the Shadowsands.

Shape Study

Now it is time to take the training wheels off, but that should be fine: you have experience with thumbnails, guidelines, points, and using extended lines to establish connections between objects. Now we're going to put it all together in this next exercise.

If you didn't use books for the last exercise have a gander at your bookshelf, and pick out some hefty tomes. Dark bindings are best because these create high contrast with the white pages. This contrast will help to make sure that the book stack presents us with nice, obvious shapes.

1 Try to forget that they are books. We're here to appreciate shapes and patterns, not objects. Take a moment to draw a thumbnail.

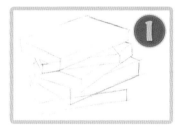

You'll find that this smaller image helps you to understand the forms in front of you, and it gives you a first pass at working out those forms on paper.

2 Use the confidence gained from your thumbnail to approach a larger study. Larger studies are always trickier because the greater distance between points creates a larger margin for error.

The practice of drawing straight-edged objects should come before drawing objects with curves. This is because the abilities we gain in producing blocky shapes will transfer seamlessly to the construction of curved objects: everything starts with points and straight lines.

Remember to use your hookshot: carry those lines on through.

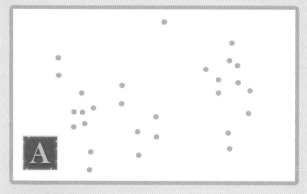

Note, I didn't begin the drawing as in (A). This is simply to show you that there are approximately 28 points to consider in this simple stack of books. If the subject included curves, then the number of variables would increase exponentially. Keep your observational drawings simple to begin with by studying mostly straight-edged objects.

A novel way to learn from a book.

You really like puns don't you...

Constellation

Reduced to Its Essence

It's time to return to the General's constellations. The constellation is a blocky shape that establishes the general placement of the subject and comes in very useful when drawing more complex subjects. The constellation surrounds the whole of your subject, whether that is one object or a collection of smaller objects. It is from this shape that we can then subdivide into smaller shapes, gradually working towards precision and detail.

> "Ten thousand formations. One suchness."
>
> — Lao Tzu

Imagined guides

Your first, most basic constellation should take the form of a six or seven-sided shape that reflects the simplest possible version of your subject's perimeter. Every composition will have its own six or seven-sided constellation to guide your drawing.

Those who follow astrology find comfort in the orderly progression of the heavens: the movements of the stars seem to offer guidance and confer a sense of order to a world which can otherwise feel chaotic and out of control. By drawing a constellation, we find our drawing's birth sign, and this will guide its development and give us a sense of order and control as we work.

The constellation is an extremely abstract, linear way of summing up an object or collection of objects. It strips away all meaning and nuance. Learning how to create and use this kind of abstraction is one of the most valuable keys to learning to draw. It is worth practicing this technique diligently: at first it will be awkward, as with all new ways of working, but once you break through that initial clumsiness, you will be truly setting yourself up for mastery.

Block-in stage one

The constellation is the first stage of what is known as the block-in. The block-in is just what it sounds like: putting in lines to build up a blocky impression of the subject. During this stage, we gather information about proportions and try to capture the dominant angles of prominent features. Establishing these large directional lines helps us to place our smaller lines, giving us a yardstick for measurement.

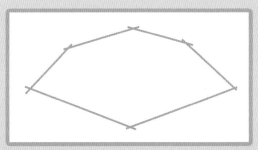

This image is the constellation that was established before commencing the eye shown previously (page 59). With the scale and placement established, work then begins over the top. If I were to draw a human head I wouldn't draw a constellation round every feature of the face. The constellation is the summation of the whole, not the parts.

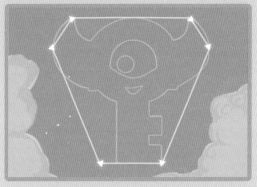

Right now we're in the business of distilling patterns into boxes. If after drawing it, we find the shape isn't in the right place, we haven't wasted too much time as this has been a basic sketch. Simply erase and re-position to your liking.

Truly, this is a thing of beauty!

Look at how the stars are sprayed out across the night sky. For astronomers to 'make sense' of the stars, they consult a stellar map to see straight lines joining the stars in various patterns that make up constellations. All of those connecting lines are, of course, simply the projections by which we make sense of the stars. If you've ever examined constellations, you know they're very basic as far as representation goes: it takes quite a lot of imagination to get from a scattering of stars to a host of mythological heroes and beasts. This is the level of approximation and roughness that we're aiming towards as we create our own constellations.

Grip I

There are lots of different ways of holding a pencil, each one suited to a different stage of drawing. The first grip we should use is what we'll call the 'constellation grip.' It's a way of holding the pencil which will allow you to keep your distance from the paper. It prevents you from becoming rigid, and it is an antidote to any temptation to get specific.

In this grip style, the pencil is held lightly between thumb, index and middle finger. The closer you get to specifics, such as a refined contour or detailed rendering of shadows, the further down the pencil your grip will move.

A pencil held at the end is perfect for the constellation phase as it creates a light and breezy stroke. The pencil has a great deal of flexibility when held in this manner, enabling you to create pencil strokes with a fluid motion that keeps things loose and open. Aim for a character of line that is confident but not certain. The constellation grip also keeps your hand out of the way so that it doesn't obscure your view. Keeping your drawing in sight as you work is important, because it allows you to remain focused on the whole.

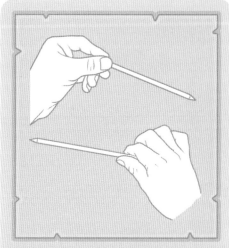

The manner in which a tool reacts with the surface can be changed just by the way you hold it. A different character and speed of pencil stroke emerge by switching to a different pencil grip.

Hold the pencil like it is a wand, right at the very end of the pencil. This should involve only your index finger and thumb and a bit of the middle finger to support the base of the pencil.

The constellation grip makes it possible to easily create lines that are both structural and highly expressive. Your aim is to capture the gesture of your subject, its movement or attitude. To be truly effective, the constellation and block-in need to summarise a lot of information. Throughout this process of reduction, your marks need to remain light: you're still working out your ideas; this early stage calls for constant re-evaluation. I tend to use a middle grade such as an F pencil for my constellations. Harder pencils should be avoided at this early stage as they can indent the paper, while softer pencils are harder to erase. At this point, you still want to be able to erase back to empty space if necessary.

When you're done insinuating I am a poison, you should consider what comes out at night when wandering in the middle of fields like this...

SHADOW DOOR

Astrological

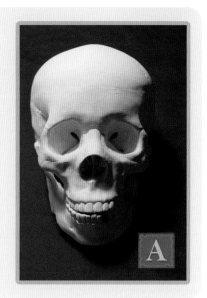

Eventually, you will become adept at drawing constellations. At first, though, drawing the simplest shape isn't an easy task: it is a sophisticated exercise. We're going to spend some time concentrating on building basic seven-sided shapes. We'll do this by eyeballing an object, finding its boldest aspects, and getting a rough idea of where seven lines can be positioned to represent these. We'll also work on eyeballing the elusive horizontal axis, using only our sight and judgement, without any devices. Later, we'll learn ways of gauging this axis with greater accuracy.

 It is a good idea to get yourself a model, an object that will serve as a teacher you can use again and again throughout your practice. I have selected this medical student model of a skull (A). I've painted it a matt white, so that its lines, shapes, shadows, reflected lights and midtones are easy to see and understand.

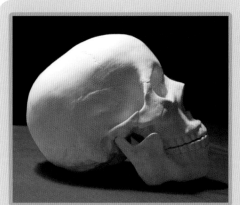 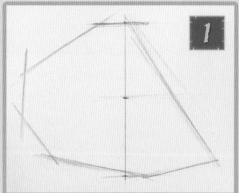 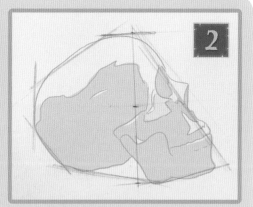

No single shape can encapsulate everything about an object, so we make a compromise. A rectangle wouldn't give us enough information, so we use six or seven-sided shapes instead. The goal is to find the most elegant possible solution, capturing the general structure and giving us a hint of where to go next.

 Patience

Take your time, relax and redraw the constellation as many times as you need to, until you're sure it's as right as can be. When you begin, keep your drawings quite small.

Before you draw lines, chart your main points. Building a scaffold using the sequential point-to-point method allows you to remain focused on your dominant line directions, and this makes it a lot easier to produce a dynamic composition.

Anyone else feel a chill?

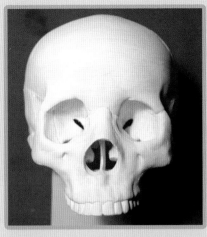
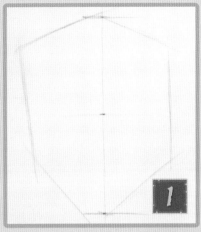
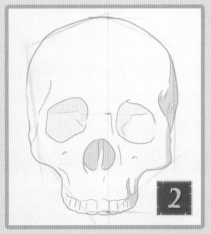

The constellation supplies the bare bones needed for us to carry on to the next stage of the block-in. A strong composition is built on a basic shape. By beginning with the constellation, we establish this basic shape at the outside. If we proceed carefully, we can maintain this powerful shape through to the end, as long as we don't let it get lost under too many small lines.

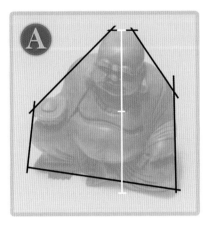
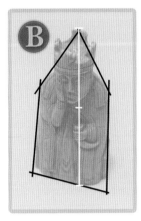
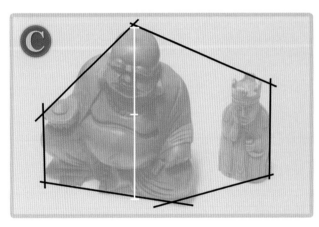

Approximation device

The constellation does not need to be an exact fit—look at Buddha's feet peeking out the bottom there (A). It is simply an approximation of the outside contour. It is also an opportunity to establish the big idea of your composition. It is a solid frame which you place around smaller ideas, and this may include separate objects, as in the example (C). Practice drawing constellations as much as you can, using lots of different objects. The elegance with which you can reduce complex forms to their essentials will determine how easily you will master the next stages. Effective constellations save you a lot of bother, because they are an exceptional method of mapping out what you hope to achieve. Your observational drawing should always start here.

LISTEN! One of the first things to do is to write a visual poem about the thing you are drawing. Poems are life stripped to its bare essentials, concentrated on the most potent images. Thinking of the constellation as a poem may help you to tackle any sense of awkwardness: this is an exercise in grace.

Easier with Practice

How are you feeling? There's a good chance that you're feeling pretty frustrated at the moment. At first, the process of drawing with straight lines may seem like an incredibly awkward way of working. Whatever drawing experience you've had in the past, it's almost certainly been nothing like this. Because it's so unfamiliar, drawing with straight lines and keeping things so extremely general can feel very artificial and stilted.

You are working against drawing habits that you've built over a lifetime. This is a challenging process. At times it may seem like you're getting worse rather than better!

Trust me, this isn't the case; you're simply training yourself in something unfamiliar, building up lots of new neural connections, changing your mind. With consistent and persistent practice, you can nudge yourself away from old habits and towards new methods. Don't worry if your workflow becomes self-conscious and clunky as you integrate your new learning. You are working to implement several principles: judging distances, deciphering orientations and trying to establish unity.

Although it's daunting at first, many tasks in our daily routines require similar levels of complex multitasking, such as cooking a meal or riding a bike. Practice causes these processes to become firmly embedded so that they become second nature. Once this happens, we can get creative and start having more fun. It takes courage and time, but it won't be impossibly difficult forever.

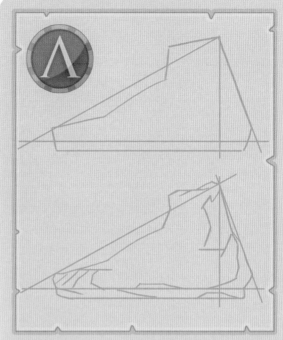

The above image is from the Charles Bargue series of academic drawings, which is a great syllabus to research. Copying the drawings will help to improve your sensitivity, focus and dexterity. It will also expose you to a number of creative solutions to problems in drawing, which can help you develop your own approaches to problem-solving. Copying these drawings is a wonderful artistic meditation that I would encourage you to try, no matter what level you are.

This particular plate shows how an artist has built up a study of a cast. Beginning with guidelines positioned at convenient places (the ankle, the sole), they have developed a constellation consisting of only three lines, which is excellent. The fewer lines we can use, the better. A great drawing has the minimum of everything: lines, values and shapes. The less information we use to get our point across, the stronger our message will be.

As we draw constellations and refine our block-in, we are taking the first steps towards using line to create a particularly useful mass. Simplicity is the road to elegance and sophistication. If you look at the block-in on the upper right, you'll see that its success is a matter of 'less is more.' A sophisticated work is one in which you are able to capture a subject using the smallest possible number of lines, lines which are well-positioned, correctly angled and proportional.

> Line is a wonderful servant but makes for a terrible master.

Sort of Harsh...

Why is line a terrible master? It's because line is not the point of our drawing in this process: lines are a tool, a way of achieving a sense of mass. Having too many lines is the same as having too many points: it becomes confusing. If we focus too much on lines, they seize control of the picture. This is one reason for limiting the number of lines in our constellation: by regulating lines, we ensure that they serve their function and convey important information, without taking over.

> If you who draw, desire to study well, and to good purpose, always go slowly to work in your drawings — Leonardo da Vinci

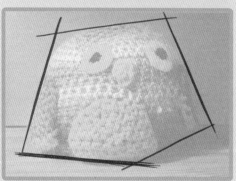

Remember: draw your constellations very lightly. Let them change. Eventually, these broad marks will either be erased or integrated into the contour. Resist the urge to try and make your basic shape fit perfectly, as this is not the goal of this exercise. As much as the constellation shape may give you anxiety at first, fear not. Over the course of using such a method, you will come to find that it functions to prevent you from becoming stressed, because when there's a big idea, things can fall into place neatly. We are creating a whole which can accommodate and anchor the smaller ideas.

Gotcha! If we can capture something within an enclosure we are in a better position to control it. You can think of constellations as nets cast over objects, or fences constructed around something.

Quick constellation studies of random objects help you to become adept at establishing quickly what is essential about a subject, and what is arbitrary.

Begin with lines that pin down the majority of the gesture or the action: everything else builds from this. Establish one main idea when you start the drawing and keep sight of it throughout your working. Essential lines are like the trunk of a tree, while details are twigs. Remember: a basic composition is a strong composition.

After a night of star gazing and capturing skeletons, we awoke refreshed the next morning. I stepped out the enclosure of the tent to see the road as clear as day, beckoning for us to continue. The Specific was nowhere to be found.

THE STRAIGHT PATH

Markers	Straight Roads	Gears of Draw	Grip II	Sharpening II	Segments
77	80	82	83	84	86

So, we set out once again on the Long Road, which stretched out for miles in a straight line. Bright sun had cleared the mists, and I could see the top of the mountain. To my supreme disappointment, however, I could also see just how far away it was. Only yesterday I'd stood at its foot! It seemed like I'd gone a long way back in order to move a little way upwards. Still, it comforted me to keep my eyes fixed on its sandy peak, and to see the road rising, so gradually it hardly seemed a climb at all. The journey was long, but it seemed possible.

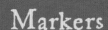

Markers

Level Up! – Marksman!

If the General asks Guido to note landmarks on their journey, think of the kinds of features he might point out. Although he can see blades of grass, twigs and bugs, he'd ignore these features for now. Instead, he would focus on major features, like boulders, great oak trees or rivers. At this stage, you need to be looking at your subject in the same way that Guido looks at the countryside, and find landmarks that best map your subject.

With your basic perimeter established, we use landmarks to begin charting the interior of our subject. Landmarks can be anything: sudden changes in shadow, creases on a person's face, the underside of the nose, the line of the mouth, the top and bottom of the ear. The simpler and broader the landmark, the better. Planning the bust of Voltaire (A), I marked off points along a vertical centreline to indicate the placement of the eye sockets and nose, as well as the general tilt of the mouth and chin. As I do this, I'm constantly reassessing my measurements. Nothing about this bust drawing is set in stone, as it were.

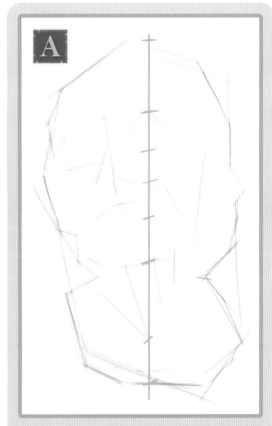

Bear in mind, this illustration shows a fairly advanced stage of blocking in general shapes. Don't worry that this image seems to skip ahead, how it came about is revealed later. Just focus on the vertical line for now, and notice how it has been plotted with points marking the position of important landmarks. These marks aren't perfectly positioned; they are just 'very good' estimates. Plotting lines in this way generates a backbone, a line of support.

> We must select the landmarks which will best guide us. Which landmarks will help us travel in the right direction?

Just in case we found ourselves lost along the road, the General thought it best to acknowledge landmarks along the way.

In Pursuit of Convenience

Now, let's take a step back for a moment. That bust of Voltaire on the previous page shows lots of lines that correspond to various landmarks, but how were they made? It isn't so easy to look at a vertical line and gauge exactly where a particular feature might be positioned along it. For this reason, let's return to basic questions, such as, what feature of the subject corresponds to the middle point along the vertical mid-line (1)? How about the thirds (2)? By discovering what lies at these places, we can better understand where other aspects are relative to these points.

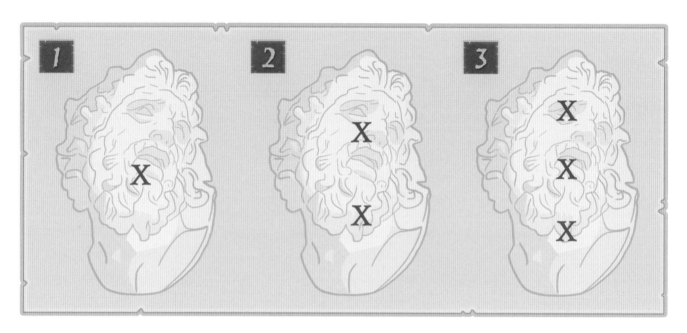

Try to understand the basic structure and locate as many tentative facts as you can. It will be a hit and miss exercise: sometimes prominent landmarks will line up with convenient ratios, and sometimes they won't. Sometimes your quarter markers will fall on completely nondescript areas, offering no useful landmarks at all. This is unlucky, but all it requires is for you to move on and find places where basic ratios and landmarks co-exist. Quarters are good (3)—there must be something among those three points that we can use. The most useful point of these three is, of course, the middle, so let's return to analysing that point.

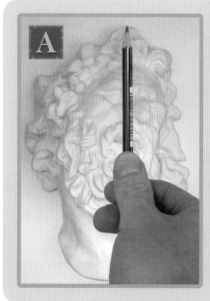

Finding the middle

It's one thing to mark the centre of your vertical line on your paper; it's another to find the midpoint of your subject. To do this, hold your pencil out at arms' length, up to your subject. Now guess where the midpoint of the subject is, just eyeballing it. Use your thumb to mark the point on your pencil that corresponds with this estimated midpoint (A).

Now you've got a pencil length corresponding to roughly half the subject's length. To check your accuracy, move the pencil down so that the tip lines up with the estimated midpoint. If your guess was accurate, your thumb should now line up with the bottom of the subject (B).

The amount of effort you put into the construction is always proportional to the amount of fun that you'll have putting in the details later on. You must first climb the ladders to be able to play on the slide.

Middles defeat muddles

Though it can be a little time consuming, we can all find our subject's midpoint, using the method described on the previous page.

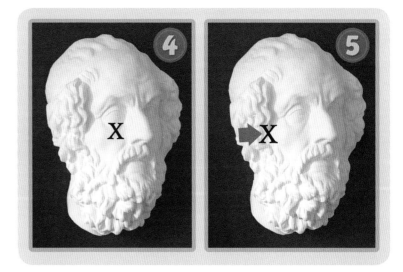

Once we've done this, we can use the same method to find quarter-points. This will give us the markers shown in image (3) on the previous page. Use the same method to find the thirds (2)—this can be a bit harder to eyeball, but just keep adjusting your thumb and be patient.

Sure, we can make these measurements, but for them to be really useful, we want them to line up with landmark features on the subject. In image (4), however, we can see that things don't always work out so neatly: here, the midpoint doesn't really match any feature. In this case, we can just shift over to the side, moving along the horizontal X axis until we find a convenient feature to use as a landmark (5).

Once we've found these basic points, they can unlock all kinds of useful measurements. In the example below, we'll see how, by finding thirds, I stumbled upon a very convenient fact about my subject.

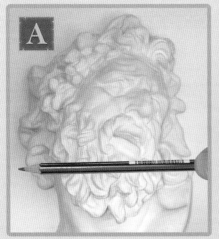
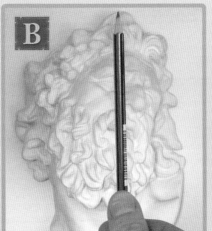
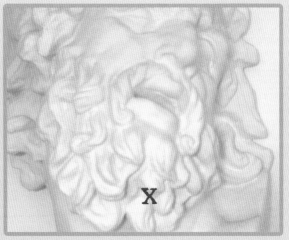

General sides

I always check how the width of the subject relates to the length as this can yield interesting information. I find the width using the same method we've been employing: I hold the pencil horizontally so that the tip lines up with one side, and my thumb marks the other side (A). I then rotate the pencil vertically so that I can check the width against vertical measurements and landmarks (B). In this case, I find that my width lines up with a point on the chin, which I'd previously found to be one of my thirds. This tells me that the cast's width is two-thirds its height. Using this information I now have a pretty solid idea of how wide to make my drawing.

No matter how daunting a subject might seem at first, its proportions may be actually very simple. Proportions won't always fall into place so easily, and later on, we will learn more precise methods of measurement we can use when the fractions don't work out so neatly. Gauging proportions allows us to piece together basic relationships, and knowing these will always help your confidence. Measuring can be tricky, and it's not much fun, but it does mean that we can feel more secure in our drawing, and knowing you have the basics right will make the latter stages of drawing all the more enjoyable.

The Shortest Path to Truth

So far we have been using lines to establish a framework upon which to build our drawing. We've divided our image into simple fractions and their corresponding landmarks. The result of this process is an image like (A), criss-crossed with a lot of seemingly technical lines. By now, these lines should hold no mystery for us: they are basic marks corresponding to landmarks along the horizontal and vertical axes. Just by asking a few elementary questions about landmarks and proportions, enough information has been gathered to make this drawing manageable.

Any prominent feature can be used as a landmark. Facial features are obvious choices for portraits, but other features can be used, such as areas of contrasting light and dark—we'll talk more about using shadows and landmarks in a later chapter.

Although we're making use of features, we're not 'drawing' them yet: our marks should still be quite abstract, just noting the most noticeable, and therefore useful, forms. It's completely up to you how you want to make these marks: they can be lines, blocked shapes or even blocks of light tone. Just keep things faint, erasable and general. Don't try to map out too many landmarks; just choose the most prominent and useful. These really can be anything, so you must use your best judgement. Once these important landmarks are securely in place, we can develop the drawing with greater confidence.

Drawing from observation takes a lot of patience and energy. This is why restraint is so important. We practice restraint by keeping our lines straight and our shapes simple, but we should look for other ways to make our drawing economical. When looking for landmarks, check to see if any other features match the tilt of the line you've just made. Limiting the number of angles helps to keep your drawing readable and workable. Finding repetition is an excellent way of establishing simple relationships.

Ahh, *you're* back.

Yes, she brought a deer, Guido. Try not to get distracted.

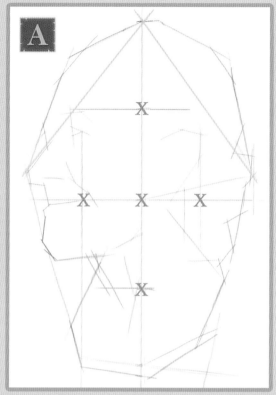

Straight offroads — Now that we've found the right and left points, we can find more proportions and landmarks along the horizontal axis. What lies at the quarter and third points along this line? These measurements can help lock in landmarks. In (A), the corner of the mouth is one-quarter of the way along the X axis. I also find that the three-quarter mark lines up with the outer edge of the ear—I make the connection with hookshot.

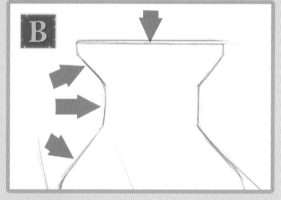

Look out for long stretches of flatness in the contour, such as the top of this vase (B). These are wonderfully convenient areas as they help us to build up a blocky outline without straying too far from the actual contour.

The images below demonstrate how to build from a constellation towards a more developed block-in. The constellation in image (A) should be familiar to us by now: this abstract shape sums up the subject using six or seven lines around a vertical guideline.* In (B) and (C), you see how I am using the block-in process to answer questions about the subject: the block-in develops as a solution to the problems and questions posed by the subject. In the following pages, we will go into this process of question and answer in much greater detail.

There is no one right way to block-in a particular subject: you will reach your own solutions based on your observations. Move slowly and carefully through these block-in phases, like a tiger stalking its prey. Carefully survey the subject before making any marks. Wait before pouncing, and you have a greater chance of capturing your subject.

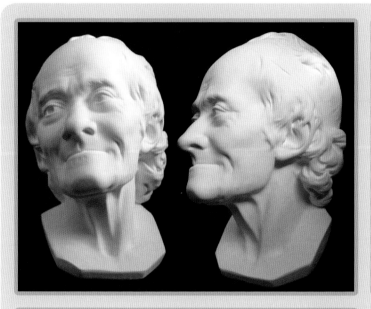
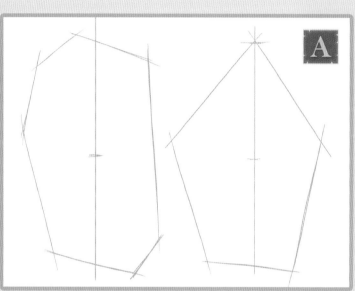
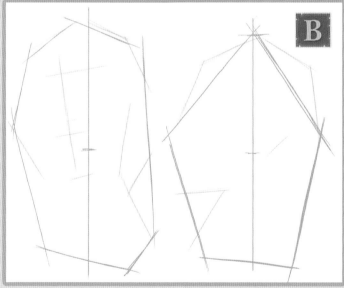

In (B), I'm beginning to mark the position of features, and this, in turn, is helping me establish the outer contour. Developing the large constellation is a sculptural process. It's like taking a chisel to a block of wood—but with the assurance that, if you go too far, you can always stick the lump back on. Erasers make this process safe. For all that it's important to take your time and be thoughtful, this is a stage where it's easy to reassess your lines.

By image (C), a likeness is forming, but although it now contains a lot of information, the drawing is still open to revision. So far, the drawing just consists of lines which approximate position, proportion and tilt. There are also hookshot lines which help me establish relationships between elements which are further away from each other.

*Or eight or nine, or even ten. Six or seven are ideal numbers though; try and aim for either of these in your constellations.

Switching Them Up

As I draw, I find that my hand automatically shifts between pencil grips as necessary. With practice, you will develop an instinct for which grip you need. For now, you can use the guide at the right. Shifting your grips is key to mastering this hierarchical approach to drawing. If you only use the contour grip, you'll make things much more difficult for yourself. At the earliest stages of the Tetraforce, you must stay loose.

Each of the different hand grip styles has an effect on how the pencil communicates with the surface. Grip isn't simply about your hand, either, or even just your arm: your entire posture matters. Relaxing your body relaxes your mind—which may or may not be what you want. Sitting down while drawing is more relaxing, but it doesn't activate the same kind of intense focus and alertness that you get from standing and working at an easel. Standing at an easel may leave you drained or tense, however, so it's useful to alternate between the two postures, if you can. This allows you to loosen and sharpen your focus and work style.

> As you become more focused on fine details such as the intricacies of the contour, your hand naturally moves closer to the tip of the pencil.

Convenient angles

Let's experiment with angles. If you're right-handed, draw a line moving upwards from the bottom right to upper left corners of your paper (lefties, do the reverse). Awkward, isn't it? While working, try to move your arm around so that you are always working at a comfortable angle with respect to a given line. This may involve angling your paper (lefties, you're probably familiar with this manoeuvre already!). Turning your paper around is much better than drawing wonky lines.

CONTOUR

BLOCK-IN

CONSTELLATION

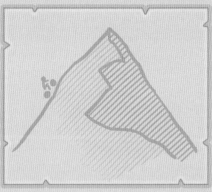

Drawing is a lot like riding a bike up a mountain. We start with the broad base shapes, and we work our way up to the smaller structures at the top.

Grip continues the analogy. We do not start by gripping the pencil near the point. Instead, we hold it way down at the base, and we gradually move our grip up the pencil.

By the time we finally reach the peak, we have a structure in place. At that point, we've reached the shadowy side of the mountain, and we're ready to begin the enjoyably technical descent of tone work.

Grip II

Mid Range of Stroke

After constructing the constellation, which serves as the foundation of the drawing, your hand should shift down the pencil, and your grip should become ever so slightly tighter. This style of pencil grip allows for lightness and manoeuvrability, while still keeping your hand from obscuring your view of the paper. Moving our hand closer to the tip enables increased precision, useful for the process of subdividing the lines.

As your grip changes, the angle of the pencil changes. The grips we use in the early stages, like the block-in grip, usually involve holding the pencil at a low angle to the page. The pencil tilts towards the horizontal, and this creates a light, loose stroke. A pencil held at a low angle leaves its graphite on the surface of the paper, rather than forcing it deep into the tooth. This means we can erase easily.

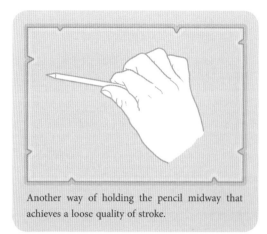

Another way of holding the pencil midway that achieves a loose quality of stroke.

Loose control

In drawing, it is critical to stay in control, while at the same time remaining loose. This may seem paradoxical. It's easy to assume that being in control requires a firm grip and that we show control by attacking all the tiny details. In fact, the opposite is true. A tight grip betrays anxiety, while a relaxed, loose grip can release a marvellous freedom of style, which is not at all reckless or inaccurate.

A drawing should maintain a sense of looseness and generality even when finished, although it should also display clarity, focus and intelligence. A finished drawing should feel loose, but that doesn't mean its creation has been haphazard: a loose grip and sense of ease display an artist's true assurance.

HEAVY HANDED

Try your best to avoid heavy statements. Certainty can be a brave thing, but it is mostly apt to be foolishness.

> Draw vigorously: be unrestrained, yet careful. Always strive for control and precision.

You must also allow a degree of looseness into your thinking: when you apply pencil to paper, there's always an irreducible element of unpredictability. As long as you trust your ability to make the marks you intend to make, a little surprise is no bad thing. As you gain confidence, you'll also speed up, and at certain times your pencil will move faster than your conscious mind. Let yourself go—trust to speed, ability and chance.

This may seem like a lot to think about now, and the Tetra-force structures may also seem a little clumsy at first. With time, however, you'll develop an almost instinctive awareness of when to change grip, grade of pencil or level of the Tetra-force. You'll also get a better sense of when a mistake is large enough to require major correction. For now, let's sum up the different key stages of grip:

Distance

The further your hand is from the tip, the more open your style can be. Gain even more distance by regularly walking back from your work to check it. Keep your pressure light.

Broadness

Remember, keeping things general does not mean losing control. By moving down the pencil, we will find that our lines become a little tighter.

Angle

As you move closer to the precise contour grip, the angle of the pencil will become more and more vertical. When you have reached the stage where precise marks are required, you'll also find that your drawing slows down dramatically.

Working with details takes a huge amount of energy, whether you are creating or correcting them. This is even truer if we try to establish details on a shaky foundation. However, if we progress systematically through our pencil grips and through the stages of the Tetraforce, by the time it comes to detail work, it should feel like a plane coming in for a smooth landing on a nice, clear airstrip. Look ahead at image (A) on page 89 to see the kind of line you get if you try to land without having established a runway.

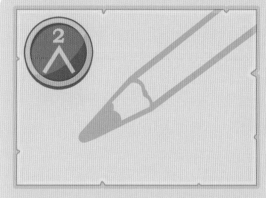

Sharpening II (A General Tip) — The Specific has made many errors. She has gotten us interested in equipment and sharp pencils before explaining the process of drawing itself.

The General will now undo some of the damage she's done, starting with the pencil tip. You may find it better to begin your drawings with a 'general tip,' which is softer and blunter.

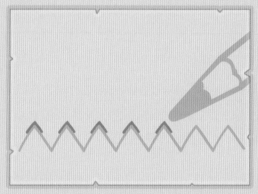

We're always told by art tutors that we need a sharp tip for accuracy, but when we're sketching a general idea, we don't need that kind of accuracy. A blunt tip doesn't risk indenting the tooth. It also won't embed graphite into the tooth, because the tip will happily skip over the tops of the paper's teeth.

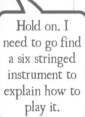

Hold on. I need to go find a six stringed instrument to explain how to play it.

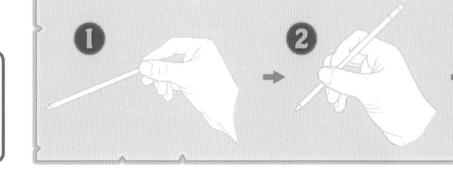

Play it? It's a pencil.

Music of Line

The discipline of drawing has many parallels with playing a musical instrument. When we draw a constellation, we are tuning the six strings of our drawing. By combining lines, playing these strings together, we are playing chords, and these can eventually come together to create a harmonious image. As we learn to play our drawings, there are a few common pitfalls we should try to avoid.

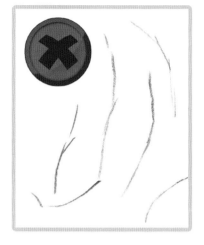

Ukulele method (little dashes)

The tight contour grip, shown in (3) on the previous page, leads us to make tiny little lines, like those pictured on the left. This style is typical of an anxious beginner, who is trying to follow the instruction to 'use straight lines' without understanding the purpose of this. They are playing the song one note at a time, forming each note very carefully. They hope that this meticulous, incremental approach will yield accuracy, but it's impossible to establish broad relationships with this jittery style. There's no sense of the whole, just a nervous attention to one small part at a time, in the hope that it will all fit together. The result is jolty and disjointed—and the process is exhausting.

Lemmy method (lots of noise)

As a student learns to draw, they are as susceptible to creating accidental noise as a beginner who has just picked up the guitar. By 'noise,' I mean lines which are inaccurate, discordant and distracting. A wrong note can disrupt a song momentarily, but, in drawing, an incorrect line, if allowed to remain, can throw things totally off course. This is because the incorrect line will form the basis for subsequent lines; every further calculation based on this error will also be wrong. In the early stages of drawing, the eraser is your best friend.

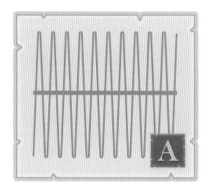

There's another way drawings can get noisy. The visual depiction of noise (A) will be familiar to musicians. We face a similar problem in drawing: using too many lines all at once creates a noise which drowns out any true notes. Some students, trying to get a line right, will draw over it again and again, getting darker and darker. If they finally manage to get the line right, it can scarcely be seen in all the scribbly visual noise they've generated.

With these potential problems in mind, let's see if the General has found his guitar and learn to play some chords. With these next lines, we'll begin to describe what is interesting and unique about our subjects.

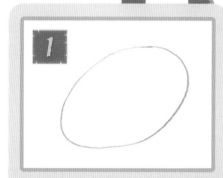

Any shape should be thought of as a song. Okay, so this egg shape may not the most exciting music in the world, but what if we wanted to 'play' it using the straight-line method?

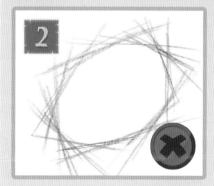

The drawing above is an example of how not to use the straight line method. The inner shape is a decent attempt but what about all that mess that surrounds the shape. This isn't an efficient way to go about drawing the shape.

> Are you sure the ukulele is the six stringed instrument the General was referring to?

> Yeah, you're right. Six strings are dull. How about twelve!

General's Musical String Theory

Once the constellation is in place and judged to be accurate, it's time to analyse smaller sections of the contour. In this next phase, we will continue to use straight lines, letting them function as an abbreviation of a particular segment's curvature. We can see in example (A) how a complex S curve has been abbreviated into three line segments. In (B), you can see how an another subtle curve has been simplified into a single straight line. Deciding how to divide the curve into segments is a matter of individual judgement, but generally, you should be looking for sharp changes of angle or direction as good points for dividing your line segments.

A rule of thumb

As a general rule, when I'm constructing the scaffolding of my picture, I try not to use any lines less than a couple of inches long. Once I've satisfactorily roughed in the larger shape, I reduce this a little. Working in this way, I gradually deal with ever smaller shapes, ensuring that everything is growing at the same pace and that the work is checked at every stage.

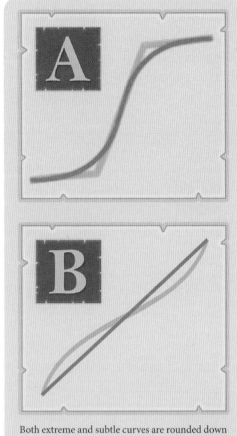

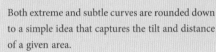

Both extreme and subtle curves are rounded down to a simple idea that captures the tilt and distance of a given area.

This kind of dark, ruler-straight line is not what we're after. A line like this is almost as closed and definite as a curve.

This line is too small. Avoid trying to incorporate little dashes like this into your scaffolding. Short lines like this don't help with judging general relationships. Remember your hookshot: a line with follow-through makes it much clearer how different components are positioned relative to one another.

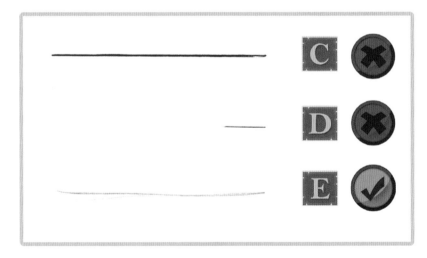

This is the perfect sort of line. It's light and very general, and it's a good length: it doesn't describe too much all at once, nor does it get too dark.

And now for some chords!

Practice playing chords

This exercise explores the relationship between block-in lines and curves. Begin with two lightly drawn, intersecting lines (1). You can add a third to bring it closer to the curve you're going to draw (2). Once you've got your lines in place, try to draw a curve that fits those lines (3). This will give you a sense of how it feels to draw confidently: the line is so much more sure of itself because guesswork is reduced to a minimum. The lines in this series have been darkened to help you see what's going on.

Next, take an eraser and remove the guidelines (4). Simple exercises such as this will help you get a feel for how straight lines and curves can be used harmoniously to develop a confidently drawn line.

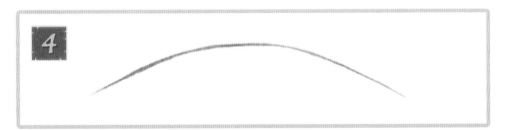

You can also try to work backwards: once you've drawn a curve, try to replicate it on another sheet of paper, starting again with straight lines. Is there another configuration of straight lines that could sum up this curve?

This technique is just as crucial to incorporate into your working method as the constellation.

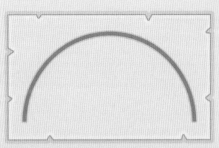

Let's say we want to draw this curve. How many strings will I need? How many lines will it take to block-in this curve?

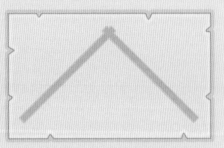

Well, let's try with just two. It's definitely always good to try to state things as simply as possible—but this is a bit too reductive. It would be incredibly tricky to then draw the curve using these two lines as your only guides.

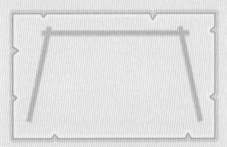

What about three stings? This is somewhat better, but it still doesn't really seem to capture the curve.

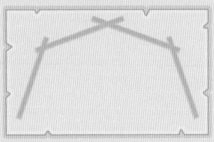

Four lines, it would appear, is the perfect solution for this curve. It gives us a good approximation of the curve, and it will serve us well as we try to recreate the curve.

Well, I suppose you could do it that way.

Look where you're going

As you train yourself in this 'straight path' method of line making, you'll find it helpful to keep your eye on your destination. That is to say, when you move to draw a line, look at the point you're drawing a line towards, rather than keeping your eyes fixed on the tip of your pencil. It's like when you drive a car or ride a bike: you'll go straighter if you keep your eyes on the road ahead, instead of staring at your hands.

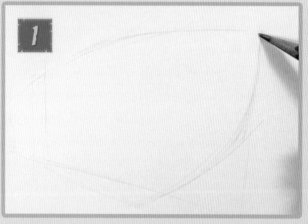

My lines are made quickly, with my eye fixed on the destination. This stops the line from looking anxious or shaky.

Light, breezy and open: that's the trick here. My lines are not perfect, and I know they never will be. That's alright, because as I work and rework them, they become accurate enough to be good guides. The first lines are simply a sort of preliminary, which I know I'll be revising. Knowing this from the beginning means that there's no reason to be nervous. —And, yes, there is a big jump to (4). This image is here simply to show you what can come from building a basic foundation. As we continue, we'll be breaking down the many gradual steps that lead our drawings to this point.

Nerves

If you're finding the block-in difficult, don't worry; it's probably a very new way of drawing. Remember: simple is best. You will get there eventually. If you're struggling, it may well be because you're trying to do too much too fast: trying to pin everything down all at once, rather than gradually capturing what is essential. Your early attempts may look like the effort pictured here (A). The lines in this study are not the product of careful analysis, and they aren't useful. The student has taken the words 'blocky' and 'straight' and run off with them in a bit of a blind panic. Flailing about, they've drawn heavy lines with rapid, stiff, jerky motions of the pencil. Avoid this kind of mark-making at all costs.

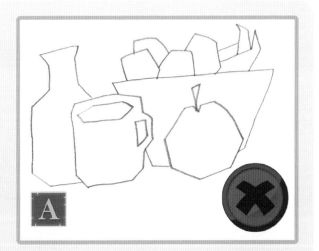

Holding the pencil lightly and thinking carefully, we should make our lines one at a time. Each stroke is a thought. Don't demand too much from a moment's analysis or from any one line. Give yourself time. You may find yourself clutching the pencil tightly, like you're holding on for dear life. This is the stress of trying to learn a new skill. Relax, take a deep breath, and loosen your grip: this is how you stay in control. The fear will pass in time.

. . .An organically grown apple

Throughout this drawing of an apple (1, 2, 3), my lines stay sketchy, light and breezy. Because this object is simple, I've begun with a four-sided shape, which is a good match for an object like this. I carve away at the corners little by little, and this is how I create a sense of roundness. The gradual and economical addition of details means that even this line drawing conveys a sense of solidity and mass.

 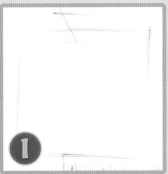 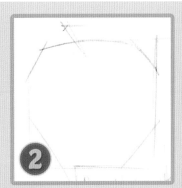 

Straight lines are an organisational tool, and they need to be coherent. Refinement is easy: the intellectual challenge lies in constructing a scaffold which will support the intuitive and expressive processes of refinement.

The Bargue Plates

The images on this page are taken from an incredibly influential classical drawing course, developed in the 1870's by Charles Bargue and his buddy Jean-Léon Gérôme.

His course included a number of illustrations (now known as Bargue plates) which demonstrate the construction of a drawing.* Working from these plates is an excellent way to build a sophisticated understanding of block-ins.

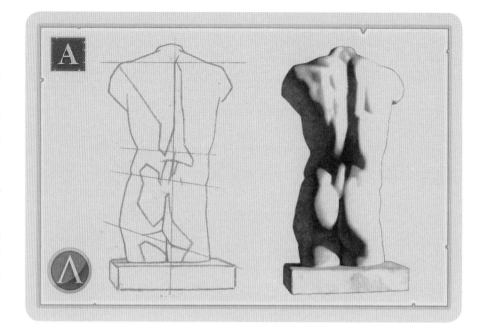

The Bargue drawing (A) shows the construction lines that were used in building this torso. Construction lines aren't a part of the drawing; they are guides, attempts at organising a solution to help solve the visual problem and recreate the image. Guidelines like these help reveal the unique features of your subject, so that your block-in can capture its essentials.

> In the Void we established basic placement and size. The block-in deals with the first lines, describing tilt, action, proportion and distances between key points. Until these relationships have been established, we shouldn't go further.

There's no one right way to construct a block-in for any subject. The Bargue plates (A, B) merely show elegant solutions. A block-in represents your own understanding of a subject, the unique result of analysis, intuition and emotional response—all distilled to their essence in a kind of shorthand.

The block-in gives a drawing its energy and strength. Once you become skilled at the block-in, you truly have mastered drawing: nothing else will cause you any real trouble. Nevertheless, no matter how adept you become at block-ins, making mistakes will always remain an inevitable part of this process.

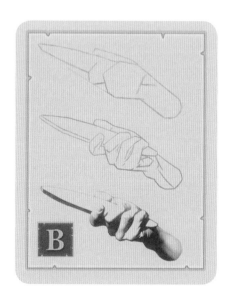

DRAW LIKE A BOSS

*Some of the best artists of the twentieth century have cut their teeth on Bargue plates. They certainly still have a lot to teach any aspiring artist, but do be aware that they represent quite an advanced level of study. This is complex stuff, so tread carefully.

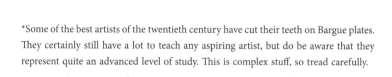

A process of revision

Making mistakes and fixing them is an integral part of the drawing process. We should never feel bad about reaching for an eraser—making changes and correcting errors is not a mark of failure, but of success. The removal of misleading lines will have a positive impact on our work. During the block-in phase, we're just looking for a good approximation. It doesn't need to be perfect—in some ways, imperfection actually serves us, because it means we're keeping things open, and this openness allows us to continue making important decisions about placement.

> The block-in is carried out at an even tempo. These early stages are absolutely crucial, so really do your best not to rush through them. Patience is such a key element in learning.

Why is are the initial stages of a drawing so vital? Well, think of starting a crossword by putting in the wrong word—it will throw the whole puzzle off. If we make a mistake early in our drawing and fail to correct it, we'll carry it with us, using it as the basis for subsequent decisions. Error will pile upon error, and we'll be getting more and more lost.

As a wise man once said, "It is the little mistakes at the beginning that will mess you up most in the end." By putting the hard work in at the beginning, guarding against lazy, careless mistakes, you make things much easier for yourself later on, when you'll be more tired. If an early mistake persists, it can take hours to fix—rather than the minutes it would have taken to catch and correct it right at the beginning.

There will always be a difference between your drawing and the subject you are trying to represent. We're trying to build our skills so that we can be as accurate as possible, but at the same time, we should understand that no drawing, no matter how refined, is perfect. And this is fine. It gives us some space to relax. Everything human is imperfect, and that includes every drawing ever made.

Rather than striving for perfection, aim to root out the implausible, the radical deviations from observed reality. Practice assessing your work critically: the key is to remain unsatisfied for as long as possible before moving on to the next stage. In these early stages, our primary focus is on the unification of lines and shapes. Your mantra should be, "Relationships, not things."

As we pressed on, the Specific took a relaxed role, which allowed us to make great strides towards our goal. Even on the straight road, though, I managed to tumble every now and again.

Think Two-Dimensionally

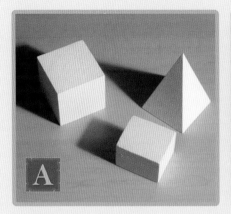

We have spoken at length about how we can handle the curve by following the straight path. There is much more to drawing than this, of course, but this basic knowledge is fundamental. Once we know how to go about representing curves with straight lines, we can combine this with our understanding of guidelines in order to generate a still life.

As you gather objects for your own still life composition, consider the two examples shown here. Image (A) shows a collection of simple still life objects. They have straight, regular edges, and because they are painted matt white, they stand out clearly against the background, making it easy to assess their perimeter. Image (B), however, is more difficult, not only because it contains curved forms but also because the objects are similar in colour to the background, meaning that their edges are not so clearly defined—at times their outlines become vague or disappear.

Copying from a setup like (A) might be a little boring, but it has a lot to teach. I'll be drawing from image (B), which is more interesting and much more of a challenge. This is so that you can see how we go about working with trickier subject matter. For your first still life I would advise starting with geometric solids, as pictured in (A).

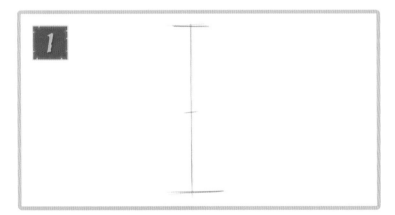

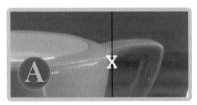

I begin by drawing lines to represent the top and base of the subject; then I draw a vertical midline between them. This will be the standard upon which I base my measurements.

Confusingly, the "mid-line" does not necessarily need to be in the centre of the image. You may choose to line it up with a convenient landmark. In this instance, I've drawn my mid-line to intersect with the edge of the cream jug (A), the point marked (X).

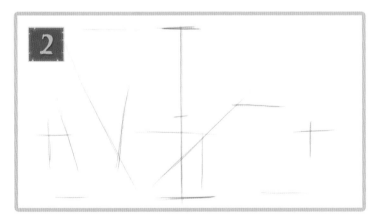

Next, I describe the most prominent structures using large, broad lines. At the same time, sweeping lines note angles and distances. These initial lines may look sketchy or even haphazard, but they are actually the result of a lot of careful consideration.

What you don't see here is how many times I rubbed out and reassessed these lines. I can tell you, I revised these lines many, many times before I finally considered them to be accurate. For now, I am eyeballing angles and distances. We'll learn more accurate ways of taking these measurements in the next chapter.

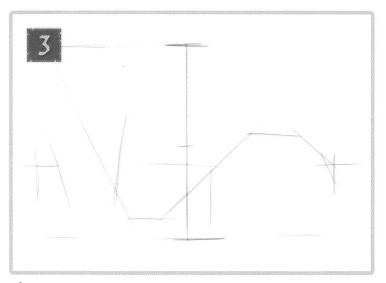

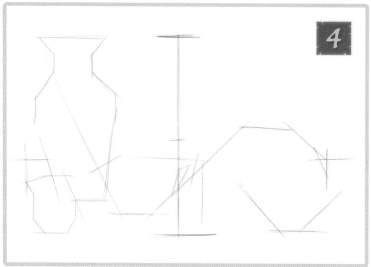

Hookshot reminder : Follow through with the line — All of these lines represent a process of approximation. Because of this, I cannot be quite certain where any of them should end. For this reason, I carry my lines through past the place where I think they might end. These extended hookshot lines also serve as construction lines, guiding my positioning. As always, imagine that you are simply copying from a series of cardboard cut-outs.

Note that the illustrations over the course of this still life exercise show the lines that are darker than they actually were. Anyway, good news! All this measuring has initiated a Level Up!

INTO THE WOODS

Accuracy

95

Unity

96

Distance

98

Generalising

100

Measuring I

102

Measuring II

104

Specific's Diagonals

106

Limiting Perspective

108

We entered the woods in high spirits, although I soon realised that the road was no longer so straight and clear. The path crept round the trees, broken by roots and sometimes blocked by low-hanging branches. The General, in particular, had to pick his way carefully among the tangled boughs. It was no longer possible to see far into the distance; countless rows of trees now obscured the path up ahead.

Accuracy

Level Up! — Measurementalist!

The human eye is not infallible, but learning to take and apply measurements in our drawings allows us to check our observations and to create the firmest possible foundations for our work. In the early stages, drawing is basically a process of making and recording measurements—expressiveness comes later (although, as we've noted, there's a certain individual flair to knowing which lines matter most, which relationships really count, and noting these economically).

Observation is key, but simply looking isn't enough to ensure accuracy: optical illusions occur all the time. Our eyes are constantly compensating and improvising, meaning that placement, lighting and prior experience can all result in distorted perceptions. Having systems of measurement in place helps to make sure that we're not caught out when our eyes play tricks on us.

Measuring can be a harsh corrective to conclusions reached through intuition, but we should refrain from becoming overly self-critical when we find things to be incorrect. Furthermore, through practice and use of measurement, our powers of observation will become more sensitive.

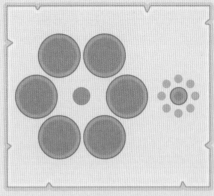

Shapes can appear bigger or smaller depending on surrounding objects. Eyeballing is all very well and good, but the eye can easily be fooled. Take into consideration multiple ways of taking measurements—that way you'll have a fail-safe method for achieving accurate proportions in your work.

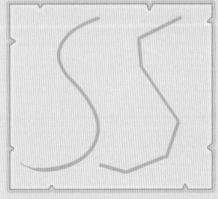

Throughout this chapter, we're still only concerned with straight lines. This is a good thing because it means we are in a better place to judge whether or not a section of line is the correct length. For example, trying to measure the sections of an 'S' shape is much more difficult than the straight-line version, with its clearly defined segments.

Proportion

To achieve a unified drawing, it's essential to consider the relationships between parts, and the relationships of these parts to the whole. These relationships are called proportion. By keeping our lines simple—reducing curves into sections, general lines and tilts—we make it much easier to understand and judge proportion.

Harnessing familiarity

Although many beginning artists feel daunted by proportion, almost everyone already has an acute sense of proportion, built up through everyday experience. Whether adding milk to tea, tossing something into the bin, or slicing cake, we are constantly evaluating scale, distance, amounts and size. The trick is learning to apply this natural sense of proportion to our drawings: although it may be difficult at first, the skill is already there, just waiting to be harnessed. Your everyday spatial awareness means that you are already skilled at knowing the distance between A and B, understanding the angle of a line and understanding the relationship between two given objects. Translating this awareness onto paper requires a few additional methods, many of which build on familiar techniques.

Unity

Building a Strong Whole

We've been talking a fair bit about trying to understand and construct 'the whole,' but what does this actually mean? By understanding the drawing as a whole, we're striving for unity, so that all parts of the drawing are strongly related to one another. Drawing the whole means that we don't attempt to draw separate things in the picture one at a time. Instead, we always strive to capture the relationship between elements of the composition. This is the purpose behind using constellations to block-in a general mass, within which we position smaller parts. By beginning with a large shape, we start to generate a network of interacting elements.

Say you start a portrait by drawing a fully-rendered eye, before working on any of the other features. Without establishing a framework that takes into account value and line relationships of the entire face, it will be extremely difficult to draw the rest of portrait. It becomes a struggle to make areas of the portrait that have catching up to do genuinely connect with the finished eye. By working in this way, the artist has not been focused on the bigger picture, this will often result in a collection of disjointed parts.

> "Deal with the big while it is still very small." — Lao Tzu

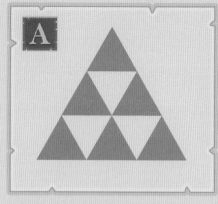

All individual parts of the drawing are related to one another as well as to the whole.

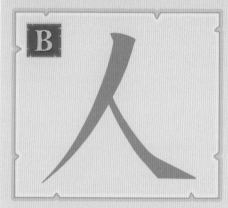

The Chinese symbol for 'man' shows two mutually supportive sticks: take one stick away, and the other falls. This pictogram is a useful image for thinking about relationships: not only is every part connected, they all rely on each other.

The whole philosophy

The ability to see the big picture, and keep that in view at all times while you are working, is a great practice to cultivate. Look at the Tetraforce symbol to the upper right (A): to see the whole is to see this as one and ten triangles simultaneously. The six dark triangles represent positive space, while the three light triangles represent negative space. Their unity creates the tenth triangle, composed of the entire network of relationships.

> "In good work, unity is the dominating quality, all variety being done in conformity to some large idea of the whole, which is never lost sight of, even in the smallest detail of the work."
> — Harold Speed

So, in this drawing process everything should grow together. This simply means that every part of the drawing needs to develop at the same time: you should never spend a prolonged period of time focussing on only one small area. It's tempting to 'finish up' small areas bit by bit, but this is a case of details leading you astray. If you let yourself lose sight of the bigger picture, not only does it become more difficult to produce a unified whole, you might also end up with some early mistakes becoming deeply embedded and hard to fix.

To develop your drawing in a unified way, it's helpful to think of the drawing process as a series of stages, as in the Tetraforce. You should aim to complete each stage to the highest possible standard across the entire drawing before advancing to the next stage on any one part of the drawing.

The image on the right shows me not following this advice. This is a master copy that I attempted some years ago, before I knew the secret of getting my drawing to grow as a whole. Instead, I worked left to right, meaning that some parts are fully rendered, while others have barely been blocked in!

In the case of the *Nymphs and Satyr* copy, I abandoned it about halfway through, exhausted and discouraged. The resulting image, however, does serve as an interesting cross-section of the various stages a drawing must go through in order to develop into a strong piece of work.

Although the earliest constellation lines have disappeared, it is still possible to make out some rudimentary blocking in, as well as some area of refined contour lines. These are the scaffolding that underpins the high polish of the fully-rendered nymph and satyr.

An incomplete master copy after Bouguereau's *Nymphs and Satyr*. You should be able to make out some of the stages that the picture went through in order to get to the finished stage on the left side.

Can you really blame people for wanting to see quick results?

This kind of disjointed method illustrated here can be tempting: it offers quick, satisfying results. The trouble is, it ultimately becomes exhausting. Mistakes become impossible to correct, and different parts don't hang together. Harmony is established when elements, in all their apparent diversity, are brought together as one.

"Every part is disposed to unite with the whole, that it may thereby escape from its own incompleteness." — Leonardo da Vinci

The black Derwent extender made to hold a wood-encased pencil.

Pencil Extenders

Remember how in the last chapter we discussed the importance of varying your pencil grip? The further back you hold your pencil, the more general your stroke. You can enhance these benefits even further by deploying a pencil extender. This creates a wand-like grip which grants you even more looseness, lightness and freedom—absolutely perfect for the beginning stages of your drawing.

The extender tool is very cheap and should last you forever.* There are different sizes available, and the large, silver Derwent pencil extender is big enough to fit a clutch pencil, such as the Staedtler clutch (B). This picture also shows another way of getting distance: extending the pencil lead. This does increase the risk of your lead snapping, so if you try this, keep the pressure light.

The pencil extender also opens up a helpful distance between you and your drawing, which makes it much easier, both physically and psychologically, to maintain attention on the whole.

Clip tip — Attaching a pencil extender to a clutch pencil gives you access to a whole new range of expressive strokes. However, Staedtler one comes with an annoying little clip that gets in the way. Fortunately, you can just ping this off. I like using an extended clutch not only for early line-work but also later on when I'm applying really light, delicate washes of tone.

We pressed on through the woods. I considered climbing a tree to get a better look at what was coming up ahead.

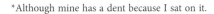
*Although mine has a dent because I sat on it.

Draw with your arm

Another way to keep your lines nice and loose is to draw using your whole arm: larger movements mean looser drawings. Drawing with your wrist produces tight, fiddly strokes.

In these early stages, then, let your drawing flow from the shoulder. Keep your elbow still and your wrist locked. Moving these smaller joints gives you access to gestures that are way too subtle and complex for right now. Keeping your movements simple gives you greater control, and it allows you to make the large, smooth gestures that produce large, smooth and confident shapes.

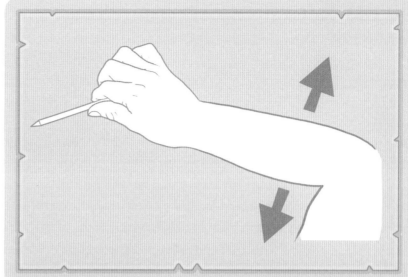

This early process blocking in is rather mechanical and your arm should movements should reflect this. The important thing is a nice fluid line, though, so don't make your movements jerkily robotic. A general rule I like to follow is that any lines longer than a few inches should be drawn from the shoulder; the wrist should be left to express smaller lines.

Test your work by just walking away. If something looks correct when viewed from a distance, you know you're on the right track.

Distance Makes the Eye Grow Stronger

Distance really helps put things into perspective. It's so often the case: if things aren't working, put a bit of distance between yourself and that problem. It lets you see things more clearly.

With distance and time, you'll be able to see whether difficulties can be resolved, or in extreme cases, whether you should just start over. Distance gives us the space to work out problems.

This is part of why thumbnails are so useful: they mimic the effect of seeing something from a great distance.

DISTANCE

+10 Fonder of
the drawing.

Taking Aim

The name for this process of checking that our drawings match our observations is 'sighting.' Sighting is a general term referring to all the methods of measuring and checking the accuracy of drawings. Sighting requires care and focus, but it's fairly straightforward: it's basically just a process of making comparisons.

Sighting is a critical skill for any artist, and it's one that can be developed through practice, as well as the mastery of some helpful tools and tricks. Sighting is about checking proportions, working out how each part relates to every other, by means of comparisons. Knowing how to measure makes this much easier, as it allows us to find accurate height-to-width ratios, and it makes it possible to locate the positions of various components with greater confidence.

General Comparisons

Measurements made in the following ways are only 'so-so' accurate.

Cut off point

The exercises we have encountered thus far shouldn't have taken very long to accomplish. It's crucial to note that, as you practice measuring and gauging accurate proportions, you should study for no more than 30 minutes at a time. The reason for this is that, if we study for too long, after a certain point, we're not training the eye, we're simply trying to finish the exercise while no longer getting the benefit from it.

> Measuring builds our powers of sensitivity, and sensitivity must always come before self-expression. Later, a combination of these two things will produce unique artwork. Constant practice will ensure you master and maintain a consistently sensitive expertise.

So, as we travel through this forest, we will learn different ways of measuring. The methods we'll now explore range in accuracy from the very general to the more specific. We will also pick up some very helpful pieces of equipment, including compasses, needles and plumb lines. As your sighting skills develop, you will become less and less reliant on these tools and techniques, but they are a great help at first. With these goals in mind, let's begin to look at some of the fundamentals of measuring beginning with some very basic ways of checking.

Squinting

Paradoxically, sometimes the best way to see something more accurately is to see it less clearly. Squinting is a technique which lets you better judge masses because it prevents you from seeing detail. Squinting changes our eyes' focus, making it broader and more generalised (B). By squinting, we are politely asking the Specific to stand aside for a moment, so we can adopt the General's vision.

Squinting also flattens our vision, which is a great help in trying to render the world in two-dimensions. By removing depth perception, squinting allows us to assess visual rather than spatial relations. Squinting helps us notice shape patterns, and later, as we begin grappling with shadows, it will help us see generalised values as well.

Head tilt

Another way of checking is to tip your head: if you tilt your head back a bit as you squint, you'll often perceive aspects of the subject you'd initially overlooked.

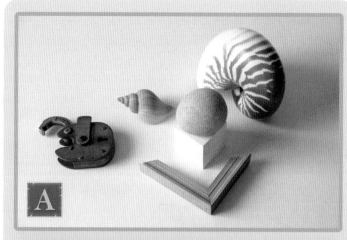

Whole view check — Squinting at the subject also reduces brightness and contrast, because our eyelashes filter out a lot of the light, dimming what we are viewing. By sacrificing detailed focus, we broaden our view, which helps us to take in everything all at once.

Two approaches

There are two main approaches to sighting: the general and the specific. We begin with the general measurement, known as 'comparative measuring,' and then we reinforce this with a more specific and precise method known as 'triangulation.' It's just as well that we have these two approaches—the old carpenters' adage, "measure twice, cut once," definitely applies in drawing. Comparative measuring and triangulation both have their own particular advantages, so it benefits us to integrate both into our working practice.

"An artist must have his measuring tools not in the hand, but in the eye."

— Michelangelo.

Gotta tell ya'. You look super creepy right now.

Measuring Level I

Eyeballing

Observational drawing without the use of any mechanical device to guide us is known as 'eyeballing.' It is, in some ways, the simplest method, yet it is also one of the trickiest, requiring great sensitivity. To complete an accurate drawing using only eyeballing would require a lot of time and patience, and many slight adjustments. It's strange, then, that most art teachers insist that students start off this way. To place students around a still life and insist that they capture the scene by purely eyeballing it is actually pretty hardcore stuff for beginners.

There are lots of ways things can go wrong with eyeballing. As previously mentioned, we can be thrown off by optical illusions, as in (A), or we can be misled by assumptions, as in (B). For instance, we may 'know' that two objects are the same size, and thus not realise that perspective is causing them to appear to be different sizes.

Eyeballing shouldn't stand alone as our only method of measurement, but it's still well worth practicing, as its practical applications are immense. Being able to tell whether or not a drawing is accurate, just by looking at it, is a very cool feeling indeed. Cultivating this ability also means that you will know exactly when you need to reach for measuring tools, and just which areas need righting.

Proportion checker

To check any assessments made by eyeballing, you can use a tool like the academic divider, to the left. This tool allows you to easily compare proportions—rather more easily than using a pencil and your thumb.

A trained eye will help you find things that were not so obvious at first glance.

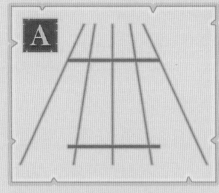

When eyeballing, we naturally compare the thing we are measuring to its surroundings, but it's critical to remember that these comparisons can sometimes be misleading. Image (A) above, known as the Ponzo illustration, shows two horizontal lines of equal length. They appear to be different lengths, however, because the diagonal lines fool us into reading this as a three-dimensional environment. Following perceptual clues, we assume that the top line must be further away and thus, also, longer. Measuring can help to counteract misleading cues and contexts.

Our eyes can also lead us astray when perceiving values. Later we will look at how a grey value can appear to look lighter or darker depending on what value surrounds it.

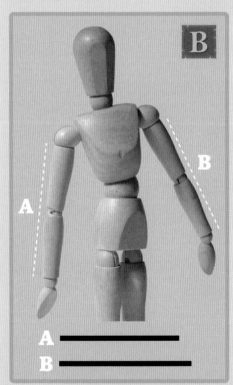

Context is extremely important in drawing. You might think that, on the mannequin above, lines A and B would be the same length, because they are both arms on the same model. It's a natural assumption, but it isn't the case. Because of how the model is turned, line A is slightly shorter. We need to take measurements to help distinguish between observation and preconception.

Judging Distance

Now it's time to get some eyeballing practice. As we've seen on the previous page, eyeballing is not an exact science, but you shouldn't let this put you off. Most people are very good at sensing balance, distance and symmetry, and these senses become more acute with training. With drawing, the trick is learning to translate our visual spatial awareness into an ability to judge proportion in two dimensions. The following exercise lets you check your aptitude for seeing proportions correctly.

1 First, draw a horizontal line, as straight as you can possibly make it. Make the line as long as you can while keeping it straight. The smaller the line, the easier this should be.

2 Look at the line now in front of you. Where is the middle point? Find it and mark it with a dash.

3 Next, try to draw another line the same length as your first line, but this time, make the line vertical. Eyeball your lines and make any adjustments. Now, use a ruler or academic divider to check and see how accurate your eyeballing was.

4 Can you find thirds along a horizontal line?

5 How about finding the quarters?

6 Judging proportions along a straight horizontal or vertical axis is one thing, but things are not usually this straightforward, so we're going to try something a little trickier. Finish this very basic exercise by drawing a diagonal line. Now, try and draw a horizontal line of the same length. After trying this, use a ruler to see how far off you were, if at all.

It is basic skills like this that we need to make use of in drawing, and hopefully this simple exercise will have helped you realise how good you already are at judging proportion. If you found this exercise difficult and your line measurements were pretty far off, don't worry: practice will definitely help you there.

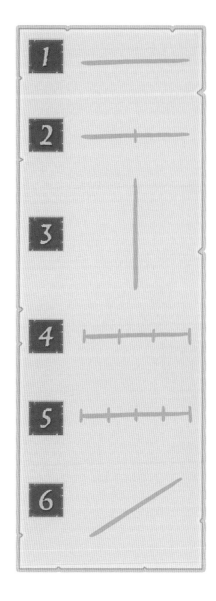

You're right! I found a bow!

Measuring Level II

General Comparisons

The 'comparative method' is one level up from eyeballing. The comparative method is rather like a longbow: it's excellent for covering great distances, but it's very difficult to achieve accurate results.

The comparative method is, as you'd guess, a way of finding measurements by making comparisons and establishing relationships. It's a very natural progression from eyeballing, and it's useful in establishing a general sense of the relationships within the image, as well as getting a broad idea of how basic shapes are angled and positioned.

We make these measurements using a straight object, such as a pencil or knitting needle. Start by holding it out in front of you with an outstretched arm. Hold it up against some aspect of the drawing that you want to measure, and mark the measurement with your thumb. Now you can hold this 'ruler' against other aspects of the subject, allowing you to figure out the size of one aspect relative to another. This will allow you to replicate these proportions in your drawing.

This method works very well when the units you're measuring are exactly the same size. Frequently, though, you will find that things are of slightly different sizes. The key is to seek out the most critical and convenient relationships. It is very handy when we find that two aspects are exactly the same size.

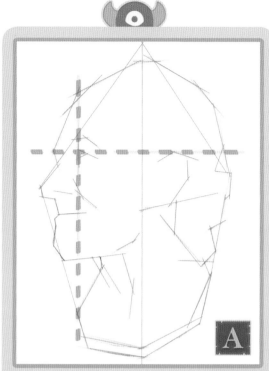

Elementary comparisons — Horizontal and vertical checks are simple ways of discovering the most basic relationships within our subject. Simply using your pencil or needle to see how one thing sits either above, or below, or along the lateral line can really aid us in building an accurate drawing.

In the drawing above I have held the needle vertically against my subject and established that the eye is directly above the lower edge of the cast's neck. All I have to do then is see if this is the case on my drawing. If it isn't, then I have made a mistake.

The trouble is that more often though, the sizes will be fractionally different. For instance, I might say that the height of my subject is 'one and a bit' its width. Is it one and a half? One and a third? One and five-eighths? We're not always quite sure. The problem with these 'and a bits' is that, bit by bit, these rough measurements can throw the whole drawing off.

One way to counteract the inaccuracy of these approximations is by making lots of comparative measurements. This allows you to assess your comparisons, and it also allows you to build up a more accurate cumulative sense of relationships. Another problem with the comparative method is that you can't transfer your measurements directly to your drawing: your measurements are relative rather than absolute, and your drawing probably will be a different size than your subject. Comparative measuring is only one method, however, and shouldn't be used exclusively.

 Close one eye in order to flatten the image. Hold the needle at arm's length so it lines up between your eye and the subject. Make sure it is perpendicular to your line of vision (don't let the needle lean forwards or backwards).

 Make measurements using an outstretched arm and locked elbow; this means that you will always be measuring from a consistent viewing point. Try not to feel too self-conscious about standing like a cartoon artist—there's a good reason they're always shown like this!

 Line up the point of your needle with the edge of the object you're measuring. Now, with your thumb, mark the other side of the object. The distance between your thumb and the point of the needle now matches the length of the object.

 With your arm still outstretched, compare this length with other line segments throughout the subject. What distances match? By what fraction do other sizes differ?

 Make lots of comparisons, and add them together to create a cumulative sense of how sizes relate to each other. Just remember that the comparative method of measuring is best used for making large, general comparisons rather than for fine measurements.

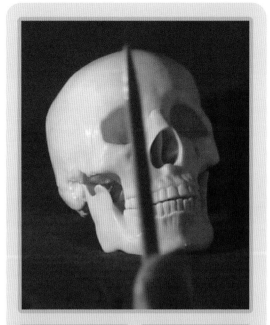

 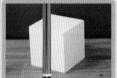

Pencil check — A general check made by holding up my pencil to see how various points align.

Basic alignments

 Let's take this cube as an example of basic relationships, looking specifically at the top plane.

 In (B), I've sketched the top plane. To check it, I ask, "How do the four corners relate to each other? How do they line up on the horizontal and vertical axes?" In this instance, none of the corners should be aligned on either of the axes. If they were, I'd know I had made an error.

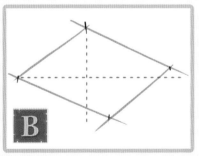

 Now let's consider another shape, such as the one shown in (C). If we were to use comparative measuring within this shape, which angles and axes might we consider? We've talked about using horizontal and vertical checks, but as we can see in this illustration, there may also be diagonal measurements to consider.

Crafting — The knitting needle is a classic, but we can also use another device known as the plumb-line. This is a great tool for both horizontal, vertical and diagonal checks. If you want to try this excellent tool, just find yourself some thread and something heavy to attach it to. I'll meet you on the next page.

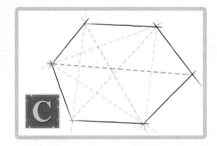

A Complete Check

The General would have you keep an eye on the basic horizontal and vertical axis, these are the easiest relationships to check, but it is of paramount importance that you also check the diagonals. If you only measure along the X and Y axes, you can still end up with a terribly skewed image. Slight exaggerations of tilt can add up to big distortions. Happily, though, you can use your horizontal and vertical reference lines to check diagonal relationships as well. As always in drawing, use the facts you've established to figure out the things you're unsure of.

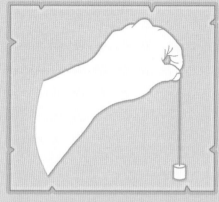

A plumb-line consists of a string with a weight attached. Gravity will cause this line to always hang vertically meaning that you can confident when assessing relationships on the Y axis.

> Get the angle and distance right in your
> block-in lines, and you'll draw more accurately.

Plumb-line

Did you find your thread and a small heavy object to attach it to? Good, now you've got a plumb-line! The plumb-line is most easily used to check vertical relationships. We can also use it to check horizontal and diagonal relationships by holding it taut between both hands.

GRAVITY

Harness the gravitational power of the whole world!

Knotting your plumb-line

You can give yourself additional reference points by making knots in your plumb-line. My plumb-line, for instance, has a knot which I line up with the top of my subject. Then there are several other knots below it, which help me gauge proportions.

It's a bit over the top but, some artists have plumb-lines hung from the ceiling during life drawing classes so that they always have this line in front of them to check any vertical alignment on the model: they can simply move so that the line aligns with different parts of the model. You might try this if you happen to have a ceiling beam handy.

...I like the castle.

You do know that you can use all the pieces, not just the castle?

You Found a Compass!

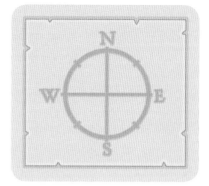

The compass, shown to the right, is a useful little tool for helping us work out the angle or 'tilt' of lines. As we should be well aware now, drawing an accurate line is about more than getting the length right. Unless you get the angles right, your carefully measured proportions won't help much. Finding angles does not have to difficult if we employ basic aids such as this.

1 Begin by drawing a compass on a separate sheet of paper (or in the top corner of your drawing paper, if you're working rough). This is now your designated tilt-checker. It's useful to draw it in ink so that you can use your eraser without destroying it. You don't need to label the directions unless that's helpful. Some people even use a clock face for thinking of tilt: five o'clock is a lot more refined than south-east.

2 Hold your pencil or needle out in front of you, between your thumb and index finger. While looking with one eye closed, tilt it so that it matches the angle of the line you wish to check.

3 Here's the tricky bit. Without altering its angle, line up your pencil with your compass. What's its direction? Make a mental note of this so that you're able to mark the compass lightly with your pencil. If you struggle to memorise the angle, you might want to hold your measuring tool against the compass while marking with pencil held in your other hand.

4 Hold up your measuring tool once again, and compare the line you made on the compass with the line you made on your block-in drawing. If the line is off, amend as required.

This may seem labour intensive, but recording a line's angle is something you should aim to master, because this is essential to accurate drawings. Practice so that this process of measuring tilts becomes habitual: this is an aspect of drawing that will always require careful attention. Remember, even lines which you might assume were totally horizontal or vertical may actually have significant degrees of tilt.

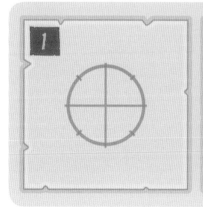

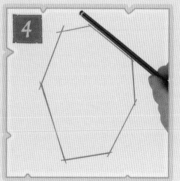

Limiting Perspective

Looking Specifically

Sit still and look at an object. You might feel as though you're seeing it from a single point of view, but that isn't the case. In reality, your eyes are actually producing two images, which your brain combines into a third image, giving the illusion of depth. To produce a flat image, however, it's useful to bypass this excellent system. The best way to do this is by closing one eye, thus flattening the world and making it easier to draw.

> Copying from one image is hard enough without involving a second slightly different image into the mix.

General's viewing (softened gaze)

Now, reducing our view to one single specific image is good, but we also need to generalise, and for that, we have the 'soft eyes' method. My tutors at college would always tell the class to observe with 'soft eyes,' which basically means to let your eyes go blurry, so that you look at the subject in an unfocused, general sort of way. This was good advice: letting the eyes go soft eliminates superfluous details and emphasises the whole, much as squinting does.

Some other teachers, however, gave conflicting advice, telling the class that all we had to do was 'really look' at the thing in front of is. The trouble is, this would cause us to strain, and that caused tension—and tension actually creates a mental blockage, making it much more difficult to function well. You've probably experienced this when trying really hard to remember some piece of information: it never comes while you're trying to force it, but once you let your mind go soft and remove this tight focus, the information will float to the surface. Similarly, we can reduce the tension around our vision by letting our eyes drift out of focus, giving us a vision of the object in its entirety.

Looks all nice and flat doesn't it? Well, that's obviously down to the camera's single viewpoint.

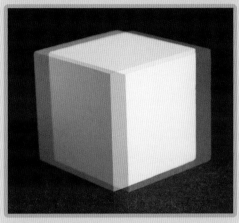

If we were viewing the cube in real life, we'd be seeing the cube from two different angles at once, something like the image above. By closing one eye, we unburden our minds of the task of synthesising these two images into an illusion of depth.

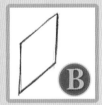

Make a practice of viewing things not as three-dimensional objects, but rather as collections of simple flat shapes. If we interpret our vision as a collage of simple shapes, it becomes easier to check what we see against what we've drawn.

For instance, in the above images (A, B), I haven't tried to draw the whole cube, I've just practiced drawing one face. It's easy to see that this shape on the right does not match the corresponding shape on the left. The differences are probably pretty clear even with binocular vision, but if you close one eye, they'll become still more obvious.

Specific begins to take charge

By now, it should be clear that both the General and the Specific are necessary for a good picture. The Specific leads us to drawings which are intricately detailed and highly rendered, whereas the General leads us to something more like a rough impression. Each of these outcomes is perfectly fine—but the overly general sketch feels unfinished, while the overly specific drawing lacks vigour and vitality. For that reason, we should seek to combine the two. We should strive to access the most helpful and visually pleasing qualities of both of these characters, while making sure that the essence of them shows through at the conclusion of the picture.

The General has given us a broad plan, a general map of which way to go. He has imparted many usefully general ways of measuring, which will aid us in creating a strong foundation to build from. This will allow us to take our drawing further and add elements of interest. No matter how experienced we become, in order to achieve finely rendered drawings without getting lost along the way, we always need to go through planning stages led by the General.

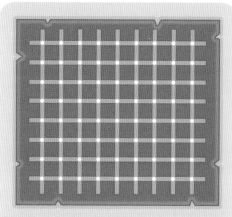

Look at the centre of this grid. You can see both the lines and the circles. The circles further from the centre, however, disappear, leaving only the high contrast pattern. Peripheral vision doesn't deal in details. The Specific lives in the centre of our vision, and even if we created a picture that was superbly detailed to the point of hyper-realism, there will always be a blurred generality about it because the eye cannot focus on the whole picture at the same time.

After a broad plan has been established, there comes a point when we need to take advice from our Specific companion. To remain general would leave our drawing as something resembling a sketch. We're now approaching methods of measuring that will deliver more accurate results. This will enable us to establish an accurate system of relationships. It is important to note that although we're about to gain knowledge of taking precise measurements, the Specific will not yet be taking over the character of our line. The reason for that is that, to make the most of the measuring technique she's about to reveal, we still need to use straight lines. We're not ditching the General yet; he still has an important role to play.

I'm lost. I guess we have no choice but to let her lead the way.

DEEPER INTO THE WOODS

Measuring III	Ellipses	2.5D Drawing
111	114	117

The General had led us in a vague direction, but now it was time for the Specific to take the lead and plot a more definite path. Colossal fragments of sculpture littered the forest like boulders. "Where did all of these come from?" I asked. "Are these the last, humbling remnants of a great, fallen civilisation? Like, 'Look on my works, ye mighty and despair'?"

"Um, maybe?" the Specific said, hopping onto a giant face. "That or Medusa's been petrifying Titans again."

I laughed; she did not. She was peering ahead, deep in concentration.

Triangulation

From her vantage point atop the stone, the Specific plots their course using an advanced measurement technique, known as triangulation. Taken from a branch of mathematics known as trigonometry, triangulation has long been used by cartographers and surveyors. It involves using the position of known landmarks to determine the precise location of some unknown feature. It may sound tricky at first, but if you stick with it, you'll find that not only is it quite manageable, it's actually a bit of a revelation.

So how does it work? Triangulation involves taking two known points and, from them, making a triangle to the third, unknown point. This process allows us to nail down the relationships between separate parts of the image, helping us to check the outline and lines within the contour. Perhaps its most important application is allowing us to determine the location of the sides with a high level of accuracy. It is a method that lets us cross-check relationships between individual parts while also keeping an eye on the image as a whole.

Weapons Grade Marksmanship

Triangulation increases your chances of accuracy tenfold.

Measure twice, draw once.

Work methodically, double-checking yourself against key landmarks. Use a couple of points on the X or Y guidelines that you are fairly sure of as a basis for triangulation.

The General has taught us how to see large relationships, using eyeballing and comparative needle measurements. Triangulation allows the General and the Specific to come together, calculating large relationships with a high degree of exactitude.

In the example to the left, we are using two known points, (a) and (b), to find the unknown point (c). You might think of this as the top and bottom points, connected by a mid-line, with (c) representing the right hand side edge of the subject. Taking the needle, we then measure the angles between both of these known points and the unknown point, (c). Using these angles, we then draw lines connecting these two points to (c). Where the lines intersect, we have found (c). This is an extremely useful method of measurement, particularly for portraiture, as we'll soon discover. We can triangulate all kinds of points within the face, such as tear ducts, the corners of the mouth and the sides of the nose.

Uhh.. any chance of a visual demonstration?

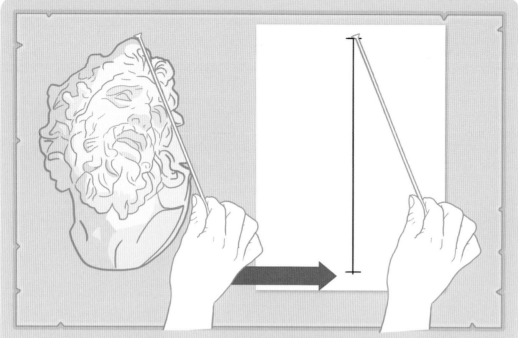

I am now using the knitting needle, which was so helpful for general tilt assessments, to locate the furthest left and right-hand points on this cast. The diagram above shows the movement my arm makes when I record the tilt of a given line segment. Because angles don't change with distance, it's not necessary to hold your arm outstretched for these measurements. Try to move your hand between the subject and your paper using a fluid motion, memorise the angle, then note it with your pencil. After doing this, use the needle again to check your accuracy.

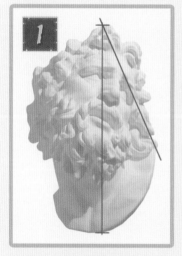

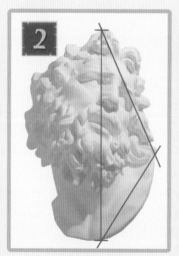

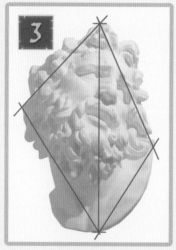

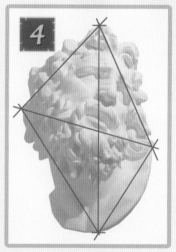

The top and bottom points are already established facts on our drawing, so we can use them to triangulate the sides. Using the action demonstrated above, I measure the angle of the line that joins the top point to furthest right-hand point, then repeat this, measuring from the bottom.

Once I have measured the angle from the top and bottom points to the right-hand side, I find the point where the angles intersect. This is the location of the right-hand point.

I then repeat the process with the left-hand side. Now I have four points I can be sure of, along with four lines connected to my mid-line whose angles and proportions I feel confident about.

Checking the angle between the two horizontal extremities is also always a very good idea: it helps to lock those points even more firmly into place, and it gives you yet another helpful guideline.

Gauging Tilt

There can be no better exercise for practicing gauging tilt than the drawing of triangles. Learning to gauge tilt is the key to accurate copying of shapes, which is, in its turn, a fundamental drawing skill. The triangle is at once the simplest shape and the most important to master, because it unlocks the ability to perform precise measurements in drawing. Triangulating within a form enables you to locate key points with a high degree of accuracy. With this in mind, let's draw some triangles.

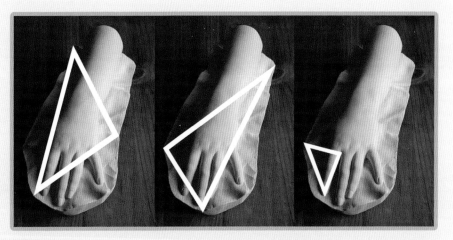

We can use triangles to check the accuracy of large-scale relationships, as well as relationships across short distances.

A For this exercise in triangulation, begin by taking a pencil and ruler and drawing two straight lines about 6cms apart (A). These can be either horizontal or vertical; it makes little difference for this exercise.

B Now, on the other side of your paper, draw two more lines, the same distance apart (B). Using a ruler, populate the space between these two lines with various different triangles. Make sure that at least one line touches both of your initial parallel lines—as shown by the bold line in the example on your right.

C Once you have your triangles in place, move back to your first set of parallel lines (A). Try to copy the triangles you have just drawn. Start by positioning the side in bold, that runs between both (B) lines. Once this first side is correctly place, draw the next two sides by gauging their tilt. The place where they intersect is your third and final point.

In this exercise, your hookshot will come in handy once again. In this instance, you are simply overshooting the lines, drawing them a little longer than they actually are—this helps with finding intersections. Anyway, your goal at this point should be to get the angle your lines right, rather than worrying about measuring their length, as the place where your two lines cross will denote the correct length of each line.

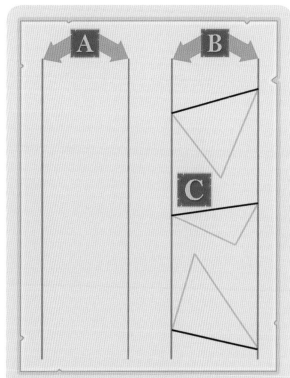

In the course of studying the usefulness of straight lines, we have already practiced copying complicated, six-sided shapes. By regressing back to triangles, however, we have a chance to really train ourselves in the accurate perception of tilt.

I saw you back on page 87 making curves. You're ready for this.

Level Up! — Portal Opener!

Now that we've spent time mastering the simplest shape, the triangle, let's take a flying leap at a shape which is much more advanced, yet also common and important: the ellipse. The wonky ellipse is a problem that many students face, and it's worth learning to solve it.

An ellipse is a circle which has been uniformly squashed—or, to put it another way, it's a circle seen at an angle. This means that ellipses are governed by the same laws as a circle: they have no straight lines, and like circles, ellipses are very difficult to draw freehand.

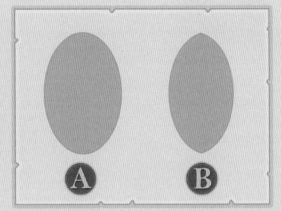

The line of the ellipse is a seamless curve (A). Ellipses never have pinched, pointed ends as shown in (B)—this is an incredibly common misconception.

I'm sure we've all had the experience of trying to draw a mug—it seems so simple, but the rim ends up looking like a child's first clay pot. In a cruel irony, as difficult as they are to draw accurately, errors in ellipses are very easy to spot.

You should be careful when opening portals. Without a system you could end up summoning monsters.

> Because an ellipse is essentially a circle seen from an angle, it must abide by the same rules as a circle.

The wonky ellipse can really damage the believability of your drawing: having spotted a problem there, the viewer will go on to question other aspects of the drawing that they might have otherwise accepted.

Although the ellipse is always challenging, there are some techniques which make it a more manageable challenge, as well as some common mistakes you can learn to avoid. Fortunately, this is an area where the General has some simple wisdom to impart. He also said something about using the ellipse as a portal . . .

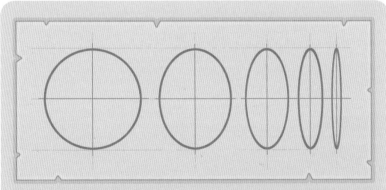

The ellipse always consists of four identical segments. By drawing vertical and horizontal guidelines through the centre, we can check to ensure all four segments are identical.

An easy way of studying ellipses is to pick up a cup and rotate it, noticing the various ovals formed by the mouth. Notice that none of these shapes, no matter how narrow, has pinched, point sides.

Mechanical Ellipses

Now, let's learn how to construct these common, tricky shapes. By now you know that straight lines are important tools in drawing, and, surprise, here they come to our aid yet again. Boxing up ovals can help us make sense of them. As well as helping to guide our construction of ellipses, boxes create negative shapes around the ellipses, which we can use to further gauge our accuracy.

Boxes will also help us handle the further challenge of applying perspective to ellipses. Perspective on an oval can be a very subtle thing. Using a box to help guide and regulate our construction of the oval can make the process a lot less frustrating.

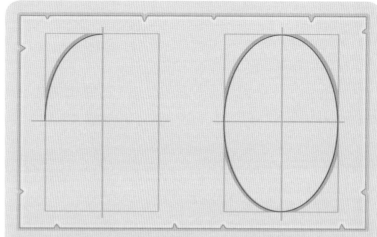

The ellipse should never taper to a point, so be sure to make the arc a continuous curving line. Even though the line may seem to square off where it meets the edges of the box, there is always still a curve, even if it is slight.

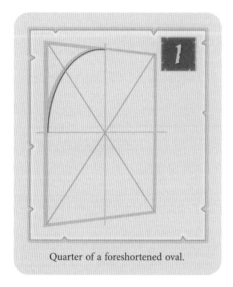

Quarter of a foreshortened oval.

Foreshortening ovals (1)

Begin by drawing a square as it would be seen in one-point perspective—you can see an example of this to the left.* Because the box is receding away from us, draw an X that links each of the corners so that the center of this box that is consistent with the way it appears in perspective can be found. Using this center point, we can then divide this box into quarters using a vertical and horizontal line.

Starting in the top left segment, draw an arc connecting the top and left points. I begin here because I am right-handed, so I find the top left arc the easiest. Try reversing this if you are left-handed. Try your best to get this arc right, because it will set the standard for the other arcs to follow. The curve should be very slight to begin with, reaching its greatest curvature at 45 degrees. After that, it again becomes more gentle as it approaches the edge.

You can now go around the square, drawing curves in the same manner (2). You will find this easier to do if you rotate your paper, so that you are always drawing in the direction that comes most naturally.

Check your oval by looking in a mirror. This will make it easier to spot any errors quickly. Because we so readily spot mistakes in ovals, it means that when it looks right, it is right. If a mirror is your friend in drawing, a living, breathing best friend is even better. They'll be glad to point out any errors!

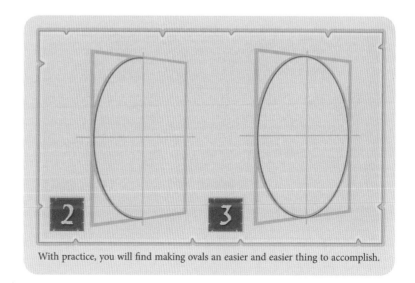

With practice, you will find making ovals an easier and easier thing to accomplish.

*Page 191 shows an example of two-point perspective. The only difference between these is that one-point perspective uses a single vanishing point, rather than two.

Ellipses for Cylinders

Once you know how to draw foreshortened ovals, you can construct a cylinder! In the diagram below, a vanishing point has been introduced: that horizontal line across the middle of the image represents the horizon, towards which the perspective converges; it should be understood as being in the distance. Drawing a vanishing point can be an incredibly useful way of guiding your drawing, making sure it remains consistent within the laws of perspective.

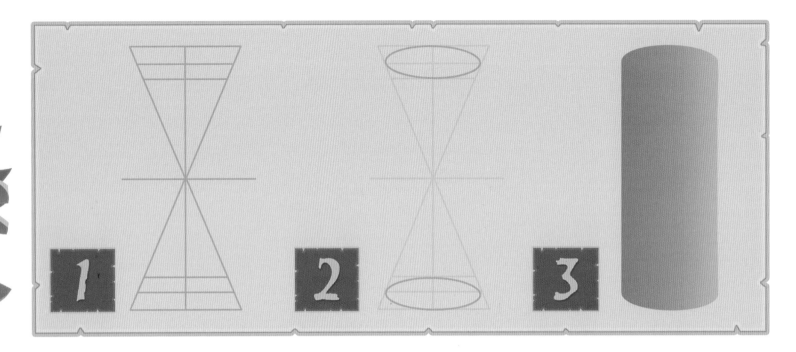

It seemed so exciting, the chance to open portals here, there and everywhere. I soon realised, however, that building ellipses using the General's mechanical formula was incredibly dull. What was the point of opening portals if they just showed me how to draw the lip of a cup or rim of a bucket with the correct perspective? Surely there must be more to these mystical, swirling ovals than this?

2.5 Dimensional Drawing

Playful Ovals

We've been looking at some very practical and quite mechanical drawing challenges, but let's take a step back and think about some of the larger challenges that face us in drawing. One big question people ask is, "But what should I draw?" So far, we've been looking at ways of drawing from objects around us—this is a practice that can give immense enjoyment, as well as honing our sensitivities, helping us become aware of things we might not otherwise give a second thought to. Our adventures in drawings are not, however, limited to everyday objects. Sometimes we might want to draw on our inner worlds, to project our imaginations onto paper. Once we set out to draw from the imagination, we again face the question of, "But what do I draw?" This time, it can pose an even bigger obstacle.

You've already come a long way in drawing, and it's time to play around a little. We're going to take a break from measurement and look at a very different kind of drawing, which is quick, organic and intuitive. I use this style whenever I want to conjure an object from my imagination onto paper.

This style involves using ovals to construct forms that have a nice fullness to them. These construction-ovals are very different from the mechanical ellipses we've been working on. Using ovals is a great method for getting ideas down as fast as possible. As a method for generating objects from the imagination, it's pretty much the complete package: not only do the ovals give us a mouldable form, drawing the ovals serves as a super quick warm-up, getting our hands in gear. Ovals let us feel out what needs to happen in a given area, and they give us clues as to what should happen next.

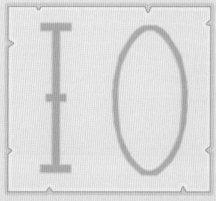

The Tetraforce isn't like the alphabet. Here, the 'I' is for observation, and 'O' is for imagination. The straight lined 'I', with its top and bottom points, is the ideal device for beginning a drawing from observation. The 'O' of the oval, meanwhile, is a fantastic tool for generating imaginative drawings. We need both of them to get anywhere in drawing.

The oval has something 2.5-dimensional about it: it's a flat shape, yet it hints at the idea of a round object in space. This effect becomes all the more pronounced when you start to link ovals together.

Working just with flat shapes, we start to get the idea of something that is either moving away from us or reaching out towards us. Ovals make foreshortening much easier to describe.

What makes ovals so special is that they carry with them a sense of volume and fullness while still belonging to the two-dimensional stage of drawing. They also have a great advantage over straight lines when it comes to constructing organic forms. They serve as a kind of intermediary stage between straight lines and curves. The key here, as with all preliminary drawing, is to make your marks very lightly: these are just your initial impressions.

In this style, a free hand is complemented by a controlled one. The free hand throws out lots of ideas and experimental ovals, creating vague impressions. These ideas can then be harnessed and shaped using straight lines. The interplay of freedom and control allows us to feel out the forms of our drawings. Be aware that if you fill the page with too many ideas, it can become difficult to pin down the right one. Use the eraser to avoid excessive ovals leading you astray: if a series of ovals doesn't work, get rid of them so that you can see clearly and start again.

Golem Technique

This is one of my absolute favourite ways to draw. The organic yet mechanical process involves placing down ovals of various different shapes and sizes in a way which feels a lot like working with lumps of clay. Over the top of these ovals, I use straight lines to bake this mould into a definite shape, whatever I wish that to be. The oval acts as a sort of quick estimation: it gives a basic idea of shape size and placement and also a very basic feeling of perspective. As we saw on the last page, connecting ovals together can quickly generate the idea of an object moving towards or away from view. I place lots and lots of ovals all around, and then finally engage in the process of squaring these off and firming them up, almost like baking the clay. The more straightness I add to the oval, the firmer and more fixed it becomes.

So I've set down what we can think of as a big blob of clay (1). In (2) I have attached a smaller lump of clay. Gradually, I add more and more little blobs and lumps, building up a larger structure (3). This method of imaginative drawing is all the more effective if you have some references images close by—you don't copy from them, but they inform your imagination. These references, which can all be images around a theme, give you something to riff on.

I proceed with the drawing, attaching smaller forms onto a larger one (4). When everything seems to be in place, I build on top of the ovals with blocky straight lines, which give the form some firmness and definition (5). I find that drawing without any sort of preliminary sketch in place is close to impossible. This 'Golem technique', however, allows me to generate sketches of just about any form I wish, very quickly and easily.

Imaginative ovals in creature creation

I brought forth this very silly looking Cthulhu (D) using the Golem technique. Without such a method I would have found it very hard to construct objects, such as the tentacles, from imagination (A).

The image (A) is a scrap of paper I had nearby while I worked, so that I could experiment with various shapes of tentacles before deciding on the kind I wanted to place in next. It would of course be possible to try things out and then trace the image into the main work, except for the fact that Bristol board is quite a heavy paper and doesn't allow for tracing.

Using the ovals, I establish line-work (B) that is strong enough for me to begin the process of shading. Shading, as you'll discover, is actually a relatively easy and fun part of drawing. We're not quite ready for shading yet, though: first we have to Level Up from the oval and find an imaginative use for the cylinder!

Bloody hell!

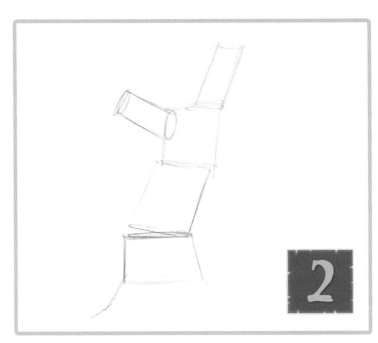

I begin the process of drawing a tree by placing basic cylindrical forms (1). These basic shapes give me a sense of how the trunk and various branches are angled and arranged (2).

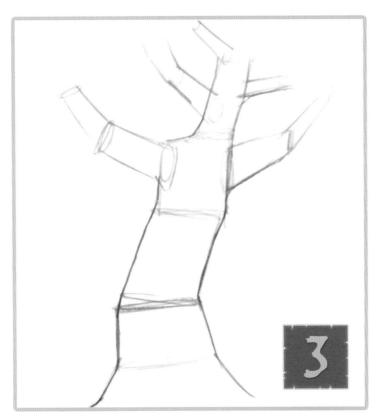

Trees are complex, with hundreds of branches, twigs and leaves. For this reason, when drawing a tree, it's essential to keep the shapes to a minimum, so that I don't become overwhelmed (3). I begin to erase some of my shape-guides by dabbing at them with a kneaded eraser (4). I don't remove them completely, however, as they can still give me important information about how a particular shape is oriented in space. By reducing their darkness, though, I keep them from becoming too distracting as the drawing advances.

From this point on, I'm going to advance the tree in ways we will cover in later chapters—this just gives us a chance to see where we're headed. By using cylinders, I've gotten a basic understanding of the tree as a three-dimensional object. Now I begin to block-in some basic shadow shapes to give a sense of how the object is lit within its environment (5). With these shadow shapes in place, I begin placing some heavy darks to begin defining the shadows (6). Every stage thus far has been bold: bold geometric shapes, bold lines, bold shadow shapes, and finally, bold, dark hatching. Even though a tree is intricate, there is nothing fiddly about its construction.

The bold, general nature of the tree's construction ensures that when the more specific phases do occur, as in these last two panels, the details are resting upon a solid structure that can hold them up and hold them together (7). There's nothing worse than getting to the decoration phase (8), and finding that all your lovely details aren't sitting on the object's surface in a way that is believable.

PORTRAITURE

Portraiture

123

All this talk of opening portals and dabbling in shadow magic had gotten the attention of someone nearby.
A woman stepped towards us through the trees. Her hair looked—weirdly alive. "Don't look!" the Specific cried.
"But he must look," the woman said, and I could hear hissing behind her voice. "I've been watching this budding artist with interest.
It seems to me that he is ready for a true challenge. If you wish to pass, you must draw my portrait."

Level Up! — Soul Stealer

The difficulties of portraiture can be truly paralysing. We'll proceed slowly: in this chapter, we're just going to learn some basic anatomy, see how triangulation applies to portraiture, then finish with a rough sketch. This will form the basis of the portrait we'll pick up again later on, once we've reached the realms of three dimensions.

Portraiture utilises the same Tetraforce processes that we've been applying to inanimate objects. The difficulty inherent to drawing a portrait of a person is that we are also seeking to capture something that lies beyond two or even three dimensions: a person's inner light, that something which animates their features and forms their personality. Without considering this, you cannot capture a true likeness.

Thus, as well as capturing physical appearances, the truly successful portrait contains psychological truth. This is one reason why it may be easier to draw people you know. It can also be easier to elicit a natural pose from someone you're already comfortable with.*

MEDUSA

You must capture her likeness. But... how do you draw something you can't see?

Detail of 'Robert' in progress, 2015 — Graphite pencil on Bristol board, 30 x 42cms.

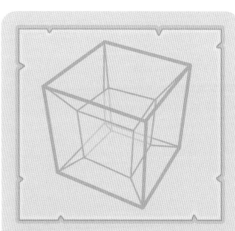

Another Dimension — This illustration shows a tesseract, or hypercube, which is used to represent dimensions beyond our usual three. When attempt to draw a portrait, a person's inner life creates an extra dimension we must contend with. The outer cube represents a person's physical appearance, while the inner cube represents the person's inner life, which we must strive to represent in two dimensions. This is a deep challenge indeed.

*If you come to do portrait commissions, try to get to the know the sitter and see what makes them tick so you can reflect this in the work. Without inclusion of the inner workings of the person, you may end up just drawing a shell and fail to capture the full depth of the sitter.

General's Knowledge

There's a world of difference between a bowl of fruit and a human body. Human anatomy is so beautifully complex that it's useful for an artist to be armed with at least a general theoretical understanding, as well as a few rules of proportion, before attempting to reproduce it. Knowing what's causing all those lumps and bumps can be a real help when trying to solve certain visual problems. There are a few proportional rules of thumb to the right, but do be aware that these are only broad guidelines. People's faces are wonderfully varied, so you will encounter many exceptions to these rules. Nevertheless, these will give you a good starting point.

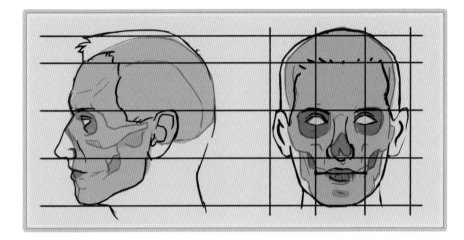

Idealism

Oliver Cromwell famously asked to be painted "warts and all." It's a line which goes to the heart of a conflict within the act of portraiture, that of realism versus idealism.

The desire to record an honest, accurate likeness runs up against several competing urges: first, there is the impulse to please the subject, leading to a sort of Photoshop effect; and then, there is a desire to capture a deeper, inner reality, to give a sense of their personality. Not surprisingly, the self-portrait is the most susceptible to such distortions. Not only is there an obvious temptation towards idealisation, there is also the simple fact that we cannot see our own faces except through the lens of our self-conception.

Our brains are powerfully predisposed towards recognising facial patterns. You've almost certainly seen faces staring out at you from wallpaper patterns, coffee stains and other inanimate objects. Because this is such a powerful symbolic pattern, we see faces everywhere and yet, paradoxically, it can be very difficult to truly see a face, without preconceptions. Observational practice is the only way to overcome this.

Head height — Seen from the front, the head is five eye-widths wide.

Eye position — The eyes are located halfway down the head. Hair can disguise this, but it really is the case. The eyes are usually spaced one eye-width apart.

Nose — The base of the nose is halfway between the eyes and the chin. The sides of the nose fall under the tear ducts in the inner corner of the eyes.

Mouth — The corners of the mouth fall directly below the pupils. The mouth is closer to the nose than to the chin.

Lip — The bottom lip is located halfway between the base of the nose and chin.

Ears — The tops of the ears are level with the eyebrows, and the earlobes line up with the bottom of the nose.

Head size — The distance from the tip of the nose to the back of the head is longer than the distance from the crown of the head to the chin.

Face is angled — The head pitches forward somewhat. The angle can vary greatly, with the jaw becoming totally recessed in some cases.

Further reading — These are some very basic guidelines for portraiture. For an in-depth exploration of proportion, of the body and the face, seek out Andrew Loomis' classic *Drawing the Head and Hands*. It offers a formula for building human heads without a reference.

Hey! Good to see you using dead guys to help you draw! You can also use a photo if you find looking at me too hazardous.

Choice of Reference

Drawing from photographs is controversial. Most traditional ateliers don't like it, while plenty of other people think it's great and get a lot of pleasure from it. My own preference is for a way of working which makes the most of both photographic references and drawing from life. They've each got different things going for them, and I enjoy them both. The challenge of drawing from life is exhilarating: you're capturing a moment right in front of you, working against time. Photo references afford us the chance for relaxing, private and potentially long term studies.

For some highly detailed drawings, I do the initial work from life, establishing the general gesture and so on. I then use a photograph for the more detailed work, building on what I've established drawing from life. This helps to counteract one of the problems with photographic references, their tendency to flatten things out. Working from life puts us more in touch with the mass and volume of our subject.

Copying from photos means that we can quickly get great results—which leads to encouraging feedback and increased confidence, all of which is helpful in motivating us to continue drawing.

Spoiler alert for later portrait: there are drawbacks to this method—drawing from photos can produce a simulacrum.

Flat image reference

Drawing from a two-dimensional photo of a person or object makes it hard to understand the subject as a rounded object within space. It can also make it harder to see depth and perspective properly. Drawing from life avoids these problems, but it throws up very real challenges of its own. Although we've been working hard to see our subjects as flat, in later stages of the drawing, it becomes important to appreciate the subject's three-dimensionality."

In some ways, drawing from life creates the opposite problem, that of translating a three-dimensional subject into a two-dimensional drawing: this poses a lot of intellectual challenges, and drawing from life really does make you think. Another challenge, which arises in part from the sheer difficulty of the process, is fatigue. Fatigue can also be a real issue for your model. There are many important lessons to be learnt by drawing from life, but it is genuinely hard. Don't feel bad if you find progress slow in this department.

We can also think about the unique advantages offered by digital photographic references. With these, it's easy to convert colour images to greyscale, making it that much easier to see values. I particularly like working from photo references on a digital pad: not only is this easily portable, it also lets me zoom in to high-definition images, which is really helpful for detail work. There's a risk here, however, of overworking: it's easy to get into the mindset that everything in the picture needs to be drawn. Photos are a wonderful tool, but don't use them to the exclusion of life drawing.

So, to escape my captor, I had to capture her—all without looking straight at her. If only I had some kind of device which could create an unmoving image of her, just as she petrified those she gazed upon. In the absence of such great magic, I used a mirror. Standing amongst the eerie stone forms of my predecessors, I triangulated carefully, hoping to avoid their fate.

Accurate Portraiture

A truly accurate drawing begins by looking nothing like the subject. While building the scaffolding, it's important to have patience with the process, and not to worry about whether or not the drawing looks good yet. We're about to take a look at a portrait I did of Elinor, which went through a lengthy process of preparation. These early stages involved a lot of calculation, correction and re-evaluation. As ever, accuracy only comes with patience: you have to make the mistakes before you can correct them! The key is to keep your strokes broad, work lightly, and have patience.

Recommended beginning — Start with a self-portrait: you're your own most patient and available model, and your mistakes won't cause any offence! Place a mirror just beyond your easel, taking care to place it so that you can see yourself from your most comfortable drawing position.

Head size — How big headed are you? When doing portraits, I like to scale the head to match the span between my little finger and thumb. Much larger, and the portrait can suffer from giganticism, becoming a little uncanny. For extreme examples, see the work of Chuck Close and Robert Mueck. It's usually a good idea to draw the head either life-sized or just a little smaller. Nine-inches is a good size to aim for.

Make sure you leave enough room at the bottom of the page for the neck and shoulders—floating heads look a bit spooky. You can find a few rules of thumb below to think about when considering different compositions of a profile portrait.

1 — *Head placement*

Avoid positioning the subject's eyes at the dead centre, as in image (A) to the right. Compositionally, this is an aggressive set-up, as the subject seems to glare at the viewer. Instead, place the head a little to the left or a bit higher up (B).

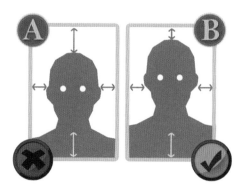

2 — *Space for gaze*

In image (C) the gaze is too close to the edge, and it looks like the subject is staring at a wall. Leaving a little distance, as shown in (D), makes room for the gaze and allows the portrait to appear more natural.

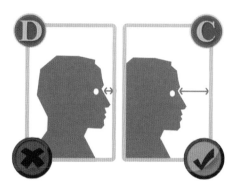

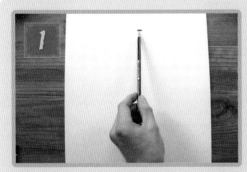

Top, bottom, middle — As usual, I begin by noting the top, bottom, and middle points. These three points are crucial to accurate measuring. I made these marks very lightly, but they have been digitally darkened in the photos so that they're easily visible.

In images (4, 5, 6), I am using my pencil to measure angles, in order to triangulate the location of the sides of the head. I held my pencil up to the model's head, then brought it down to my rest over my paper surface at the same angle. After holding the pencil against my paper, I memorised the angle and jotted it lightly on the page. I then found the points where the angled lines intersect: these are the left and right extreme points of my subject. The shape that results from this looks like (A).

A kite shape

Once you've recorded your angles, you need to run long, straight lines along them. If you find straight lines particularly difficult, it's alright to use a ruler. This process of recording and marking angles to triangulate the left and right sides is challenging, so I suggest doing plenty of practice, just on scrap paper, and working as dark as you like. This way you can see what you're doing as you build up confidence.

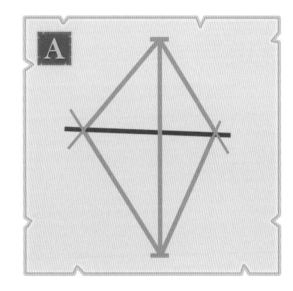

For portraits, your initial shape will probably be like a kite. The initial shape will vary from subject to subject, but what won't change is the sense of laying down firm foundations.

Here I am holding up my pencil to assess the angle that occurs between the left and right points. I then hold this up to my subject to check this is correct. If it is, then the drawing is off to a great start.

Remember the crossword puzzle: the more you get right, the more clues you have for what to do next. Hasty guesses, however, will lead you astray. Only Confucius does his crossword with a pen.

Refusing to Get Tied Down

The human head and face are so extremely familiar to us that, when drawing them, we are susceptible to drawing what we expect to see rather than what we actually see. It can help to de-familiarise the face by looking at it as a piece of architecture or a landscape: the cliff of the nose, the caverns of the eye sockets.

In portraiture, it's also especially tempting to go into too much detail too soon, because we yearn to achieve a likeness. In this portrait, I actually did fall prey to temptation, rushing ahead—as a result, the head ended up being a little too wide. This was a mistake that became embedded in the drawing as it was allowed to remain past the block-in stages. When I finally noticed it, though, I was able to regress that area back to block-in and eliminate the error.

The longer mistakes go unnoticed and the further down the Tetraforce we take things, the harder these problem areas are to correct. Still, I know that my measuring process allowed me to root out a good many errors and problems early in the process. Time devoted to measurement is time well spent.

All the lines I note down are part of a process of question and answer. These lines constitute my solution to the problem of trying to understand the face. When trying to understand the orientation of the face, the brow line is a good place to start.

Line character (reminder)

Even though I am taking care in noting my lines and proceeding slowly, I still consider my lines open to revision. They remain light and loose. When our lines communicate with each other in a true and visually pleasing way, we begin to achieve harmony. If we take measurements based on an inaccurately placed aspect, however, the sketch becomes discordant and chaotic. During this process of measuring and blocking in, remember to keep your lines at least a couple of inches long. Any smaller lines would be too much detail. Detail causes tightness, which then results in fatigue.

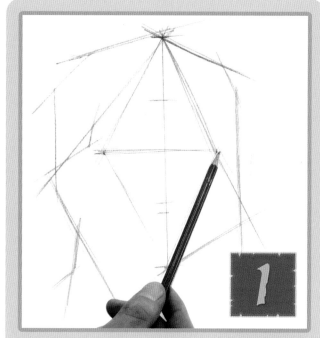

Use the chin and the mid-line to triangulate the position of the eyes. The mid-line also provides a place for noting the location of important landmarks such as the brow line, mouth and base of nose.

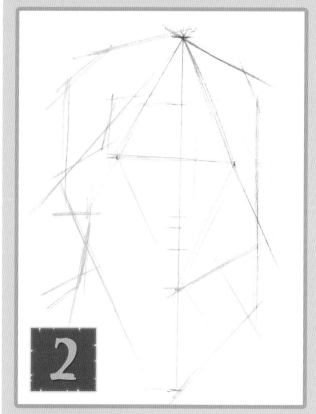

Here you can see how triangulation has enabled me to position the dominant lines of the head. The main angles and the locations of features are recorded accurately, using just a few lines. The lines of the actual sketch were also far lighter; they've been darkened here so that you can see.

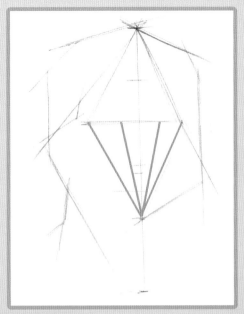 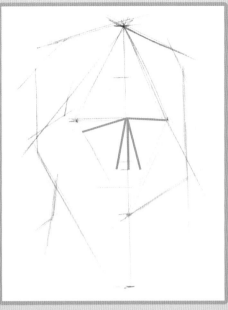 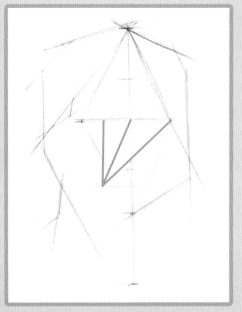

Positioning features — In portraiture, I find that certain features are critical for the purposes of measurement. These triangulation anchor points are the corners of the mouth, the tear ducts of the eyes, the base of the nose, the hairline, and the cross section of the eye. Once I find these points and cross-reference them against each other, I find that positioning everything else becomes much easier.

Portrait centre line

The line of the nose usually runs close to the mid-line we drew right at the beginning. As such, the line of the nose provides a valuable reference for placing the other features. It's best to begin by positioning the medial lines, that is, lines that are close to the mid-line. Lines further away from the mid-line are called lateral. The more medial a feature is, the easier it is to position accurately. Once your medial lines are well-placed, you can work outwards laterally.

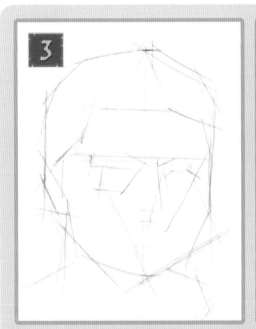  

These images show snapshots of different stages of the portrait, all darkened to help you see my workings. By image (4), I've generated a good enough likeness that I can begin venturing into the Shadows, laying in general dark masses (5). This step helps to reveal any small mistakes of positioning that may still lurk in the image.

Okay, you can be on your way now. I assume you have no idea how to proceed anyway. I'll meet you in the desert, if you actually get there that is.

Mapping the Coast

Cartographers must take care to map coastlines accurately so that ships will not run aground. In the same way, as draughtsmen, we must carefully plot our contour so that our drawings don't crash and become unsalvageable wrecks. Beware, however: there is a fractal paradox which states that the coastline of Great Britain is infinitely long, because every line of the coast can always be subdivided. Thus, the contour can become infinitely subtle and fine. Large shapes break down into smaller and smaller shapes, potentially forever.

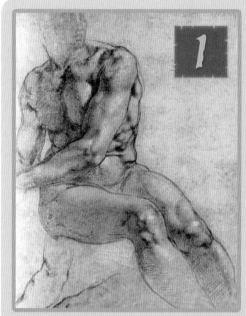

I'm now going to have a go at copying this Michelangelo drawing. With the picture placed next to my working surface, I'm ready to begin massing in the most obvious angles. As before, the lines of my block-in have been digitally darkened for visibility.

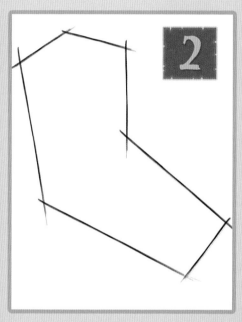

My constellation shape comprises seven line segments, capturing the most prominent angles in the original. This is my first, broad estimation, from which the drawing will grow. It is very much open to change.

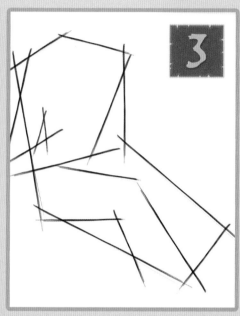

My block-in is increasing in complexity, but my lines are still light enough that I can correct them without leaving behind distracting marks.

Throughout the block-in phases, we have kept things broad and general, and we have avoided elaboration. The block-in has allowed us to manage complexity and to ensure we construct strong structures. Now, before you begin your contour, take time to reassess your block-in, checking and refining your angles in particular. There's no point decorating a building which is about to collapse.

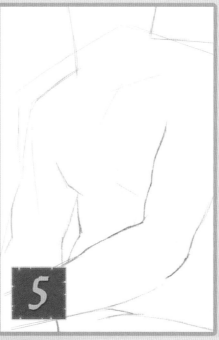

On top of the block-in, I begin overlaying the smaller line segments of the refined contour, building upon the broad structure to become more specific.

You can see here, at the left-hand shoulder, that my constellation was actually quite far off. This is a good example of the kinds of mistakes you're likely to make.

The line is becoming tighter and tighter, the more information is included. If I find that a line segment is wrong, then it's much better to regress the flawed section right back to a block-in, rather than trying to tweak a complex set of line segments.

As we walked, the path moved closer and closer to the edges of the coastal cliffs. Suddenly, to my horror, the General tripped on a tiny stone and fell! As I raced to his aid, I heard the Specific behind me. "He had to go sometime. Things can't stay sketchy and ambiguous forever, now can they?" I didn't answer. I was too busy falling over the cliff with him.

CONTOUR COAST

Desperately, I clung to the cliff-edge. The same unevenness which had tripped up my dear friend, the General, now proved my salvation, because there were lots of little nooks and crannies to dig my fingers into.

CONTOUR

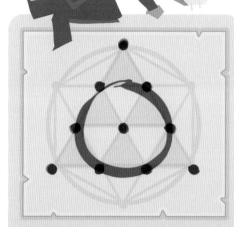

Level Up! – Contourtionist!

We've finally reached the stage at which we can move towards a precise representation, rather than a broad approximation. As we do this, our line becomes far more specific, definite and fixed. This means, however, that we're beginning to close off our options, so we must take care.

We will now also begin to leave straight lines behind. From a block-in composed of straight lines with varying degrees of tilt, we must now work with arcs of varying degrees of curvature. The angles and proportions established in our block-in will guide us as we start the tricky task of dealing with these curved lines. Eventually, every line of the block-in will acquire some degree of curvature, although by allowing some of the original blockiness to remain, we can maintain the strength of our lines.

With the contour, we are still developing the outline. As much care and time as we put into developing the outline, however, our ultimate goal is to hide it.

Having approximated the outline into a series of line segments and subdivided this account of the perimeter to a high level, the curvature of the form is the next step. The contour is basically the subject's outline. The contour marks the point at which a form turns completely away from our line of sight. It can also describe the edges of features within the subject.

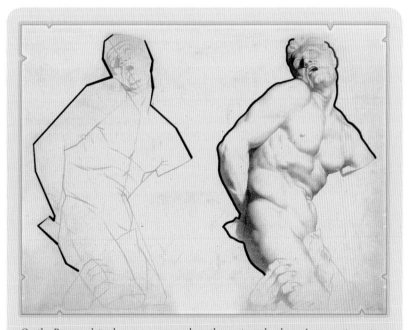

On the Bargue plate above, you can see how the contour develops. An accurate contour must be built upon the foundation of a solid block-in. Otherwise, it's impossible to capture the extremely subtle modulations of line, particularly on a subject as complex as a human body. It's almost impossible to draw such nuanced lines in a single motion. The human body is especially challenging to draw, because the line responds to rounded forms that are capable of an incredible range of gestures: there are very few places where the perimeter line of a human body is flat.

Outlines give drawings an artificial quality, so, once we've developed an accurate contour, it will be integrated into the picture. This can happen once we begin adding value.

For our purposes, line can best be understood as a means of describing an area of stark tonal contrast. When two tones are placed together, the area of distinction, along which they meet, is perceived as a line.

Along this zone of tonal difference, however, there will be stretches of lower contrast, and so the implied line will fade. Once our line takes on this characteristic of coming and going, with the subtle variations of tone, our line ceases to be sketchy and attains quite a different quality: the line transcends the symbolic and begins to depict the subtleties of visual perception more faithfully.

Lost and Found Edges

Coming and Going Away

Sometimes line, like Guido's giant companion, must leave us. For a line to become something other than a plodding progression from point A to point B, it must become a little less explicit and complete.

If every aspect of the composition is simple, if nothing is left to the imagination and everything is spelled out, we make things too easy for the observer. On this level, completeness doesn't necessarily lead to contentment: a line that dips in and out of existence has a variety that creates interest.

Compositionally, outlines are quickly and easily noticed. Strong lines, such as those in figure (A), create tracks for the gaze to follow. Used skilfully, they can guide the eye to the focal point.

> "The knowledge of the outline is of most consequence and yet may be acquired to great certainty by dint of study." — Leonardo da Vinci

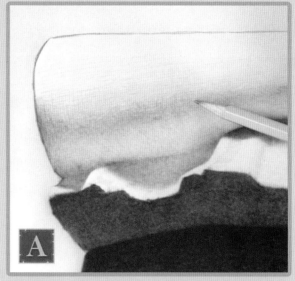

Striking line — The strong outline here captures the eye and gives it a track to run along. This is a compositionally active outline.

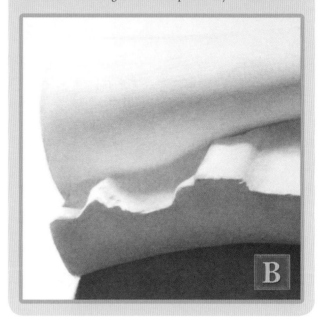

Dismantling the scaffold weakens things?

In image (B), the upper outline has been removed, creating a strikingly different effect from image (A). Without the outline, we have a much softer and more realistic effect. Compositionally, however, the image is weaker: there's nothing to catch the eye, so it simply drifts upwards in search of the object's lost limits. Greater realism, in this case, also means a weaker drawing.

How could we solve the problem raised by these two images? One solution would be to use a dark background. Then the upper line of the cast would still be clearly delineated, without the need for an outline. When using a dark background for situations like this, I make the background gradually lighter as it moves down towards the subject; this prevents the dark background from swallowing my subject, as well as any cast shadows that are to be found at the foot of the drawing.

Wish I could say this is the first time this has happened.

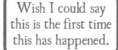

Lost edges aren't really lost at all. Instead, our brains join up the line segments, filling in the gaps. Lost edges can be a wonderful means of adding compositional interest. By suggesting detail without actually including it, we give the viewer's eye and mind playful work to do, making our drawing more interesting.

If you have a chance to imply something rather than drawing it, try taking that route instead. Drawing everything is exhausting for you and dull for viewers. Lost edges are like the silences in music and like subtext in drama. Allow the observer to become involved in your drawing by creating opportunities for discovery.

Even a finished, accurate line can create problems. In image (A), we see a darkly outlined sphere, and in image (B) we see the problems that arise if we try to add shading to this shape. If we make the shadows dark enough to match the heavy contour, then the shading becomes too dark, and the result is flat. Usually, along the edges of rounded forms, we'll find a subtle play of reflected light, as we'll learn later.

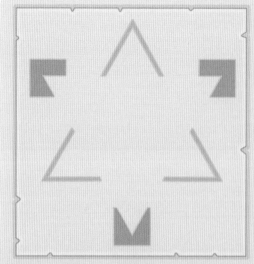

The above image contains plenty of clues, allowing our brains to piece together the idea of two triangle shapes overlapping each another. The drawing actually contains no complete triangles, but our minds can easily infer eleven if we look for them. Implying lines makes the image participatory, something the viewer co-creates with the artist.

> When borders fluctuate between the firm and the and vague, this unites the subject with the background.

Colour problem

As you evaluate your subject, colour can present an obstacle to seeing where contours come and go. If you look at the vase images to the lower right, the greyscale image clearly reveals how the large vase's outline dissolves into the background in the lower right-hand side. In the colour image, this dissolution is still perceptible, but less readily apparent. You can help yourself discover these elusive intervals by squinting at your subject.

In conclusion, when drawing the contour, look for chances to let the line get lost. This enhances the realism of your drawing, creates interesting variety, promotes unity between the subject and its background, and will be useful as you progress towards adding values.

(A) and (B) show how a dark contour makes realistic shading problematic. Aim for a medium darkness in your contour so the line can later accommodate the lighter value of the reflected lights.

Grip III

The Contour Grip

The writing style pictured in (A) is the perfect grip for constructing the contour, as it allows you to be precise with your mark making. However, we should take care that we are at this point still working at a medium light grade. I find it a good idea to keep all contour marks still fairly light because I never know when I am going to want to make them disappear later on. Before attempting the potato exercise detailed below and pictured to the right, draw a roundish shape freehand. You can compare this with the potato you make using the construction technique illustrated in (1, 2, 3).

That's a potato!

We begin with straight, general guidelines, as we've practiced (1). Over these, we then develop a precise contour (2). Using the writing grip gives us more precision and control as we refine our lines. It offers a lot less flexibility, however, so I find myself needing to switch between this and a grip about midway on the pencil.

During the contour phase, we begin to focus on small shapes, and individual forms begin to come into focus. The scaffolding fades, revealing specific forms contained within. Even as the character of our drawing changes and the general falls away, our earlier planning continues to keep us on track. Our success at the contour stage very much depends on the hard work we put in during the planning phase. Although preparation makes the contour possible, it does not remove the challenge. Take your time traversing the contour: there are usually many nuances to consider. When trouble arises in the contour, always be ready to revert back to the block-in stage to correct any errors.

Allow for variation

The purpose of the contour phase is not necessarily to replace all the broad, straight lines with curves. We must be discerning, using our knowledge of the subject to judge which of these general lines supply our image with necessary strength. If everything curves, the result will be a floppy, weak picture. Retaining a certain degree of rough straightness gives our picture structure, as well as a wonderful variety. Straight and curved lines also achieve very different expressions. Allowing the contour to remain blocky to an extent can convey boldness and solidity.

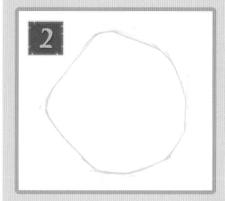

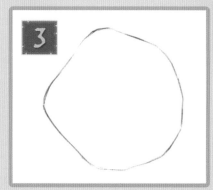

Continue to practice making random shapes in this manner. These are confidently created shapes that no longer look like a line that was created in one go. This is a shape that has had its contour developed from a plan.

The example on the previous page was about drawing the contour of a potato. When drawing subjects that have lines and shapes on the inside, such as the old man's face to the right, it is a good idea to consider the internal lines while you are also developing your outline. This way, the internal and outside lines can inform and reinforce one another.

Think about the nature of your subject and what you're trying to express: you can use the character of your line to promote the quality appropriate for your subject. Allow the music of your lines to be expressive and varied. The contour can assume a whole range of appearances, from soft and blurred to crisp and clear; it can dissolve into shadows or vanish under intense light, only to return again further down the line. The contour phase allows us to rediscover our subject, gaining renewed appreciation of its uniqueness and subtlety. There's real pleasure in capturing the contour, and it is key in portraying the true personality of your subject.

The contour, in this approach, does not simply mean the 'outline,' as in the periphery. Although some teach that you must have a refined outline before beginning to work on inner forms, I find this unnecessarily difficult. I begin work on inner forms as early as the block-in stage, marking key shapes and prominent landmarks. This way, forms on the inside support forms on the outside, and vice versa. I also find this essential to maintaining unity within the image.

Although the contour has great expressive potential, remember that we're not developing the contour in order to become attached to it; rather we are trying to make it as accurate as possible so that we can use it to build more accurate tonal masses later on. If we intend on fully rendering our drawing, then the line-work we have constructed is just a plan for the next stage. Line represents the end of one plane and the start of another, and in the coming stages, we will be representing these planes with areas of different value, rather than with line.

It is of course not just the outside edge contour that becomes fine-tuned. We approach inner contours in exactly the same way, refining them from the block-in until they reflect the specifics of the form's appearance.

The contour also refers to the shadow edges.

The contour is the final stage of line-work, and it's important to do your checks carefully at this stage. Don't be afraid to take your work back if it needs correcting, as I've done here with the eye (3).

Time

Knowing When to Quit

Timing is crucial to success. In drawing, this means knowing when to shift gear to a different pencil grade, when to change your grip, and when it's time to move to the next stage of the Tetraforce hierarchy, such as from block-in to contour. At first, all of these things will be difficult to judge. Be patient with yourself as you build up the necessary experience.

Extensive drawing sessions will dull both our pencils and our wits. One of the most important things to learn is when you need to take a break. As you work, there's an invisible, ghostly hourglass sitting beside us, the sand trickling away. Some people call this an attention span, but we're going with 'ghost hourglass'. As your hourglass runs down, your attention is dulled. You become accustomed to the mistakes you've made, and familiarity starts to seem like correctness.

Stamina

Don't work when you're tired. When we're exhausted, it's much easier to make mistakes and much harder to catch them when they happen. Sometimes, even if we catch a mistake, we won't have the energy reserves needed to correct it properly.

One counter-intuitive way I've found to help conserve my energy and attention is to build up gradually to the 'fun parts.' Once I get stuck into these satisfyingly detailed aspects of a drawing, I find that I burn energy at a tremendous rate. I'm often guilty, however, of continuing to draw long after my reserves are depleted. When this happens, I often end up 'licking' the page. Don't worry—it's not as gross as it sounds. To lick the page is to polish one area of a drawing repeatedly and absent-mindedly. It's a draughtsman's daydreaming.

Interest

Boredom and fatigue lead to impatience. Impatience tempts us to jump ahead to a more advanced stage of the drawing hierarchy before it's time. Doing this will result in a lot of mistakes, which will take huge amounts of energy

Night fell and cold cramped my fingers. I'd been holding on much too long. By the time the Specific found me, I was sorely in need of rest. "I'll make you some soup," she said. My Specific friend had not been idle all this time—she had found the path to the Shadowsands.

to correct. Instead of skipping ahead, take a break. Boredom is a signal that you need to rest. By taking breaks and advancing through the hierarchy at a steady rate, it's possible to keep a handle on boredom, rather than allowing it to seize control.

Familiarity

When we work for too long at a stretch, the drawing becomes so familiar that we hardly even see it anymore. Like the loose tile in the kitchen or the crack in the living room wall, some problems become so familiar that we just stop noticing them. The more your ghostly hourglass runs down, the more accustomed you grow to your un-corrected mistakes.

The reset button

The way to flip over your ghostly hourglass is simply to rest. Now, this may seem to contradict some of what I've said about having patience with the difficulty and frustration inherent in learning a new skill. There's an important distinction, however, between being patient and pushing too hard. Sometimes, it's enough to simply take a five-minute break. When you come back, you may very well be able to spot errors you missed before.

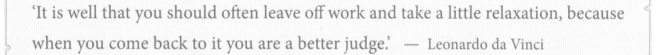

'It is well that you should often leave off work and take a little relaxation, because when you come back to it you are a better judge.' — Leonardo da Vinci

Sometimes you can also flip the hourglass by flipping your image. By turning your image upside down, you instantly refresh it, allowing yourself to see it anew. This works particularly well if you're drawing from another image, because you can flip both your drawing and the subject. Even when drawing from life, flipping the drawing can help you judge the correctness of overall composition, line structure and tonal gradation.

The only problem with this upside down vision is that it's almost too powerful: it can reveal so many problems with a drawing that you may become discouraged. Again, always respect your energy levels, and remember that being able to spot mistakes is a genuine achievement, which should be celebrated.

Momentum

What do you do when, upon returning from a break, you suddenly spot an overwhelming number of errors? Try to tackle the easiest problems first. This way, you can build momentum to carry you through the harder parts, which require full engagement. Beginning with the most difficult problems right away is a bit like starting to run full tilt without warming up.

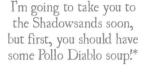

I'm going to take you to the Shadowsands soon, but first, you should have some Pollo Diablo soup!*

Using Self-Criticism

It's important to be honest with ourselves. The process of looking, clearly and critically, at our own work is known as 'self-critique.' This is not the same as giving in to our Shadow Self, with their overly harsh and destructive criticisms. Instead, genuine self-critique is a fundamentally important skill, by which we're able to check our own work, find its flaws, and judge its successes.

As well as helping you spot errors, ultimately this skill will help you to develop an authentically expressive style, one capable of communicating truths to those who view your work. The difficulty with self-critique is that it's hard to get enough distance from our own work to see it with any objectivity. In this section, we're going to look at a round-up of all the ways you can check your work. Before I elaborate on each of the ways of checking you're on track, I want to share with you a trap I often fall into which a dose of self-criticism always helps to remedy.

Making one bit really good

Part of self-critique is recognising our bad habits, so I'm going to share one of mine, a habit that makes it really difficult to correct and advance my work. As I draw, I like to focus on the things I've gotten right, pushing those further and further—while neglecting the areas that need fixing. The more I work on the parts that look good, the less I want to return to the parts that need fixing. Ignoring problems won't solve them, and that one successful element cannot rescue the rest of the picture. To avoid falling into this bad habit, methodically check your work as you progress, and make sure that every part of your picture is advancing at a unified rate. Find the worst parts of your drawing, and work on them until they equal the best parts. So, to help you in this difficult, often painful process of self-critique, here are thirteen methods I've found useful.

Cyclops vision

As we've already seen, the requirements of artistic vision are different from those of everyday sight. Our normal binocular vision works by combining the two slightly different perspectives of each eye into a single, three-dimensional image. This means that, when we look at a subject to draw it, we're actually seeing it from two perspectives at once. You can simplify things by closing one eye, which flattens your vision, as well as making it easier to see edges more clearly, which is handy for the contour stage. Bear in mind, the difference between your two eyes' perspectives—known as 'binocular disparity'—decreases with distance, so this Cyclops trick only really works with close objects. The closer your subject, the more important it is to close one eye to check it.

Squinting

Blurring your vision lets you take in the whole, with no distracting details. Let your eyes be loose, not focussing on one area. This also makes it much easier to see value: blurred vision makes patterns more readable. Use this method of

DRAW LIKE A BOSS

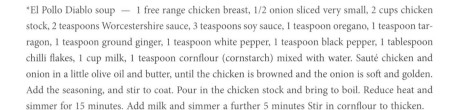

*El Pollo Diablo soup — 1 free range chicken breast, 1/2 onion sliced very small, 2 cups chicken stock, 2 teaspoons Worcestershire sauce, 3 teaspoons soy sauce, 1 teaspoon oregano, 1 teaspoon tarragon, 1 teaspoon ground ginger, 1 teaspoon white pepper, 1 teaspoon black pepper, 1 tablespoon chilli flakes, 1 cup milk, 1 teaspoon cornflour (cornstarch) mixed with water. Sauté chicken and onion in a little olive oil and butter, until the chicken is browned and the onion is soft and golden. Add the seasoning, and stir to coat. Pour in the chicken stock and bring to boil. Reduce heat and simmer for 15 minutes. Add milk and simmer a further 5 minutes Stir in cornflour to thicken.

checking throughout your drawing process, until it becomes second nature. It blocks out the inessential, simplifies the subtle, and helps you understand the basic shapes and blocks of values that make up your subject.

Analyse 'negative shapes'

Looking closely at the negative space surrounding your subject is an excellent way of cross-checking the accuracy of your contour: it allows you to come at the problem from another angle.

Persistence of vision

This is a nifty trick that makes use of a neurological quirk called 'persistence of vision': for the briefest moment after you look at something, your eye seems to retain that image. Thus, if you flick your eyes quickly enough between your subject and the drawing, one image seems superimposed upon the other. When you move your eyes back and forth rapidly and repeatedly, your mind will try to combine the two images, making any differences very noticeable. The effect is almost like a little animation. Sometimes, I blink between the two, and this helps me see differences more clearly.

> 'Sitting too close at work may greatly deceive you.' — Leonardo da Vinci

Stand at a distance and view your work

If the picture reads well from a distance, it will also work well up close. Viewing your drawing from a distance also gives you a valuable opportunity to take pride in your progress. One problem that I run into a lot—and this might just be me—is that as I walk back from my work, I often bump into things, which really breaks my concentration. Focussing on the picture while I'm backing away is an important part of this check, and tripping up breaks that focus. Basically, make sure the coast is clear before you start walking backwards.

View your drawing through a mirror

This is a trick from none other than Leonardo da Vinci, and it's almost too effective. Looking in the mirror instantly highlights all mistakes, so it can be a bit devastating. It provides you with fresh perspective without the need for taking a break.

The Shadowsands were aptly named—they were a dessert shrouded in permanent night. The dark sands were illuminated only by the pale, reflected light of the Moon. A domed building stood alone among the shadowy dunes.

7

Work upside down

There are a couple of good reasons for turning your drawing on its head. From a purely practical point of view, turning the drawing will allow you comfortable access to areas that would otherwise be hard to reach. If you find yourself contorting to reach a particular area, it's a sign you need to rotate your drawing board.

If you're drawing from a photograph, turning both the photo and your drawing upside down is a great way to sidestep your assumptions: it de-contextualises the image, making it easier to see both the subject and your work as abstracted shapes, patterns and tones. When I turn the picture right-side up again, I'm always surprised, both by all the new work that seems to have magically manifested by itself, and also by all the errors that suddenly jump out at me, almost as if I had taken time away from the work.

Walking away from the drawing is a good way of checking the whole, but what if we want to look more closely, to better see our details? Well, we can of course use a magnifying glass to observe a little closer if we need to. I like to use a magnification sheet that is often advertised as a reading aid instead of a draughtsman's seeing device.

'We know well that errors are better recognised in the works of others than in our own; and often by reproving little faults in others, we may ignore great ones in ourselves.' — Leonardo da Vinci

8

Analyse from different angles

If you only view your work from one angle, it may end up only working from that angle! Try to get into the habit of looking at your drawings from many different angles. Remember the lesson of Hans Holbein's distorted skull, and don't produce images that only work from a single vantage point.

Tilt your head 45 degrees

Tilting your head is one of the quickest ways of spotting inaccuracies as you work. As a method of checking, I use it as often as I squint, which is very often. It allows you to get another perspective without the need for actually detaching your drawing from its surface and physically rotating it.

"This is the Shadow Observatory," the Specific whispered. *"This is where we'll find the General." I couldn't imagine what she meant. I'd seen him fall off a cliff. I guess if there were a place where we might once again meet the dead, this ghastly building would be it.*

Checking angles with a compass (page 107)

Use your compass often to check your tilts. Eventually, you may find you're able to do this without actually drawing the cross, but in the early stages of your development, keep this device by your side.

Ask a friend to point out possible errors

Thankfully, everyone is a critic. Anyone can spot inaccuracies, even without any artistic training, and this means that, whether they draw or not, your family and friends will be able to offer you valuable insight and feedback. Most people will have a good enough eye for proportion, for example, that they'll be able to point out areas that 'just don't look right.' Showing your work can be scary, but this kind of honest appraisal is an important part of your development, and courageously confronting errors is crucial to attaining mastery. Fight the impulse to hide your work 'until it's ready': while you're still practicing is one of the most important times to share. When showing your work, try not to betray too much discomfort—you want your critic to feel it's completely fine to point out areas that need work. Find enjoyment in sharing your work, both throughout its development and when it's completed.

Image bank

Ideally, you should constantly be expanding your image bank, either in a sketchbook or digitally, collecting images that inspire you. This image bank can serve as a reference and inspiration, as well as firing your competitive spirit, helping you to keep pushing until you reach the standard of the work you admire.

Take a break

Get up and walk away from your drawing for a bit: make a brew, check your email, walk your dog. We've looked at lots of methods that mimic the effects of a break, but sometimes it really is necessary to take a rest. A good time for a break is when things don't seem to improve no matter what you do.

A break allows frustration to dissipate, and new solutions will often present themselves when you return. As Leonardo noted in his diary, "Men [and women] of genius sometimes accomplish most when they work least, for they are thinking out inventions and forming in their minds the perfect ideas which they subsequently express and reproduce in their hands." When things get too rough, don't be hard on yourself. Take a break, have some Pollo Diablo soup, and let your subconscious get to work.

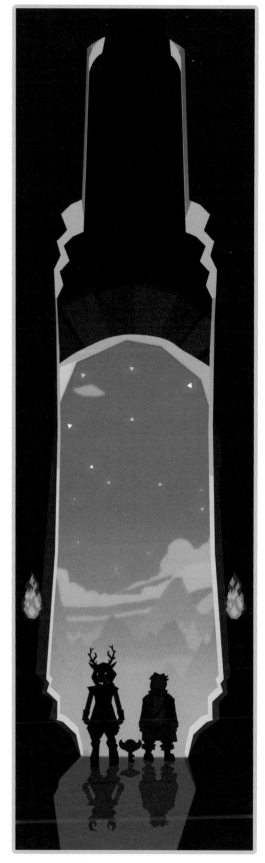

The Specific doused her lantern, out of respect for the shades. In the silence of a great hall, the darkness seemed thick with the weight of unfathomable aeons. The floating blue lights were strange yet somehow welcoming . . .

SHADOW OBSERVATORY

"I've never really known my way around the Shadowsands," the Specific confessed. Her voice echoed weirdly in the cavernous stone chamber. "We'll need the General if we're going to make it through this temple." The darkness was too much for me—against the Specific's warnings, I lit my torch again. Dense carvings crowded the stone walls, mysterious shapes dancing in the torchlight. I was getting creeped out—kept feeling like there was someone behind me.

Tetraforce of Shadow

As Above, So Below

With the contour drawn to an acceptable standard, we completed the first half of our quest—but now we must confront the Tetraforce once more, in its inverse shadow form. As Guido enters the silent, dank, Shadow Observatory, we will begin to consider the interior of our drawing, mapping out the shadows. The Shadow Tetraforce will be our guide. Let us now begin by considering the first three levels.

Shadow Point

Our quest through the Shadow Realms begins with the shadow point. Here we must ask, "Where is the focal point of the picture?" If we know this, then we generally also know where to place our deepest darks. This is because of the gravitational force exerted by the deepest darks: they pull the viewer's eye towards them. Careful consideration of their placement is an important factor in establishing a good composition.

Shadow Line

The shadow line marks the boundary between light and shadow, and it is an absolutely critical landmark to acknowledge. By simply drawing a line to represent the shadow-edges on the subject, we subdivide our drawing into regions of light and dark. This is the final preparation stage before we begin adding value.

Shadow Shape

The shadow line creates the idea of a division between light and dark. It only really begins to take form, though, when we add a basic value to the areas of shadow, creating the shadow shape. This is when we start to get a proper idea of the subject as an object interacting with a light source.

Shadow shapes are not just about dividing an object into light and dark. The shadow shape also divides the image between matter and anti-matter. By 'anti-matter', I mean any dark, negative space surrounding the object. We should also note that at this stage we are still only dealing with areas of flat value, interlocking jigsaw pieces of light and dark. This simple two-tone division creates the basis for beginning to add midtone values later.

Through a doorway, I caught sight of a familiar symbol. "Oh, thank goodness," I cried, rushing forwards into the darkened room. Finally, we were back on the trail of the Tetraforce! Yet something was wrong. As I puzzled over the inscriptions, I realised: everything was upside down.

V

SHADOW POINT

If you want to weild the focal point, you first have to ask yourself some specific questions.

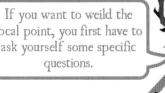

Level Up! — Dark Arts!

The first lesson of the Shadow Tetraforce is brief and, er, to the point, but it is crucial. Before we add any shadows, we need to figure out where our focal point is. Because of the way darks draw the eye, any shadows we add will carry a certain weight. What does this mean in terms of our composition?

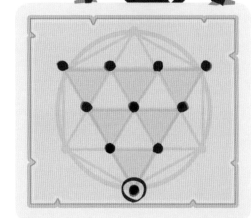

Where's the point?

The focal point is a basic compositional device that designates the main point of interest in the picture. The most important function of composition is to ensure that the viewer understands the picture's message, and the focal point is a key part of conveying this message. If it isn't clear what the message is, the image will fail. Equally, if a picture has too many focal points, it's like having many people speaking all at once: the messages become confused, and nothing gets communicated.

Composition is the means by which the artist guides the viewer's eye through the image. It may be true that not all who wander are lost, but we don't want to leave the viewer's eye wandering for too long. Instead, we want to give it something to latch onto; this will guide the viewer into the picture. This attention-grabbing 'something' might be an area of interesting pattern, texture, high contrast, leading lines, highlights or deep darks.

For this reason, the placement of interesting elements, such as deep darks and highlights, is often dictated by the location of the focal point. Darkness is very eye-catching: think of darkness as a black hole, pulling the viewer's gaze. It makes sense, then, to place it near our focal point, so that the viewer's eye will be drawn to the most important place.

Thinking about the compositional value of darks will serve you well as you work out the arrangement of tones in your image, considering which elements are most interesting, and which should fade into the background.

I gazed in bewilderment at the mysterious runes surrounding the Tetraforce. "They tell of a shadowy hall," the Specific said, reading over my shoulder, "where we may find the Focal Point. It has the power to guide the eyes."

What's the point?

Any picture begins with the simple question, "What is my subject?" From this, the story of the picture unfolds. Our intention is to create a composition around the main subject, constructing an aesthetically pleasing combination of light and dark shapes, leading lines, pattern and textures.

These elements can be thought of as forming paths within the landscape of the picture, leading the eye towards the focal point. You can't build a path by scattering paving stones around haphazardly, and a good path shouldn't be broken and full of gaps. When composing a picture, we need to make sure that we've created a network of relationships between the interesting elements, so that they guide the eye along a smooth, clear pathway, rather than leading it down a bumpy road full of boulders and potholes. When elements within an image don't relate harmoniously to one another, reading the image becomes a difficult, energy-sapping experience.

Continuing to think of our surface as a landscape, it's a general rule that lighter areas advance towards us, while darker areas recede. Look at the line in (A): the eye is drawn towards the darker half of the line, almost as though it is rolling down an incline, as shown in image (B). The deeper the dark, the deeper the trough; the more abrupt the gradient, the steeper the drop (C, D). Darker areas seem further away, and, at the same time, they exert a pull on the eye, almost like they're warping the fabric of the paper. Thus, when we add shadows, we are almost constructing a topography, a terrain that the eye moves across.

If we have a lot of scattered areas of dark, we create a landscape pocked with ditches and holes. Instead, we want to simplify and unify, joining our darks together so that they create channels, all flowing towards a single focal point. We also don't want to direct the eye off the edge of the page. We should try to arrange our highlights and deep darks in such a way that the focus is directed towards the focal point, which should be towards the centre of the image.

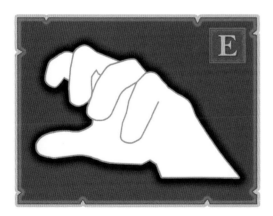

Because lights advance and darks recede, by placing a highlight next to a deep dark, we can create a mountain/valley effect. This is a trick classical artists used to give their paintings striking depth. Once, in the British National Gallery, I was struck by a Diego Velásquez painting, in which a person's hand seemed to reach right out of the picture, roughly as in image (E).

A guide approached and explained how the effect had been achieved: by placing a trough of deepest dark around the light hand, Velásquez had created such a contrast that the hand appeared to advance out of the picture plane. Deep darks are an extremely powerful compositional tool, so don't go splashing them around. Use them wisely.

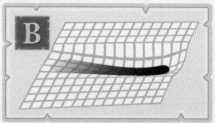

As the line gets darker, it seems to recede away from us. Placing a deep dark like this too near the edge can cause the eye to fall out of the picture.

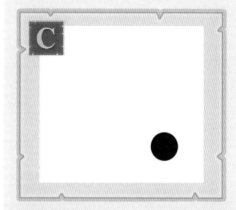

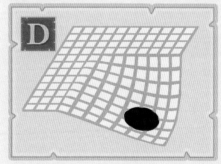

This black circle represents the focal point. It captivates us as soon as we look at the white square (C). Imagine if there were another black circle in the opposite corner: we would have a picture at cross purposes with itself, and we wouldn't know where to focus. When thinking about composition, it can be useful to imagine things as simply as this: where are you going to place your black circle? Is it too close to the edge? Are there any other, confusing dots floating around?

SHADOW LINE

Following a Dark Path

Contrary to what you might think, shadow is not first added to a drawing by way of blocks of value; it is first described with line. Remember, we're not painters, and we have to be a bit inventive when it comes to describing mass. This is what the shadow line is for: it describes the edges of the shadow, where a surface turns away from the light and falls into shadow.

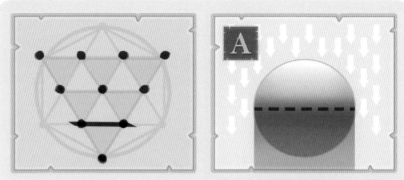

The dotted horizontal line pictured in (A) shows where the core shadow lies on this sphere. This is where light rays hit the edge of the form at a tangent. Beyond this point, the form is cut off from any light emitted from the primary light source. This is what makes them so dark and, therefore, a massively useful landmark.

This area of a form, commonly referred to as a 'core shadow', is a critical line. Like all lines, it begins as blocky and general, then eventually attains a softer, more variable quality, becoming a lost and found edge.

Strong lighting will produce a crisp shadow edge, but in dimmer light, the transition into shadow will be drawn out, so to speak.

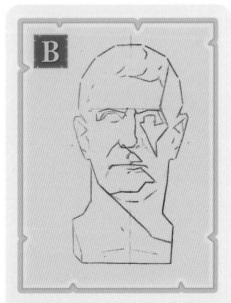

By putting this line in, we end up with something like a jigsaw puzzle that consists of two large pieces. A jigsaw with only a few shapes to join is a very easy puzzle indeed, and this is just the way we want it, simple and manageable.

When considering shadow masses it is best to look for the most convenient shadow elements, the boldest shapes and cleanest core shadow lines. We will go about blocking in the shadow lines just as we developed the contour. It's also worth noting that the shadow line is such a key landmark that it can be blocked-in at the same time as other key features and internal landmarks.

It is common practice for artists to mark off the border between light and dark by first blocking in the shadow edges, as we see in the Bargue image (B). This image is like a very short story: spare and concise, containing only the most essential information. A fully rendered drawing is more like a complete novel, more fully realised and rounded. As ever, though, the more complex an image becomes, the harder it is to correct any mistakes.

Oh, there you are!

Straight lines, yadah yadah.

General Shadows

Do this...

Night Excursions

By drawing the shadow edges, we start to get an idea of light on the subject, while still mostly remaining in the realm of line. This stage allows us to map in the shadow shapes before fully committing to a wash of tone—lines are much easier to erase and correct than big blocks of value! Marking the shadow lines creates a sort of half-dimension between two and three-dimensional drawing. We're approaching three-dimensional drawing cautiously—jumping dimensions is no mean feat!

We treat shadow edges exactly as we would we would any linework: we begin with straight, general lines. Essentially, all we're doing now is blocking in the outline of the shadows. Using broad, straight lines, we reduce the shadow to a manageable level of complexity. Build the shadow lines using the process you've already learned: start with line sections that simply record general position and tilt; measure often, and avoid small line segments or curves.

While blocking in the shadow map, it's also important to recognise where there are breaks in the core shadow. The shadow line is not always continuous, and there may be places where sharp-edged shadows become diffuse. Line may not be the best way to represent these softer areas of shadow.

> Look at your subject and seek out as many core shadows as you can. Make it your mission to map their locations; this will be essential to building value later on.

Core shadows are key landmarks, and, fortunately, they're some of the easiest to spot. Marking them broadly will give us a good map to follow as we pass through the shadow realms. Once we've got our general, blocky shadow map refined to an acceptable degree, we can think about adding value. But how do we go about refining the shadow map? What does a refined shadow map look like?

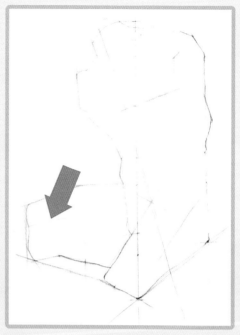

A lightly drawn line gives a very basic idea of where the form falls into shadow.

Sometimes a form will turn away from the light so quickly that it creates a clear division between the realms of light and dark. The sharper the turn, the more defined the shadow core.

Even when forms are curved and their shadows are softer, it can be helpful to think of them as if they were blocky, angular shapes, with a clearly divided light and dark side.

We can also help ourselves out by lighting our subjects properly: the brighter the light, the sharper the line between light and shadow. This is one way of reducing the difficulty of drawing from life.

Permeable hatches (A) or walls of lines (B)?

Bold, straight lines don't suit all shadow edges. Depending on the nature of the form and the line, core shadows may be either defined or diffuse. Straight lines are great for the former, but not so good for the latter.

A particular form may even contain both defined and diffuse core shadows, and we need a way to note this distinction. Think of farmer's fields in the countryside: not every boundary is marked with walls; some are marked with hedges, which serve as a softer edge-marker.

Soft cores (hedges)

We can use dashes or hatches to form a hedge, marking a more subtle or gradual transition from dark to light. Noting these kinds of transitions more softly will help when it comes time to actually replicate the softer tonal shifts.

Hard cores (walls)

Lines make excellent markers for sharp, clear core shadows. If the core shadow is particularly dark, it's best to mark it using a softer grade of pencil: this allows you to get a darker line without scarring the paper and creating problems for yourself later on. Using a fairly dark line makes these more dramatic core shadows stand out nice and clear.

Deciding where to use a line and where to use a diffuse hatch is a matter of judgement. Either way, you want your core shadows to be marked clearly enough that they're easily visible, without being misleading. Applying a dark line to all shadow edges eliminates nuance and can form a barrier to creating the slow, gradual tonal transitions you need.

These lines are crucial preparation for the challenging process of modeling. Successful modeling is about more than simply recording the values you see: instead, you are using these values to sculpt the form on your page.

Shadows can be tricky, so before we advance to modeling, let's take a moment to practice with a basic geometric shape. This will let us get to grips with the blocked-in, sharp-edged shadow shapes.

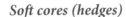

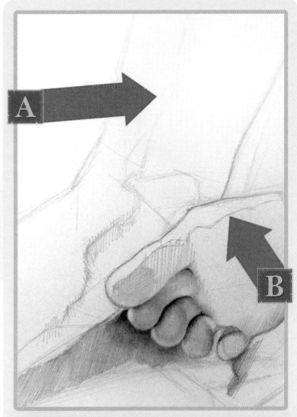

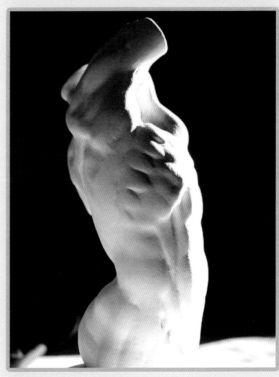

Quite often, shadow edges become washed out by powerful reflected lights, as is the case with the lower half of this model of a human torso..

Is this like in Buffy where when someone comes back from the dead, they come back all sad and moody?

He seems fine to me.

The First Geometric Shape

Geometric shapes are important tools for developing our observational skills. In the woods, we used a triangle to practice checking tilt accurately. We also used the triangle to practice triangulation, using two known positions to find the location of a third, unknown landmark.

Now we are advancing from triangles to pyramids. If you look at (A), you will see that a pyramid can be drawn very simply using just two triangles, one light and one dark.

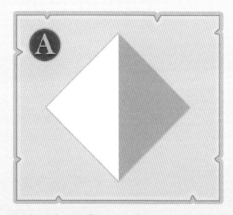
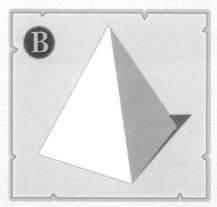

It takes only a small amount of imagination to see this shape as a three-dimensional object, like a pyramid as seen by someone in a plane flying overhead and looking down. We all have this imaginative power, and it certainly comes in handy when we mass in the dark shapes, allowing the lights to suddenly flick on in our image. The presence of a shadow shape triangle (B) displays the cast shadow's grounding ability.

By including shadow—even in this basic, single-value form—we are moving into the third dimension. This is the simplest possible introduction to shadow shapes, but if you can accurately copy a pyramid and wash in its shadow side with a single, consistent tone, then you're off to a great start. In this exercise we will also look at taking things a little further by adding a cast shadow (B), thus locating our object within an environment.

To begin

Grab some paper, an HB pencil and, if you have one, a pyramid. If not, it's fine to work from the illustrations here. Begin by checking its angles: close one eye, hold your pencil out in front of you, and line it up with the sides (1). Align this angle with the paper surface, memorise the tilt, then mark it down (2). Use the same method to measure the next two light sides (3). Find the proportions using triangulation, as discussed on page 112.

Triangulate the shadow side in exactly the same way (4). Next, wash this area in, using a single, even tone (5). You have now completed your first shadow shape. Take it one step further by measuring the angles of the cast shadow, then filling that with a darker area of tone (6). Congratulations: by completing this exercise, you have just Levelled Up.

VII

SHADOW SHAPE

Level Up! — Darkitect!

We have now begun to start thinking about laying down a value for our shadow shapes. Eventually, we will be applying the full spectrum of values, communicating all the subtle ways in which light plays upon a form. For now, though, we're going to keep it simple, working with only two tones: light and shade. Remember, keep it general to begin. Filling in our shadow map with a single, general wash of tone creates shadow shapes. These shapes make it easier to see any inaccuracies in our shadow map, and this allows us to correct them before we add a third tone, the midtone, and leap into the third dimension.

> The dark line and dark shape are two of the most important landmarks to recognise.

Mapping two continents

Look around you. Every object has a light and dark side. When you begin to include these two realms within your drawing, something wondrous starts to happen: your drawing begins to shift into a different dimension.

Look at the Bargue copy (A): there are only two tones here, but already the object has taken on a whole new level of realism. Our brains recognise and respond to even the simplest description of light and shadow. Build the general shadow as carefully and methodically as you built your general form. From general lines and general shadows, we achieve the foundation necessary for awakening the third dimension.

By washing in the shadow shape with a value, we emphasise the patterning of light and dark within the form. As we saw earlier, it's easier to compare shapes than lines, and just like in any other stage of the Tetraforce we need to be continuously checking for accuracy.

This stage is a last chance to correct mistakes before things get more complicated. Of course, it's always possible to regress any line or washes of tone, should you need to, but it's best to have your line structure at a decent, stable level before you begin working with value.

This is the smallest range possible: two tones, conveying a basic representation of the two sides of light and shadow. The tones found in the shadow side are generally much simpler those in the light side, and this is a good thing as it gives the eye a place to rest a while. Be aware, though, of the subtleties of the lost and found shadows, as some planes alternate between varying degrees of light, shadow and midtone.

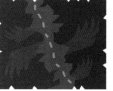

You Found the Map of Shadows!

When we start mapping out these two continents of light and shadow, we create what is known as a chiaroscuro effect, which basically means a high-contrast image. Light and dark, plain and simple. Now, I say 'high-contrast,' but a gentle wash of tone is all it takes—you shouldn't go overly dark. That's because you will almost certainly need to adjust the shadow shape with a kneaded eraser. What you find when you begin to hatch in shadow shapes is that a lot of monsters will jump out at you. It's astounding how many monstrous mistakes can be revealed by toning in one area of shadow. Unless, that is, you already got everything right before shading—which I never do. There are always corrections to be made.

To map a shadow shape, you need to produce one single value, evenly distributed across all your shadow shapes, using only your pencil—no blenders yet.

These areas of flat tone will serve as a base for more complex variations of tone later on, as we try to depict the nuances of value created by the changing relationships between the surface and its light source.

For this reason, do not go round making all your shadows jet black, as in (A). The tone we add now is just a foundation. How dark I go with this initial wash is usually dictated by what the lightest tone found in the shadow shape is.

In the early stages, keep your tone range to a minimum. Say as much as you can with a few tones before adding more.

It's worth noting that, as we define our shadow shapes, the midtone is treated as part of the light side. This means that, for now, they should be left alone. It's important to get a clear sense of what's going on in the shadows before we engage with subtle transitions into light.

Searching for Patterns

There is a pattern of light and dark to be found on all objects, but sometimes this will be clearer than others. The definition of light and shadow depend on lighting conditions. The image above is an example of high intensity light, which creates a distinct separation between light and dark. As we begin studying shadow shapes, this is the kind of lighting we want: it's best to practice with clearly delineated areas of light and shadow.

> Just as a straight line is the foundation for curves, a general shadow map provides the scaffolding for a later, subtle exploration of a subject's full range of values.

Large washes can be obstacles

Why do we add a general wash of tone over the shadow side, but not the light side? The shadow side is usually simpler than the light side: it has fewer tonal variations, so it's easier to generalise. If I were to add a wash of tone over the light side as well, it would make it harder to describe the often subtle variations of tone found on this side.

The images on this page show how I begin to progress my shadow work from the most basic single-tone wash, by adding simple blocks of tonal variation.

> As with our line-work, our shadow work will be easier and more accurate if we can think in terms of abstract shapes and patterns, rather than automatically labelling objects as 'beard,' 'nose' and so on.

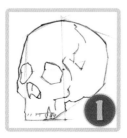 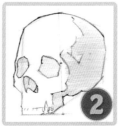 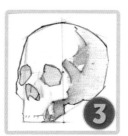

I start adding some tonal variety by returning to my core shadow line, starting to work in some areas of darker tone. These are the tonal progressions that will begin to capture the form's curvature. I keep my light sides fairly clean of pencil marks until I feel ready to tackle its greater subtleties.

> A lot of skulls round here... Pretty ominous.

Hatching a plan — Blocked-in shadow shapes make the lights explode. It is always a moment look forward to in a drawing. The blocks of value here are basic, and the number of values I am distributing is kept to a minimum. The upward direction of my hatching isn't random—it is an attempt to follow the feel of the picture, the upward tilt of the face.

Signal of fatigue

I find that if I work when I'm tired, I'm more prone to laying down huge washes: there's something easy about the process—it's a bit like colouring by numbers, and this means we can veer into thoughtlessness.

Be particularly cautious of making large washes of darker tones: not only are these hard to work back from, they also have the effect of bleaching their surroundings, creating a distractingly high contrast.

Just as we need to see objects as two-dimensional to begin drawing them, we have to see shadows as flat, abstract patterns in order to fully realise the potential of shadow shapes. It's only later, when we've advanced to the next level of the Tetraforce, that we will think about creating the illusion of roundedness.

It's the abstractness of the shadow shape that makes it so powerful. Because it's divorced from symbolic systems, the shadow shape is easy to see objectively, and this makes it an effective device for checking the accuracy of our work. The shadow shape is an even better tool for revealing mistakes than the shadow line. This is because, as we've learned, shapes are easier to see than lines.

Notice how the shadow shapes have been washed in with a limited palette of light greys. What we really don't want to do is 'colour in' our shadow shapes, filling them totally with tone, especially not a dark tone. This will flatten the image and make it very hard to progress to the next stage. Instead, make an 'open' wash: a loose, light hatching which gives the impression of shadow tones without becoming rigid.

Balancing darkness

As abstract patterns, shadow shapes not only help us check accuracy, they also reveal the aesthetically pleasing potential of shadows, their decorative power. Are the shadows balanced with the light sides, or do they overwhelm them?

Balance doesn't mean a half-and-half division—this tends to look static and boring. There are no strict rules for achieving balance, but as a very general rule of thumb, aim to have about 25% of your image in shadow, 75% in light. This is a ratio taken from traditional portraiture, but it applies well to other subjects, too.

How dare he bring torch light into the temple. Let's eat him.

DARK SIGHT

+10 Unity - Becoming suddenly aware of negative space can reveal many problems. However, it is better to see them than not!

Patience. We will.

23) Eye I

Let's take a momentary break from discussing shadow shapes and put some of these ideas into practice with this eye demonstration. In this demo, we'll be getting ahead of ourselves a little with mention of blenders, but don't worry: we'll get to a full explanation of those when we reach the land of light. I want you to see how shadow shapes help to build a drawing. After this we will return to more concrete practicalities.

 To prepare for adding value, we map out the areas of shadow following exactly the same process we used to develop our linework. Begin with simple, straight lines, checking for accuracy, and gradually develop this into a refined scaffolding for your shadow work.

 Once you have your shadows mapped, use light hatching to lay down blocks of tone. Think of this as a tonal block-in: keep it basic, and keep it flat. Use just one, light value if you can. The idea is to generate a simplified pattern of light and shade. This should help us see any errors we've made in mapping out the areas of shadow. The value at this stage is still two-dimensional, giving no sense of roundedness.

 Start adding a few very dark values, as above the eye. This process, known as 'keying', creates a standard against which we can judge all the other values.

 Pay attention to the direction of your hatching. To successfully describe a topography, we need to consider the flows upon its surface: make sure the lines of your hatching flow properly across the 'landscape' you are creating. To ignore this flow and direction will destroy any sense of roundedness.

Think large.
Masses of Shadow.
Blah blah blah.

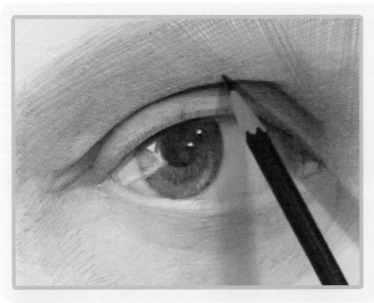

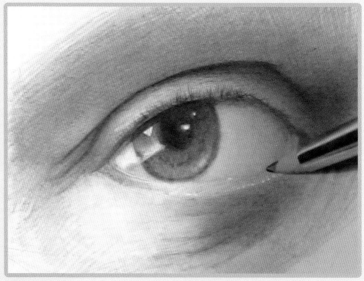

 As shadows develop, you'll find that one of your most valuable blenders is the pencil itself. As it passes over areas filled with graphite, it breaks down the granules and softens them. This blending effect is especially valuable when your pencil use takes into account the subtle directional flows within the image. It's possible to create a realistic drawing simply using the pencil, if it's deployed sensitively enough.

In the later stages, we use a range of tools known as blenders. These move us to a whole new level of realism, elevating our work to full three-dimensionality. The blender in the image above is known as a colour shaper. This versatile tool is also useful for working with coloured pencil and even clay.

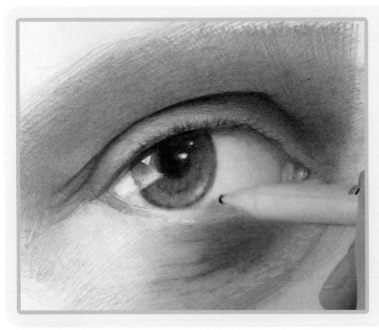

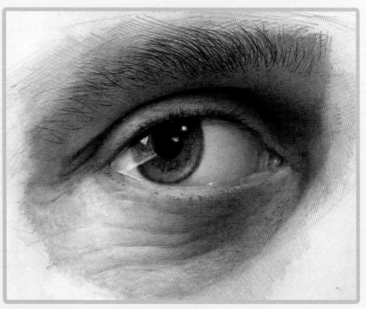

 Here I am using a blending stump, which produces a different effect to the shaper, because of the feathery way that it interacts with the graphite—not quite so smooth as the shaper. I have also deployed the eraser stick, which is a firm tube of plastic eraser. Its sharp edge enables you to carve out white lines from the surface of graphite, which adds definition to areas blurred by blender.

All manner of textures are available to the artist who understands their tools. Drawing done solely with pencil can be a wonderful thing, but the pencil cannot go it alone when trying to create a proper sense of realism, as things like pencil grain are indicators that this is a drawing rather than reality. We'll cover this in detail soon, but for now, let's return to building our shadows.

You should be less concerned about the General and more concerned with the Candlestick man who walks these halls.

Under Stark Light

We've been looking at some pretty challenging examples in this section—human eyes, complex casts. This is because, even in the most advanced subjects, we can see the same basic principles at work.

To actually begin putting these principles into practice, however, we're going to work with a simple yet classic study: drapery.

In the Dark Pyramid exercise, we captured the light and dark sides of the simplest of three-dimensional objects. Now it's time to tackle the complicated ripples and folds of rumpled fabric. Brightly lit drapery provides a perfect opportunity to practice shadow shapes: white sheets show value changes clearly, and it's easy to generate almost infinitely variable forms. It's a great place to start, but it's also an excellent preparation for the challenging forms you'll encounter in figure drawing or portraiture.

Artists have been making studies of drapery for centuries, and with good reason. Fabric has the potential to generate all kinds of dramatic, sweeping forms within itself. In studies of drapery, we see how an ordinary sheet can be graceful or expressive; it can easily become a landscape of ridges and valleys, or waves crashing against the shore.

To make the most of your drapery study, use dramatic lighting. You need a harsh, directional light source so that there will be a clear division between lights and darks. You want the shadows to be as pronounced as possible.

The first time you try this exercise, you may just want to choose one shadow shape to focus on and practice with. It's hard enough to replicate a single shape without also worrying about whether its proportions are correct in relation to everything else. Drawing just one shadow shape removes some of the pressure, making it an excellent way you start your shadow practice.

See? Even Leonardo da Vinci practiced drapery. Back then, it was especially important to be good at drawing fabric, because it featured heavily in commissioned portraits: fancy fabrics were expensive, and the posh people wanted to display their wealth. For our part, however, we're interested in drapery because it's a cheap way of studying the twists and turns of surface topography.

Standard drapery study

Throw a white sheet over a chair. Set up a bright lamp to one side and shine it at your drapery. Make sure the light brings out strong, clear shadow shapes.

Normally this wouldn't be a great lighting set-up for a still life study, because the harsh light bleaches out the midtones. For our purposes, however, this lack of subtlety is exactly what we want. You can arrange the fabric however you like; enjoy the range of possibilities.

Drapery study variant

You can also use a piece of striped or patterned cloth for this exercise. These patterns can serve as a visual aid, helping you to understand the structure of the material and to make sense of its complex surface topography.

Leonardo hardcore variant

If you're a bit insane, you can try to arrange your drapery to match Leonardo's. I've never seen anyone attempt this before, and now that I have, I can tell you why: it's ridiculously hard.

However, by attempting this, I did gain insight into the process he might have used. Now, when I look at his drapery, I can visualise his hands and the motions they would have made, pulling the cloth taut around each leg, then building up those little ripples in the base of the cloth. So, if you want a mental and rather sculptural challenge, you can try to replicate his forms and enjoy the new level of intimate appreciation this affords.

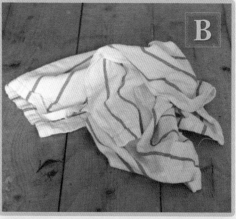

Dark Matters

So far we've been focussing on objects, what we might call positive forms. The emptiness that surrounds these positive forms is known as 'negative space.' I don't really like this term, however—it sounds too, you know, negative, which isn't fair, given that drawing the negative space can have such a positive impact on our work. I prefer to think of it as 'dark matter,' because, like dark matter, negative space surrounds everything and holds it all together.

We've learned about defining an object's perimeter, and we've begun mapping its interior. No drawing is complete, however, unless we consider the background. The time has come to look at the non-shape or anti-shape of the dark matter, and to learn how this can be yet another way of checking and correcting the lines we've used to describe the positive forms.

The consideration of the background as an important shape, worthy of attention in and of itself, is called negative drawing. This area of our drawing is another void, a space of emptiness and absence, the space where things aren't. This actually makes it much easier to draw: it's already abstracted, outside of symbols and object names, and, as we've learned, this facilitates more accurate observation.

The shape of the space that surrounds our object serves to regulate and check the object itself: it becomes another standard against which to check the accuracy of our contour.

> "Form is emptiness, emptiness is form.
> Emptiness is not separate from form; form is not separate from emptiness. Whatever is form is emptiness, whatever is emptiness is form."
> — Lao Tzu

We've talked before about the problems that arise from naming our subject. Now we encounter yet another difficulty: when we name the subject, we automatically grant that named object more importance than the unnamed space surrounding it.

The air around me suddenly took on an oppressive feel. I was surrounded by something that I could not put a name to.

The negative space is literally pushed into the background. Of course, the subject is important, and it will deservedly take prominence when the drawing is finished. While we're constructing the drawing, however, we need to consider all angles and aspects. Just because you're not focused on an area doesn't mean that it's empty, that nothing is happening there. Think, for instance, of developers destroying a meadow or some woods because there's "nothing" there—only a complex ecosystem. What we emphasise, where we choose to focus, what we decide to value: these are choices with consequences, in drawing and in life. In our drawings, as in life, if we are blind to our surroundings, we're going to get into serious trouble. So let's learn some ways to avoid this.

Level 1 — *The Candlestick man*

This one should feel familiar by now: using the power of abstraction to simplify something apparently difficult. Naming objects makes them harder to draw. By shifting our focus from positive to negative space, we can bypass the symbolic, naming impulse.

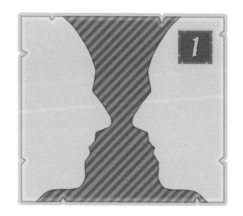

Take the image on the right: you can flip between seeing it as two faces in profile or as a candlestick. It is much easier to draw the 'candlestick' of negative space than to draw the two profiles—in part because, when we draw faces, we have to deal with lots of symbolic preconceptions about how things are meant to look. We have far fewer expectations about the negative space candlestick, meaning that there are fewer obstacles to direct observation: all our information comes from the image, not from ourselves. Being able to flip your focus between object and background is a useful skill to develop.

Level 2 — *The third piece of the puzzle*

While learning about the shadow line and shadow shape, we looked at an image as consisting of two jigsaw pieces: the light side and the dark side. We can think of negative space as the third puzzle piece—as represented by the brown area in the image on the right. This piece holds the other two within it; their shapes all fit snugly together. We can think of a picture as an alternation between light, dark and void.

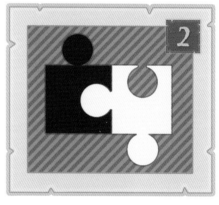

Level 3 — *Dark matter on the inside*

Sometimes there will be little islands of negative space encircled by the object, as in the vase on the right. These trapped negative shapes are a gift as we're trying to determine accuracy: they serve as convenient regulators, smaller shapes that can help to gauge the accuracy of the larger shapes. Trapped negative spaces are especially helpful when drawing complicated subject matter, such as hands, branches and foliage.

Thinking about negative space can be very helpful when drawing, and now we have three ways of looking at it. Being aware of negative space can simplify complex subjects, making sure we never go too far astray.

Do you see us now little man?

Dark Matters

Now that we've learned a few ways of spotting dark matter, let's practice focussing on negative spaces while drawing. We're going to draw from this photograph of a chair (A).

Drawing an object like this becomes a real debate between positive and negative space—you serve as a mediator, trying to balance the push and pull between both sides. It can be a challenge to see both the object and its background at the same time. The trick is to switch your focus between them regularly. Line is nothing more than a shared boundary between positive and negative shapes.

The above image (B) is the result of drawing the trapped negative shapes in the lower part of the chair (A). To draw these, you just need to squint and measure with your pencil, as usual. Very simple. You'll soon find that by maintaining an awareness of both perspectives, you get a far more unified picture.

A drawing by an artist who doesn't take negative space into consideration will be much weaker for it. It will produce distortions, just as if you only listened to one side of a debate.

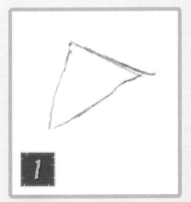
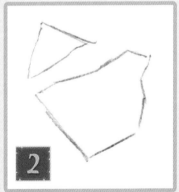
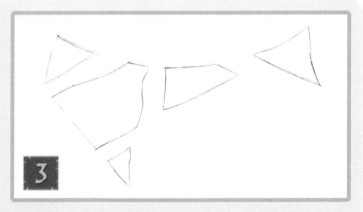

Negative chair shapes

For this simple study, I placed a photograph of the chair next to a sheet of drawing paper, roughly equal to the size of the photo. I then proceeded to try and draw an area of closely positioned negative shapes such as those just under the seat of this chair. Needless to say, I'm not saying you should normally draw this way, but this exercise does let you get a sense of just how powerful negative space is, and it underlines the idea that, at the end of the day, we're just copying shape patterns.

If we were in the middle of drawing a subject like the chair, where there are especially pronounced internal shapes, we might consider taking a moment to doodle a thumbnail of how the internal shapes appear to us. We can then compare this with what we have already established in our drawing proper. This sidesteps the comparison between the object of the chair with all its attached symbolism but of course introduces a greater margin of error since your thumbnail might be a little off.

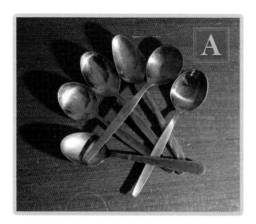

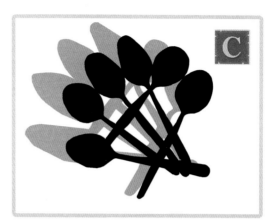

Drawn your chair shapes? Great! Now go grab all your spoons! Scatter them on your table under some harsh light. Start off by drawing these spoons freehand. Concentrate on each spoon. It's hard, isn't it? Really hard. I want you to remember how difficult it is, so that you'll truly feel the benefit of working with dark matter.

Try again, this time focussing on the negative shapes and copying them. The key to this study? Realising that there are no spoons. Rather than seeing a tangle of objects, see the small, trapped negative spaces instead. This second attempt will almost certainly be better, and easier, than your first.

You've truly begun to integrate dark matter into your drawing practice. To take this further, you can try to capture the shadows as well. Accomplishing this will ready you for what is coming next. However, before that, you need to remember that when it comes to dark matter . . .

Don't allow dark void to dominate

So if dark matter is so helpful, how come the candlestick men were so creepy and strangle-happy? Well, there's always the danger that negative space can take over your drawing and squeeze the life out of it. Seeing negative shapes affords us a greater degree of accuracy, but it can also have a flattening effect. For example, the negative space around a sphere will seem to describe a circle: to capture the roundedness of the sphere, you have to pay attention to the object's specific structure.

Flattening and abstraction are useful tools, vital for the early stages of a drawing—but we must be able to switch out of them, to tap into our understanding of how an object behaves in space. At the highest levels of drawing, we should be aware not only of what we see but of the parts of the object we can't see, and how these inform the position of the object in space and with regards to light.

Shadow Anatomy

Dark Components

In the previous pages, we've been dealing with shadows in a deliberately simplified, generalised way. We've been concerned with the shape of shadows, not with their tones or the varieties of their edges. Now, however, it's time to learn the different parts of the shadow.

The quality of a shadow varies according to the quality of light. A shadow's tone is determined by two factors: the amount of reflected light and the local value of the object on which the shadow is cast. Although there is tonal variety within the shadowed side of an object, the range is far narrower than on the light side of an object, where the nuances of value may become extremely fine.

This simplicity and unity of value is one reason that shadows are such a fundamental element of composition: they help to divide up and organise space within the image. This means that, even as we subdivide our shadows, we'll still be basing our value work on clear, basic categories of shadows. This will make life much easier later on, when we begin dealing with far more nuanced value scales on the light side.

'Cast shadow,' or 'umbra,' refers only to the dark body of the shadow, not to its fainter edges. These edges are known as the 'penumbra'.

Cast shadows are already distortions of the subject's form, and their shape changes all the time with the angle of the light. For this reason, it's not easy to look at a drawing of a cast shadow and tell whether or not it's accurate. We can use this to our advantage.

Obviously, the cast shadow needs to adhere to some kind of logic, but because it's already such an abstracted shape, it can be altered to promote other aspects of the drawing.

Cast shadow

The cast shadow, or 'umbra,' is not attached to the topography of a given subject: it falls on the ground and surrounding objects, similar to a beam of light but inverted.

Cast shadows are caused when the path of light is blocked by an object. The shape of the cast shadow is determined by the shape of the object casting it. The cast shadow visually anchors an object to its surroundings. This is what makes cast shadows so important in drawing: they are necessary for giving the illusion of objects existing in space.

Was this what was getting you down? He shouldn't be a problem now I've captured him.

*Local value refers to the essential value of an object's surface, without taking into account shadows, textures or lighting. An object's local value can usually be found in the midtones, so it is not within extreme light nor is it in shadow.

The shape of the cast shadow changes according to the angle of light. Every child has watched their shadow shrink at noon and stretch out into evening. The edges of the umbra also vary according to the nature of the light source. The stronger and closer the light, the crisper the shadow will be. When the light is more distant, the edges of the shadow will be blurred, becoming more indistinct the further they extend.

Shadowy adaptation

Artists often exercise creative license with their cast shadows. They may change their shape or even remove them completely, depending on their aims. What might be some cases in which you'd want to adapt or remove shadows? Sometimes, a cast shadow will obscure an important form, or disrupt a line. The shadow might hide a key highlight which would otherwise tell us a lot about the roundedness of an object. In portraiture, it's often necessary to adapt the shadows under people's noses—these can have the unfortunate effect of causing people to look a little too much like a notable silent film performer.

Harvester of Shadows

+10 Fluency in the language of the shadow realm.

The cast shadow is crucial to creating realism: it links together the object, its environment and the light. The cast shadow also offers surprising opportunities for making creative choices, however. Because cast shadows vary so greatly in everyday experience, it's possible to alter them in your drawing without your viewers noticing anything amiss. This means you can change the angle of a shadow to better direct the eye towards a focal point, for example. You can also change the shadow to improve the general abstract design of your image. This is the paradoxical magic of the umbra: it allows you to simultaneously enhance realism while also manipulating reality to serve your creative purposes.

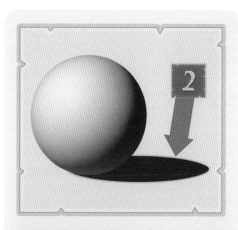

Penumbra (Latin for 'partial shadow')

The penumbra surrounds the umbra. It is the lighter, softer edge of the dark umbra. In the penumbra, only some of the light is being blocked. We can generate this feathery, diffuse effect either by applying a blending stump to our shadow edge or by using any of the H range of pencils to fade out the shadow.

In the illustration above, you can see the cast shadow transitioning into a penumbra, which gets more blurred the further out it goes. Whether you have an incredibly diffuse penumbra, or a very crisp-edged one, there is always some sort of transition from light to dark to consider.

Sometimes, I just wonder if everyone thinks I'm dull. If I could just find my keyboard... I could show you there's another side to me.

Form shadow

A form shadow has two main parts: the shadow core, and the reflected or 'bounce' light. The form shadow edge is where the form begins to turn away from the light, into shadow.

Unlike the cast shadow, the form shadow is, in effect, attached to the surface of the object: it is a darkness caused by the object turning away from the light.

As with cast shadows, the nature of form shadows is effected by the character of the light source. Strong lighting produces sharp shadows. Softer lighting results in diffuse shadows, with a gradual transition between light and shadow.

Just as cast shadows give a form gravity and weight, form shadows create a sense of volume and fullness. These shadows belong to the realm of the Specific: they communicate the nuanced variation and individual characteristics of a form's surface.

Squinting

Identifying all these different types of shadows may be overwhelming at first. Remember, squinting is powerful. Squinting helps to simplify things, making it easier to perceive patterns. It also flattens what we are seeing into manageable planes—even now that we're beginning to consider volume and roundedness, this is useful, because we're still drawing in two dimensions.

Occlusion shadow (dark accent)

The occlusion shadow, also known as the dark accent, is the darkest part of the shadow: this is the place that no light touches. It is blocked from both the primary light source and all secondary or reflected light. The occlusion shadow is a very helpful shadow landmark to locate, because it will usually be the darkest part of our subject, and we can use its value as a standard against which to compare other values.

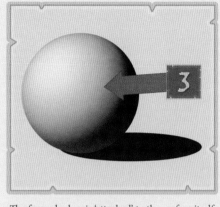

The form shadow is 'attached' to the surface itself. It is created by the very forms that make up the object.

Sometimes a cast shadow from another object will merge with a form shadow, as in the above photo of a stone.

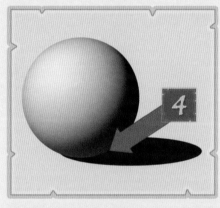

Putting in the deep darks, such as occlusion shadows, early on is known as 'keying.' Keying creates a tonal map by distributing a few 'key' values, providing standards of comparison.

The underside of this stone receives no light and becomes very dark indeed. This is referred to as an occlusion shadow,

Core shadow

The core shadow is another very dark part of the shadow, and it falls on the border between light and shadow. When we mark shadow lines, we are indicating the position of the core shadow. The reason the core shadow is so dark is that it falls between two areas of light: the primary light source, and the reflected light bouncing back from another direction. The core shadow therefore denotes an area that is receiving very little light from either of these sources.

As we've already seen, the core shadow is a key landmark. Once we pencil it in, the object's structure really starts to become evident. In fact, because the core shadow is such a clear and important landmark, it can be marked any time, even during the block-in phase: it can be a great reference point for working out the overall shape of the drawing as a whole. With shadows, as with all forms, begin by focussing on the largest shapes. Let smaller shadows be subsumed within larger ones to start with. As with every part of the process, always work from general to the specific.

In your practice drawings and sketches, you can use medium-heavy lines to describe shadow cores, so that you can see them easily. In your proper drawings, however, core shadows should be pencilled in very faintly, like the rest of your organisational lines: this lets them serve as a guide to later shading without committing you too soon.

Remember what we said earlier about hedges and walls—sometimes your core shadow will be broken or indistinct. On rounded forms, shadows usually dissolve into soft transitions, and if we've scored the core shadow with a heavy line, this can make those subtle shifts difficult. Because core shadows fall on the boundary between light and dark, they serve as a point of departure from we will begin to extend our pencil washes out into the light section.

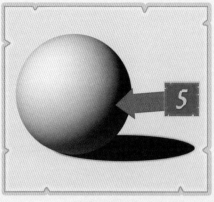

The core shadow is the most pronounced area of the shadow shape. This is the area where the form has completely turned away from the light.

A final test: can you name all the different kinds of shadows in this image?

Where Texture Is Revealed

Where light strikes an object tangentially, it reveals a lot about the nature of the surface. Strong light produces a strong core shadow, and where there is a strong core, there is strong texture. The dips and ridges of the core shadow's line reveal so much about the surface of the object. An obvious example of this is the Moon and the way its craters appear to us.

You couldn't have a look in this hatch for my keyboard could you?

Secret Hatches

Exploring Hatches

169

Open Hatches

172

Hatch Direction

174

Dark Unity

176

Keying

178

Reflected Light

180

We had discovered the Focal point, and we had successfully captured dark matter. The way cleared, we pressed on through the shadowy halls, until we came upon a series of hatches. They were all facing different directions, and some even stood open. Had someone been here before us? "Don't worry about that now," the Specific said, heaving at a heavy trap door. "We need to find the right hatch to get us out of this dungeon."

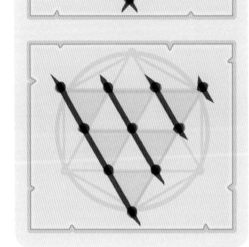

Exploring Hatches

The Value of Line

We've been working with value for a while now, but now it's time to think about how we add value and to finesse our technique. We're going to be working with a technique known as 'hatching'. Hatching is simply shading using evenly spaced parallel lines, which you generate by moving your pencil rhythmically back and forth across the paper. There are a number of ways to vary the tone of hatching—the three listed here are incredibly useful. Each has its benefits and drawbacks, and in time, you'll develop an instinct for knowing when to use each.

Space between the lines

The distance between the lines determines how dark the hatch is. The closer the lines, the darker the value. We will refer to a hatch with large spaces between the lies as being 'open'. A more open hatch produces lighter values. One advantage to leaving your hatch more widely spaced is that this will make it easier to integrate these open hatches into even areas of tone.

Pressure that is applied

You can vary the value across a single line by changing your pencil pressure. To avoid damaging the paper, never apply more than medium pressure. The value your pencil produces under medium pressure is the limit of its grade—don't push your pencil beyond its grade. (Changing grades is of course another way to change tone!)

Hatching and cross-hatching

Layering the hatching will also gradually darken the area. This is my favourite way to build tone: layer by layer, rather than trying to nail it in the first wash. This lets me find the right value bit by bit, rather than accidentally making an area of my drawing too dark.

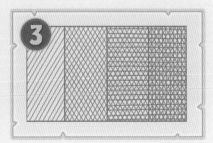

When hatches are layered one over the other, they should eventually form a seamlessly integrated fabric of tone. Example (3), on the previous page, shows a uniform progression of lines, but ours won't be so mechanically accurate. What we should aim for is to be as consistent as possible, while also recreating the flow of the surface.

Overlap (A)

Sometimes overlaps like the one pictured in (A) happen. Obviously, this is because two hatches close to one another have overlapped, and the double layer has resulted in a darker value. This is usually an unwanted accident, but it's possible to correct.

Of course, if the value created by the overlap matches the tone you need, then there's no problem at all. Simply darken the values on either side of the overlap to even out the transition.

If, however, the tone in the middle is not what you require, you can go in with a kneaded eraser to tidy things up.

It's also worth noting that the hatch in example (A) is very dense indeed. Such thick, close hatching is not always the most practical way of applying tone. In fact, one advantage of using more open hatching, with more space between the lines, is that this makes it easier to knit together patches of hatch. This can avoid the problem of overlap.

Stippling (B, C)

Stippling is a method of laying down tone by dotting at the paper with a sharp pencil (B). This technique can, of course, damage the paper, resulting in marks which may be very difficult to remove later on. I reserve this technique for creating textures. For instance, it's useful when creating the impression of brickwork or adding texture to gravel and rock. This method works especially well in conjunction with erasers, as these add some variety to the dots.

It's also possible to create textured value by dabbing at the paper with tools such as a colour shaper (C), blending stump or kneadable eraser. The shaper can deposit graphite it has collected on the tip and spread it around with a nice textural effect that the pencil alone can't generate. The shaper leaves a smooth smear, while the stump makes a feathery, blurred mark. I can then hatch over these effects, building value over an interesting textural foundation. It's worth playing with these tools, experimenting with the effects you can achieve. We will delve more into these topics later, when we discuss blenders in more detail.

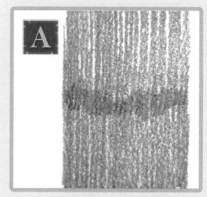

The place where two hatches intersect can throw up some horrible dark areas

Pencil stippling is useful in texture generation.

Here we can see the colour shaper is being used in a stipple fashion, laying down graphite in a light smear. Effects like this are useful when generating textures. They also work nicely at the edges of the picture, where we want things to be a little out of focus.

Zigzag approach (B)

You've probably used the zigzag method as a child, while colouring in. This hatching method involves sweeping the pencil back and forth without lifting the tip from the paper. The trouble is that the pencil goes over the same area twice when changing direction, leaving darker areas around the edges. These darker overlaps are one of the small details that make smooth tonal transitions difficult. If I use this technique at all, it is in areas of tone between two contours (A), so that the darker points of the zigzag are hidden along existing shadow edges (B).

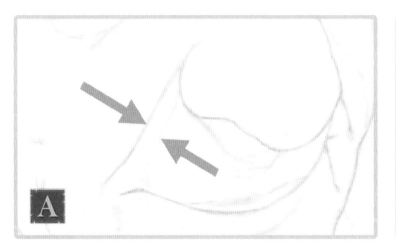

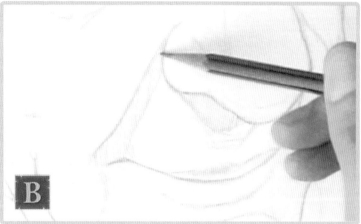

Open hatch (C)

Using open, widely-spaced hatching (C) makes it easier to knit together areas of different value. The wider the hatching, the more open it is, and the lighter it will appear. Remember that the direction of the hatching is determined by the curves of the surface being described. These open hatches create an initial, suggestive wash of value, which can be built up gradually and subtly.

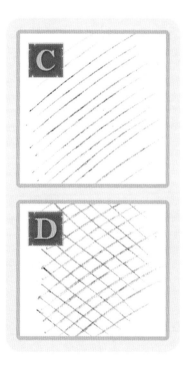

As well as creating value, the lines of hatching have their own compositional importance. As we've seen, diagonal lines create a sense of motion and energy. The swift, repeated diagonals of hatching thus add a liveliness and vibrancy to any drawing. This is a good argument against the over use of blenders, which will blur or even totally obscure the lines of hatching.

This may very well be what you want. It is worth considering, however, that hatching not only imparts energy, it can also create a sense of strength and structure. Polishing a drawing may actually weaken it. This, of course, is a matter of personal preference, and you will need to draw your own conclusions about how much hatching to leave visible. Be ready to experiment with different finishes and approaches.

The cross-hatch (D)

In cross-hatching, we place one hatch over another (D), creating a darker value. This is a more sculptural method of adding tone. The angles of cross-hatch needn't be as perpendicular as in (D), but it's good to keep your angles fairly uniform at first. As I start my drawings, I often look to begin with planes that have a similar angle, so that their hatching will have relatively unified flow. Watch out for having hatching and cross-hatching moving in too many different directions at once.

Open Hatches

Interlocking Hatchery

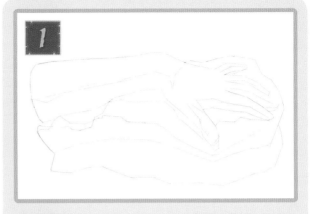

Let's take a practical look at how to apply open hatches. Using this line drawing of a plaster cast (I), I am going to show you how to use open hatching to generate a sense of form. I will also show you how to deal with the problem of overlap. For this demo, I will be using a 2B, a nice middle grade pencil that will let me build up the shadows in a uniform manner.

Of course it is not just the space between the lines that makes a hatch open, it is also the lightness of the marks. It's possible to leave a hatch too wide open, though: a very widely spaced hatch made with super faint lines will look less like shading and more like some random cat-scratches. Use your judgement and aim for moderation.

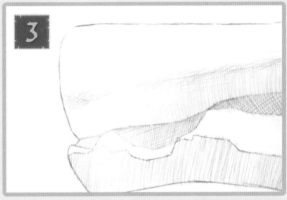

Beginning from the core shadow, I have begun lightly hatching outwards. Notice that my lines are still following the flow of the form.

Try not to overwork your hatching. Not only does this save effort and avoid mistakes, it also preserves the paper tooth Commit some time to thinking about what value an area should be before you start hatching.

I've now begun hatching in another direction, developing the shadow mass beneath the core shadow. Even though I've changed direction, my lines are still following the cylindrical form of the forearm.

One good reason for changing my hatching direction in the shadow mass is to maintain the visibility of the core shadow guideline—it also means that, where the two hatch patches intersect, I get a nice dark cross-hatch, making the darker core area still more visible. Working this way has made the area around the core shadow darker intentionally. It is not, therefore, the product of an accidental overlap. The more experienced you become the less accidental overlaps will occur. At that point, shading will have become instinctual.

Something tells me this is the wrong hatch!

You Found the Wrong Hatch!

Hatching is not just colouring in—image (A) shows what happens if you think about it like that. In fact, this image shows just about everything that can go wrong with hatching: the shadow shapes are far too dark, their values are inconsistent, and they've been hatched in at random angle.

There's really almost nowhere the drawing could go from here—its hatches lead to a dead-end. If, instead, it had been washed in with a medium-light value which takes into account the average darkness of each shadow, as well as the shape of the form being described, then it would be easy to develop onto the next stage. The door would be opened to shadows, to the actual arrangement of value in our drawing.

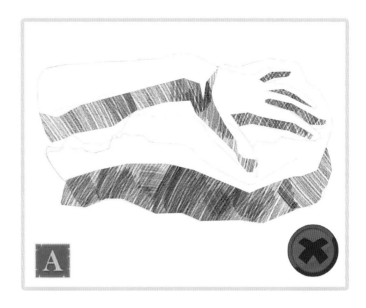

If line is music, then scribbling is noise. Hatching in every direction at once can quickly degenerate into the mess you see in image. This is no way to generate value. Having said that, scribbling does have its uses: when used carefully, it can be an excellent way of generating texture, in situations where a controlled use of chaos is welcome.

The useful scribble

When is scribbling useful? In the drawing above, I'm working with two quite involved textures—fur and grass—which might seem superficially similar. The crucial thing to bear in mind is that the more complex a form is, the more important is to have a solid idea of its basic shadow/light pattern. The fur patterns of a dog's paw are really quite complex, with hair going in lots of different directions, so I had to make sure I understood the overall shadow/light pattern first, before I started drawing each lock of hair; otherwise, it would have appeared inconsistent.

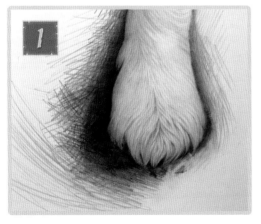
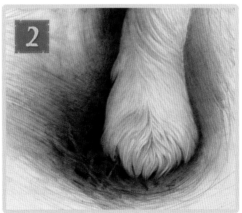
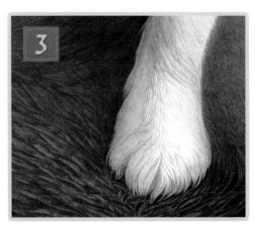

Scribbling in the hair would've been a bad idea—it would've confused the form of the limb, and it wouldn't have described the directions of hair growth. The grass, on the other hand, is a different matter. In this progression of images, you can see how scribbling has generated a useful foundation for the texture of the grass. Yet even here, the scribbling has only provided a base for much more deliberate directional work. Notice the sweeping lines of the grass: rather than copying my observations exactly, I've taken license here, using my hatch directions, built on top of the scribbles, to help move the eye around the picture. Changing hatch directions create a dynamic swirl and flow.

I refuse to say it.*

*Hold the door.

Hatch Direction

Angled to Serve Composition

Just as it's important not to scribble in every direction at once, it's also not a good idea to hatch in only one direction. The hand is naturally inclined towards a downwards stroke, but it's important to work against this tendency a little and introduce some variety. Otherwise, your hatching will become too linear, flat and predictable. Try an upwards stroke, for example.

As we've seen, the best approach is to hatch across or along the form. Combine moderate variation with consistency to achieve a dynamic flow. This may sound daunting, but there are a few simple rules you can remember to help make your hatching successful:

1 Keep your pressure uniform.

2 Avoid cutting into the tooth.

3 Work lightly and build up in layers.

Even though we want our hatching to go with the flow, the first layers of hatching don't have to be a perfect replica of your model's surface. Cross-hatching is a process that allows you to build things up gradually, as long as you work lightly.

Adding value while staying in control of the picture only becomes difficult when we hatch in randomly. Don't work chaotically. Try to understand the general flow of the surface and how it is oriented towards the light-source—build from that.

This drawing of the *Laocoön* sculpture has been digitally darkened so you can see the direction of my hatching more clearly. Notice how this first wash of shadow both moves with the flow of the form and aims towards the focal point.

The flow of the hatch can be a useful way of guiding the viewer. In this case, I want the eye to move upwards, across the neck and beard, towards the face proper.

Dark energy

You can see the compositional effects of hatch direction in the two drawings to the left. In (A), the lines aim towards the eye, and in (B), a drawing by Michelangelo, the hatches not only follow the form, they also direct attention towards the face. The goal is to have hatching enhance rather than confuse the drawing's gesture. If Michelangelo had shaded, say, vertically, it would have detracted from the drawing's dynamism.

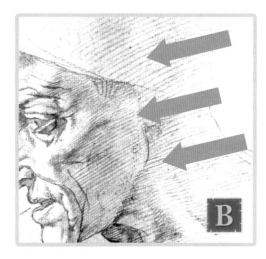

Tool direction

Direction is an important consideration when using other tools as well. The marks made in (C) were made with a blending stump. Notice how the lines are darker at the beginning and ends of each pass: this effect can be quite noticeable, making any shadows you blend look quite patchy.

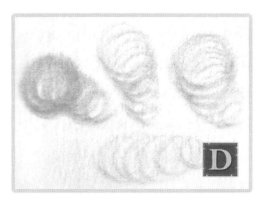

Rather than zigzagging your blender, use a hatching motion, going lightly when touching down and lifting off. As when hatching, blend along the grain of your subject. If your blending doesn't follow the flow of the hatches, you could end up destroying all the careful descriptive work you've done, rubbing it right out. As you blend, imagine you're sanding a wooden sculpture, going with the grain and gradually smoothing the forms. When blending the background, you can move your stump in small circular motions, as in (D).

Early intro to stumps

This image of the *Laocoön* bust (E) shows the stage just after the image has had its shadows blended with the stump. Blending isn't just a way of smoothing things out: the blending stump helps to unify shadow areas, as well as removing the grain. I use them to simplify matters when the shadows get too complicated, with too many different tones. I like to try to maintain a contrast between a bold, basic dark side, complementing a more subtly sophisticated light side.

Blending stumps are also great for nocturnal scenes. Objects seen in dim light lack definition, their edges blurred. Low-light photography doesn't have this same fuzzy quality, and this can actually distort our perception of our own perception. Pay attention to the details and textures of your own visual experience, and start to think about ways of conveying them.

Dark Unity

Every Dark Side Has a Light Side

As we move towards adding more values to our drawing, moving beyond the simplified arrangement of dark and light, we need to change how we think about our drawing. We need to think sculpturally: rather than merely making a two-dimensional copy, we are in fact modeling the forms.

Modeling the values in your drawing involves the use of knowledge and understanding to create a truer, more accurate depiction of your subject. The opposite of modeling would be 'shading,' which is a purely optical attempt to copy values. When modeling, we are still comparing values between our drawing and the subject, but we are also using our knowledge of how forms work in light, thinking conceptually about how forms are turning.

All the abstraction we've been struggling to cultivate—the flattening, the divorcing of visual perception from three-dimensional knowledge: it's time to set that aside. Modeling involves the conscious, deliberate use of what we know about objects in reality. These might be basic things, such as, "This vase is all white, so I know that it's local value is consistent," or "A surface will always become darker as it turns away from the light source."

Modeling is about using value to sculpt your subject. This means using the shape, position and relative darkness of values to maximum effect, so that they are not just accurate, they do the work you need them to do in your image. Modeling sees values as part of a relationship between form and light, and it uses value to depict the dark and light side of an object's forms. Drawing from observation is always a shifting combination of knowledge and perception, a blend of the purely optical with the formal and theoretical.

> Modeling is about properly describing the surface; in other words, tones should not be put in indiscriminately but should rather take into account the shape and turn of each individual form.

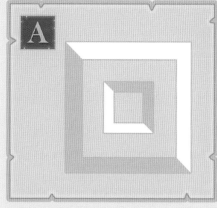

An example of a simple, readable arrangement of light and shadow, giving the basic idea of an object in a light source.

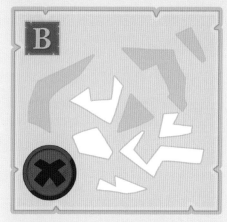

In (B), we have an a series of light and dark shapes, but they are incoherent. They do not convey the sense of a three-dimensional structure, because the patches of light and dark do not relate to each other. There's no sense of light and shadow, just random, floating patches of value. This is why we build our shadow maps, so that we can see clearly whether or not we have a value pattern that makes sense.

We also need our values to make sense in relation to one another, to be unified. 'Over-modeling' describes a situation in which the values lose unity due to being over extended. For instance, the lights might be too light relative to the darks, or vice versa. When this happens, there is a loss of unity between the values and the form they are meant to describe.

To avoid over-modeling, remember that not every drawing needs to contain the full range of values, from white to black. Over-modeling can also result if we neglect the balance between light and dark—if, for instance, we adjust the light side but forget to compensate but altering the dark values also. It's important to preserve the overall contrast between the light and dark sides of a given form.

Modeling

Modeling is where drawing begins to resemble sculpture. If you could reach out and touch the object in your drawing, what would it feel like? Drawing, through modeling, becomes an almost tactile experience.

You should aim for a work which both looks and feels like the subject. By this, I mean that values should be applied in such a way that it looks as if the objects in your drawings truly are three-dimensional, that they could be lifted out of the drawing, rather than remaining the cardboard cutouts we pretended they were during our preliminary work. I once heard an actor praised because, every time he came on stage, you fully believed he had just been out in the world living a fully realised life. Strive to give your objects the same kind of reality and weight, so that even the sides which aren't visible have an implied presence within the drawing.

Achieving this requires us to pay attention to what happens as a form turns away from the light. Is it moving into full shadow, or is it moving into an area of reflected light? In both cases, there will be a shift in the value of the shadows, as they get either darker or lighter. Either way, keeping the shadow shape as a single, flat plane of value will destroy the sense of three-dimensionality.

Which is the best way to hatch a cylinder? Curved hatches are too difficult to pull off consistently. A horizontal hatch is flattening. In this instance, the vertical hatch is the best solution.

Because curvy hatches are difficult to do consistently, I only find them useful for subjects like grass, where consistency isn't paramount. On regular objects, like a true cylinder, keep it straight.

Multiple directions

You have an array of line directions to you, just as you have a palette of tones. Using a variety of hatching directions is another valuable way of adding interest. It's perfectly fine to rotate the paper if you find a certain angle awkward. While varying angles is a good idea, you should, for the most part, stick to using straight lines: these are easier to keep regular and consistent. At the same time, don't worry if your hatches aren't precise: we're not aiming for a mechanical conformity.

Right and sinister

Whether you're right or left-handed plays no part in making you a better artist. There's a popular conception that creativity lies in the right hemisphere of the brain, which controls the left hand, and that therefore left-handed people are more artistic. Well, being left-handed in a right-handed world is difficult, so it's easy to see why this cheering idea has gained traction—and history certainly offers an impressive list of highly accomplished lefties in all fields. I would venture to say, though, that the most solid difference that handedness will make to your drawing is in determining which hatching direction you prefer. Lefties prefer a hatch that moves from lower right to upper left, while right-handed people favour the opposite. Whichever angle you are predisposed towards, try not to get stuck moving in just that one direction. Variety is the spice of drawing.

Can I ask that you NOT whistle. I want to get out of here alive.

I can see a door up ahead.

Keying

Where to Put the Key?

Once we've mapped the shadows and hatched in these shadow shapes, it's finally time to start getting more specific. We do this by placing a key, that is, by developing a specific area of high value, as I've done in (A). This is the secret to tonal accuracy, and it's really quite simple: find the darkest shadow tone on your image, and use this as a standard against which to gauge the rest of your tones. This darkest area serves as a tonal key, a basis of comparison. If we were using toned paper, we might also consider developing an area of highlight, but this is unnecessary with white paper.

What makes this 'key' so useful is that, once we've established the lightest and darkest tones, all the others fall into place far more easily. Using keys prevents you from over-modeling, because you've already established the extreme limits of your tonal range for the drawing, and all the other lights and darks must adhere to that scale.

Take time to consider before establishing your key. Take stock of the subject as a whole, noticing how light is effecting each part. Judge carefully: you don't want to have to change the key later on. Changing the key is a lot like changing the ending of a story—you'll probably wind up having to change much of the rest of the story, too. Amending the key means altering all the rest of the tonal relationships. It's also important to maintain the balance between the light and dark sides of your image: if you alter one, you must reconsider the other, to make sure the balance stays consistent.

We've already seen the finish for this study (page 175) but I want to rewind to an earlier state to show you the key I established for it. Having checked the shadow shapes for accuracy and established the proportions of light and shadow, we can begin to develop a key, otherwise known as a tonal standard. For the key, we choose the area of darkest shadow—in this case, located under the nose. This location is convenient: I want my deepest darks to be around the centre of the picture in order to draw the eye to this area.

> Your deepest dark should be matched by an equally bright highest light. Maintain balance between the dark side and the light side.

This is also a time when you may decide to stray a little from your observation. It isn't always necessary to faithfully record exactly what you see. You may, for instance, choose to make your value scheme far darker than the one you observe. I often choose to darken things to some degree, to increase the impact—it can be difficult to achieve ideal lighting, and I often find my subjects look a little flat and low-contrast for my liking. The ability to choose a darker value scheme and to deviate successfully from your observations is something that comes with knowledge and experience. You need a firm grasp of how value works, and a control over your use of value, developed through exercises such as sphere studies and cast drawings.

Shadowy Recap

Let's pause and review what we've learned so far about putting in shadows.

General wash

We begin shadow work once we're satisfied with our contour. As we now know, we begin by blocking in the core shadow and develop the shadow line to a good degree of accuracy.

Then, we use a wash of open hatching to fill in the shadow shapes, switching on the lights (A). Just use a single layer so that things are still easy to change. Use this stage to check that your lines and shapes are accurate. Check the relationship between the outline and internal structures; see if the shadow shapes are correct; and use negative space checks as well. At this stage, hatching in values is rather like trying out a move in chess—keeping your hand on the piece so that you aren't truly committed. Sometimes it's necessary to see the move in order to tell whether it's right or not. Mental images and ideas are much too slippery to check.

Specific key

Once we're happy that everything is as it should be, we can key in the darkest places of the drawing (B). These should be important landmarks, and ones that receive almost no light. The key will set the standard for all other tones. We know that nothing should go darker than this area. This helps us avoid over-modeling.

We inserted the key. What other surprises could the shadow realm have in store?

A

The longer that your drawing can remain in a state that resembles the image above, the better. This image simply shows a basic shadow map. The light and dark shapes help me see the object as three-dimensional, and I can clearly spot any mistakes. I have a pretty good idea of how to develop any area of the drawing from here.

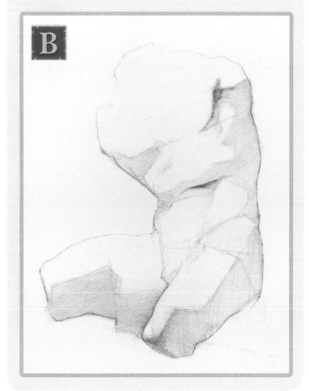

B

Reflected Light

You Found the Lights in the Shadows!

Since entering the shadow realm, we have been treating shadows as large blocks with one or two values. This has been a necessary simplification. However, the shadow side of an object is rarely completely dark—it is usually illuminated by some degree of reflected light.

We can think of the primary light source as being like the Sun, and of reflected light as like the Moon, casting its pale light over those regions of the planet which have fallen into shadow.

Just as moonlight is much dimmer and softer than sunlight, the reflected light we find in the shadows can be very subtle indeed. It's usually easiest to spot reflected light near the edges of the form, right along the contour. You can see an example of this in the diagrams below.

Over-estimating the power of the Moon (A)

The Moon isn't as bright as the Sun, and if you make reflected lights seem as bright as your primary light source, it will spoil the illusion of roundedness, flattening your drawing. This kind of mistake is easier to make than you might expect—it may not be very obvious as you draw, but a viewer observing with fresh eyes will spot it right away.

In figure (A), the reflected light on the right side is so bright that it could only be coming from a mirror or highly polished surface. When light is reflected, it loses energy, and part of the light is lost, bounced off in different directions. This is why reflected light is always weaker than the primary light source.

LANTERN BEARERS

Shadows that might at first appear to be black or incredibly dark will usually contain light to some extent.

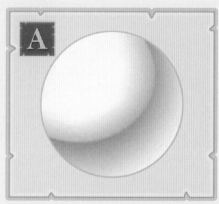

Drawn correctly, reflected light can accentuate an object's roundedness. Too much reflected light, however, can have an adverse effect. In the above example, the reflected light is so bright on the underside of the ball that it seems to bend towards the viewer, rather than curving away as it ought to.

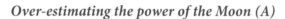

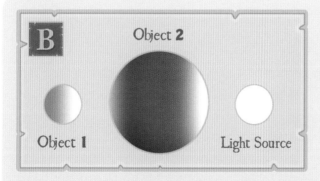

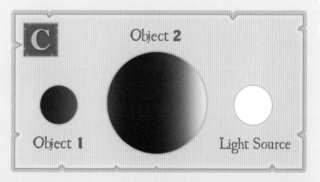

The strength of the reflected light on an object is dependent on the local value of the surface that it reflects off. A lighter local value reflects more light, while a darker surface will absorb more light. You can see this effect illustrated above. In image (B), the light is bouncing off Object 1, which is white, and casting a noticeable reflected light on Object 2. In (C), Object 1 is black and reflects far less light back onto Object 2—the reflected light is still there, but it is far more subtle.

People often overestimate the brightness of reflected lights due to an effect known as relative brightness: we perceive a value differently, depending on the other values around it. A value which, on the light side would seem dark, can look quite bright when surrounded by shadows. This phenomenon can have strange and confusing effects, but we can also turn it to our advantage. We'll consider it in more detail on page 243.

By now we should have a handle on the specifics of the shadows, but it's worth remembering that things never get too specific in the shadow realms. There is often far less detail visible on the shadow side than on the light side.

Note the subtle shifts of tone in this mask of Voltaire. Those shadows aren't simply flat tones; they have a shimmering sophistication.

The whiteness of the plaster really helps to bring out the glow and glint of the reflected lights, making them a real pleasure to attempt.

Once you have done the necessary work of simplifying and generalising, take time to appreciate what's really going on in the shadows.

Think of a half Moon: on the illuminated side, you can make out the topography quite clearly, while the shadow side reveals very little. Having said that, the dark side is not flatly black—it has a subtle luminosity which is really quite beautiful, and this is something we should attempt to capture in our shadows. The blending stump is fantastic tool for working with your shadows. It smoothes out the pencil grain, while also simplifying and unifying areas which may have become over-modelled.

The Potato (Continued)

It's our old friend potato, fresh from the Contour Coast! Let's give him some value. Image (1) is where we left off, and in image (2), I have blocked the shadow shape and hatched it in with a 3B midtone. Image (3) shows how I have begun to add some tonal progressions, moving outwards from the core shadow. This example gives a simple idea of how shadows can be developed. In this demonstration I have drawn my core shadow a little more clean cut than I normally would. Still, it will suffice as a place of departure for the next stage which involves an excursion into the land of light.

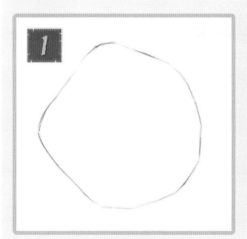 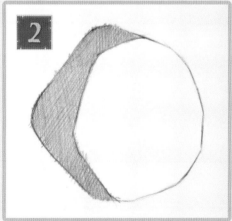 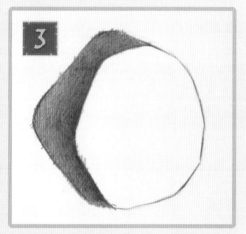

Now this shape has a light side and a dark side, and there is some progression within the dark side: the shadows are darkest at the core shadow, and they fade out into reflected light. We begin to get the sense of a three-dimensional potato. The trouble is, because the light side has no tonal variation, it looks completely flat, as if the potato had been sliced in half. We'll remedy this soon enough.

The downside to finding the light in the darkness is that we can now be seen...

 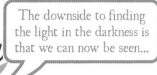

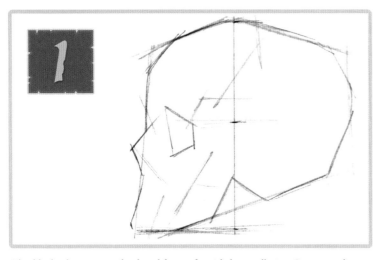

This blocky drawing was developed from a five sided constellation. Can you make out the five sides? Here, phase two of the block-in has been initiated, in which important inner shapes and lines have also been noted.

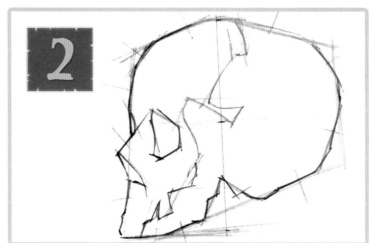

With a workable contour in place, I carve out the shadow shapes, dividing this skull into continents of light and dark. My lines are a bit too dark and overpowering, but that's alright—this is just a study, and I want to be able to see everything clearly.

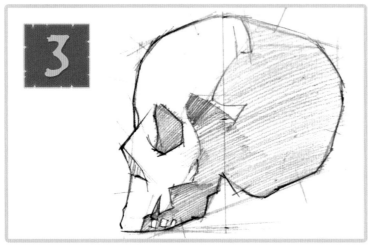

Shadow shapes are now loosely hatched in with a wash that approximates the average tone of the shadows. I'm not shading too darkly yet, as I want to creep up on the specific tones of the shadows. There are a few overlaps, but they won't be there for long.

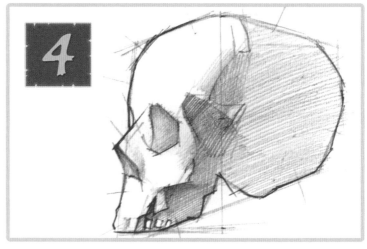

With the dark shapes in place, I then begin to work outwards, using the core shadow as the basis for my tonal gradations.

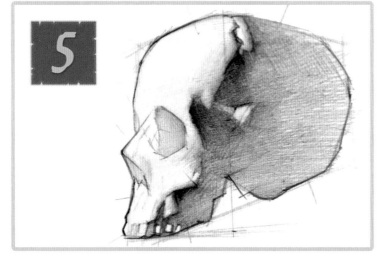

Deep darks are keyed in, giving the image a sense of drama and increased three-dimensionality. My layers of hatch take into account the skulls surface and have been done in such a way as to eliminate the overlaps from the initiate wash.

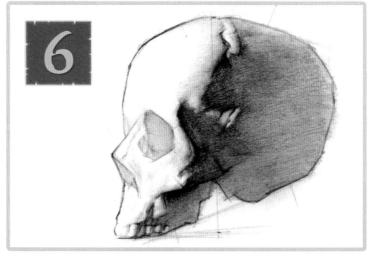

The study is complete. I like to keep the shadows basic; the limited tonal palette I have used for this drawing adds boldness, clarity and power, just as the straight, blocky lines give strength and stability to the contour.

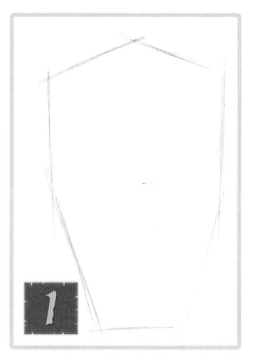  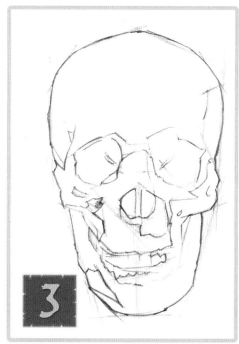

Here we see the constellation (1), block-in (2) and finally contour with shadow shapes blocked in (3). I start adding value in the shadows, using rough hatching (4). Working outwards from the shadows into the light, things become far more subtle as we start to consider midtones. Midtones bridge the gap between shadows and light, and they are very important to conjuring three-dimensionality, as we will learn in the coming chapter.

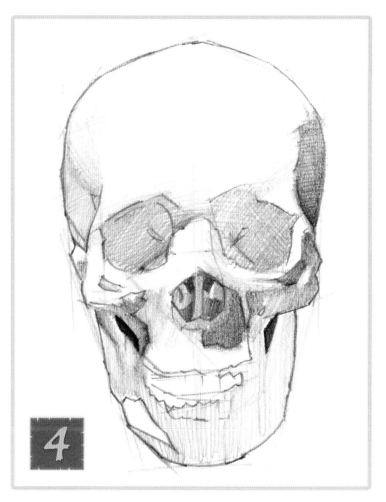 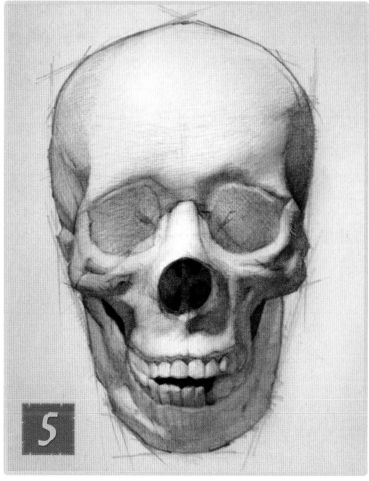

Once the midtones are in place, this skull suddenly leaps out into the third dimension (5). See how subtle these values can be? Before we attempt these fine tonal gradations, it's essential to have all the fundamentals firmly in place, so that we can keep the drawing under control.

MIDTONE BRIDGE

Tonal Triad	Midtones	Specific II	3D Elementals	Planes
185	186	189	190	192

I could hear the undead horde clattering close behind us, but I could see the light—we'd almost made it! The Specific yanked me across the bridge, just as the skeletons rushed to grab us. Shards of bone pelted us as we emerged, panting, into the hot desert sun. Was this really the right way?

TONAL TRIAD

VIII

Level Up! – Illumin-Arty!

We have passed through many gateways to reach this stage of the Tetraforce: from points, lines and shapes; through shadow lines and masses; and now, we find ourselves turning towards the light.

Tonal work is divided into three segments: shadows, midtones and lights, as you can see in the Tetraforce to the right. We have just learned about shadows. Over the next two chapters, we will consider midtone and light. The midtone acts as a kind of bridge between light and dark, between two dimensions and three.

> The midtone is essential in generating the idea of volume and fullness; it is a bridge between light and dark.

The Midtone Bridge links the Shadow Observatory to the Land of Light. Fortunately, we don't have to hurry across this border zone as quickly as Guido did, but we, too, will be guided by the Specific, leaving the Shadow General behind. We will learn to use our pencils to create a bridge of washes which extends outwards from the shadows, gradually moving into the light.

Three segments combine: shadows, midtones and the lights. Together, they open up the Tetraforce to a whole new dimension! Ka-pow wow!

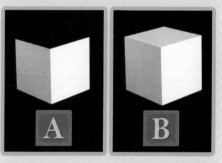

Having already considered the shadows (A) and how they can give our pictures weight, we'll now learn about midtones, and ways in which they bring volume and depth to our drawing (B).

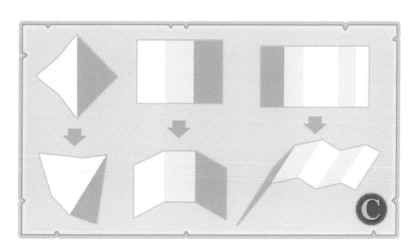

Tonal tilt (C)

We used line sections of varying degrees of tilt to describe the two-dimensional outer perimeter of an object, and now we will use tone to describe how the object is tilted in space, with respect to a light source. These two descriptions of tilt—line and tone—complement and reinforce one another, creating the illusion of depth.

Pushing out into the Light

We spent the last chapter creating nice clear shadow edges—now we're going to start messing around with them. The midtone develops outwards from the core shadow, into the light side. From a shadow line division between light and dark, we're going to create a smooth progression of values, because a shadow very rarely has such cleanly defined edges. As you can see at the foot of the page, there are many ways to create subtle transitions from shadow to light, using tools like stumps, chamois leather and even paintbrushes to push the graphite out from the core shadow, describing the diffusion of light.

Before touching these tools, however, it's important to master these tonal progressions using only your pencil. Get a feel for the modeling process, sculpting with the nib of your pencil. This puts you in control of the process of creating an impression of depth, rather than leaving you to hope for happy accidents.

DIFFUSE SHADOW

Blurry shadow edges can be created with a hard pencil, stump or chamois leather.

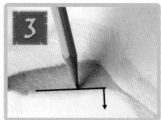

The black line in image (2) indicates the area of sharp-edged shadow that I will be diffusing, using the 2H pencil. The pencil is the best way of going about this, as it allows you to consider the topography in a gradual way, rather than smudging it up with a tool. Once you've created a carefully rendered value structure, then you can use blenders. Be careful not to go overboard with the blenders, however: smoothing everything out will weaken the drawing.

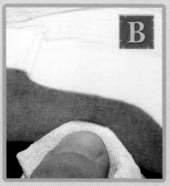
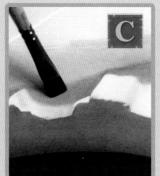

Different tools each lend their own quality to the tonal progression. For instance, using a pencil alone may result in an unwanted graininess. While it's useful to finesse your pencil work with blenders, you shouldn't rely on blenders to actually create your midtones, as this is likely to result in sloppy work. Blenders can be very useful in giving your shadows and midtones softened, feathered edges. Combining these slightly blurred areas of tone with sharp shadows is a remarkably effective way of creating depth. Notice how, in (C) and (D), these contrasts make it seem as though the tools are actually reaching into the picture and working on a three-dimensional sculpture.

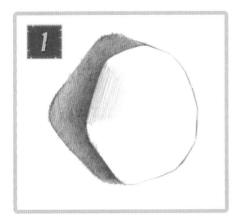

I generally add my midtone by working outwards from the core shadow, the wash of tone becoming lighter and lighter as I go. This gives the impression of a rounded object turning towards a light source. As well as working outwards from the shadow line, I also work back into the dark area to soften the shadow core.

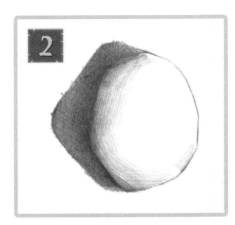

As always, my midtone washes take into consideration the flow of the surface. Obviously, since this is an imaginary potato shape thing, I am just following the general rules a rounded object should follow. For example, I am changing my pencil directions to describe a roundness, rather than just hatching straight across.

Over the top of the first hatching, I am now putting in a second layer to create a cross-hatch. This darkens the area adjacent to the core shadow while also having the effect of developing the surface texture.

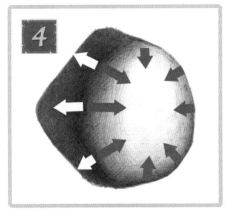

I am continuing to work inwards from the shadows (4). Eventually, my potato boasts a subtle reflected light on its left hand side, a distinct core shadow and a progression of middle values spreading from the core into the light side. To finish, I tidy up my highlight, using a kneaded eraser to make it a little more prominent (5).

Reflected light, core shadow, midtone and highlight: these four aspects are crucial to creating a sense of three-dimensionality. There is one more thing to consider, however, and that is ambience—and here, my imaginary potato runs into difficulties. The reflected light gives some sense of interacting with the surroundings, but the edges are just too dark. It doesn't fit convincingly with its surroundings, and this flattens out the shape, making it less convincing. These are not insurmountable problems however: the dark outline is an issue that can be dealt with later on when we consider final adjustments.

The light side is composed of midtones and highlights, while the dark side consists of the core shadow and the reflected light. These four tonal zones are all you need to know to be able to depict form convincingly. Everything after that just comes down to careful observation of the particular ways different objects relate to their light sources.

Why am I suddenly sinking? Also why are you grinning at me like that?

Finally! I get to properly Level Up!

Gradients Are Tonal Curves

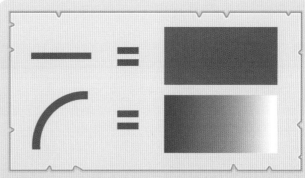

Uh oh, the Specific seems to have metamorphosed into a Djinn of Garish Awesomeness. Those robes sure are embellished—and check out her wings! Meanwhile, Guido has sunk eye-deep in the ultra-fine sand. Chances are, you may be feeling a little like Guido by now. Not only have we been meddling with blenders, we've also begun dealing with tonal gradients, and these things can be subdivided into way more than fifty shades of grey. This is great news for the Specific—but for students, not so much.

A tonal gradient is a lot like a curve: the seemingly infinite subdivisions of tone are a lot like the infinitely many tiny line segments that make a curve. Dealing with too many values all at once is just as confusing as too many curves.

There are lots of good reasons not to let either curves or tonal gradients into our work too early. Both can cause paralysing information-overload. Curves and gradients also have a dangerously finished feel to them. They close us off, leaving our picture too little room to grow. As we work, it's important to keep our drawings in a place where change and development are still possible.

The simple straight line is related to the flat tone and the curve, with all its complexity, is related to the tonal gradient. Values convey symbolic information in much the same way as lines. We are adept at interpreting tonal gradients on two-dimensions into representations of three-dimensional forms. For example, look at the shaded square above. It's just a square that goes from black to white, but it's easy to interpret it as a cylinder.

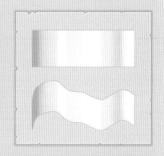

Values communicate the angle of a plane with relation to a light source. When the planes are curved, the shifts in angle will be almost infinitely subtle, just like the changes in the angle of the curve. When you're trying to get infinitely many things right all at once, it's easy to mess up.

Fortunately, we don't have to get it all right at once. Just as we blocked in lines to get curves right, there's also a process for blocking in values.

Tonal gradients also give the impression that a certain part is finished. That 'finished' bit becomes the standard against which all the rest of the picture is measured, to which all the other parts must relate. Now that bit of the picture is in control of the whole process, dictating all the rest of the picture's development. Suddenly, you've lost control of your work.

A curve in Z space

Drawing the line-work has been a process of arranging lines and curves on an X and Y axis. Tonal gradients are our way of expressing the angles and curves of planes on the X, Y and Z axis. Once we start adding value, we've begun describing a whole new dimension. This is some seriously advanced stuff we're getting into now, so tread carefully.

You're so self absor... damn I love these new shoes!

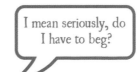

I mean seriously, do I have to beg?

3D Elementals

Excellent Teachers

Maybe Guido shouldn't have followed the Specific into this the land of light. He definitely can't cross this desert if he keeps sinking into the sand with all its teeny-tiny grains. We also need to take a moment to plan a better route through the wilderness of tonal gradients.

The answer is child's play . . . well, children's building blocks, to be more exact. They come in a wide variety of geometric forms, each one offering its own particular challenges and lessons. Studying these geometric shapes helps to give us a firm understanding of how light interacts with basic forms, which is a starting point for understanding more complex ones.

Acquire geometric shapes

With these forms arranged in front of us, we can begin to understand them as building blocks of the world, so to speak. There is a study, known as the 'form principle,' which considers nature as composed of these simplified forms. Through sustained study of geometric forms, we will eventually be able to look at any object and translate it into these basic geometric shapes. Not only that, we will have an understanding of how light interacts with these simple forms. For representational artists, this skill is vital.

The effects of light upon three-dimensional objects are predictable and orderly. We can learn them through study. Once we have grasped the principles of light's effects on geometric forms, we will be much better able to understand and represent the tones we encounter in drawing.

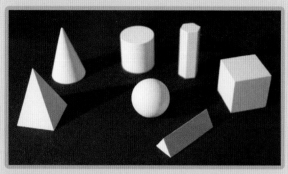

By studying simple geometric shapes, you can study the effects of light on forms while keeping variables to a minimum. To truly benefit from this study, you need to be able to draw these forms from different angles and under different lighting conditions. I implore you: get some building blocks, and paint them a matt white. You will benefit immensely.

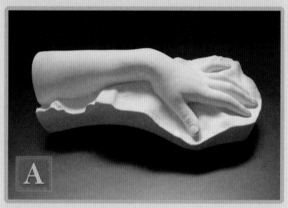

The geometry of reality isn't so neatly ordered or simple. Nevertheless, you will find it is possible to describe complex structures in terms of these simple forms. For instance, here a hand (A) has been translated into a series of cylinders, each slightly tapered (B). This kind of exercise is obviously useful in imaginative drawing, but it also has benefits when drawing from life.

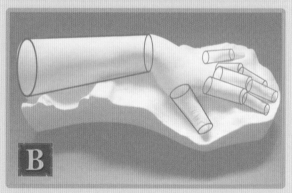

It's not necessary to actually draw the geometric forms each time. Once we've recognised them, however, we are better able to understand the forms before us. This kind of analysis is a helpful problem solving tool. It also ensures that we understand the objects in our drawings as full, rounded objects. After we've spent so long learning to look at our subjects as flattened abstractions, this can be a helpful corrective, one which also keeps things fairly simple.

Don't cross the sand yet until we have a found a solid plane to walk on.

Do I look different to you?

Standing on a Solid Plane

So you've got your blocks? Great. Now, find all the ones with curved sides and throw those across the room—we aren't touching them yet! We're going to start really simple. Now, find yourself a cube. Place it in front of you so you can see three sides. Each one is a different value: light, shadow, and midtone.

Earlier in this chapter, we looked at the pyramid. Drawing cubes is a step up from pyramids, however, because there are more angles to get right in relation to one another, and there is also one more visible plane. In this exercise, first we will practice getting accurate tilts, and then we will 'block'-in our three basic values.

With this in mind, we're now going to take a very brief, very basic look at linear perspective. This is, I'm afraid, all the perspective we have space for in this book. There are, however, many excellent resources available if you want to take your study of perspective further.

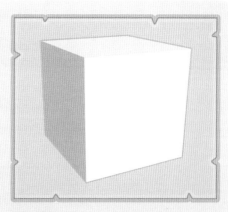

The side that faces the light the most will always be brightest. The side that faces us less directly will be darker and the one turned most away from the light source will fall into the darkest shadow. A cube placed near the light will have its light sides appear very light, while a cube that is placed further away from the source will be darker. Obvious, but easily forgotten.

We should avoid drawing an isometric diagram of a cube. This comes about when we ignore the slight change in angles, and the sides are drawn parallel.

The tricky thing about drawing a cube is getting the linear perspective right. Every object adheres to this visual law, but with a very regular form such as the cube, it's more obvious when the rules are broken. Linear perspective states that lines which are parallel will converge towards a single point on the horizon, known as the vanishing point.

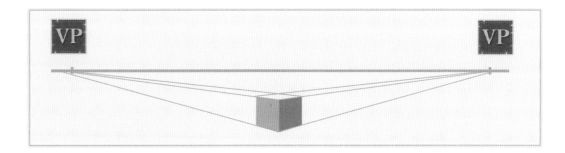

Think of train tracks seeming to become narrower as they stretch into the distance. When drawing a cube, however, you have two different sets of parallel lines, so you're working with two separate vanishing points. This is known as 'two-point perspective.' For our purposes, this is all you need to know. It's important to check the tilt of your lines, or else the cube will look weird, and it helps to know that the sets of parallel lines are converging towards their separate vanishing points—this helps you avoid drawing an isometric cube.

What matters here and now, however, is not the precision of your technical drawing. Draw a cube. Check your tilts, keep two-point perspective in mind, and get a basic form down. Now comes the important part, for this stage of our study. Block-in your values: a solid block of shadow, and another block of midtone. Get comfortable with this, with using your pencil to make these blocks of value. By shading in the values on the cube, we have completed the most basic possible expression of midtone. Things will steadily get trickier from here on . . .

Facets of Value

When we talk about planes, with objects that aren't blocky and regular such as the cube, we're really talking conceptually. It is a way of thinking, generalising the sides of an object as if they were flat, in order to get a rough account of their values. If you look at the series of objects below, you can see how we might think of a sphere in terms of planes, but this is not how we would actually go about drawing a sphere. It's just a way of thinking that helps to simplify values—and also helps us appreciate their complexity. When we draw, we block in the shadow shapes and wash them with value, but it isn't helpful to then segregate the light side into blocks, as in the images below. To actually represent the tonal transitions within the light side of a smooth, rounded object, we would use light washes of tone, rather than blocking in planes.

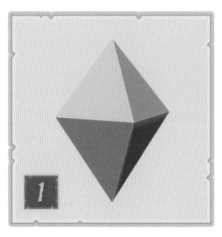
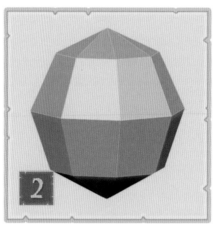

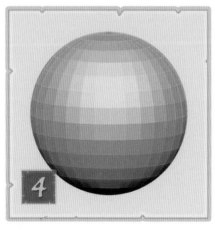
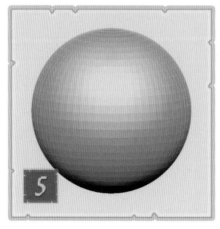

This progression of images, from the 'digital sculpting' program ZBrush, shows the progression from simple polygon to sphere, much as we've already practiced the progression from blocky to curved lines.

ZBrush operates through a 'subdivide' button: every time you press it, each polygon is divided into four. By approaching the sphere from this perspective, we can appreciate just how astonishingly complex its values really are. Looking at those last three images emphasises how difficult it is to manage all of this tonal information. This is why it's important to slow down and get our tonal structures blocked in as firmly as our shapes. Decorative flourishes come later.

I kinda like this new me actually!

The best way to think about planes is in terms of the front, back, sides, top and bottom. From these simple planes, it is much easier to go about creating believably structured values.

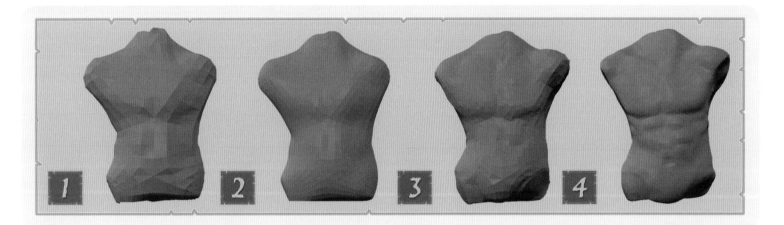

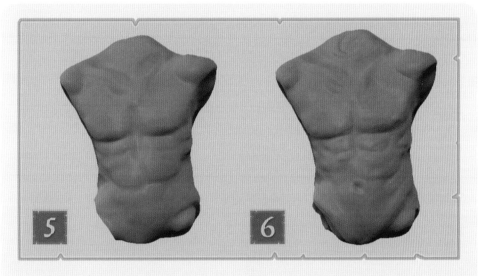

In this series of images, I've sculpted a torso using ZBrush software. This image actually began as a cube: each of its six planes was increasingly subdivided and manipulated to create the complexity you see here.

It's traditional—and true—to say that good draughtsmanship is an essential foundation for sculptors. I have also found, however, that practicing digital sculpting has improved my drawing abilities. It has helped to force me to begin from simplicity, where both form and value are concerned.

ROBOTICS

Making the most of 3D software like ZBrush can improve your grasp of drawing three-dimensional objects.

Cubes? Really? I seriously think you traded down.

Gauging Tilt in the Third Dimension

Simple fold

When it comes to studying planes, subjects don't come cheaper or more valuable than a sheet of creased paper. This can be a great little exercise to practice applying values in a consistent manner. Make some folds in a sheet of paper. Now, squint at the subject and block-in the values as best you can, choosing one value for each plane.

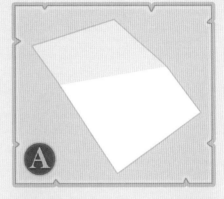

Subtle facets

We can take this a little further and attempt to capture what's really going on within these planes—when we fold paper this way, the planes that form aren't necessarily flat; there's often a slight bow to them. This allows us to begin investigations into subtle transitions of tone within each facet.

The eye is extraordinarily sensitive to differences in tone and tilt. It's not necessary, however, to record every infinitesimal degree of variation. Exercises like this help us to become sensitive and analytical observers, able to decide what truly matters about a subject, which nuances and details are important and which are irrelevant.

Random facets (1,2,3)

Remember the 'Points' exercise on page 55? We can use a similar approach to practice adding tone imaginatively. In this exercise, you will generate a form composed of random triangular planes (1). You will then imagine a light source, and shade in the faces appropriately.

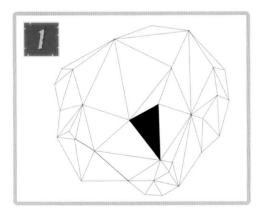

I begin by deciding where to place my heaviest shadow. This serves as my key. It doesn't have to be jet black, just a nice bold dark. This gives me a reference point.

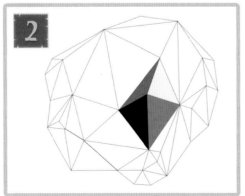

Looking at this darkness, I then decide what might be happening around it. I choose a plane facing in the opposite direction from my dark key, and I decide that the light will be hitting this plane almost directly. From this decision, I've begun to map out my shadow side and my light side. Now I can see where a midtone value would fall.

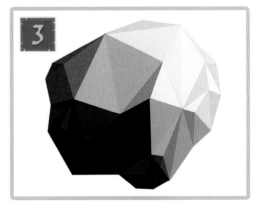

Every plane on this imaginary polygon is tilted in space, so each one will vary in value to some degree. Exercises like this help us to advance from the generalisations of shadow side/light side, and to really get a feel for the particularities of a surface.

Tonal Progressions

Now that we've considered flat planes, we are finally ready for tonal progressions. The cylinder is the ideal subject for this study because, unlike the sphere, the cylinder has a single curvature, producing one band of tonal progression. So, place the shape in front of you and let's begin.

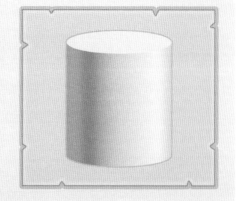

When drawing your cylinder, refer to the demonstration of ellipses on pages 114 - 116 to avoid some common pitfalls. Remember, an ellipse is a circle seen in perspective, which means it should demonstrate no flattening (A), lopsided asymmetry (B) or pointy, tapered ends (C).

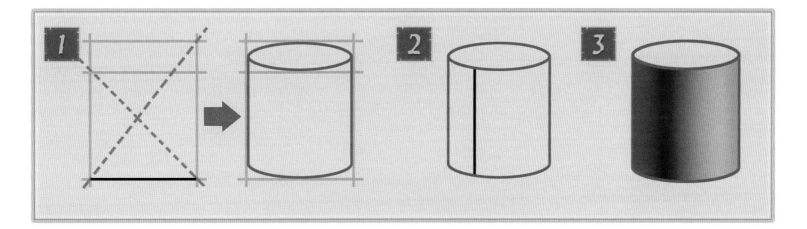

1 Block-in the shape of the cylinder, thinking of it as a rectangle to begin with. If, while making your measurements, you find that the ratio of width to height isn't a whole number (like, the width is three times the height), you can always use triangulation to find the correct proportions instead, as I have done in image (1). To triangulate, I start with a baseline. Working from the bottom left corner, I measure across to the top right corner, then record that angle. This gives me the far edge of the ellipse. Then, working from the bottom right corner, I measure across to the near edge of the top left corner. As you can see in the diagram, this marks the near and far points of the ellipse that forms the top of the cylinder.

2 With your cylinder drawn, erase your construction lines. Then draw a third vertical line on the cylinder: this line will represent the location of the core shadow, and it will be the point of departure for our washes of value as we attempt to describe the object's curvature. Your tones will be darkest here, becoming gradually lighter as you progress towards the places that are turned towards the light source.

3 For this part, my washes spread outwards from the core shadow in a vertical zigzag manner. I generally use B pencils for shadows, switching to H pencils for areas that come closest to the light. I also use washes of H pencil over the top of the shadows to break down the granules of B graphite, filling in the gaps. Our aim in this exercise is to achieve a smooth progression of values as we work from the core shadow, out into the midtones and towards the highlight.

Into the Light

I was feeling much more surefooted now that the General had guided me onto the solid planes. He seemed a lot more cheerful, too, out in the light. "It's been a while since I played my guitar," he mused. "Guido, what do you say I teach you to play a few tones?"

IX

SPECTRUM

Level Up! — Enlightened One!

When we look around, we don't see things, we see light. We see light interacting with things—bouncing off, partially absorbed, scattered, blocked—until it's reflected into our eyes, focused on our retinas, then interpreted and named by our brains. Throughout this course, we've been working to unhook the naming stage of this process, to focus instead on an intense and analytical interpretation of light interacting with matter. The study of drawing is, largely, the investigation of how light plays upon surfaces.

We have seen, by now, that shadows are really quite simple. Much more descriptive and varied, however, is the light side. This is the region where we will learn much more about the topography of our subject. The light side adds information and character, but it doesn't have to be complicated.

Whether or not things get complicated depends, as always, on our planning. How well have we developed our tonal scaffold? We constructed accurate curves by averaging out the lines' scale and tilt. Similarly, by averaging out the tones, we will create a structure which remains consistent as we add more and more values. We never want to suddenly flood our line drawing with thousands of values because, sing it with me now, "Complexity is not manageable!"

Happily, to study light and realistically describe its appearance in drawing, we only need a very basic amount of knowledge. Even better, the best way to apply this knowledge is simply. You can say so much with so little.

A picture's success does not depend upon the fanatical recording of every minute tonal shift. You can say so much with so little, and the more experienced you become, the more you will feel this to be true. In art, it's always better to imply something than hammer it home.

Looks like he found the keyboard afterall.

See the cube in the middle? This symbol represents the rays of light, of varying direction and intensity, which hit an object from every angle. Nine lines converge in the centre, representing the nine tones we will use in our studies.

Although the Tetraforce symbol above depicts a cube, it is the sphere that we will be studying now, as we advance our study of light's effects upon the three-dimensional form.

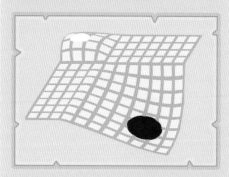

In this section of the Tetraforce we will encounter the highlight for the first time. As we have seen, dark values give the effect of receding into the distance whereas the lights have the opposite effect in that they create areas that appear to advance towards us. This is a simple and yet very useful device to consider when arranging a composition.

A · B · C

Play It

Using your imagination for a moment, tap the piano key farthest to the left. A nice rumbling, ominous growl of a sound—lovely. Now that you've heard 'black,' I want you to tap the key farthest to the right. It's a tinny little squeak of a note, this is 'white.' Next, just go flipping crazy and swipe your hand all the way from left to right. Whoof! It's a scale with too many notes, and this chaos of a sound is like the gradient from black to white (C).

If I were to ask you to use the full range of values in (C), and use them correctly, to depict an object under light in the real world, that would be like asking a beginner piano student to play a Rachmaninoff piece, after hearing it just once.

As we've already seen, there is a music to lines, and lots of miscalculated lines add up to noise. Tones can be equally musical, and if we misjudge them or use them randomly with no understanding of their relationships, the result will be just as noisy. Lots of disconnected tones will be discordant. It's better to be selective, playing a simple tune with a few well chosen, harmonious tones.

Judgement is key here. We learned the importance of judicial selection when we tried to capture a curve using straight line segments: we had to decide what was important, and what to leave out. We need to go through a similar decision making process when it comes to values.

Eyeballing values — The trouble with midtones is that they're often quite difficult to see. If you do find it difficult to see them, don't worry. Once again, squinting can help you make out these values. To carry out this check, squint at your subject and then at your drawing. Are the edges of your shadows more clearly defined than those of the subject? If so, then your midtones are probably not dark enough, and you need to go in and darken the transition, working from the cores once more into the light.

Boldness and clarity are vital in creating the illusion of three-dimensionality. Steer clear of using excessive and unnecessary values: these create confusion about a plane's orientation in space.

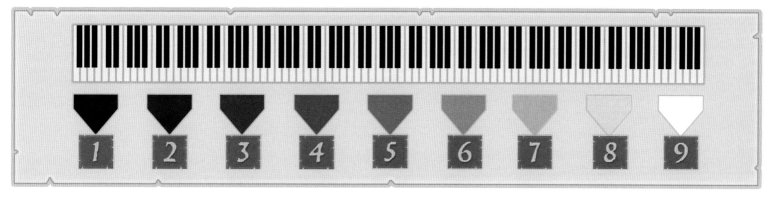

We're going to make values manageable by creating intervals: nine values will serve to represent their general area of 'visual sound.' By selecting just nine representative values, and leaving out the many shades in between, we can create a workable value structure to serve as our scaffolding.

Melody of shadow

You're probably familiar with the song 'Chopsticks,' a jolly beginner's number that can be played with just two fingers pressing two piano keys at the same time. So far, our venture into values has basically been 'Chopsticks': two tones, light and dark, which still manage to convey something recognisable and pleasing.

From three tones that represent shadow, midtone and light, we're now going to expand our palette of greys to nine tones. This is the value equivalent of the block-in stage: subdividing the long, straight lines of the constellation into smaller line segments. Just as we looked for convenient angles and landmarks, we're now looking for convenient and prominent values.

We're also looking for repeated values. Just as we found lengths or angles that were repeated throughout the form, we are now looking for areas of similar value. These are best found by squinting. Once we've found these areas of similarity, we're no longer dealing with lots of individual values; instead, we've just got a few values, repeated across the form.

Ordering your values into this compressed, generalised range is instrumental to being able to manage a potentially dizzying array of values.

1 — Dark shadow (occlusion)
2 — Half shadow (the core)
3 — Light shadow

4 — Dark halftone
5 — Light halftone

6 — Dark light
7 — Half light
8 — Light light
9 — High light

Light

Behaviour of Light

As we get ready to expand our palette of values, let's pause for a moment and consider the behaviour of light. Illumination from primary or secondary light sources can throw up all kinds of visual surprises, but nonetheless, light's behaviour isn't random—it follows certain basic rules. For our purposes, we can understand light travelling from a light source as moving in a straight line. As we can see in (A), this simple fact helps explain the shape of cast shadows.

Things get a little more complicated once the light interacts with an object. When light hits an object, it then bounces back off it. The angle at which the light made contact with the object determines the angle at which the light is reflected off it, as seen in (B).

Where the light hits the object directly, it bounces right back in the same direction, creating a highlight. If the light hits at an angle, however, it bounces off at an angle. The greater the angle, the less light we get back to us, and the darker the surface appears. This is a massive simplification of optics, of course, but it will serve for our purposes.

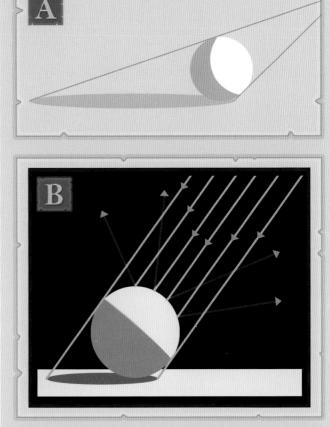

The side of the object turned towards the light is known as the front plane. Within a light source, values inform us of the geometry of objects because differently orientated surfaces receive different amounts of light.

As the surface of the object turns away from the light, then the amount of light received by planes decreases, either gradually or abruptly, until the surface falls into shadow.

When an object's surface has different curves, like the human body, the degrees of reflection vary greatly. This is one reason that life drawing is so difficult: the angle of the surface with regards to the light source is constantly changing, meaning that the tone is also always changing.

A particle AND a wave

Light is made of fascinating subatomic particles called photons. They have no mass, move faster than anything else, and behave at once like particles and like waves. They move in straight lines and in curves, simultaneously. This apparent paradox was the subject of controversy for years, among the scientific community and between the General and the Specific. It turns out that they're both right.

Here comes the sun, doo doo doo doo.

The dual nature of light is fascinating, but what relevance does it have for artists? A very direct and observable one, it turns out. The particle nature of light means it moves in a straight line, allowing it to hit an object and cast a sharp shadow, as we saw previously in (A). Ah, but there is a problem: even the sharpest shadows have slightly blurred edges. This fuzziness is due to the wave action of light, resulting in a slight spreading effect called diffraction. (Remember this when we reach the pebble demo on page 206.)

Psst... Dual nature. Told you punk!

Introverted and extroverted surfaces

A shiny object tells you a lot about its environment, whereas a matt surface gives more information about itself, its own volume and topographical detail. Matt surfaces are rough, meaning that light reflecting off of them is scattered in lots of different directions at once, resulting in a diffuse light. The appearance of this diffuse, scattered light on the object is known as 'form light.' Light shining onto a smooth, glossy surface, however, is reflected directly back, producing a highlight.

When light hits a modern mirror (C), the light is reflected right back, so that the angle of reflection is equal to the angle from which the light hit it (the angle of incidence). When light hits a rough texture, such as our toothy paper surface, it's scattered (D). The reason you don't see a reflection on an unlaminated paper is that light is being ping-ponged off it in all directions. This is what makes paper such an excellent medium for the printed word: you can read, even in direct light, without having a glare of concentrated light shoot right back at you.

The contrast between these two objects is obvious, but what is not so apparent is that there are midtones on the glossy vase just as on the matt stone. Squinting at these objects can aid in seeing the subtle mid-values.

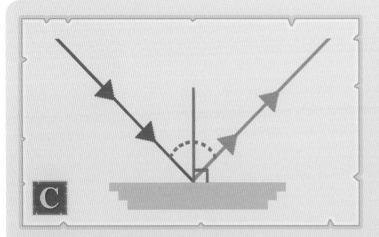

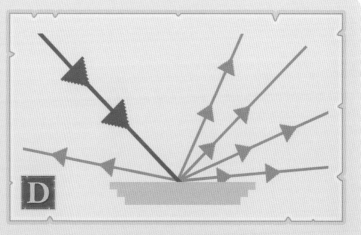

As we know from the Shadow Observatory, light can be either primary or secondary. Primary light is emitted from a light source, such as the Sun or a lamp. Secondary light is light reflected off another object—the Moon's light, for instance, is secondary. We already know that the angle of incidence, the angle at which the light hits the object, determines the angle of reflection. In the case of a smooth surface (C), the angle of incidence and reflection are equal, and the object will appear shiny. If the surface is rough (D), the light is actually hitting a surface which, rather than having one angle (and feeling smooth), has lots of tiny little different angles all at once. The irregular surface scatters light in multiple different directions, meaning that the reflection of light will not be nearly so concentrated and won't appear nearly so bright.

Yoo hoo! Over here! This dark, dead people filled dungeon won't explore itself.

Light can be pushy

Although light has no mass, it has a fair bit of momentum, meaning that when it hits an object, it actually pushes it—just a teeny, tiny bit, exerting half a billionth of a kilogram of pressure. Therefore, on a sunny day, a city will weigh ever so slightly more than it does at night. Because light travels even faster in a vacuum (299,792,458m/s) than it does through Earth's atmosphere (298,925,574m/s), light pushes with a bit more oomph in space. Taking advantage of this, NASA has begun equipping space craft with sails, to catch the gusts of light coming from the Sun. None of which has any direct bearing on our drawing, except, perhaps, to emphasise the point that light has a genuine impact.

Direction, Intensity, Quality

Lighting direction has a great impact on how a subject is perceived, and we must take lighting into account when arranging our compositions. The phrase 'seeing something in a different light' acknowledges the emotional tenor of light on an image. Lighting also determines how easily an image can be read. For best effect and greatest legibility, artists have traditionally chosen to use a light source in either of the upper corners.

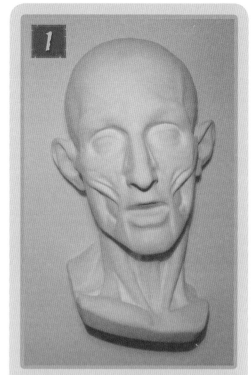

Light hitting this bust from the front results in flattened forms.

Front lighting

Front lighting has the effect of bleaching and flattening out a subject, reducing its interest. This is because, as we have seen, a light shone directly on a subject will tend to bounce right back at the viewer. Lighting from this angle means that the shadows, which could provide a sense of roundedness, are all out of sight.

Side lighting

Creating an image which is half in light, half in shadow, side lighting can be very dramatic. The trouble is, it splits the image in half, which goes against the rules of composition. In general, it's best to avoid compositions which are split in two, because they are too evenly balanced. Compositional rules are only ever guidelines, however, and there may be instances where side lighting serves your purposes.

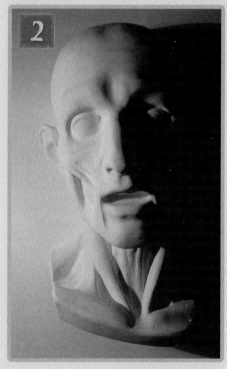

Side lighting creates a stark division in the picture.

3

Overhead lighting

Because of the position of the Sun and overhead lights, this is the lighting we're most used to. This lighting casts certain shadow shapes on the human face, but these are familiar to us. This is quite an everyday and comforting lighting setup, one that keeps an image comfortably within the constraints of normality—unlike, for example, the sense of unreality created by upward lighting. Be aware, however, that overhead lighting can have undesirable effects, such as casting a dark shadow under the nose.

Bleaching out

Consider the strength as well as the position of your light source. A powerful light source can create dramatic effects, with sharp contrasts and well defined shadow shapes. However, it can also potentially bleach out the forms of your subject, creating a glare that destroys definition and nuance.

 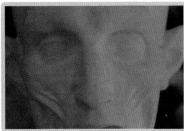

Baroque

The Baroque setup puts a twist on everyday overhead lighting. By putting the light in the upper left hand corner, we create an image that is read from left to right, the same way that Westerners would read a text.

Light shining down at a 45 degree angle is the setup most commonly chosen by artists. In this arrangement, the light is placed slightly in front of the subject, to avoid side lighting. This places about two-thirds of the subject in light, with one-third in shadow. This proportion of light and shadow is optimal for revealing form, giving a sense of solidity and creating interest.

(4) This is the most common lighting setup for portraiture, as it makes the most of the subject. It creates a pleasing proportion of shadow and light, with about one third of the image in shadow.

Baroque lighting brings out the subject's character through a dynamic composition, making it easy to see why this has become such a common lighting choice for portraiture. It's worth noting, however, that some masters of the past departed from this convention: Rembrandt favoured side lighting, while Van Dyke preferred front lighting.

If you've ever seen beautiful light transfigure an ugly town, you know the power of light to elevate the most unsightly or mundane subjects. This is what makes light such an important consideration for artists. As powerful as good lighting is, bad lighting has just as great an effect—just think of the horrifying visions captured in the mirror of a spot-lit changing room. Bad lighting can ruin the most wonderful subject. Make sure your lighting serves your subject rather than doing it an injustice.

Fluorescence

Fluorescent lighting is terrible for drawing, but, ironically, it's very common in schools and studios. In a room brightly illuminated with fluorescent strip lighting, the light comes from everywhere at once: the effect is flat and uninformative.

Shadows are vital in describing a form, and the direction of light and shadow creates a kind of narrative flow within an image, revealing how forms flow. Strip lighting disrupts this narrative, producing a disorderly image, devoid of informative, consistent shadows. In such a situation, important information is lost and critical landmarks become unreadable.

Character and personality can become lost in bad lighting; it is distracting. Forms can be broken up and made hard to read.

> Choose lighting conditions that serve your subject and your theme. Angle your light in a way that highlights important structures and casts interesting shadows.

White card

One trick you can use to enhance your lighting is a reflective white card. I used a white card, positioned off camera, to the right, in the previous example of Baroque lighting. This amplifies the effect of the reflected light, helping to reveal form all the more.

 Insufficient light — If you don't have enough light, the important aspects of your form will be less visible. Dim lighting flattens out forms and obscures much of what makes a subject special.

 Too much light — Too much light obscures almost as much as too little light. An excessively bright light source also produces intense reflected light, and all this glare will bleach your subject and reduce its shadows.

 Unfocused light — Undirected, ambient light, such as you get on a cloudy day or with fluorescent bulbs, casts few useful shadows. It does nothing to promote or distinguish your subject's character. By contrast, strongly focused directional light throws a subject into dramatic relief, especially when set against a dark backdrop. It can serve as a spotlight to emphasise your focal point.

Lit from below

Light from below is extremely unusual, and it has the effect of rendering objects unfamiliar, creating an unnatural, unnerving feeling. Think of the classic pose for telling scary stories: a torch held under the chin, casting a mask of weird shadows over the face. You're unlikely to use upwards lighting often, but it is perfect for images which call for an otherworldly, mysterious or haunting atmosphere.

Taking note

As well as taking a mental note of the position and angle of the light source, it can be helpful to make a physical note in the top corner of your paper. You can use a cone shape like the ones shown below.

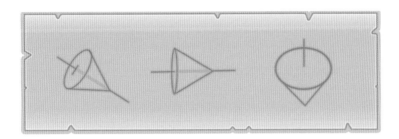

Even people we know well become unrecognisable with a such an extreme change in lighting that creates shapes unfamiliar to us. In this way upward lighting reveals unfamiliarity which is quite alienating.

When we are properly aware of the light—its position, character and distance—we become able to consciously and deliberately construct the light in our image, rather than simply copying what we see. We gain a more active, structural control over light and shadow.

Human Écorché

The rather strange looking cast featured in this section, by Jean-Antoine Houden, is a type of model called the 'écorché,' from the French meaning 'to flay,' and they represent subjects with skin removed. As well as looking rather ghoulish, the écorché can inform our understanding of anatomical structures. A basic knowledge of anatomy is extremely useful for an artist, as it helps us to understand why bodies behave as they do, as well as what causes a body's many lumps and bumps. Knowing the human body inside and out can be especially beneficial should we wish to develop characters purely from our imaginations. The full medical écorché is mostly useful for the study of muscular anatomy, while a white écorché is good for understanding a body's planar geometry.

As learning resources, they don't come cheap, so do be prepared for a hefty price tag. If you purchase cheaper casts, be aware that you may end up with a copy of a copy of a copy, many generations removed from the original. Such casts make for poor and inaccurate references, with a good chance of major distortions.

Learning from Pebbles

The life of an artist is full of drama. The sequence of photographs on the right, for instance, is the product of an afternoon I spent waiting for clouds to move away from the Sun. Over the course of this action-packed few hours, I was able to document the changing effects of clouded and direct sunlight from a single window upon a single pebble.

Although you don't have to go to these hair-raising extremes, it is important for all of us to become naturalists of light, noticing what light does in various different situations. Leonardo's journals, for instance, are full of observations about the behaviour of light . . .

"When the Sun is covered by clouds, objects are less conspicuous, because there is little difference between the light and shade of the trees and the buildings being illuminated by the brightness of the atmosphere which surrounds the objects in such a way that the shadows are few, and these few fade away so that their outline is lost in haze."

Sharp and diffuse

So what can we learn from my epic afternoon? The edge of a cast shadow is well-defined with a hard edge in bright sunlight, but it becomes ever more blurry and diffuse as cloud cover increases. The darkness of the shadow also varies dramatically.

As the Sun comes out, the shadows darken, the reflected light becomes brighter, the core shadow sharpens. The highlight brightens so much that the right edge of the pebble is nearly lost, fading into the similarly coloured background.

> Ignore her.
> A few minutes
> spent observing is
> very important.

Easier Than Spheres

It's your turn now to study the noble pebble. There's a wonderful simplicity to this study because, unlike with spheres and other geometric forms, you can't get the shape wrong. Freed from this pressure, we can instead concentrate on studying the laws of light and shadow. This demo was produced in about 10 minutes on scrap printer paper.

 Cheap low quality paper such as this doesn't allow for a smooth textured pebble, which explains the dark dots on the final image.

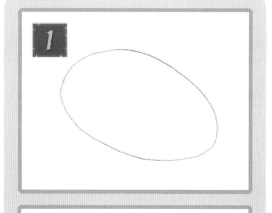

 Using a single line, lightly draw an oval like the one shown here. Don't be precious about the shape: it doesn't matter here. Use a mid-range grade of pencil (F, HB or B). Make the oval about 5cm across—the smaller the study, the easier this exercise is.

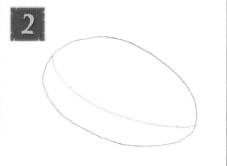

 Draw a crescent-like shape across the oval, as shown here. This serves as your core shadow marker. Again, try not to draw too slowly or be too perfectionist. Ideally, you should do a few of these pebble studies, and you'll get better results if you allow yourself a certain abandon.

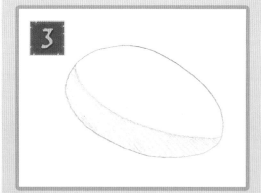

 Still with the mid-range pencil and using the zigzag approach, wash in a consistent single tone across the lower crescent shape. This hatched in area becomes our shadow shape, creating a distinction between light and dark.

Hatch over the shadow shape, this time going in a different direction, creating a cross-hatch.

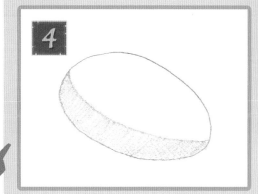

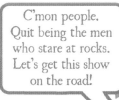 C'mon people. Quit being the men who stare at rocks. Let's get this show on the road!

5 Go back to the core shadow line. Beginning with a 2B, start hatching upwards from the core shadow, letting your lines follow the curvature of the pebble. Your hatches should become gradually lighter as you move upwards towards the highlight. Finish these hatches off with a 2H.

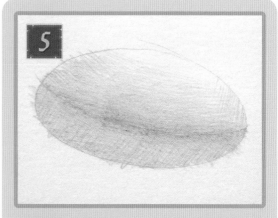

6 Return to the core shadow line, and begin hatching downwards into the shadows. Use a 2B and curving lines. Don't shade all the way down to the bottom of the pebble, though, as this underside will be catching some reflected light.

Go ahead and place the cast shadow edge now. This is represented by yet another crescent line, drawn in one motion outside the oval.

7 Using a 2B, cross-hatch a flat layer of tone to your cast shadow. Using a sharp 3B, draw a dark line where the bottom of your pebble meets the cast shadow. This will serve as the beginning of your occlusion shadow, the area of darkest shadow, places that direct or reflected light hasn't been able to reach.

8 Using a 2B, hatch outwards from the dark line into the cast shadow.

Looks a bit grainy. How about we do some brushing to smooth that out.

DRAW LIKE A BOSS

9 Continue hatching across the cast shadow, using the occlusion shadow as your starting point.

(The paper I am using for this tiny study is the cheapest possible, so the tiny black dots where I have broken the paper tooth are starting to show themselves in my cast shadow now.)

10 Finish hatching in a consistent layer of tone across your cast shadow, remembering to keep it darkest in the occlusion zone. In this image, you can see that my cast shadow has become much darker than the shadow on my pebble, so that my pebble no longer makes sense. This means I need to go back and darken it, to redress the balance between the object and its shadow.

11 Returning to the core shadow, add a dark line to enhance the core shadow if it has become obscured. From this marker, again work downwards into the form shadow. Does the reflected light need to be toned down a little to match the darkness of the shadow? If so, you can add a light wash over the entire shadow side to create unity.

12 Go back to the edges of your core shadow with a 2H: washing lightly outwards, create a subtle sense of diffusion around these edges.

Add any final touches to the pebble itself. For instance, I decided that the bottom edge of the pebble shouldn't be so clearly defined, because of the way it's curving under, so I've darkened this to give a sense of a roundness that continues underneath.

Next, we'll look at an alternate method of drawing pebbles, using our eraser in a creative rather than purely corrective capacity. This is a great way of generating textures and random shapes.

It's more important that you master generating progressions with just the pencil first!

 **W**OODEN DOOR

 Using a 3B, apply a first layer of hatching. Don't use too much pressure.

 Going in different directions, add a second and third layer of cross-hatching, again with medium pressure.

 Pass over your hatching with a hog's hair brush to fill in any gaps.

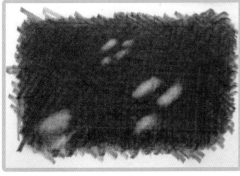

4 Now begin the process of pressing your kneadable eraser into the graphite, revealing shapes of varying texture and brightness.

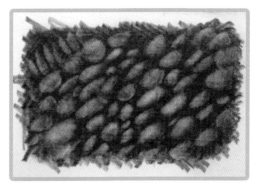

5 Repeat this process of dabbing until a mass of forms emerge. Because you've used a variety of different pressures, these stones will all look different.

6 To finish up, use a sharpened 4B to refine some of the edges and deepen the darkest shadows.

Here you can see this technique used more extensively in a larger drawing of an outdoor scene. This is a fun exercise, which allows us to achieve a great effect with relatively little effort. It serves as a nice little break before we gear up for a more intense session of observational drawing. It's time to put away our erasers for the moment. All we'll need now is pencil, paper and a mug (and maybe a second mug, for coffee).

There's usually more than one way to get the job done!

Traditional Study of Light

As we advance to drawing the sphere, the greatest challenge will be maintaining consistency in value. A sphere is absolutely regular and uniform, a form which is always turning, and always turning by exactly the same degree in every direction at once. With the cylinder, we only had to achieve a tonal progression along one curved plane. With the sphere, we must achieve that tonal progression in all directions.

For this reason, it's important to keep things simple and to progress gradually. Allow smaller shadows or tones to merge with larger ones. Begin with broad areas of simple, flat tones. Refine and differentiate these little by little. Don't try to capture everything at once. There is also a technical challenge to managing hatches on a curve. Rather than trying to hatch along the entire shape at once, work in smaller sections. Keep your hatching loose so that these sections can better mesh together. Dark patches will emerge where your sections intersect, but it should be possible to even these out as you go. If not, you can always use an eraser.

In each tiny area of a rounded object there is a different value. It is not necessary to describe every one of them in order to convey the idea of roundness.

I'm not sure there's much to be learned by drawing the circle of the sphere. For that reason we're going to skip drawing the sphere itself and jump right into toning this shape. The shortcut for doing this is as follows.

A Begin by tracing a circle around your mug or cup with an F grade pencil.

B Next, move the mug slightly towards the upper left (the direction of our light source in this exercise). Trace a crescent shape as shown here; this represents your core shadow.

C Lastly, draw an oval to serve as the edge of the cast shadow. With these three steps, you have set yourself up for this study of values on a sphere.

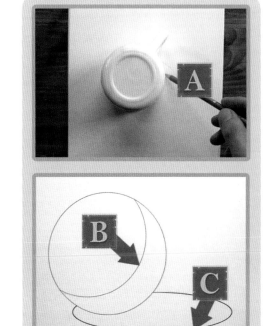

In this exercise you should aim to keep the values you place on this sphere to a minimum at first. Use just enough tones to convey the idea of a sphere without creating confusion. As you continue to study the behaviour of light, you will find yourself becoming aware of a far wider array of tones than you ever noticed before. This is a heightened sensitivity which comes through focused practice. It may, however, feel daunting to try to put this awareness into practice. It's not necessary—or even possible—to capture the full range of tones you perceive on an object right away.

 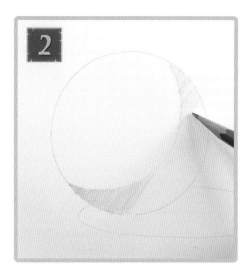 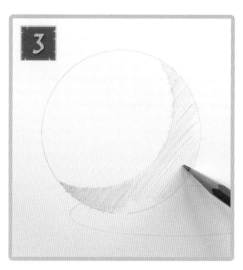

(1 - 3) Hatching in curved areas of shadow can be tricky. I begin at the bottom left of the shadow shape, then move to the top right. Finally, I merge these two areas of shadow. Working this way is more comfortable than trying to achieve a crescent-shaped wash in one pass.

 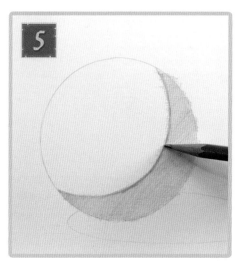 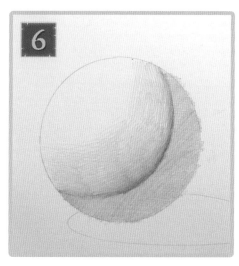

(4- 6) Having cross-hatched the shadow shape, without being too concerned about tidiness, I then move on to making my core shadow more pronounced. This dark line will become the starting point for my shading from now on.

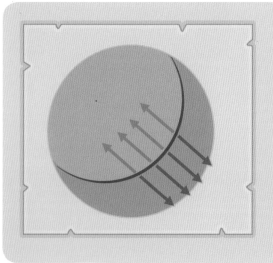

Away From the Core

The core shadow line always serves as a kind of base camp from which our hatching expeditions start out. Beginning at this darkest point, the hatches become gradually lighter as they wrap around to meet the highlight on the light side and the reflected light on the dark side.

The arrows on the diagram do not indicate the direction of your hatching lines themselves—after the initial tonal block-in, your hatches should follow and describe the curvature of the object. Instead, the arrows indicate the ways in which your hatching work should progress, moving outwards from the core shadow.

(7- 9) My washes fade out as they approach the place where I think the highlight will be. I've made this assessment based on the position of the cast shadow that I've roughed in. Once I've wrapped my hatches around the light side, I return to the core shadow and begin growing my hatches outwards into the form shadow.

(10 — 11) I finished this study by blocking in the tone of the cast shadow, beginning with the occlusion shadow right under the sphere and working outwards, gradually achieving an even tone. I then returned to my form shadow, darkening it to coordinate with the cast shadow. I then toned the background using a mask and some powdered graphite (a technique we'll discuss later). Finally, I picked out a highlight using a kneaded eraser. I did this as a timed exercise to prevent myself from becoming too precious. You may find that you want a little more than 10 minutes, simply because your hand has not yet become so practiced in making hatching motions. You may be more comfortable giving yourself 30 minutes.

Drawing Conclusions

Check your reflected lights — Make sure your reflected lights aren't too bright. This is quite an easy mistake to make.

Darken your cores if needed — Go over your core shadow a few times with a 3B, just to make sure its definition hasn't been lost during the process of darkening everything else. Some artists choose to exaggerate the value of the reflected lights and core shadows. This makes an image easier to read the image, but it sacrifices realism in favour of design. In fields such as concept design, this is a highly worthwhile trade-off, since one of the main goals of the graphic designer is to achieve pictures that communicate a message quickly.

Highlight

Speck of Light

Highlights are a powerful element in our visual language. With just a speck of white, we can communicate wetness or polish. The highlight draws immediate attention, in much the same way as the deepest dark values. This means that the placement of the highlight is an important compositional consideration: will the highlight direct attention towards your focal point, or could it become a distraction?

Highlights are not always white: the highlight's tone is a combination of the colour of the light source and the local colour of the object itself. The appearance of a highlight also depends on the texture of the object. For example, on human skin, a highlight will seem to be more fused with the form light, whereas on water, it will almost seem to float on the surface, as if detached.

Number and placement

Placing highlights is an important matter of judgement: does the highlight serve your focal point and your composition? Sometimes it may be best to omit the highlight completely. As well as placement, we also need to consider number: if a picture has too many highlights, the eye, dazzled, won't know where to land. Think of a starry sky: it's beautiful, but as a composition, it's lousy. There's no one point to draw the eye.

Speaking of skies, when drawing an outdoor scene, we need to think of how to deal with the Sun in our picture. Although it will often actually be the brightest point in an image, we don't necessarily want it to take the lead in our composition. The same, in fact, is true of any light source. One way of portraying sunlight but not the Sun is simply to position it behind the viewer, as it were, with shadows aimed off into the distance.

> Something tells me that you're building up to saying that specks of light are bad things. I don't care. I think they're awesome.

It is a wonderful thing in drawing that, by including a highlight, we can give the appearance of wetness or shininess on what is just a paper surface.

It is the planes on an object's surface that are oriented directly towards the viewer's eye that will be seen to emit the highlight.

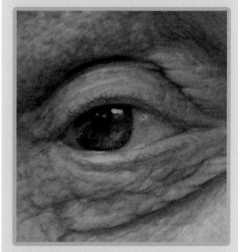

The highlight is a reflection of the light source, and the more polished the surface, the more apparent the reflection. You can see this very clearly by looking at a soap bubble or eyeball.

> Need... water...

Premature highlight = necromancy

Highlights should always be left till the final stages of a drawing, like a tiny, powerful full stop. They give a sense of completion, of realism and liveliness. In portraiture, for example, they can be found in the sitter's eye, or on the tip of the nose, where the addition of a brilliant dab of light value can enhance the feeling of realism. A specular shock of white close to a jet black iris confirms the eye both as a wet thing and as a place of interest.

> The highlight is one of the easiest things to put in, so why not wait a while before placing it in the picture?

HIGHLIGHT

Premature - A highlight placed too early can have a bad effect on unfinished work.

For all of these reasons, the highlight's effect can be terrible if it's deployed too early. For one thing, the highlight placed early is very distracting for the artist. While working with one in place, your mind keeps telling you "You're all done; it's finished now!" Sometimes we want that feeling, especially if a picture's not going so well. At first it may seem to offer a successful fix, hiding mistakes and giving the impression of a finished piece of work. This illusion is only temporary, however. Adding highlights to a drawing that isn't going to plan will not save it. A highlight has the effect of making a nearly complete work come alive—and is that really what we want to do with our seriously misshapen works? It's best not to animate the dead.

Highlights take a moment to make, and they're finished almost as soon as they're begun. They should be saved and savoured as one of the most satisfying elements in drawing, a treat we earn through all our hard work. They're almost effortless to make, yet they have such power. Resist them until the time is right, however, or you will find that they cause many problems while solving none.

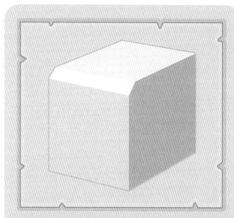

One interesting use of highlights is to create rounded or dulled edges, as we see above. Objects with totally sharp edges can look quite unnatural, so a highlight along the edge can add a glint of realism.

Conservation of ultra-white

Now, in the case of drawing something that you know has an area of highlight that you absolutely need to keep white, then it is a good idea to close off that area with a line to indicate the place that you do not want any graphite to contaminate. In the next demonstration, we'll learn how to draw a water droplet, which requires an ultra-light highlight to create the illusion of wetness. We need to keep this area pristine: if we erased to create the highlight, it would still be a little dull, and that just won't do for this subject matter.

Making water? Great!

I begin with a basic round shape for the water drop and another oval shape to signify the location of the highlight. I must try to keep this a stark white for now.

With the line-work in place, I begin by in the darkest place on the water drop, which is right next to the highlight. I use a 3B pencil to create clear, sharp contrast with the highlight.

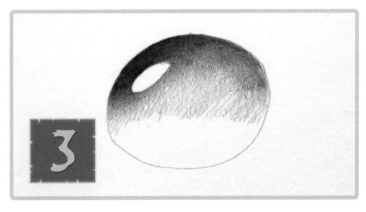

With the 3B, I outline the darkest part of the water drop's shadow. I then extend the shadow outwards from the outline to produce the beginning of the water drop's shadow.

Continuing to work downwards, lightly applying the dark 3B pencil.

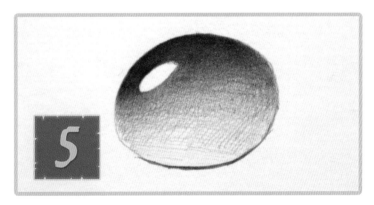

I draw a line under the droplet as a starting point for creating a cast shadow.

Working outwards from that occlusion shadow, I extend the shadow.

I roughly hatch in a background to begin placing the droplet within an environment. My next task is to remove appearance of pencil grain within the drop; otherwise the illusion will be unsuccessful.

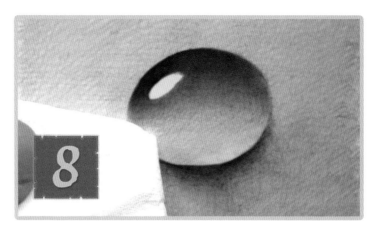

For this task, I use a sable brush and toilet roll—we'll discuss blenders next. The background in the picture should keep its grain—if I blend everything in the scene, I will lose contrast, and the effect will be less striking.

This droplet casts light as well as shadow: I use my kneaded eraser to add a burst of light within the cast shadow, focused by the shape of the water.

Lastly, I go in with a colour shaper to add some finishing touches. The colour shaper blends by smearing the graphite in a way which replicates the smooth look of water. I also added some wood-grain lines to the background, allowing these to show through, distorted, in the droplet.

Nifty distortion details

Looking through water creates a magnification effect, as shown in the final image. Including this distortion of the background surface texture adds another level of realism. This is a great exercise for practicing seamless tonal transitions. This also means that it's a great chance to let blenders do what they do best: removing pencil grain and creating smooth tonal progressions.

Grainy Texture

Once we've established our values, we're ready to start really bringing some realism to our drawings. Pencil grain can be a major barrier here, because it signals so clearly that a drawing is a drawing. This is especially true with subjects, such as water or clouds, that really require smoothness. Blenders will help us pull off the illusion. By removing pencil grain, blenders help a viewer suspend disbelief. As well as removing grain, blenders can create a blurred effect, which can add a sense of depth.

There are a range of blenders available, and which ones we choose will depend on the size of the area we're working on, as well as the particular textural effects we're trying to create. In the next pages, we'll explore these tools in detail. Once you've become skilled in the fundamentals of drawing—building constellations, creating accurate shadow maps and plotting values—I recommend you get hold of as many blending tools as possible, so that you can play around and conduct experiments with them.

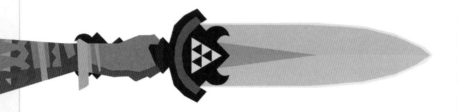

Crisp edges and sharp details are usually the province of the focal point. Any secondary components should therefore be given a slight blur: making them a little bit indistinct better promotes the focal point. And this is where blenders really come in useful.

Index Finger

Who's that climbing out of the sand? It's that Sebum guy! Yeah, he's still a threat. You should never, ever use your finger to blend. Not only is the effect rubbish, it transfers oil to the paper which will be impossible to remove.

This oil will leave a noticeable stain that gets even more obvious if you try to generate a subtle gradation of tones over a sebum-infused surface. Nevertheless, the urge to be hands-on when creating is very natural, and you can achieve a similar feel by using colour shapers, without the unwanted oiliness.

Yuck — This is not the effect we're aiming for. Let's leave finger-blending far, far behind us and look instead at ways of generating a much more pleasing blended effect.

Level I Blender

Tissue Wrap

Toilet roll and kitchen paper towels wrapped around the index finger can make for decent blenders. Paper towels blend well without absorbing too much graphite. Because paper towels often have an embossed pattern on them, they may also add a certain textural effect. Be careful that the tissue you have selected for blending doesn't contain any lotion, as this could leave behind unwanted residue.

Both toilet tissue and paper towels are very good for large scale blurring. I often use them in making objects in the distance far more vague, as shown in this misty winter scene to the right.

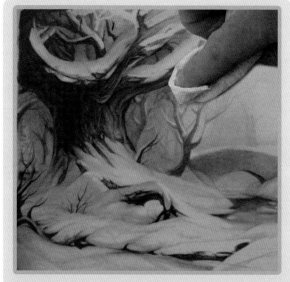

It is also possible to apply graphite powder to your drawing with tissue, but be careful not to polish the graphite too much, as this will cause burnishing and produce an unsightly shine.

Level II Blenders

Blending Stump

Also known as a torchon, the blending stump is basically a very tight roll of paper pulp, with a point at each end that can be used to blur elements of your drawing. The stump drags graphite across a surface leaving behind an even, dull patch of tone. As you use the stump, its point will gradually become more and more fuzzy, which means it will produce a less precise, more feathered effect. This can actually be of benefit if you're trying to create broader stokes. You can purchase blending stumps in a wide variety of sizes, from very broad to very thin, making it possible to achieve excellent precision.

One very useful thing about blending stumps is that it's possible to load them up with graphite. If used for blending, a fully loaded stump will remove a lot less graphite than a fresh blending stump. The loaded stump can also be used to deposit graphite throughout your drawing. The result is a nice fibrous mark, quite a painterly effect, and very different from a grainy pencil stroke, adding some nice variety to things.

Designate blenders for each tool

A note of caution: if you use a combination of mark-making tools, such as charcoal, graphite, the special 7B and 8B, carbon pencils or white chalk in your drawings, be sure to have a separate stump for each of these mediums, as they don't mix very well. This rule applies to all your blenders, from chamois to brushes. Make sure each medium has its own set of designated blenders—ideally, marked—because getting them mixed up could wreak havoc on your work.

As you begin experimenting with blenders, you may find them a little intoxicating. Don't let their power go to your head: blending effects are no substitute for solid pencil work.

Although they may at first seem to offer a short-cut, blending does not remove the need for producing accurate tonal transitions with the pencil. Achieving properly distributed tones, which clearly describe the topography of the subject, is the province of the pencil—the stump and other blenders only finish things off.

Just as we spent time practicing with the pencil, spend time engaging with your blending tools. Explore them as blenders and as mark-makers. Get to know the range of effects at your disposal—you will then know what is possible, what works, and you'll be ready to use it when the occasion arises. This is how I discovered so many of the techniques and tricks I use: by applying different pencils and tools to different paper surfaces.

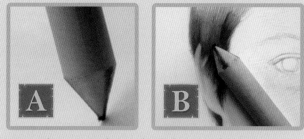

You can be precise and surgical with the point of the stump (A), or you can use the side of the point (B) for a large sweeping blend. The side of the stump is good for large patches that need to be blurred. It's always good to be on the look out for tricks like this to help you work more efficiently—I sometimes find that I get stuck in unexamined habits that end up wasting time and sapping my energy.

It's possible to clean dirty old stumps, either using a kneadable eraser or by filing it with an emery board to get back to a fresh, white tip.

Necromancy +8

Just like highlights, blenders should only be deployed when a drawing is nearly finished. Not only can they give a superficial sheen of completeness to unfinished works, if used excessively, they can also have the unfortunate effect of sucking the life right out of a drawing. Use blenders to complement and complete your hatching process, while being aware that they are never a substitute for thinking through your values properly.

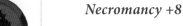

Tortillon

The stump and tortillon are often mistakenly assumed to be the same tool. When you hold them up against each other, though, they're actually pretty easy to tell apart: the blending stump is a double-pointed solid roll of paper, the tortillon is a single-pointed hollow tube of blotting or cartridge paper. Their true differences are best understood through experimentation. Although you can get tortillons at art stores, they're extremely simple to roll for yourself.

2

Because the tortillon has a longer tip, its sides can be used more effectively. Unfortunately, however, the tortillon's construction is far less sturdy than the blending stump's, meaning that they don't last nearly as long. Although it's less solid, the tortillon's surface is harder, because it's made from paper rather than pulp. This means that they don't blend as effectively as stumps. They do have their uses, however. They're good for softening edges, as well as for blurring and generally removing definition—this is useful if you want to push something into the background, either literally, by creating the appearance of distance, or figuratively, by making an element seem less important within a composition.

Making a tortillon

All kinds of papers can blend, so do some experimenting. You can even use common cartridge paper, although it's a little hard for this purpose. You'll get a better effect from softer paper, and a soft, thin paper such as blotting paper is the easiest to roll and use. If you have a used, store-bough tortillon lying around, you can always unroll it to help you understand its construction.

To make your own, you just need a sheet of paper, a ruler, a wooden skewer and some tape.

1 Grab a sheet of paper and cut it to measure 3 x 6 inches.

2 Measure to 3.5 inches on a long side and 1 inch on a short side. Draw a diagonal between these points, and cut along that line.

3 The point marked (x) will form your tip. Take a thin wooden skewer and begin rolling, as shown. Roll the paper about five times just to get it nice and curled, prepared for proper rolling.

The most important thing, when rolling, is to make sure the angle of the tip is right. If it's too steep, the tip will be too weak. If it's too shallow, a tip won't form at all. Once you've managed a decent tip, take some tape and secure the newly made tortillon tightly.

Alternative blenders

You may want to try some less traditional blending tools, especially for large patches. Makeup applicators, cotton buds, and powder puffs can all be used for your drawing as well as your face. Do be sure to test them first before you apply them to your drawing, as they may contain oils or perfumes that could damage your drawing surface.

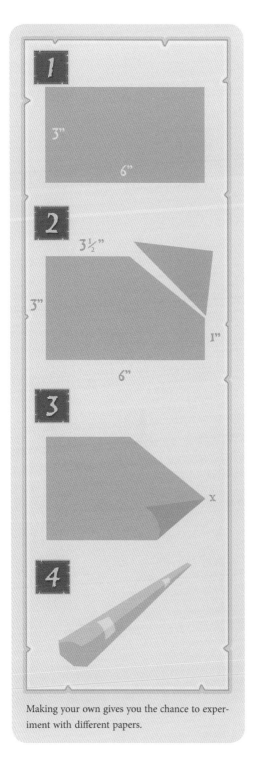

Making your own gives you the chance to experiment with different papers.

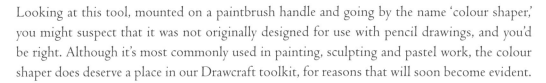

You Found the Colour Shaper!

Looking at this tool, mounted on a paintbrush handle and going by the name 'colour shaper,' you might suspect that it was not originally designed for use with pencil drawings, and you'd be right. Although it's most commonly used in painting, sculpting and pastel work, the colour shaper does deserve a place in our Drawcraft toolkit, for reasons that will soon become evident.

Varied Tips

There are many different kinds of colour shapers available, with a wide variety of shapes and sizes, ranging from the very hard to very soft. Some have chiselled heads, letting you pull broad washes of graphite all over the surface, creating large, textural washes. Some have rounded edges, creating a less defined mark. Others are sharply pointed, perfect for dealing with small areas and fine details. There is a colour shaper tip for just about any mark you may wish to make. The blending capabilities of this tool are absolutely marvellous, making them essential for anyone who wishes to achieve hyper-realism.

Although you can get huge colour shapers, I rarely use this tool for mass blending—used over too large an area, it can produce quite an ugly effect. The best thing about colour shapers is the way they allow you to, well, shape the graphite, making it easy to blend around corners. There's something about the flexibility of a colour shaper which makes it feel a lot like smudging with your fingers, without the dangers of the dreaded Sebum.

Shaping graphite

The colour shaper allows us to move graphite around in a way that blending stumps cannot. It also produces a much smoother blend than the stump, without the fibrous quality. Also, while the colour shaper does collect graphite, allowing us to deposit it elsewhere, it doesn't actually absorb any graphite, unlike blending stumps. The silicone heads of colour shapers are durable and easy to clean. I've yet to wear one out.

The colour shaper can also be used to make marks of a kind that the pencil alone cannot achieve. Loaded up with graphite, the colour shaper can be used to pull streaks of graphite across the page without leaving any grain. This is an effect which is particularly useful for edges, creating a painterly effect. Shapers are also great for capturing the very subtle tonal nuances found in the lighter areas of a picture.

The sort of edge that the colour shaper produces is less fibrous than the stump. The shaper gives a smooth blend to the edge which has a smeared quality to it.

You can easily clean the colour shaper by wiping it on a clean sheet of paper or rag (or your jeans). If you want to make sure it's really clean, you can use water. Just make sure it's absolutely dry before you let it near your drawing again.

Chamois Leather

High quality chamois leather (pronounced 'shammy') is a wonderful blender for both large and small scale work. I like using it to blur large areas, creating a sense of atmosphere. This soft cloth also works as a subtle eraser, removing excess graphite, even over large areas.

The colour shaper can be dragged along sharp edges (A) to create a blur (B). This removes unnaturally clean edges, creating a slightly blurry indistinctness which looks much more realistic. It can also be helpful in changing the depth hierarchy of objects: the more indistinct an object is, the further back it is pushed.

If there's a big, dark area which looks too bold or stark, applying the chamois will give it a far subtler appearance. Perhaps there's an area of a drawing which has become too detailed and busy: it can be simplified and given a certain ambiguity by passing over it with the chamois. In the same way, the chamois is good at pushing things back into the distance, making them seem lighter and more blurred.

There are lots of different qualities of chamois cloth available. Having experimented extensively, I would definitely recommend investing in a natural, more expensive chamois leather. This will produce a far better blending effect than the cheap, synthetic kinds that people get to use on their cars. The cheaper chamois can leave weird white streaks on your work. As with everything, always test new material on a scrap piece of paper before applying it to your drawing.

Folding the rag to a point, as shown here, increases precision. You can also use a felt pad to simulate the effects of the chamois. One of the joys of blending tools is finding new ones which suit a particular purpose or produce a certain special effect.

Over-blending with chamois

As with all blenders, there's a danger of applying chamois leather too soon, too broadly or too heavily. The chamois is not a shortcut to awesome blending—if used in place of hatching, the effect can be quite crude. Chamois also tends to be quite a broad blender, making it easy to apply too liberally. This is one reason why I like folding it into a point. Chamois also removes quite a lot of graphite compared to other blenders, so much so that, if you know you're going to use a chamois on a certain area, it can be useful to go a little darker than necessary. Otherwise, the chamois can leave the drawing looking rather washed out.

Two things are happening when chamois passes over graphite. It's blended smooth, but it also becomes lighter as the chamois removes some of the graphite (B).

Level IV Blenders

Brushes

Oh, look, it's another tool we've pinched from painting! There are lots of reasons to use brushes in drawing, including their extra subtle blending capabilities. First, though, there's a practical use that I want to share: sweeping away eraser debris. You know by now not to brush eraser crumbs away with your hands, and leaving the page littered with bits of rubber and graphite is no good either. One of my pet hates is having my pencil pass over some of this rubble, because it creates a jitter in my stroke which is hard to use or remove.

A drafting brush is ideal for the purpose of keeping things clean. At first, I used a large sable brush to sweep away debris. This was a mistake, however, because a brush such as this can pick up and redistribute particles of graphite. If you choose to sweep away with common painter's brushes, go lightly with your sweeping, just in case the brush is loaded. It took me a while, actually, to notice that my brush was depositing graphite as I swept, because the effect was extremely fine, almost indiscernible.

Other than a drafting brush, if you want to remove eraser debris absolutely cleanly, I would advise you get a blow bulb, which is basically a hollow rubber ball with a tube attached. As you squeeze the ball, air comes out of the tube, letting you shoo away debris without subtly blending with the brush or accidentally spitting on your work by blowing with your mouth.

A little secret

So, we know how important and eye-catching highlights are, right? They need to be reserved for important places. For this reason, it's a good rule to make sure that all the light areas of your page that are not a part of your focal point should be dulled just a tiny bit, even if they are supposed to be white. This lets you reserve true white for your highlight, letting you use it where it really matters. This is where the brush comes in. It's an excellent tool for just gently dulling large areas of white paper, giving them a very faint, uniform tone, a kind of glaze.

The brush is a unifier

I have all kinds of brushes in my toolkit, from a soft, small sable water-colour brush to big, bristly wall-painting brushes. They can all be used both to blend and apply graphite, and each has its own particular best use.

For maintaining harmony and unity, my go-to is a clean, dry sable brush. If a drawing starts getting a little out of hand while I'm creating texture, a sable brush helps to rein things in. For instance, when I feel my highlights have gotten too bright, I wash over them with the brush—this brings all the highlights back to a consistent level, closer to the midtone. With unity re-established, I'm able to reassess the position of my highlights.

Brushes are able to apply graphite with a very light touch. The change of value in light, for example, can be extraordinarily gradual. These transitions can be so fine that they can't be described properly with a grainy pencil. Instead, a brush can be used softly to describe this subtle range of transitions. With a brush dipped in graphite powder, you can apply delicate gradations of tone to your paper, an effect which works particularly well when describing soft clouds or objects that you want to appear hazy in the distance.

Crafting — Actually, I don't have space here to go into how I constructed this state of the art block-in device.* As I'm sure you can tell, the process was incredibly complicated. But anyway, since I spend my block-in phase continuously erasing and correcting, I'm forever sweeping away eraser debris. Combining my tools in this way just makes the process so much quicker.

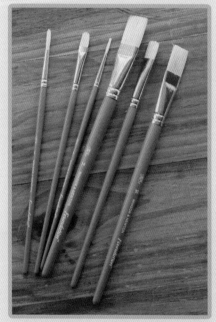

Hog's hair brushes — For applying graphite powder, I really like hog's hair brushes, because their bristles hold more graphite than a sable could. Short thick and firm bristles make this a wonderful blender.

I have a small hog's hair brush with the bristles cut down. Trimming makes the bristles more rigid and increases the amount of blending they can do.

> Blenders such as brushes have a habit of adding complexity, which is never something you want when you're trying to work out a problem area.

As we have already mentioned regarding the effect of over-stumping an area, the most dangerous thing about blending is that the process of smoothing can remove a lot of the line-work. This is a bit of a shame, because hatching can be a very refined and beautiful thing to look at in its own right. Purists will tell you to only use the pencil as hatching has an important architectural purpose within a work, giving it structure and dynamism. The extent to which we leave hatching visible depends, to a large extent, on the effect we're going for—more realistic drawings will need their hatching at least partially integrated through blending.

Even if you plan to blend your hatched in lines away completely, it's still important to blend in accordance with their structure. Our hatching should follow and describe the flow and direction of a particular surface, and as you blend, you should work along these directional lines. One reason for this is that hatching and blending in the direction of a form's flow is the best way to get yourself to treat your drawing as if it were a three-dimensional space. If you believe that you are actually moulding a three-dimensional representation, rather than just a two-dimensional depiction, then it's more likely that you will achieve realism in your work.

Not everything in a drawing should be blended. Use different approaches for different textures: to ignore these differences is to destroy the contrasts. Blending is our final task, and it requires restraint because it can be so addictive—Smudge-Sticks Anonymous is never short of members.

As with everything, blending is about finding a balance. If, as you start out, you find yourself going overboard with the blenders, this might not be such a bad thing—at least you'll get to see all the problems that come with over-blending.

Overuse of blenders such as the brush can also put a halt to your cross-hatching development. I suffered from precisely this problem, and as a result, I was always reaching for some kind of tool to do the work for me. Thankfully, I eventually realised something was wrong, so I went back and studied the basics thoroughly. By returning to subjects such as the sphere study and foregoing any temptation to use a blender, I managed to get my skills up to scratch.

The sable brush is possibly the subtlest possible way of tweaking tone. Using this tool to make such small changes is something I leave until the last stages of a drawing.

Good news!

Graphite applied to the paper with the brush is non destructive, that is simply because the tooth doesn't receive the same force as it does with the pencil and remains on the surface and therefore can always be removed.

I use a large brush for large sweeps of blending and a smaller brush when I require finer areas of blending. Used in moderation the brush can unite aspects really well in a very subtle manner, the trouble comes when it is used either too early or used excessively.

For all that the Specific loved the ultra-fine tonal progressions the brush could create, she was also getting the hang of its more practical uses.

Conjuring Depth

While discussing blenders, we've talked a lot about blurring and lightening objects to make them seem to fade further into the background. Creating a sense of depth within the frame is vital to realism, so let's take a moment to examine various ways in which we can create distance.

1   ***Line overlap*** — A very simple way of communicating depth with line is simply to have two objects overlap. Do note, however, that it's generally not a good idea to let two objects share a boundary line.

2   ***Line weight*** — Varying line thickness can also give a sense of distance: thicker lines seem closer, while thinner lines seem farther away.

3   ***Size*** — If we see two similar objects, but one of them is smaller, we often assume the smaller one is farther away, rather than just being miniaturised. A larger object will also attract more attention than a smaller one. It's fine to have two similar objects within a picture, as long as you think about varying the size or definition in order to declare which object requires more attention.

4   ***Lightness*** — Think of pale blue mountains in the distance: objects far away appear lighter and take on the colour of the atmosphere. Obviously, these effects only operate over long distances—the cup at the far side of your desk won't be showing any signs of this so-called 'atmospheric perspective'. At these greater distances, detail is also lost.

5   ***Blur*** — Combine a sharp-edged object with a blurry object or background to generate an instant illusion of depth. This is even more effective if the objects also overlap. This overlap is useful because objects can be blurred for two reasons: either they're far away, or they're too close. As you can see in image (6), overlap helps the mind decide which is the case.

6   ***Blurring makes the eye run away*** — Looking at a blurred area really isn't very pleasant, because our eyes are straining to focus on something that can't be brought into focus. The eye will tend to slip away from this unpleasant effect. Blur also conveys a sense of speed, and this implied motion also causes the eye to move on.

Veiling

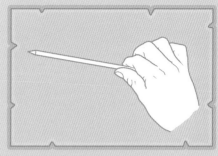

The veiling technique is a fine process that has our hand shifting right back to the constellation grip. This ensures that the application of values will be as light as can be. This general grip does sacrifice a little control and accuracy, but because your washes are so light, you can easily remove any stray marks with a kneaded eraser.

Light as a Feather

You know how we've just been talking about the limitations of pencils when it comes to fainter, softer values? There is a pencil technique for tackling these situations, known as 'veiling'. This method has the effect of very slightly adjusting the values in your drawing, almost like you're laying down a sheet of translucent material over a particular area of your drawing.

This is a slow and delicate process, one to which harder grade mechanical and clutch pencils are ideally suited. For veiling in , these should be held at the far end, as this will enable the light pressure that is required.

I know we've just been talking about fancy blenders, but the pencil itself can be a great blender. Try hatching in a patch of shade with a soft pencil, such as the 3B, then going over it with a harder pencil, like a 3H. The harder pencil works to break down the softer particles of graphite on the surface. It then moves these fine particles across the surface, filling in gaps left behind in the initial 3B hatching. This process thus acts as an incredibly subtle form of blending.

When applying the veiling method, make sure your pencil is nice and sharp.

Veiling is perfectly suited for the lighter side of the subject, where changes in form direction need to be indicated very gently. Veiling allows us register very gentle shifts in tone. Adjusting values as softly as this requires a great deal of patience and sensitivity, but when you manage it, you'll be a fine artist.

Very fine indeed.

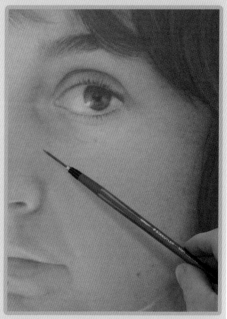

I find that large spaces with subtle tonal changes such as a person's cheek demand this sort of light touch.

Tedium

Overbearing Background

It's time to address an issue that's been lurking in the background for a while now. Namely, backgrounds. As we've seen, white is an attention-stealer, so white backgrounds can be a problem. In this cast drawing, the white background was bleaching out the subject. I decided I had to darken it. This is a long job, so be sure to cue up some background music!

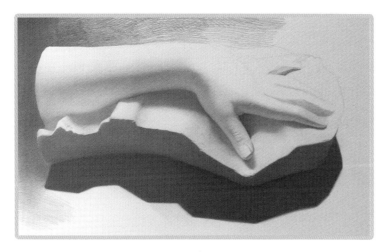

It's sensible to begin a large, dark area from the side opposite from my drawing hand, so I'll be working left to right. This cuts down on the chances of my accidentally smudging this heavy layer of graphite. In this study, I'm not actually sure how dark to make the background, because I didn't do a value thumbnail, so I'm not sure what will be appropriate.

The top edge of the cast, along the arm and wrist, is fairly straight, so I want a crisp edge. I'm using a sheet of paper as a mask over the cast so that I can stump the darker region into a nice, smooth blend without risk of smudging my lights.

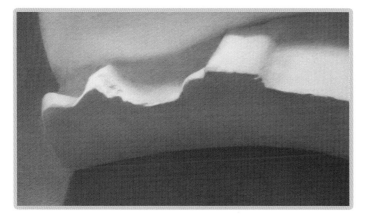

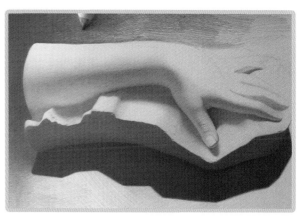

Changing the background means I need to reconsider my edges. The light edges which used to fade into the background are now sharply contrasting, but I've got some new disappearing edges in my areas of shadow.

To create a dark background, I begin by working over an area with a sharp 3B, then going over this with an H pencil. Finally, I use a stump to smudge the whole thing, completely removing any pencil grain—I don't want any sharpness or detail in my background as it will destroy the sense of depth I'm trying to create.

Level 0 Eraser

Bread

Yes, bread. For centuries, this food stuff was the eraser of choice for artists. Then rubber came along and made things sane. Some artists actually still use this. Crust off, of course. I'm marking this eraser Level Zero, because, come on, don't play with your food.

I have never tried this. Eating it, sure. Rubbing it on my work? Not so much.

Level 1 Eraser

Plastic Eraser

We're now on page 230—'tooth-hurty'— which is apt, because plastic erasers really will hurt your paper's tooth. Plastic erasers are fairly aggressive cleaners, which you should use with care and restraint. We'll talk about gentler erasers in due course. As far as plastic erasers go, my preference is for these two on the right here. Staedtler in particular can usually be trusted to make really decent, high quality erasers for a good price. Even though these are quality plastic erasers, they're still the last erasers I reach for. It's always better to begin with softer erasers, turning to plastic erasers only for final clean-up work.

Smearing

If the image on the right doesn't look familiar, you were clearly a better Maths student than me. Smearing occurs in drawing when you use a plastic eraser on an area that already contains large amounts of graphite. For effective erasing, you need to begin in an area of the paper that's still free of graphite, or which has had as much removed as possible. The trick is to use softer erasers first, removing as much graphite as possible. Then the plastic erasers can go in and do their thing without making a mess.

Goshdarnit — Things started so well! I began with a clean vinyl eraser. Gradually, though, it got dirty, then graphite started to smear, and the whole situation deteriorated from there. A clean eraser can create happy accidents. A dirty eraser is just an accident waiting to happen. The tragic irony of smears caused by erasers is that these marks are darn difficult to erase.

The image on the left shows a dirty plastic eraser. These erasers pick up graphite, which they can then redistribute in smears across your working surface. Clean them by rubbing them on a blank sheet of paper.

Erasing is fundamental to drawing, not only as a way of removing mistakes but also as a means of developing ideas. Be careful with erasers, though: they are the type of tool which can do most harm, especially if cheap materials are used. The general rule to remember is that, the harder the eraser, the more it will push graphite down into the tooth of the paper, causing it to become embedded. Conversely, softer erasers are able to more delicately remove the top layer of graphite without pushing the medium deeper into the paper—these erasers manage this due to their stickiness. The goal with erasing is to remove graphite gently, while causing the least possible amount of damage to the surface. Erasers that embed graphite or damage the surface are self-defeating.

 Level II Erasers

Stick Eraser

The material in the stick eraser is basically the same as in the block erasers discussed on the previous page. The stick eraser is an upgrade simply because it's much more comfortable to use. It's a very versatile piece of equipment, because it's possible to shape its tip with a pocket knife, or even with a small metal pencil sharpener. When it's sharpened or given an edge, it becomes an excellent tool for cutting into the graphite with a precise white line.

For the both the fat Derwent and the slender Tombow eraser, all we really need to do is just snip off the end with scissors to keep it maintained and ready for the next pass. Stick erasers, like other plastic or vinyl erasers, leave an annoying trail of debris in their wake. Be sure to brush this away with your drafting brush or else it could cause your pencil to skip.

Sharpening

A sharp-edged stick eraser is an ideal tool for working on subjects like hair and grass. We can give the larger Derwent eraser the same kind of chiselled edge that we used with pencils. A chiselled edge is sharp enough to be precise but wide enough to be strong.

When we draw with softer grades of pencil, our edges get a little rough and fuzzy. We can use the eraser stick to clean these edges up. The precision of the stick eraser is also good for counteracting the kind of haziness that can arise from using the kneaded eraser too heavily.

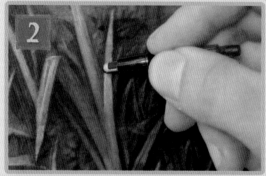

The stick eraser used in this example is from a mechanical pencil. The one I use most often is the Tombow Mono pictured right at the top there.

Rather like a pencil's point, the edge of a stick eraser can be very precise if it's maintained with a knife or metal sharpener. A stick eraser will produce a sharper line than a kneaded eraser, but there's still a certain softness to any erased line. To create really sharp, fine white lines, use the stick eraser in conjunction with a pencil: this combination of tools will produce a very clean effect. We'll explore the usefulness of creating fine lines and edges later in our discussion of portraiture.

Putty Rubber

The kneaded eraser, also known as a putty rubber, is a wonderfully versatile eraser. You can sculpt these erasers into many forms (A), allowing you to make it chiselled, pinched, spiked, flat or blobby. You can make it as pointed as you like for the purposes of plucking out highlights, or even shape it into a leaf to dapple textures.

Another handy thing about them is that kneaded erasers don't leave behind debris, making them nice and neat to use. When you want to clean them, just roll the dirty area on a clean surface, then pull at it to reshape the eraser. As with all erasers and blenders, keep your graphite putty rubber for graphite only—if you're drawing with charcoal and chalk as well, keep separate erasers for separate mediums.

The putty rubber has a strange unpredictability about it, which I find fascinating but which you may initially find disturbing. When you erase with a putty rubber, you can never be entirely certain what effect it will produce. It introduces an element of chaos into proceedings which can lead a drawing in exciting, unforeseen directions. The eraser becomes a complement to the pencil when you learn how to make the most of accidents that arise.

In my drawing style, I eventually come to use the eraser almost as much as the pencil. It's not just about removing lines at this point, it's about making them as well. I find that the kneaded eraser enables me to take a sort of push-pull approach to values, where I fluctuate between extremes in order to arrive, eventually, at an appropriate middle ground. I intentionally over-apply graphite, creating a ground upon which my erasers can work: the excess graphite becomes a medium I can almost sculpt with my malleable erasers.

Leonardo da Vinci method — One of the master's most closely guarded secrets, there is no mention in any of his notebooks of these little hands made from kneaded eraser. Indeed, no shred of evidence for this practice has ever been uncovered—proof of the lengths to which he went to protect this valuable and mysterious technique.

The kneaded eraser can be sculpted into any shape you need, but because it's so soft, it's necessary to remould these shapes every so often. This isn't a bad thing; the firmness of the stick eraser complements this quality.

You can form it into a ball or rolling pin shape, which you can then roll over the surface to remove large swathes of graphite. This paves the way for using harder erasers to bring the area back to brilliant white.

The putty rubber will become saturated with graphite as you use it, so it's important every so often to change the area you're using to erase. Eventually, kneaded erasers become so saturated with graphite that they just need to be replaced.

Hey look! Ruins!

Portrait background

The putty rubber can also be used for controlling edges. This is especially useful if you have decided to maintain your background as a stark white. In these situations, leaving a solid perimeter line around the subject can make it look rather flat and unconvincing.

A bright, white background has a huge effect on an object's contour, making it disappear in places, as the light bursts over the surface. To mimic this effect, you can dab a putty rubber around the edges to remove the outline wholly or partially, unifying the object with its background. It's also possible that you'll find the white background a little overpowering—you can always tone it down slightly by using a sable brush to apply small amounts of graphite powder as I did in the concluding stage of the sphere.

Light wrap

The back-lit effect that occurs when an object is placed against a bright, primary light source is called 'contre-jour,' meaning, 'against daylight.' If a person stands against the Sun, the light wraps around them, creating a very dramatic halo effect.

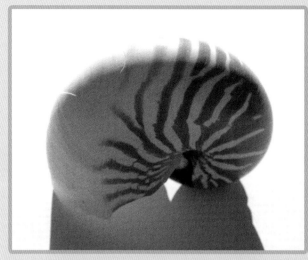

We can unify an object with its white background by dabbing at the contour line with a kneaded eraser, making it far less visible. This can be a powerful effect, but be aware that it can also greatly increase the power of your light source—which may come to overwhelm your subject.

It's also worth remembering the importance of line in strengthening our drawings. If an object's surrounding lines are totally removed, it becomes hazy and indistinct—our eye drifts away from it, wandering in search of a subject to hold it. Line is a pathway for the eye, a necessary compositional device. It's important to preserve it as much as necessary.

In contre-jour, the edges of the subject become fused with the light source. Depending on the power of the light source, the edges of the subject may be completely dissolved. Even as the edges disappear, the silhouette is pronounced, because the light hits the subject like a crashing ocean wave. This effect can really help to make an object look convincingly rounded.

The contour of this potato was initially very sharp (1), until the kneaded eraser was used to soften it (2). By doing this, the three-dimensional quality was greatly enhanced. Surface texture was also added with the eraser and then refined with the 2B pencil (3).

SHADOW DOOR

1 This demo is focussing on eraser work, so our initial pencil work can be pretty loose. Sketch in a few angular lines to make up the beginnings of a brick wall—nothing too fancy.

2 Scribble in a layer of hatch. This puts a ground of graphite in place for us to work with, but there's no need to make everything tidy at this point.

3 Lay down a cross-hatch. The sort of bricks we're going to draw will be pretty decked in, so we're going to let this rough ground show through to some extent.

4 Now outline some major shadows. The ones I've placed here are totally random. I've just tried to distribute them in a way that looks sort of balanced, without seeming too regular.

5 Go ahead and scribble a hatch into those shadow shapes. This drawing is going to be quite chaotic, so rough pencil work will help create the right texture.

6 Smudge with a stump, then add some lines to indicate the brickwork. Be careful to keep the lines irregular, letting them disappear at intervals. This ensures that it won't look like a cartoon outline of a brick wall.

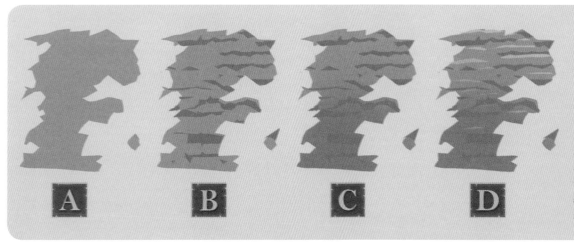

Organised chaos — This progression of images shows the basic thinking beneath the creation of this detailed, chaotic image.

By progressing according to these clear stages, I've been able to keep my lighting consistent. I begin with a foundation shape (A), move on to a shadow map (B), to which I add some tonal variation (C). Finally, I add some basic light shapes (D), which really brings it into three dimensions.

7 Decide on your light direction. Here, I want the lower part of the wall to be darker, so, starting at the bottom, I do a wash of darker pencil. I let this fade out as I move upwards. I go over this with hog's hair and sable brushes to blend it in.

8 Use a sharp, dark pencil—I'm using a 4B clutch—to key in some darks, getting a sense of the structure and depth of the cracks. Remember to think of your wall in terms of basic planes: how are different blocks angled? As you can see here, some of them are tilting upwards, some turn in, and others face outwards.

9 Begin to cut into the darks with an eraser stick, creating shapes of light. The result will be too bright, but that's alright for now: the goal is to get the shape of the bricks that face the light. Later, we can go back and adjust the values so that they make sense together.

10 With chaotic textures like this, we can go into so much detail—and this means it's easy for things to get out of hand. The more complicated the surface, the more difficult it becomes to ensure everything is still consistent with the light source. If you've blocked in your value structure beforehand, things are far more manageable.

1

Blu-Tack

You probably know Blu-Tack for sticking things on walls, but it also makes an incredibly effective kneadable eraser. It's capable of bringing even quite dark marks back very close to the original white. As with putty rubbers, Blu-Tack does a good job of removing the majority of graphite from an area, so that we can use a plastic eraser to finish up the job.

Blu-Tack is a bit firmer than most kneaded erasers, but I find it is even less destructive to paper fibres. It removes graphite very readily, and it leaves no residue on the paper (unlike on walls!). If you want to clean it, just stretch it and roll it on a surface, as you would with a kneaded eraser. It's also non-toxic, which is nice, and it works well with acid-free paper—so it won't hurt our drawings or the environment.

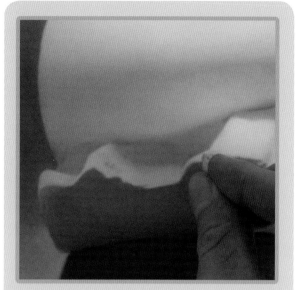

The special property of Blu-Tack that makes it so effective is its stickiness.

Dabbing

We apply Blu-Tack with a dabbing rather than a rubbing action, which means we avoid embedding graphite in the tooth. Go lightly with the dabbing: it only takes the slightest pressure. This means that it won't pull at the surface, making Blu-Tack a very non-destructive eraser.

Because of its wonderful stickiness, Blu-Tack allows us to remove graphite, even on a very heavily built-up area, with very little pressure. Unlike blending tools, Blu-Tack won't damage your line-work. This means it's possible to fade out an area without destroying the detail. Applying this substance to your work gently allows you to make subtle changes, little by little, while staying in complete control. This will enable you to achieve some remarkably delicate effects.

There are several different ways of using Blu-Tack, and older Blu-Tack will develop its own particular qualities as you use it. One of the best ways of deploying Blu-Tack is to roll it over an area. If you roll a fresh piece of Blu-Tack over an area, it can create a softened atmospheric effect, toning down contrast without removing detail. If you want to remove all traces of graphite, the best way is to roll your Blu-Tack or putty rubber over the area, just as you might roll snakes of clay. This will remove a great deal of graphite—clearing the way for you to go in with your eraser stick, and finally a harder vinyl eraser, if necessary. If your Blu-Tack is getting dirty, stretching and rolling it a little will refresh it—and when it comes to erasing cleanly, fresher Blu-Tack is far more effective.

What is this stuck on my shoe?

Great for skin

Blu-Tack is an excellent tool for creating believable skin texture. Skin is rarely perfectly smooth: even quite young skin is full of little bumps and pores. To mimic this irregularity, pinch your Blu-Tack into a spike and dab at the area. Next, pass over the area with a brush, removing the white dots and bringing everything back together again. This creates a subtle, skin-like effect.

While we're on the subject, there is a paradoxical quality to skin that we ought to consider. If you remember, when light hits a matt surface, the irregular texture scatters the photons all over. When light hits a shiny object, it bounces right back, focused into a highlight. Well, the anomaly of human skin is that it has characteristics of both a matt and a glossy surface. This means that, for the most part, light has a soft effect on skin, but that there are areas where the skin becomes shiny, with sharp-edged highlights.

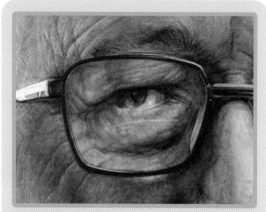

Detail of 'Robert' 2015, — Graphite pencil on Bristol board, 30 x 42cms.

Any putty eraser will become grubby after a time, as the substance gradually takes on more and more graphite. Eventually it will become dark and saturated. To restore it, pull and roll it until it becomes cleaner.

Detail of 'Kev' 2013, — Graphite pencil on Bristol board, 30 x 42cms.

Aye, got me too.

Far Less Destructive to Tooth

Everyone knows how to erase: you take rubber in hand and you scrub at the paper furiously until your mistake disappears into a blur of graphite, ripped paper and regret. Well, we're going to set that method aside for now, and learn how to apply kneadable erasers and Blu-Tack. Rather than rubbing, we use a gentle, dabbing action that lifts away the topmost layers of graphite. Blu-Tack is so sticky that the lightest touch will have an impact.

 I've gone over this area several times with a 3B, hatching it roughly in all directions to make sure the graphite has been thoroughly worked into the area.

 To begin, I roll my Blu-Tack into a tube and roll it over the area I want to return to white. The action is a like using a tiny rolling pin. Once I've passed over it several times, the area is becoming noticeably clearer.

 By now, the Blu-Tack is grubby with graphite and is becoming less effective, so I stretch it a bit to create a fresh surface area on the eraser so I can continue erasing.

 After a while, my rolling and dabbing is no longer having an effect. This is when I know it's time to go in with some harder stuff.

 Using a plastic or vinyl eraser, I rub at the area, though not too roughly. I use a clean brush to clean away the debris. (Don't blow away the eraser crumbs, because you might accidentally spit on your drawing.)

 The area is getting substantially clearer, especially considering how it started. I keep going like this until it reaches the level of white we see in the final image.

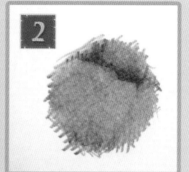

Erasing aggressively can break the paper fibres, resulting in a gritty effect when you try to pass over it with a fresh wash of graphite.

With ordinary paper, this kind of destruction can happen pretty quickly. With Bristol Board, however, it would take quite a lot of effort to do that much damage.

Electric Eraser

The electric eraser is a handy, quite specialised tool. It's particularly adept at picking out tiny highlights. As with Blu-Tack, its ability to pick out highlights makes it useful for creating textures. Sometimes I also use it for my final level of erasure, after the putty rubber and stick eraser—but only if it's really needed. Where the electric eraser really excels is in giving sharp-edged definition.

It's best to use the electric eraser a little cautiously, and not over large areas, because it's possible to inadvertently do damage. When using it on a large scale, it's much too easy to accidentally dig into the paper surface. This is also why I use a sequential method of erasure, moving gradually from the softest to hardest erasers. It's a lot easier to damage your paper with an electric eraser than any manual one, because your arm normally isn't spinning at 12,000 rotations per minute.

Masks

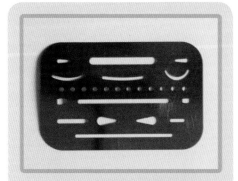

The electric eraser can be used in conjunction with a masking tool to create crisp lines in areas where precision is required. Masking tools, such as the one pictured on the right, come in many shapes and sizes. I use quite a flat one because the thicker ones tend to blunt my eraser fairly quickly.

You can improvise your own masking tools as well. A mask can be as simple as a piece of paper shaped to fit the area you wish to cover. A transparent ruler makes a good straight-edged mask. You may find it useful, however, to have the wider variety of shapes offered in stencil form, particularly the wide variety of curves found on tools such as the French Curve.

A basic metal mask tool such as this can be occasionally handy when precision is important. French curves (not pictured) can also be a very useful thing to have around when there comes a need for exact curves.

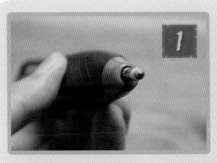

Blu-Tack as a cleaner — Blu-Tack can be used to clean other erasers such as the electric eraser. I keep a blob of Blu-Tack stretched out to the right of my working area for cleaning my erasers. Keeping your erasers clean avoids accidentally transferring graphite onto the paper from the dirty eraser.

Dude, it's alright. I have contact lenses in. You can look at me. You can even draw my eye if you wish!

Messy at First

I've mentioned that, at a certain point in a drawing, I begin to use my eraser almost as much as my pencil, and to use it constructively, rather than just to remove mistakes. This technique of working with the eraser is known as reductive drawing. To practice it, we're going to use a subject that we've already worked with, the eye—but this time, we're going to approach it in a completely different way. For this demonstration, I'm using graphite powder, a hog's hair brush, blending stump and various erasers. This demo involves the application of a ground of tone with the hog's hair brush. I then work over this tone with both pencil and eraser, building up the darks and carving out the lights.

I construct the line-work, using the usual process. I then proceed to apply graphite powder with a hog's hair brush (I), which holds more graphite and produces a darker tone than a sable brush. It's important to do my line-work before I scrub in a tone, because it means I'm able to erase and fix my lines as necessary. If I laid down the tone first, fixing my line-work would also require fixing my tone—it's easy to see how this would become a headache.

I apply the graphite powder using a gentle swirling motion (I). See all those dark specks in the first picture? I try to break these down with the brush, spreading the tone. I need to get all these clumps of graphite broken down before I go any further.

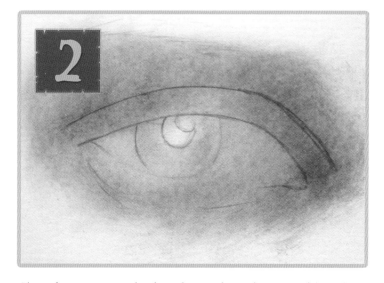

The surface is now covered with graphite powder. In the process of doing this, I caused the line-work to become far less obvious, so in this image I have darkened it so I can still see the main guidelines.

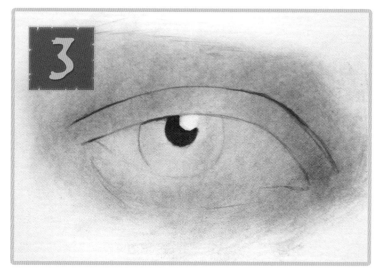

This image shows that I have keyed in the darkest area of the eye, the pupil. I have also dabbed at the highlight just to give it a clean because some powder has made its way there. This is one of the problems with graphite powder—it can be hard to control. But not to worry, it's usually very easy to remove, as it is still pretty much just resting on the tooth, rather than being embedded.

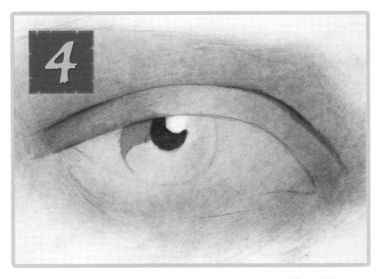

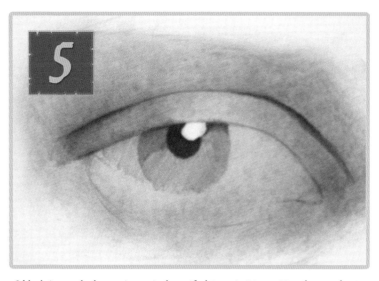

I continue to work at my darks, using a 4B. For the shadow of the eyelid crease, notice that I haven't just put a big black line to mark the fold. Instead, I let the line of shadow vary in thickness and darkness. This adds realism.

I block-in my shadows using a single, unified tone, just to position them and get a better sense of how the light is playing on this form. One of my main goals here is to stay in control of my tones. I can't allow them to get too numerous, otherwise things will get out of hand.

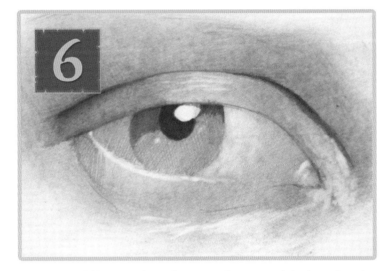

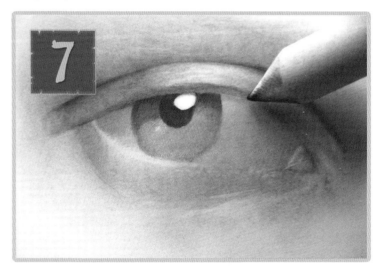

With the kneadable eraser, I begin the process of carving out light shapes from the ground of tone (6). I also begin to use the stump to blend tones together (7). This blending serves as a helpful process of simplification: if I've ended up with too many tones, the stump will bring things back together. A good composition depends on a basic structure of lines, and a good tonal composition is based on a few tones that work well together to create both contrast and harmony.

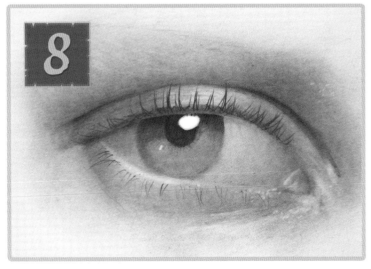

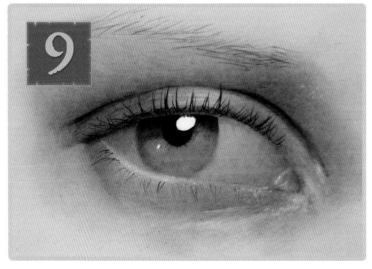

I have carefully applied the sable brush over most of the drawing to get rid of all the white space (8). I've avoided brushing over the highlight, however, which helps bring it out, leaving no confusion over where the eye should land in the picture. I've also added the eyelashes and eyebrow (9). With these, note that you should proceed gradually. It's very easy to put in too many lines and to make them too dark. One good way to go about it is to add a few strands with a very sharp pencil, then leave it, and work on something else. You can check back later to see if you need more. To make the lines for eyelashes or eyebrows, let your stroke begin dark, but tail it off at the end so that it finishes finer and lighter.

Tonal Trickery

Judging values is a tricky business, because of the phenomenon of relative brightness: a value can appear to shift in brightness depending on the other values nearby. This is easy to understand if you imagine a candle in a dark room: it seems very bright, because of its relative brightness compared to the shadows around it. In the daylight, however, the same candle wouldn't appear nearly as bright. Of course, this creates difficulties of judgement for us in drawing. It has one advantage, though: you can make an area appear darker or lighter without actually changing its value at all; instead, you can simply change the values surrounding it.

Local value

In pencil drawing, we face the additional challenge of rendering coloured objects in black and white. The greyscale value of an object, independent of lighting or shadow, is known as its 'local value.' An object's surface pigmentation absorbs a certain amount of light; the amount absorbed or reflected determines its local value.

Unless the object is actually black or white, the local value will be found somewhere in the midtones. As colours change, so too will the local value. For example, on a light-skinned person, the relative value of the lips will be darker compared to the face, because of the difference in local value between the skin and lips. The lips will also be darkened in places by shadow, however.

This interaction between shadow and local value is where things get a little more complicated. On a uniformly coloured object, such as a white sphere, we know that any change in value is related to light and shade. If we were drawing a rainbow-striped ball, however, changes in value would be determined not only by lighting but also by different local values. This is why it's useful to study single-toned objects first, before embarking on multicoloured forms: a single local value lets us concentrate on the effects of light without distraction.

Tonal strip (A)

A tonal strip is a tool to help us deal with the difficulties caused by relative brightness and local value. It is a piece of card, which can be rectangular or round, containing different shades of grey, and each patch of tone has a hole punched out, allowing you to hold it up to your subject and check particular values against this more absolute scale. This will

The tone of the rectangle to the left is sampled from the dark side of the cast on the above where the arrow points to.

This is the lightest light caused by a secondary source that occurs on the right hand side of this cast. The dark value of this square is surprising because on the cast it looks really quite light. The shadow appears light simply because it is surrounded by darker values. Whereas, when this shadow value is seen, in isolation against lighter values, as it is above, it appears dark.

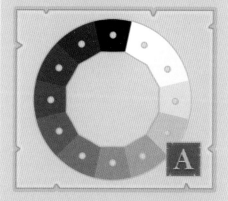

Tonal Strip — If you make one of these I would recommend using paint rather than graphite to make the individual blocks of tones, as paint won't shine and confuse you while checking.

help you see and assess values in areas where it's not so easy to evaluate the differences. I found this tool very useful when I was starting out, although, as with many aids, I find myself using it less often as I become more experienced. It's certainly worth trying, and it can really help you train you to distinguish between values that may seem very similar.

Edge lighting

The image to the right is an example of edge lighting, a type of back lighting that highlights the contour with striking detail. Also known as rim lighting, this creates a narrow, bright sliver of light running along the contour, while the bulk of the object is left in shadow.

The effect is intensified when set against a dark background. This is one way we can use relative brightness to our advantage, using it to increase drama and contrast. Take note, however, that rim lighting does not create a flattened white outline around your subject. Rather, it creates an illuminated edge which varies in breadth and brightness.

The above square of tone is taken from the brightest area on the cheek.

This is the brightest the rim light gets lower down. This makes it clear how much tonal variety there can be, even within narrow areas of brightness. They seem more similar than they are, in part, because of the effects of relative brightness.

Tonal relativism

Tones are not absolute. Each individual tone is perceived within the context of its environment; it's determined by local value, lighting, and its relative brightness compared to the tones around it. This has an interesting implication for our drawings: by making use of relative brightness, we can create the appearance of greater tonal variation while still using only a very few tones. This is made clear in the image below, based on Edward H. Adelson's optical illusion:

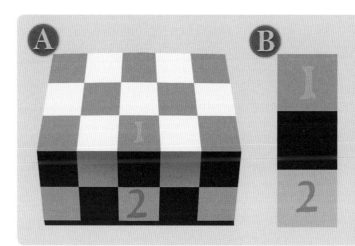

The three squares on the left (B) show these values as they appear on the chequered cube (A). The top square looks a lot darker than the bottom square.

The image on the right (C) show the reality of the situation. The Squares (1, 2) in (A) are actually the same value, only the context of what is surrounds these squares in (A) misleads our eye. The lower square in (A) is in a part of the image that we perceive as being in shadow and so we assume it must be darker.

Portrait Continued

Starting With the Hair

We're now going to pick up where we left off with the portrait we made back in the swamp. This demonstration will be mostly about blending, and over the course of building this image I will be breaking a few rules so I can complete each part in sections. For instance, I don't normally begin a portrait with the hair as in (A). We know by now that working on the drawing as a whole is the best way to go, but for the purposes of demonstration, I want to focus on explaining each part separately, to help you get a handle on how to tackle some common textures in portraiture. As a result of working like this, however, the finished portrait is ultimately weaker, in my opinion. Nevertheless, the goal here is instructive: showing you how to blend, and at the same time demonstrate the dangers of over-blending, becoming too fussy and working in parts.

Hair texture seems to trip a lot of people up, but it shouldn't really. We're going to spend some time getting to grips with this subject, not because it's particularly difficult, but just to help overcome this common anxiety. Drawing the hair follows the same process as building up any other form in a drawing. Remember to seek guidance from the General first: think of hair in terms of a large mass rather than individual strands. Focus on establishing the basic structure of the hair, the placement of light and shade—only then can we heed the Specific's call to add individual strands.

As well as roughing in value, I am selectively removing outlines with the kneaded eraser. It's useful to use an eraser to tidy things up every now and again. You can see here how I've hatched in a big, dark mass—this is how I'm going to begin describing the shadowed side of the hair. I'm working with a 4B pencil, being careful not to press down too hard. This is especially important here because I want to come back later on with the eraser stick to pick out some white strands of hair. If the graphite's been laid on too thick, the eraser would skid over the surface without removing the fine lines I'm looking for.

Harder grades of pencils can be used along with a brush to begin blending.

When drawing hair, is very easy to end up with way too many values. That is to say, it's easy to resort to putting in more information than you actually need.

At this early stage of adding value (B), I am trying to keep the shadows limited to a single consistent value. I'm using the hair to key in the drawing, since this is the darkest part of the drawing. This means I'm now establishing my deepest darks, which will serve as a reference point for all other darks in the drawing: I'm making use of relative brightness. In (B), I've gone over my 4B foundation with some harder grades, brushes and also—a little prematurely—with my mechanical pencils. This has broken down the soft 4B graphite, beginning to blend it.

Modeling Hair

Hair is one of those times when our ideas get in the way of our drawing. Because we know that the hair is composed of individual strands, people try to draw it that way, line by straggly line (A). Think of the hair as a mass. It has a structure, just like the head itself, which needs to be communicated, like any other form. To model hair well, it needs to be understood first as a unified, solid shape, and then as locks: every lock has its own planes that reflect light and turn away into shadow (B): every lock has its own planes that reflect light and turn away into shadow. As always, begin with the largest forms, and only gradually work down to more specific details.

This general approach to hair is the most practical. Think of sculpting hair in clay: the sculptor doesn't roll lots of spaghetti strands to stick onto the head. Instead, they create masses which are later given definition as hair. Locks, not wires. Stray strands of hair—which are loose, or darker or lighter—can be picked out later, as telling details.

Once we've established the masses of hair and are looking to establish these characteristic details with a few sharp, crisp lines, there's no better tool than the stick eraser. For this kind of work, the edge of the stick should be ultra-sharp: sharpen any dull edges with a knife. As well as sharpness, you need strength and stiffness. Make sure there's only a small amount of the eraser showing above the barrel. This gives the stiffness needed to create sharp white lines.

> When trying to create the impression of hair, the eraser stick marks should be quick and confident, made with one fluid, flicking motion.

The above image shows the way people often tackle hair. We need to avoid this method.

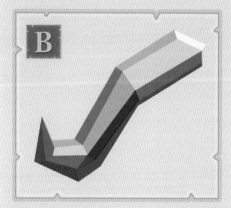

Hair can be thought of as a mass, just like any other object. Squinting can help us to see it in this more helpful way. Masses of hair abide by the same rules as any other mass: they have a highlight, midtone, shadow and an area of reflective light.

The stick eraser works wonders for adding highlights to hair. Another method of creating brilliant, fine streaks of white is called indenting, which we'll look at next.

Valleys of White

Indenting is another way of adding fine, white lines to a drawing. Although it's not a method I favour, let's have a look anyway, just in case the occasion ever arises. Indenting is the practice of creating a fine, uniform white line by dragging a pointed instrument over the surface of the paper (I use a needle embedded in a wooden stick). This is a technique that works well for some effects, such as animals' whiskers, stitches in clothing, or sharp scratches in wood or metal.

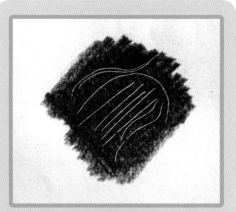

It is possible to draw within these bright white lines in order to create some variation: this is useful because we rarely need such stark white lines. It's also possible to completely fill in an indentation if we need to remove it altogether.

Indenting process

The goal is to press the line into the paper, rather than cutting it, producing a distinct white line, while controlling the damage to the paper. Indenting is far more effective on compressed papers than on loosely toothed or textured papers.

You want to be working on a hard surface. Although it is possible to indent directly onto the surface of your drawing, I prefer to place a sheet of tracing paper between my drawing and the needle—I guess it depends how squeamish you are about direct contact between needle and paper. In this example, we're going to use tracing paper.

Blunt tips generally skip over indents very well. Harder pencils will skip over the indent too, just make sure the indent is deep and narrow enough for this to happen.

To begin indenting

Place the tracing paper over your drawing, then use masking tape to secure it. To make the indentation, you will need a sharp, pointed object, such as a needle or a very hard pencil, like a 9H.

Take care not to tear the tracing paper. The angle at which you make your mark will be important here. In this case, it is better to pull the drawing tool towards you rather than pushing it.

Now, when you work over the surface with a softer grade, you will find that the grooves you have made act as a mask that the softer pencils cannot enter. This is a striking effect, but also one that requires a good deal of consideration.

Indentations are not wholly permanent, however. It is possible to modify these indentations by reaching into the white grooves with a sharp HB and purposefully shading in the area you wish to be toned.

 DRAW LIKE A BOSS

In this image, it may look like I'm drawing the individual strands of hair, but I'm actually just using some 3B hatching to lay down the tone in an area I know to be very dark.

The direction of my hatching is very important here: it needs to match the direction of the hair. I'm not drawing the individual strands, but I am making use of the similarity between pencil strokes and hair.

At this stage I am attempting to build an appropriate tone in this area, using the clutch pencil to break down the grainy 3B foundation, then sweeping in with a sable brush to spread the graphite further into the white spaces.

Letting the tone build gradually, I'm creeping up on the darks rather than just hammering in a huge dark cross-hatch. By being gentle with the surface, I make sure it will respond to the flicks of the eraser stick later on, allowing me to add striking, highlighted strands of hair.

Continuing upwards, I go both darker and lighter. I'm letting my 3B describe the darker values, as before, but I'm also using the HB clutch to create the midtones in areas where the light begins to hit.

I've also begun cutting out the highlights: using quick, aggressive sweeps of the stick eraser to carve out streaks of white, which I can then amend and shape with my clutch pencil.

As dust settles

Drawings can sometimes take a long time, stretching out over many sessions. During the intervals, if you leave the drawing on a horizontal desk, dust will begin to collect on the surface—this happens surprisingly quickly. When you return to your drawing, your pencil will interact with any dust that has gathered, creating unpredictable, disruptive effects. This problem is easily avoided, however, if you put your work away between sessions, or simply place a piece of paper over it to shield it from foreign particles or sticky-handed nephews.

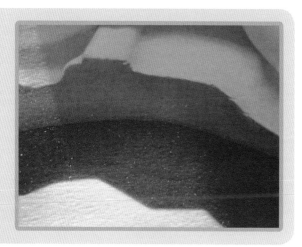

I feel like you got distracted and made a big jump between 3 and 4...

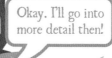
Okay. I'll go into more detail then!

Locks of hair — Longer hair is built up lock by lock. In the following images, we'll look at the process of drawing just one lock in isolation, to give you a sense of the process.

Don't be tempted to rush the hair, scribbling it in at random. Here, more than ever, the angle and direction of our pencil strokes are critical. These lines describe the surface. Any deviation from the correct angles will break the illusion.

For additional practice, look at the photo to the left and decide how you would break it down into locks.

With a 3B pencil, I begin to indicate where my darks are on the lock of hair.

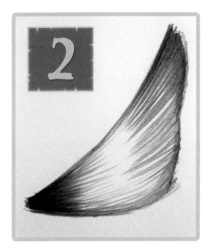

I begin making sweeping strokes across the lock, still using my 3B—which, I might add, is not particularly sharp.

Hair that is clumped up in this fashion tends to have core shadows going on, which I begin to indicate on the right.

The core shadow is now a lot more obvious. I'm still using the 3B at this stage, although I am also using a harder pencil at intervals to begin blending.

That harder pencil is the HB clutch pencil; I'm using it to begin breaking down the 3B, and also to add strands of detail within the highlight. I use the HB clutch throughout the drawing, pulling lines from the shadow into that highlight, as well as breaking down and refining the shadow side so that it becomes less grainy.

Much better.

De-Glaring the Hair

At this point, the lock of hair is too shiny, thanks to the bright white highlight you can see in (6). To tone this down, I use the 2H clutch pencil in conjunction with the sable brush; both applied quite gently. As you can see in (7), the highlight is muted. I could then go into this softened highlight with the sharp edge of an eraser stick and pick out just a few strands of brightness.

Flicking

When describing hair, we want to use light flicks of the pencil. A normal pencil stroke is blunt at the beginning and end, as in (A). The trouble with a flick, however, is that although it has a delicate end, the beginning is still blunt and broad, as you can see in (B). This looks unnatural for hair. We want a mark that begins lightly, gradually gets darker, then fades away—but how can we produce this kind of double flick?

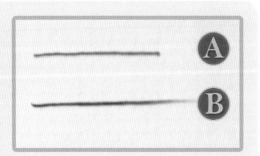

I've developed a really effective trick for this. First, I make a mark using the normal flicking action (and it's worth practicing this). Then I return to the beginning of the line, and I flick in the opposite direction. I've now got a nice double flick.

The trouble is, as the flicks tail off, the quality of the line becomes a little grainy; it loses definition. To improve this and create a softer gradation, I switch pencils. My first lines, in this example, were made using a 2B clutch. Changing to a nice, sharp F, I return to my flicks, and I go over them with this harder, lighter pencil. This acts as a micro-blending tool, and it creates a more subtle tonal shift. I can even use this sharp F to continue the line a little further in either direction.

At this point, we were definitely in the realm of the Specific, with an incredibly fine attention to detail. This kind of precision manoeuvre gives a drawing an impressive level of finesse, but it's easy to see how, if initiated too early, it could become distracting, exhausting and maddening. Save these flourishes for late in the game, when they will really count.

Dang! I like, totally lost my hat!

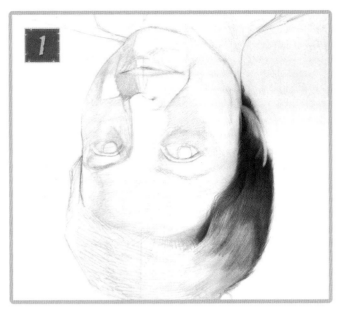

At this point, I have reversed the image, so I am working on it upside down. My reference image is, of course, also turned around. I suddenly see the image anew, and I have a good idea of what parts need urgent attention.

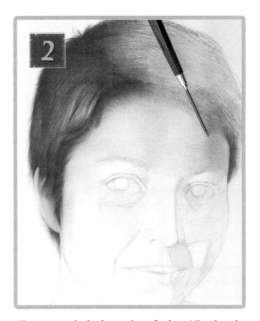

I've extended the nib of the 2B clutch pencil to help me veil in the lightness of the skin texture. We can look at the human skin is as an incredibly complex sheet of material, the slightest change in tone will give an idea of change in plane, angled differently to the light source.

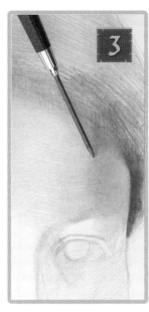

Working out from the core shadow, I attempt to describe the curvature of the forehead, veiling in tone with thin lines that move in the direction of the topography.

With the image now turned upside down, the highlights that have been added prematurely are starting to bother me. I have been excessive with the brightness—which is fine as I try things out, but I need to knock them down with the sable brush, as the brightness looks quite unnatural. These stark whites should really be applied at the end anyway.

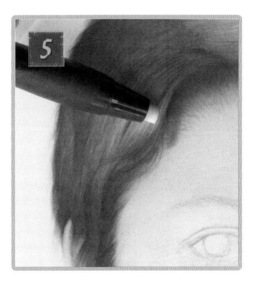

With everything now reduced to a consistent midtone level, I can come in with the sharp stick eraser and decide where to place a subtle highlight, amongst the now subdued lights.

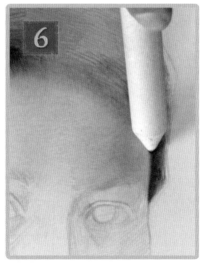

The left-hand side is going to be ultra sharp and the main focus of interest. The far right will be more blurry and out of focus, so some of the time I draw with the stump as I want all the features around this area to appear indistinct.

Specific Transitions

Effective tonal transitions require a combination of softer and harder grades. Creating seamless tonal transitions is a skill worth practicing, as inconsistencies will be easily spotted by viewers. In this simple demonstration, we will build up a series of tones using harder pencils layered over softer pencil. Building up value in this way can create its own details as an interesting by-product.

 This first image shows a tonal progression created with a wash of 3B, through varying pressure. This is how the progression begins, but not how it has to end.

 Now, a wash of HB has been added, beginning from the top and moving down. This wash fills in the gaps, breaking down the graphite and blending it a little. It also gives a more subtle tonal transition. The HB reaches further down into the tooth of the paper, whilst crumbling some of that 3B wash into finer graphite particles.

Next, I add a layer of 2H to further blend this hatching. If we want to, we can go on to use the brush, stump and/or colour shaper to continue blending, until we reach the smoothness we need. Layers of hatch can also be blended with a hog's hair brush, which creates a nice even tone. It's then possible to work over this, adding darks with a soft pencil and erasing to create highlights or random texture.

 ### *Grade hierarchy*

When layering, it's important to know which pencil to begin with. Going in first with a harder grade of pencil will make it harder for the darker grades to perform—they'll just skid over the top of the initial layer.

To see this in practice, cover a small patch of paper with a dense cross-hatching of 4H, then go over it with a 4B. Darker pencil grades need a fuller tooth to deposit their heavy load of graphite. In this case, the tooth has been blocked up by the 4H, making it very difficult for any further graphite to adhere. The quality of the 4B's mark is seriously compromised.

Thus, when I say we need to build up layers, I don't mean for us to start very lightly with a 6H and work our way all the way to the 8B. Nor should we always start with a 6B. Instead, we should think about where the shadows and light fall, and how dark the shadows will be. From this, we can judge what grade to begin with and, subsequently, how to end.

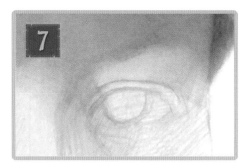

At this stage, I have outlined the shape of the iris as well as drawn a ring around the place where I want my super bright white highlight to be.

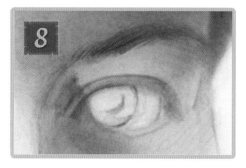

The ring around the highlight that we put in at the beginning helps to keep our hatching away from the area we wish to remain a bright white. However, the 4B doesn't leave the tidiest edge, so I go in with the mechanical pencil to sharpen this up.

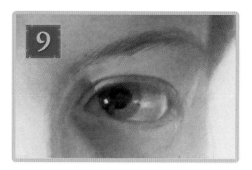

The pupil is drawn in with 4B pencil and then worked over with a H clutch pencil. I did this to reduce the grain on what I wish to be a smooth eyeball.

Here I am using a 2H clutch pencil to veil in a subtle tone that describes the turning of the cheek within the shadow shape. As always, I progress from dark to light, veiling in more and more subtly. I am trying my best not to leave any dark marks behind.

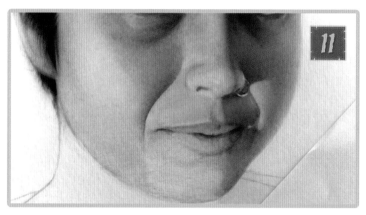

Building from simple blocks of value, I use softer grades over that to describe the surface. I continue the meticulous hatching process.

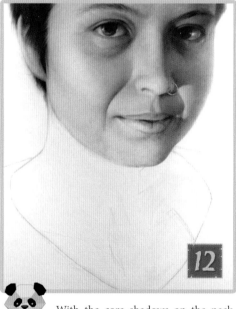

With the core shadows on the neck mapped out I'm ready to begin toning that area. I rather like drawings that have a balance between an area that is fully toned and areas that are left as line, but that wouldn't work in this case as the head would appear to float.

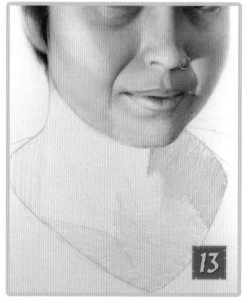

So that I can get a general idea of how shadows will look, I mass in shadows taking into account the general directional flow of the surface and how this can promote an upward flow, back to the face.

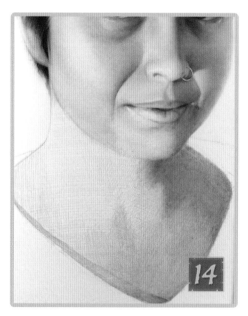

The easy stuff has been left till the last with this basic block-in of the neck values. There's a logic to tackling the harder stuff to begin with when you are full of energy. The manner in which I've worked up to the point has enabled me to bring this portrait to a conclusion with minimum frustration.

Check your darks

One of the most common changes in drawing in the closing stages, as we saw when doing the sphere exercise, is that it is often found that we haven't put the darks in dark enough, along the core shadows. For that reason, we might want to consider darkening these if the picture needs a little extra punch . If we do make a change to any of the dark places, there comes a need to take into account the light side and alter that too in order to maintain tonal balance between our light and dark values.

Ideally, we should have been reserving our deepest darks and highlights till the very last, and now is the time to put in those tiny highlights in the eye or nose. This is a special moment—I find it far more satisfying than scribbling a signature at the foot of the drawing. On a portrait there are other little touches we can add to increase surface interest, freckles, moles, warts, random hairs as well as finer hairs on the edges of the hair mass. We can go on indefinitely to the point of taking things too far, so we must cultivate the ability to call time on the picture lest we go too far. Restraint being just as important at the end as it was when we reigned in the exuberance of the curve and the gradient of values.

Finally, we have a finished portrait. The procedures and tools that went behind making this image should no longer be a mystery, however, Medusa looks like she has an opinion to share about the portrait . . .

Once again, critical old me... You're going to hate me now...
I think what you've made is a bit of a simulacrum, you
know? How about you set all your blenders to one side for a
moment and return to just pencil, paper and eraser.
You'll need to get back to basics for the challenges ahead.

CAPTURING COLOSSI

Mastery

255

Level I
Copying

256

Level II
2D Copying

258

Level III
3D Copying

266

Level IV
Sight-Size

268

I'd reached the end of the road. The path I'd been following so long gave way to clouds. Way off in the mist, on a separate peak, I saw a girl, her back to me. I called to her, and though her collie's ears twitched, she must not have heard me, because she never looked up. What was she drawing? What could have so captivated her? I couldn't see anything at all.

MASTERY

Level Up! – Drawing from the Past!

On our journey so far, we have been working to fine-tune and appreciate our powers of observation. We've also been learning a system for breaking down the problems of drawing, an approach derived from a centuries' old academic tradition. Although the twentieth century saw academic methods displaced from the centre of artistic practice, many contemporary realist artists and theorists will tell you that academic study is an essential precursor for developing a freer, more personally expressive style. The study of academic drawing will enable us to face and overcome many of the challenges we'll face in our artistic development—without these skills, all the freedom in the world will not be enough to help us surmount certain difficulties, and we may find our development stagnating.

In this final chapter, we're going to look at a small curriculum for continued development, based on the practices of academic Ateliers. We'll begin with some very basic methods that shouldn't pose much of a challenge, and will eventually advance to some truly challenging practices that will require many hours of concentration and effort. In facing these advanced challenges, frustration is perhaps inevitable, but remember, every obstacle you face is an opportunity to Level Up. Every door that blocks your path will eventually open. Persistence is the key to advancing in any field.

The academic training methods we are about to look at might feel rigid and formulaic, but they are the backbone of realist drawing: they add structure while promoting dexterity and creative intellect. Creative flourishes we add later on will be all the more powerful for being based on a solid foundation of time-tested methods. Achieving technical mastery will allow us to express our unique visions of the world fully and truthfully.

Geometric shapes, master drawings, sculptures, still lifes: these are typical subjects of study for academic artists. We advance in drawing through the practice and consistent application of sound principles. Each of these subjects pose their own special challenge, presenting us valuable ways to develop our skills.

If you wish to accurately represent the visual world, I can think of no better program of study than a combination of direct, natural observation and copying from great works. Drawing from great works increases sensitivity and understanding. This is a formal and formulaic drawing process, but its principles are sound and require no alteration. Eventually, with practice, you will hone your direct observation, and when combined with the techniques discussed in the coming pages, your work will be on exceptionally solid footing. Where you go next is entirely up to you: and you will be well equipped for your journey.

Without the strength and ability provided by drawing principles, artists are frozen in a kind of creative adolescence, not knowing how to challenge themselves, develop further or advance their artistic capabilities. As Cicero said, "To be ignorant of what came before you is to remain always as a child." There is a momentum and energy stored in the knowledge of the past that we can use to propel our work forward. These exercises may feel like backwards steps—but think of them as the few steps you take back before taking a running leap.

Cartone Method

As we begin to dabble in mastery, we're going to try out a method that Michelangelo used for generating his frescos.

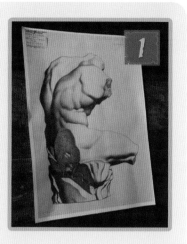

Known as the 'cartone' or cartoon method ('cartone' is Italian for 'a very large sheet of paper'), it involved making a preliminary sketch which was the same size as the finished work will be. A needle was then used to prick tiny holes all along its lines, allowing the cartoon to function as a kind of stencil. The paper was then attached the wall, where the fresco would be painted, and a bag of charcoal dust was 'pounced' upon the cartoon. When the cartoon was removed, the charcoal dust could be seen along all the tiny pinpricks, so that the image was transferred onto the wall.

We will be doing something similar in this exercise, minus the walls and pounce bag. Only pencil and paper are required here. The first thing I want you to do is to grab yourself a nice image. I have once again selected a Bargue plate of the Belvedere torso (I), so you can follow along with me, if you happen to pick up Gerald M. Ackerman's reissue of *Charles Bargue's Drawing Course*. Any image with nice, clear line-work is fine, though—you can print one from Pinterest if you wish.

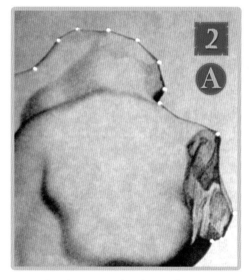

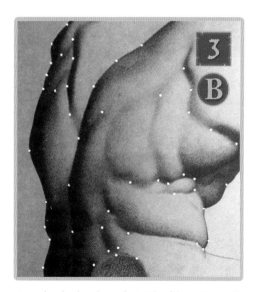

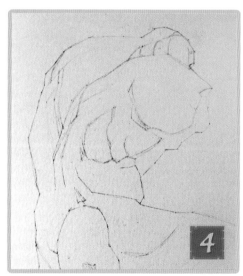

Remember how we reduced curved contours to straight lines? This step is an exercise in picking out the important points along the perimeter, places where the line changes angle or direction. You can see above the points I thought it was helpful to mark.

If you want a challenge, you can choose to simply prick the image along its perimeter, leaving you to place the features on the inside unaided. Alternately, if you'd prefer to get on with the value study more quickly, you can complete the next step and record the internal landmarks, too. These dots will greatly assist us in creating the shadow shapes that are such a vital part of the value phase.

Recording landmarks on the inside of the contour will make this exercise a little easier. When you are satisfied that you have pricked a hole through all the important landmarks, then you're ready for the next step, which is to attach this image to your drawing surface, and, with a HB pencil, mark a dot through each hole.

When you're done, don't throw this pricked image away as we still need to use it as a guide for when you join the dots up.

Now we play connect the dots, joining up our marks with lightly drawn straight lines, again using a HB pencil. This gives you a block-in that you can refine into a more accurate contour, using your original image as a reference.

This phase of drawing the line-work is not wholly without challenges: there will be instances where you have neglected to record a particular landmark, and you will need to draw in the missing feature, working from your original.

I fail to see how cheating will lead to mastery...

Cool! It's like a cheat mode for the times you end up doing your Art homework the night before.

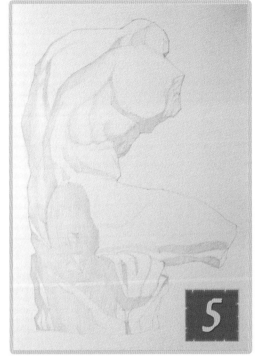

5

Having marked your shadow shapes, use a 2H pencil to fill them in with a nice consistent wash. One of the great things about this exercise is that it is so relaxing. We can sit or slump at our desk without any fear of any distortion occurring, because our line-work has been taken care of with the cartoon study.

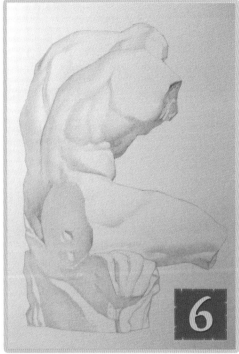

6

Crank the darkness up a bit by going in with the HB to darken the core shadows and shadow shapes in general. Now, I don't usually add value in such a regimented way, moving from 2H down the grades till I get to the 2B, but I'll do it this way here, as it's a method you may wish to adopt.

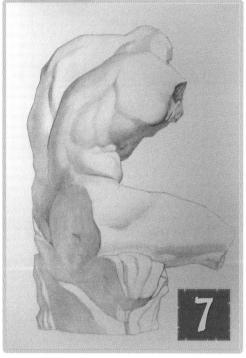

7

With the 2B, continue to develop areas. Things are getting darker gradually; each area is treated with a layer of 2H, HB and then 2B pencil.

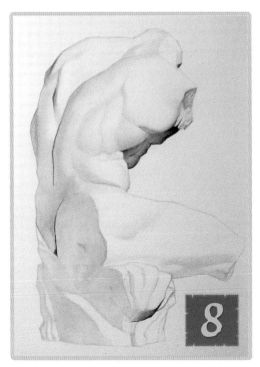

8

Time for a big jump. Take a sharp 5B and lay down some dark keys to represent the darkest areas of our subject.

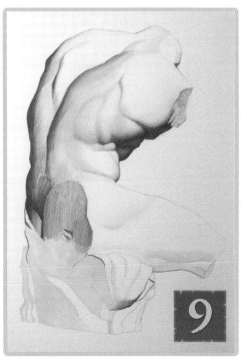

9

Continue growing the deep darks with the 5B and 3B. I can feel the layers of 2H under my pencil as I go in with 5B. It's a little too skiddy for my liking but everything seems to be going okay so far.

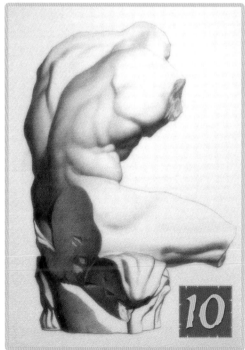

10

Here we have a completed master copy. Its values developed in layers, beginning with a simple 2H foundation. Timescale on this? Well, I managed to watch all of The Fellowship of the Ring in the time it took me to finish.

Shoulders of Giants!

Like many of the bosses we have already faced, this next boss arises from the past. You will be up against great artworks by some master artists. To defeat these colossi, as always, you must capture them.

This might seem daunting, but if you set your sights high, you will rapidly achieve fantastic progress. My own experience of studying and copying master drawings and sculptures has completely changed the way I see art. By drawing from the past, I am not only able to appreciate these artworks, I am sometimes able to learn their deeper lessons.

As you work through increasingly challenging master copies, you will find yourself suddenly seeing once-hidden aspects of paintings: wholly new things will appear within the work, new shapes will emerge, and art will become all the more incredible. Master copies are not an easy challenge, but by this stage, nothing worthy of our skills should be easy.

A well-trodden path

The practice of drawing from master copies has been around for centuries, and it continues today in Ateliers all around the globe. This study will give you a whole new way of looking at the originals you copy from. Instead of being an external, passive observer, you will get right inside the mechanics of the artwork, investigating the artists' methods of problem-solving.

Many artists have come to this cliff in the past: Picasso, Cezanne, Matisse, Joshua Reynolds, Michelangelo, Leonardo da Vinci, Edgar Degas, John Singer Sargent, Édouard Manet, Eugène Delacroix, to name only a few of them.

As I stood trembling at the cliff edge, the mists suddenly cleared, allowing me to glimpse the full majesty of the colossus I was to face. "Go get 'er!" the Specific cheered. Despite the heckling from below, I readied myself to leap onto the giant's curved back.

They have all stared out over this wide vista and dreamed of capturing a colossus for themselves. As you may have noticed, the artists I just listed belong to radically different movements and represent extremely diverse artistic philosophies. All of them, however, shared the same core skills we have been working to master. All have practiced, strengthened and enhanced these core skills through master copies.

As we strive to capture the colossi, we will be working through a series of classic Atelier exercises. Take note: although some of these challenges may seem brief or simple, they are actually more extended than any exercises we have yet undertaken. The benefits, however, are great. The study of geometric forms marked the first stage of this advanced stage of drawing. As we have been doing so far, we will continue to work through a number of stages, each a little more difficult than the last and each posing its own unique challenge.

This is the first master copy I ever attempted, after *Patroclus* by the 18th century colossus Jacques-Louis David. I was in my early twenties and had just discovered that copying could actually be a good thing. With master copies, as with all drawing, the key is to keep trying until you get it right. Don't settle for 'almost'—if you have to erase something twenty times, do it. Don't worry about damaging the paper; this is just a study, and you're learning. Try not to think of academic principles as rules but rather as tools that can, when you know how to use them, make the experience of drawing much less frustrating and much more enjoyably rewarding. It's a myth that drawing principles will block artistic sensibilities and individual creativity.

We will begin by copying a two-dimensional colossus. After that, we will draw from a three-dimensional colossus. Finally, we will conclude with a challenge known as 'sight-size drawing.' As we move through these challenges, we will have a chance to compare and contrast the processes of drawing from two and three-dimensional subjects. Despite the differences in subject matter, each exercise will follow a similar procedure, one which should be relatively familiar to you already. These exercises will give you a good chance to apply and reinforce skills you have learned so far, while also stretching yourself still further.

Master copies will also hone your perception in general, helping you to become more aware of the world around you, with all its wealth of visual pattern and complexity.

Be warned! The following pages feature nudity, so those troubled by bums should skip straight to drawing the lion on page 266—Oh, whoops, there's a bum on this page, too. I guess the damage has already been done. Sorry about that.

I closed my eyes and made a leap of faith . . .

Flat Colossus

Choose your colossus with care. For any master copy, ensure that you are working from a high-quality reproduction. Look for a work with strong directional lines and powerful, dynamic and well-defined gestures. Also look for easily read line-work and an interesting narrative. Seek out artists that inspire you, and study them intently.

For my colossus from the second dimension, I have chosen a 2009 figure drawing by the artist Colleen Barry. I especially like the powerful, clear line-work, because that's the aspect I want to concentrate on. The original is 18 x 24 inches, but my copy will be substantially smaller. Consider scaling down your copies at first: smaller copies are less difficult and less likely to overwhelm you.

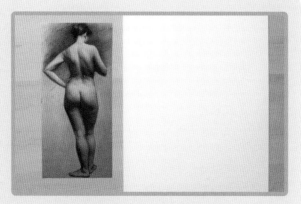

Because I'm right-handed, my Bristol board is placed on the right side, with the reference on the left. This keeps my arm from blocking my view of the reference as I work. Lefties should reverse accordingly.

To begin

I have marked the top and bottom of the picture. Then I dropped a vertical guideline down through a convenient part of the drawing. In this case, the vertical line generally follows the line of the woman's spine and left leg.

My initial guideline placement follows the strong vertical line running through Barry's own composition, and it passes through several useful landmarks. The more landmarks you can locate along your vertical guideline, the better.

Working down this guideline, I have marked the position of useful landmarks. I've chosen a variety of landmarks: features on the model, places where lines end, and areas of obvious tonal contrast.

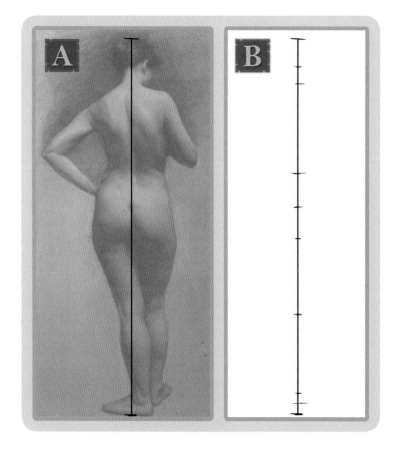

"Hey! What gives?" I hear you cry. "This panel's empty!" Well, not quite. This panel is actually full of lines, but I'm keeping them extremely light at this point, in case I need to change them. I've included this photo so that you can see just how light I keep my guidelines.

My actual pencil lines are barely visible, so once again they have been enhanced so that you can see what's going on.

In the centre is my vertical guideline, full of points.

I've triangulated the positions of the left and right extremities. These are useful points to establish early on because they form the basis for my constellation shape.

We've come a long way since encountering the Vase of Doom, but this exercise is pretty much just that. The difference is that now we have a process in place which allows us to properly measure and describe the angles and proportions of particular line segments.

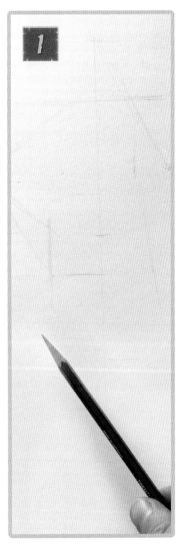

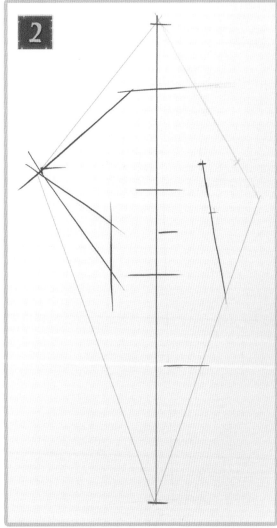

My pencil glides from the reference, which I have placed on the left of my desk, over to my drawing. This is a quick check to establish that I have correctly placed and angled the dominant line of the left thigh. This process is carried on throughout the creation of this master copy.

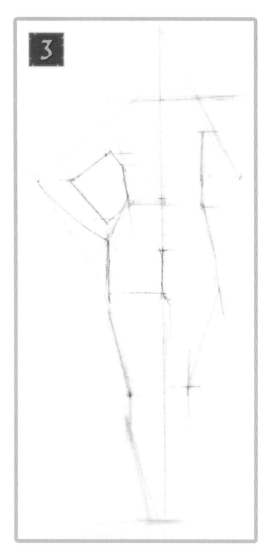

3 The block-in is becoming more complex now, and a curvaceous contour is beginning to emerge. Thanks to the triangulation of many measurements, I'm now more confident in the accuracy of my marks, so I'm letting them become darker (although the actual marks are not as dark as you see here—I've darkened the image to help you see). At this point, I am also systematically removing any inaccurate or unhelpful guidelines because they can be distracting.

4 By now I'm sure we're all super aware that core shadows are very important landmarks: they help us gauge positions as well as helping us compare light and dark shapes. For this reason, I'm always on the lookout for core shadows within my subject. Here you can see where I've begun to note their location.

5 I'm now happy with the contours of both the outside perimeter and of the shadow shapes. This image is ready for value to be added.

6 Adding value begins with the shadows. Also, because the reference image is fairly dark, I've gone over the light sides of my copy with a couple of washes of 2H, just to remove those harsh lights that are nowhere to be found in the original. When drawing, always look for opportunities to add what's useful and remove what isn't. In this case, the stark white of my drawing surface was definitely not useful and needed to be taken care of.

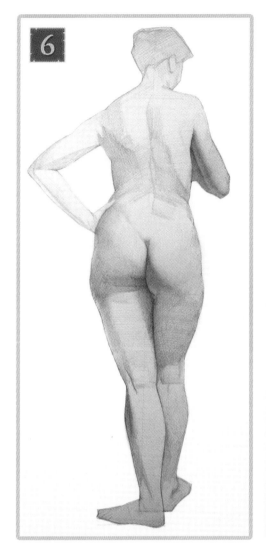
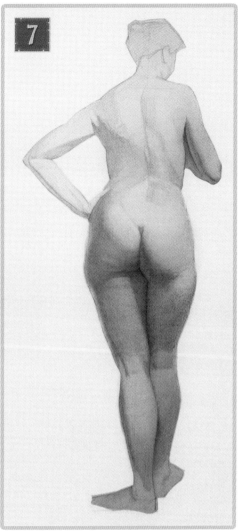
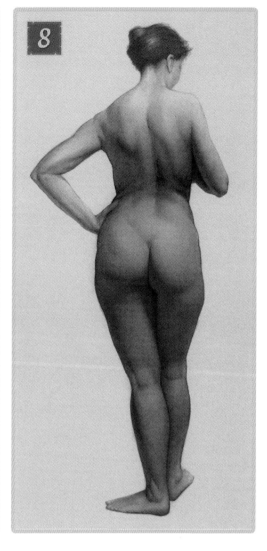

7 I'm gradually darkening the shadows, and as I work, I'm also breaking down the graphite particles and filling in those little gaps. I'm making sure that my value structures are well established before jumping ahead into refinement. I notice that the lower part of my copy is getting too far ahead, so I move back to the areas that need to catch up, such as the head, torso and left arm.

8 I've reserved highlights and deepest darks for the model's head. In this image, it's a little hard to make out, but the deepest darks are on the hair. This wasn't quite clear on the original, so I've had to make a decision. I decided I would rather my focal point be the woman's head, rather than the crease of her bum.

Capturing a Winged Lion

Master copies take a while, so choose artworks that interest you. For this study into shadow, therefore, I have opted for the only thing scarier than an airborne shark: a Venetian winged lion.* That's my child-self's reasoning. My mature reasoning thinks that this image makes for an excellent study because it manages to convey strength and power, even though most of its lines are curved and its forms are softly rounded. How does this piece get away with breaking such a basic rule? The forms might be rounded, but they are contained within a solid rectangular shape, which adds a lot of stability to this image. The composition and pose, as well as the subject matter itself, bring a lot of force to this image.

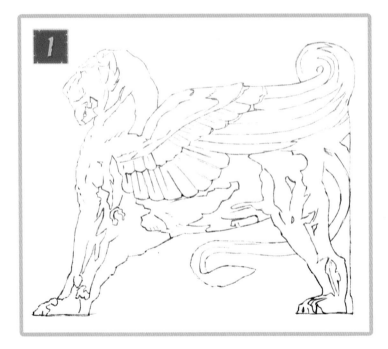

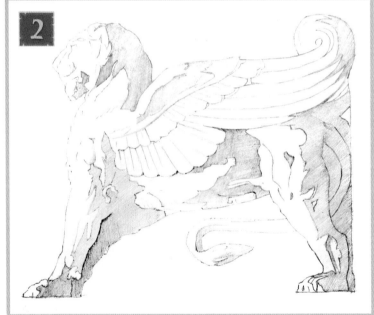

1 I've established the line-work in the same way as in the previous demonstration, following the processes we've already explored. With my contour and shadow shapes established, I'm ready to start adding value.

2 As always, I begin by applying value to the shadow shapes. This is always one of my favourite parts of the drawing process, simply because you get such quick results with very little effort. Once I've roughed in an average level of darkness for each area of shadow, I begin to key in a dark around the front leg. From this point, I am starting to carve out the specifics of how these shadows will appear.

*You may beg to differ.

The key grows, informing other shadows, which are in turn deepened and darkened. I can't resist developing the lights, and so my midtones also begin to grow and spread. One thing to note is that for this image I'm using a paper with a more pronounced tooth than usual, which you can see particularly well in the close-up. I chose this paper because, this stone sculpture is quite grainy, and I wanted to replicate that lovely texture. One way I make the most of this rough, gritty effect is by using a hog's hair brush to apply some graphite powder.

 Using the brush and powder allows me to mass in my values quickly. I then make adjustments with the blending stump. In contrast to this rapid, mass approach, though, I'm also working out from the shadow cores into the midtones with my H to produce a delicate, intricate veiling of tone.

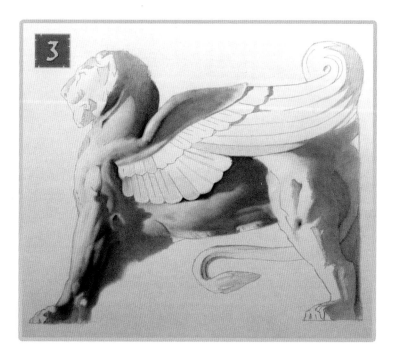

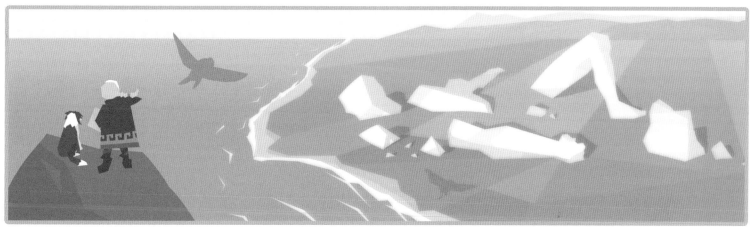

The lion leapt into the air, and we clutched tight to his mane. He flew right past a girl on her who appeared to be still drawing—the collie tilted his head in confusion as we soared over the water, towards a strange sight: a plain littered with gigantic, oddly-shaped boulders. "That," the Specific shouted, over the roaring wind, "is a shattered Stone Titan. You gotta catch it—it's gonna be awesome!" Uh oh. The thing was huge. Somehow, the fact that it was immobile didn't make it seem any easier to handle.

Level III Copying

Belvedere Torso II

Drawing from sculptures and casts forms the natural progression from the two-dimensional master copy, and it will serve as a basis from which to move on to life drawing. Once you have mastered drawing from casts, learning to take accurate measurements and assessing values, you will find no inanimate subject difficult.

You may face practical difficulties in accessing high-quality casts, as they are quite expensive. We've already looked at some low-cost hacks, such as using white sheets for drapery and slapping a coat of white paint over objects. For cast drawing, you might also try going to a museum or gallery. Even small town museums are likely to have several casts. If you need a chair, just ask: museums are usually glad to accommodate artists. Bear in mind that it may be necessary to make several trips, as good master copies take time. Working in public can also invite some curiosity, which may or may not be a problem, depending on how you feel about attention. Try not to let it distract or discourage you: you're here to work, and it's an important task.

By drawing from casts of great sculptures such as the Belvedere Torso, you will be following a great tradition. Many great artists have drawn from sculptures as a means of furthering their abilities, and all have built their images using the techniques that we have studied.

How do you choose which cast or sculpture to draw from? Avoid dark surfaces, as well as anything made of metal or glass. On shiny surfaces, midtones are hard to see. Even worse, qualities such as reflectivity and transparency actively confuse us, making it hard to understand exactly what's going on with the surface and form. Take this shiny, black owl, for example: looking at him, we can tell a lot about the sunny day around him, but it's much harder to make out the details of his structure, and the high gloss removes any tonal subtlety.

Instead of gleaming fence post owls, opt for sculptures with a matt, white patina. This is the best surface for revealing form. Reflected lights and half-tones will be much clearer than usual, helping you to develop the ability to see them even when they are less noticeable.

This particular cast is from the statue known as the Belvedere Torso, by the sculptor Apollonius. This work had a massive impact on art history. It profoundly influenced Renaissance artists, most notably Michelangelo, who studied it extensively. I didn't fly out to the Vatican City to study it, but acquiring this cast was a significant investment. It's well worth working from if you have the chance, however: no matter how it is angled, there are beautiful shapes and lines to study. This variety of possible perspectives is one of the reasons that drawing from sculptures is so rewarding.

When working from three-dimensional subjects, stages like the block-in become even more important—and challenging. Labouring over painstaking measurements may not feel glamorous, but remember that every great work depended on its scaffolding. Michelangelo's 'David' will have literally been surrounded by scaffolds to help him access it, and though that framework has long since vanished into some Vatican bin, the success of the work depended on it. Note that in the pages which follow, I have digitally enhanced the scaffolding lines so that they are visible; they were actually much fainter.

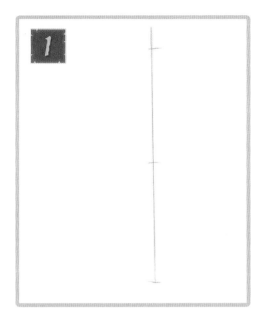

Top, base and middle points are put in with little fuss. From these, I have triangulated the positions of the right and left sides and marked in these estimates as well.

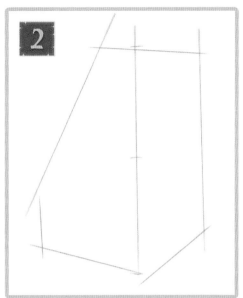

Holding the pencil at the far end, I construct the constellation with broad strokes. I've chosen five lines to convey the most salient information about the torso, noting its broadest angles and proportions. You get bonus points if you manage to construct a constellation with fewer than six sides. Things are still very broad and unfocused at this point. Nice and open, ready to be corrected.

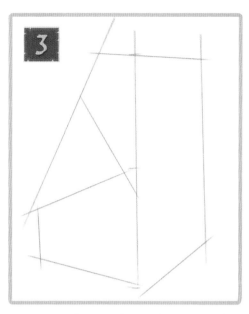

I carve into the constellation shape with a few more lines—eight perimeter lines now, things are hotting up. These lines are not meant to be accurate visual representations of anything yet. Rather, they are devices for finding the largest relationships and reducing them to their essence: basic length and tilt. The visual experience is a puzzle, a sort of lock that needs picking, and right now I'm feeling it out, trying to see how it works so that I can crack it.

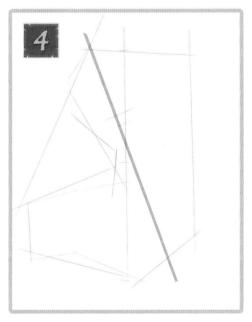

I keep subdividing the shape and lines. The dark diagonal running through the shape indicates a (very light) guideline I ran through the torso to get an idea of the central line that runs through the chest. This helps me understand the orientation of the torso and keep track of which way it's facing as it twists.

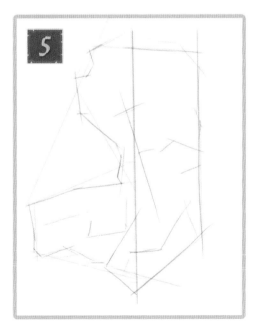

Now I block-in the position of the darkest shadows. These are crucial marks, as they help me to reassess the accuracy of my contour. I am always thinking in terms of patterns: patterns of positive and negative space, patterns of light and dark.

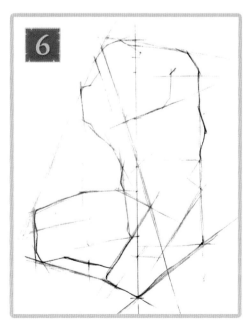

Here you can see the completed line-work. Core shadows, or rather, shadow edges, are great for assessing the accuracy of the perimeter line. In the actual drawing, all of these lines were still very light, of course: they're darkened here so that you can make them out. And with that, I have seen The Return of the King. Go Frodo!

4

Level IV Copying

Sight-Size

Sight-size drawing is a staple of Atelier practice. It is an approach in which you create a 1:1 replica of your subject. This means that you place the subject right beside your drawing, and produce a drawing which is exactly the same size as the subject. This very literal method of drawing is excellent training for the eye, helping us to understand relationships in the subject and make the most of them within our drawing.

In the D-Lab

Sight-size is a controlled and precise drawing practice, which means you need to be able to regulate all aspects of your environment. The studio needs almost laboratory conditions. Because the proportions depend on position, it's essential that both the subject and the drawing surface remain in exactly the same positions. One of the most crucial (and difficult) elements to control is lighting. It is critical in sight-size that we be able to control the lighting conditions, making sure they remain consistent over the course of this extended study. Windows must be covered, as the angle of sunlight will change over the course of the day. Good artificial lighting is key.

CASTS!

Let's make further use of casts and try an altogether different approach with them.

From this controlled environment, we are able to develop and fine-tune our artistic sight. By practicing this method, you will become adept at making accurate measurements, choosing reference points and problem-solving. Sight-size is also an excellent way to train yourself in preparing drawings precisely and efficiently.

Making accurate measurements early on in the drawing will eventually become second nature. Take your time and don't rush. This is a training exercise—it's not about creating pretty pictures, although many artists do eventually use it for that purpose. Teachers love this method because it allows them to see very quickly where the student has made an incorrect observation.

> This process doesn't deviate from what you observe. The principle of this exercise is to try to nail down exactly what you see, in order to build your powers of observation. This isn't a time for flourishes of creativity; this is eye training.

The tricky thing about sight-size is that you are not allowed to look at your subject while you are working at your drawing surface. You will only view your subject from a specific viewing point, several steps back from both the subject and your work. You step back, look; step forward, draw; then step back and look again. This process develops a very particular lock-step connection between observation and drawing, and because it's so particular, it's important not to practice this method too exclusively. If you neglect other ways of training yourself to see proportion, you may find that you come to rely on this method entirely, so be sure to change it up!

Lighting

For sight-size, we need a few constant, controlled elements: at least one steady light source, one subject, and one viewpoint. Cover any windows as completely as you can—it's important to block out the changeable daylight. Set up your lamp or lamps so that the light is evenly distributed between your subject and your drawing surface. The light should be placed on the side of your non-dominant hand, so that your drawing hand won't cast a shadow on the surface. If you want to replicate Atelier conditions precisely, get a bulb equivalent to an old 75-100 watt light bulb (1100-1600 lumens), which is what these workshops use. You want strong, directional lighting on your subject, and you want the light source positioned so that it creates simple areas of light and dark on your subject.

Choice of subject

The classic subject for sight-size is a cast, but, as we've discussed, there are a number of good substitutes you can use. Choose a subject which is the same size as the drawing you will do, so roughly the same size as your paper. The best subjects are matt and white of course. Place your subject on a stable surface which raises it to eye level. You want to use a dark background simply because this creates a nice contrast and makes the silhouette stand out clearly to us as we view from a distance.

Choice of easel

Because you need to be able to line your drawing up side by side with your subject, it's important to work on an easel for this practice. For sight-size, your easel needs to be sturdy and stable so that it doesn't rock around while you work. It should be absolutely vertical—check with a spirit level or plumb-line to be sure. The easel needs to be able to hold your drawing board high up, at eye level. Position your easel next to your cast, so that your drawing board is halfway between the front and back of your cast. Affix your paper to the board using artists' tape, as discussed in the beginning chapter on surfaces.

The viewpoint

This is the part that makes sight-size really special. You'll only be viewing your subject from this position, so you need to measure and mark it clearly. There is a tradition, noted in Leonardo's writings, that the distance you step back should be three times the height of the subject. So, if you are drawing an object 30cm high, step back 90cm. Once you have this measurement, you can use masking tape to mark a viewing point on the floor (A). In the sight-size method, unlike normal drawing, we see the subject and the drawing simultaneously, and because they're side by side, our eyes don't have to refocus to adjust to different distances.

Sight-size involves a fair bit of standing, so choose some comfortable footwear. Get yourself some awesome slippers like these bad boys (they're fluffy on the inside!).

A few pointers and recaps

Because I'm right-handed, I always have my subject on my left side. Left-handed people should reverse this. This is a comfortable way of working because it means that you're not having to look over your working hand.

Distance is so important to sight-size: all your observation, analysis and corrections take place from a distance. You want to get into a rhythm of walking away from the work, comparing the subject and drawing, walking back and adjusting anything that's off, then walking away again to check. As well as your viewpoint, you also need room to take a nice long walk backwards, at least eight feet, so a 12-foot room would be ideal.

When checking, close one eye—and make sure it's always the same eye. Use your dominant eye, if you know it. (To check: hold your thumb outstretched. Close one eye, then the other. When your thumb jumps most, the eye you've shut is your dominant one.)

RIGHT HANDED SETUP

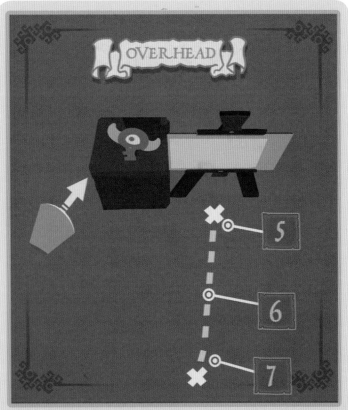

OVERHEAD

The correct setup for this approach is to have the subject and the drawing surface placed side by side. Then, from a distance, both the work and the drawing can be viewed simultaneously, or rather as quick to simultaneous as we can get. In this way, we're not turning our head, refocusing or peering around easels.

1   **Light source** — Positioned so you never walk across it, placed high above the subject, and not shining into your eyes when you're in drawing position.

2   **Subject** — Traditionally a cast is chosen for this purpose, but you can use anything really. A two-dimensional subject is completely fine to use also.

3   **Drawing board** — Paper large enough to contain the subject fastened to the board with artists' tape.

4   **Easel** — Vertical, to avoid any distortions.

5   **Working point** — We should at no point allow ourselves to take a peek at the subject while at this position, working at the easel.

6   **Walking distance** — This distance should be three times the length of the subject.

7   **Viewing point** — This is where you view the subject from, making observations, before returning to your working point to mark those observations down.

Surface — Use a good quality white paper; leave toned papers for later explorations, as grey paper requires a different process than we've been exploring so far.

Monocular vision — When you look at your subject, only view it with one eye open, and use the same eye each time, preferably your dominant eye.

Pressure — Work as lightly as possible, while still working darkly enough that you can see your drawing from your viewing spot. The peculiarities of this exercise make it especially important that you always keep your work open to correction.

Be true to the subject — Deviation from what you see in nature must be a choice and not an accident. When first beginning such studies, try to be as accurate as you can—design is something that comes after we mastered observation.

The cast is angled so that it is shown in its best light.

First things first

Careful observation is essential if we're going to get anywhere. Before making any sort of mark on the paper, you should take some time to look over your subject; you will probably make surprising discoveries. This is a time of analysis free from commitment or anxiety: there's no need to worry about mistakes, because we haven't even begun.

During this analytical, observational phase, we can make some initial decisions, planning possible routes our drawing can take.

We can look for landmarks: which features are interesting, basic and prominent enough for us to use? Look for fundamental shapes, repeated angles, and relationships between large forms.

Pole and plumb

Before we begin you might consider upgrading your easel by affixing a pole to the top (A). It should extend far enough out to the side that you can hang a plumb-line from it, to fall across your subject. This plumb-line will serve as a guideline when you step back to your viewing point. This set up ensures that your central guideline remains concrete, clear and fixed, rather than being a vague, general idea. It can also be helpful to stick a bit of Blu-Tack to the plumb-line thread at a point where it intersects a useful landmark.

This just makes it even easier to line things up while you're at your viewing position. Having a plumb-line hung up becomes important in the next steps, because it keeps your hands free to make other measurements.

Find the centre line

We begin sight-size by standing at our viewpoint, holding the plumb-line straight out in front of us, and finding the vertical mid-line. Remember, this may not be right in the middle of the cast: you get to choose it, based on your assessment of important landmarks.

Holding the plumb-line nice and steady, move your arm across the cast until the line falls across a place where it's hitting two important points. On a human head, this might be the edge of the nose and the corner of the mouth, for instance—you can choose anything, as long as the points are nice and obvious, and are as close as possible to the middle. This is an important line which you'll use for a lot of future measurements.

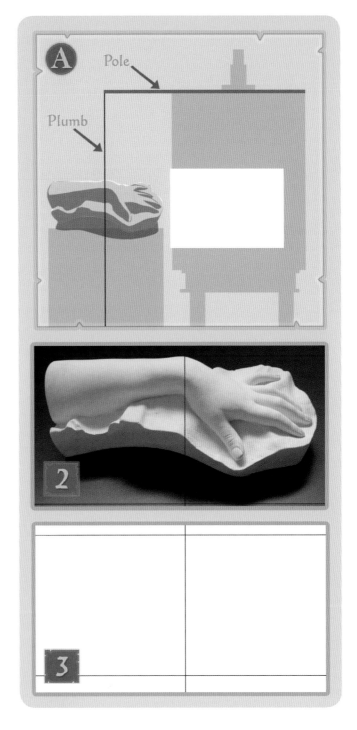

Drop a guideline

Now, moving back to your easel, use a yard stick to mark your own vertical, central guideline, corresponding to the plumb-line observation you just made. This is just a reference line, so mark it very lightly. Step back to your viewing position and use the plumb-line to make sure that your guideline is properly vertical.

Top and base points

In our drawings so far, the placement of top and bottom points has been up to us. In sight-size, however, they have a definite position that we must discover. To find the top and bottom points, take your plumb-line by its ends, stretch it out tight horizontally, and hold it with your arms outstretched. From your viewing position, align the taut plumb-line so that it lines up with the top edge of your paper. Slowly bring the line down until it meets the top of the cast. Holding the line in place, notice where it intersects your vertical line. Now look at your paper and find the same place on your vertical guideline. Keeping your eye on that point, walk back to your easel and mark it. Repeat this process to find the bottom. Once you're happy with the placement of these two points, you can continue to use this process to mark the position of other landmarks along the central guideline.

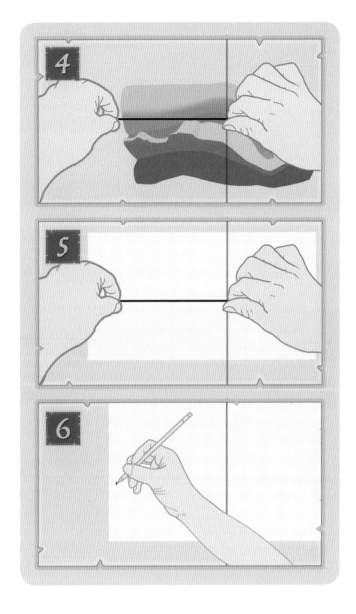

 Find the sides — A similar process lets us find the sides. Outstretch your arms with a strand of black cotton pulled between them. Line one end up with a side point and the other end with the vertical guideline. Mark the distance with your thumbs.

 Keeping your arms outstretched, move this length of cotton so that it is now in front of the drawing surface, lined up with your guideline. Look at the point that your thumb has marked as the side. Keeping your gaze locked on this point, return to your easel and mark the point.

 Once you've marked several landmarks using this process, walk back to your viewing point and use the plumb-line measurement technique to check the accuracy of your marks.

Remember — Use a mirror often to compare your drawing with the cast. As we should already be aware, this is a very effective way to check your accuracy: it allows you to see your work with fresh eyes, as if you'd taken a break. Doing this frequently will let you catch mistakes before they become too entrenched.

Everything at once — All areas are worked at a similar rate. Don't let any area get too far ahead of the rest. The drawing needs to progress at a unified rate; otherwise, one part might come to dominate the image, which can cause catastrophic distortions, especially if the dominating part contains any errors.

Think in abstract terms — Don't draw nouns. Rather than thinking in terms of drawing named features on your subject, think in terms of abstract shapes. In the example shown here, I am never thinking "This is the index finger, and now I'm drawing the knuckle . . ." Let your hand be guided by strict observation, not stored knowledge of your subject.

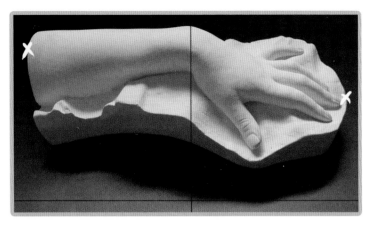

You can see where I've dropped two corresponding central guidelines. Using the method described on the previous page, I've marked the left and right-hand side points.

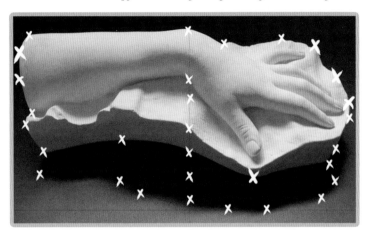
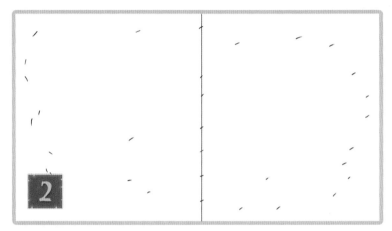

Using the same process of measurement, I locate many other useful landmarks. As a useful exercise, examine each of these points and ask yourself why I decided it was significant. Does it mark an extreme outer point? A change in tilt? A shift in tone? You should aim to begin line-work before the points become too numerous.

Once I've mapped out my many landmarks, I begin the block-in phase by lightly joining up these points. This gives me a highly generalised idea of the cast. Now that I've marked out some basic line segments, recording their lengths and angles, I can return to my viewing position to double check their accuracy. Using my plumb-line, I can repeat the process of vertical and horizontal measurements. This is the easiest way of checking my accuracy. I then systematically check the correctness of my lines by using the plumb-line to compare the location of points with relation to one another, cross-checking with several different points, not just the ones adjacent.

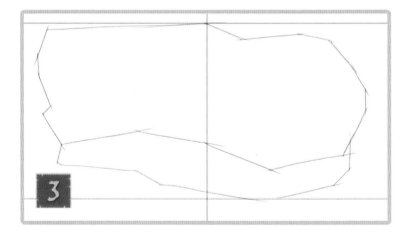

I have at this point clearly defined the contour, and I have also included a faint line indicating the edges of shadows. Reaching this level of detail takes a great deal of time and concentration. Even at this stage, it is still possible to make out the individual line segments. The reason for not converting all straight lines to curves is that I usually want to retain some strength to the line. This is one instance where I do exercise some stylistic choice, as I decide what degree of straightness to retain.

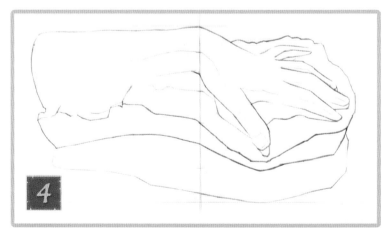

THE END

**Discovering
a Studio
278**

After my attempt to capture the scattered limbs and pieces of the Stone Titan, I felt drained. Did I have the heart to go on? Marius hopped up onto my shoulder. "Look up," the General said. My breath caught: we had reached the end of the road. Below us, I could see all the ground we had covered. Before us stood a little house on a hill, a place to rest.

Be afraid of the child who can draw the cube accurately. It could very well mean they are some kind of genius.

Cube Boss Beats Child?

When starting out, I had two aims for this book. First, to teach drawing in a new way. Second, for this to be the first drawing book to use no puns at all. One out of two isn't bad. As I began researching for this book, I decided to look into ways of seeing, particularly the ways that children see. There's been a lot of fascinating research into the stages that children's drawings progress through. I'd never seen anything, however, on how a child would respond to a classic Atelier exercise, such as drawing a cube. Could a child, unfettered by hang ups and preconceptions, tap into direct observation? Thinking that this might provide some interesting opening remarks for the book, I grabbed a cube and my nephew Mason, who was at the time five years old.

I wanted to see how Mason would deal with the visual problem of the cube, set up as in illustration (A). I wanted a fancy pants opening, but with his five valiant attempts, Mason actually reminded me of something profoundly important instead, which is the message I want to leave you with. We've talked about drawing as a way of solving problems, but the truth is, there is no problem. Drawing is just drawing. There are degrees of technical sophistication, but in the end, we can all pick up a pencil and communicate something with line.

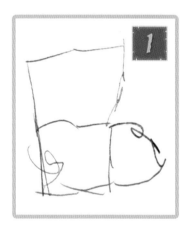
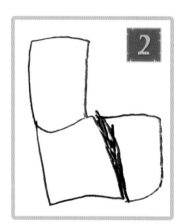
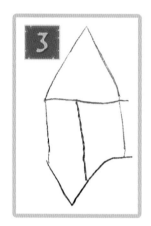

In his first three attempts, we get an interesting glimpse into his problem-solving efforts. In these drawings, with small anxious lines, he's trying to reconcile what he knows about cubes (that their faces are square) with what he sees in front of him. By the third drawing, he's begun to recognise the ways that the angles are actually skewed by perspective. In the fourth drawing, however, something quite new emerges: bored of my exercise, he starts riffing on the shape: a face appears, and the facets grow into legs.

By the fifth drawing, his frustration has blossomed into spectacular, defiant playfulness. Drawing from observation, using the methods and exercises in this book, will make you a better draughtsman. It can also be aggravatingly difficult. Amidst all the technical discipline, make room for play, for creativity and spontaneous fun. Drawing is one of the first ways we learn to play and a place we can all return to whenever we want.

So, at the crossroads between play and discipline, we've reached the end of this book. By now, you should feel that you have a firm grasp on the fundamental principles of drawing. Throughout the course of this adventurous Tetraforce Atelier, I've tried to break the process down into simple steps. If you can really integrate this philosophy into your work, you will find that you have a secure, solid foundation from which to leap to new heights.

Although this is the end of the book, it should not be the end of your journey in drawing. Take the principles you've learned here and push them further, drawing more objects from life. You should no longer be tormented by the thought, "But I can't draw." Instead, hopefully, you will feel confident and peaceful as you decide to set aside an 30 minutes or so to meditate with pencil and paper.

> This is a subject we can all enjoy. We don't need expensive kit. All we need is to is grab some pencils and paper, and choose an interesting object to serve as our teacher.

Many of the exercises in this book are useful to return to time and again, throughout your artistic development. Whether it be geometric solids, still lifes or master copies, these exercises constantly provide new opportunities for development. Every time you return to them, you will discover something new within the practice. These exercises will become constant companions in your artistic adventures, always offering a fresh challenge. Repetition is key to developing a strong set of skills—and each time you repeat, it will be new. Keep your eyes on the path, don't lose sight of the General, and don't let the Specific carry you away. Give your hands a good shake, remember to breathe and resist the temptation to get fiddly. Be bold, take courage, and don't forget to have fun.

We reached the top of the hill where the house stood. From within, I heard a faint and familiar sound: the scratching of a pencil on paper. Marius bouncing along ahead of me, I mounted the steps.

1. Sturdy bookshelves

These hold research material, sculptures, plaster casts and books containing images such as anatomy or natural forms you might wish to reference.

2. High ceilings

A big space allows space for thought and makes you feel freer. See David's 'Tennis Court Oath' for a good illustration of big ideas swirling overhead.

3. Overhead north light

A studio with a north-facing window doesn't allow direct sunlight to enter, which is good because direct sunlight would shift over the course of the day. Light striking your paper causes a glare, making it difficult to see what you're doing. North-facing windows cast a soft, even light throughout the studio.

4. Plants

You don't need ivy growing from your roof, but greenery is always a nice, oxygenating addition. Beware the wickedness of plants at night, when they shift their alignment to chaotic-evil and begin trying to poison you with murderous exhalations of carbon dioxide.

5. Noiseless

Seal your studio off as best you can from unwelcome auditory distractions.

6. Sight-size location

It's nice to have a safe, out of the way place with controllable lighting where you can leave your sight-size set up for long periods of time. This is useful because, as we've just seen, sight-size study can be a long-term process.

7. Ventilation

Breathing in graphite dust is quite horrible. Dry lips and a sore throat are indications of breathing in too much graphite. Can't be healthy.

8. Wall colour

A light wall colouring maximises the effect of the light. White is the best choice for studio walls.

9. Table

You want a large table that can hold your materials. Even better is one that can be tilted, allowing you to work at an angle. Keep an empty space on one side for the inevitable accumulation of tools.

10. Carpet

If you have hard floors, consider putting a rug in your studio. I am forever dropping pencils, and if they fall onto a carpeted surface, the leads inside are a lot less likely to break.

11. Artificial light

We've already talked about the problems with sunlight. Good artificial light lets you work at any time of the day or night. Position it on the opposite side from your drawing hand. Consider the quality of your bulb, because you'll be working under this for long periods. A really high quality LED is a great bet.

12. Walkway

As part of your sight-size area, you should have a clear walkway about three times the height of your subject.

13. Plan chest

I'm still aspiring to a proper plan chest, but you do need at least two storages places: one for papers and another, larger cabinet for tools.

14. Good acoustics

This is for when you need musical inspiration. If you decide to have music, opt for some without lyrics. Songs with lyrics activate the verbal part of the brain.

15. Wall space

You'll want to hang completed work, as well as images that inspire you. This can also be a place to hang brainstorming images. Make sure it's somewhere you can actually reach, so you can change it up as needed.

Index

RELEASE THE KRAKEN!

Amanda Lee
Hillary Summerton
Maximilian Thornhill
Olle Lyberg
Wolfgang Müller
Paul Weinandt
Zachary Weiss
Eryka Sanchez Mejia
Jason Cunningham
Mark Giordano
Duncan Mellonie
Helen Carey
Faramaz Jean baptiste
Dorothy Smith
Shuwei Zhang
Moriah Trostler
Lai Cheong Sang
Sasathorn Phaspinyo
Andreas Moll
Arnfinn Moseng
Morten Birch
Melanie Nadeau
Jonas Wollmen
Keith Kritselis
Henning Rieche
Afzal Mussa
Raphaëlle Jubault
Lynne Schaffstall
Dahyun Kim
Sutee
John Forsyth
Marcus Pehrsson
Nicholas Green
Carl Going
Rowan Gray
Scott Strbik
Martin Clapson
Jon Bloom
Per Fagrell
Miles Meeks
Joshua Balboa
Shawn Aronson
Michael Kayson
Jérôme Argot
Robert Jones
Keven Welch
David W Luna
Omar Khalil
Daniel Ihrke
Joshua Cooper
Jenny Warner
Angel Luis Diez Hernandez
Michelle van Voorhies
Jose Antonio Diaz Cañas
Kevin McCormick
Angela Titus
Shannon Groff
Matthew Hudson
Brandon Brown
Chris Vasicek
Michael Goldman
Gilles Philippart
Will Whittaker
Ged Trias
Minesh Chauhan
Jayant Menon
Tim Betz
Adam Skoglund
Craig Hackl
Calum Thompson
Samuel Allemann
Ryan Lok
Mark Anderson
Iris Close
Michael H. Stubbs
Jarryd Peterson
Melissa Alvarez
Alexander Noot
Massera Massimo
Alex Luzi
Lakshman Shantakumar
Renee Rijff
William Lamming
Sam Forsyth
Matthew Morris
Stefan Liden
Niran Lohmaneeratana
Chad Pierce
Amanda McKenzie
Charles Fugitt
Katherine Hatton
Matt Golins
Derek Young
Edward Winder
Pan Seng Tat
Bruce Johnson

Robert Schipano
Alicia Petroff
Lauren Alexandra
Ricardo Carvalho
Nancy Dillon
Zheng Gin
Jesus Rodriguez
Steve Baker
Sean Brightman
Marc von Martial
Dale Cook
Tony Sturtevant
Joseph Budovec
Priska Knaus
Nick Bers
Christopher Povinelli
Ian Nicolle
Andy Baker
K Wilson
Dave Sawyer
Julija Skvorc
Paul Anguiano
Nestor Miyares
Katharina J Vikholt
Jacqueline Low
Chris Mack-Riddell
Jerrod Jackson
Ryan Miesen
Dan Connolly
Nikolai Schlegel
Paul Counter
John Wertz
John Fawcett
Anton Brink
Yannick Bertrand
Jean-Marc Giorgi
Julia Benson-Slaughter
Elizabeth Liew
Frank Suyker
LaVar J Foxworth
Andrew Hunter
Juan Enrique Leon Navarrete
Kieron Briggs
Miss Katherine Usher
Alec Swiniarski
Quek Soo Kiat
Ovittayakul Tanachai
Anders Pedersen
James Holland
Karin Marie Jacobsen
Rhonda Bender
Joan Andelin
Jason Wiggins
Abby Hadden
David Pérez Gutiérrez
Swisslab Gmbh
Jenny Hall
Matt House
Soon Wei Song
Henry Clark
Vincent Tee
Steve Henson
Vryce Hough
Ben Waxman
Mike Barnes
Andrew Corrigan
Hugo Mota Prego de Faria
Aleksander Kenton
Melissa Polkey
Robert Lewis
Sven Liepertz
Joachim Irgens
Tom McIntyre
Andrea Kulpa
Geert-Jan Bekman, de bieb
David Berchelmann
Patrick McCook
Aaron M. Batman
Sophie Gelhar
Jerry Fuchs
Richard Fowler
Tyler Hass
Tara J Kohinski
Andreas Müürsepp
Chen Yu-Shuo
Stan Pelikys
Dave Owens
Alex Van Boxel
Eric Stafford
Levi Greaves
Deborah Wunder
André Kishimoto
Ryan Mose
David Fooden
Shannon McGuire
Chris Bennett
Yuriko Coenen
Valerie Little
Davis Agle
Dennis Timm
Lee Engelhardt
Daniel Sullivan
Nigel Man
Benjamin A. Russell
Mike Clarke
Ric Paul
Ihyoson Yamanaka
Greg Forbes

Dan Pollack
Justin J. Walsh
Dan Walker
Ian Holt
Stephen Ross
Mermet
Thomas Callahan
Mark Flisher
Laura Grenot Jones
Corey Williams
Tracy Tavis
Kneubuhler Romain
Gordon Brander
Kelly Klingenberg
Leobardo salcido
Rebecca Price
Richard Mansfield
Grant Raifstanger
Robin Marshall
Stuart Lafferty
Christine Louise Hansen
Philip Smyth
Aron Chan
Gregory L Box
Trey Ratcliff
Danielle Bynoe
Derwin Galen
Alexander O. Smith
K.M. Franken
Ashley Nichole Mirasol Wheeler
Tara Yoo
Thomas Chang
Kyra Jaeger
Richard Muncy
Alexandra Jomini
Rachel Hahn
Christopher Fodge
Ivan Å Ivak
Vincent Pang
Thomas Brown
Mario Salamanca
Tom Brown
Pam Waite
Santo-Matei Alexandru
Peter Snares
Amber Corlett
Courtney Pennington
Lisandro Gutierrez
Adriane Ruzak
Sarah Humphreys
Eric Koboldt
Kimberly Sward
Rob Lascola
Sam Bauc
Keith Ambrose
Mark Magagna
Martin Mederly
Kasper Holm Christiansen
Renée-Claude Dostie
Jason Emery
Ulises Troyo
Ian Noble
Stephen Kan
Michael Datler
Kristan Stewart
Mitchell Ballew
Alexandra Jeschke
Todd Steen
Carrie Ho
Colton West
Robert Biskup
Iven Bryer
Simon Carter
Anthony Cacella
Declan Ryan
Lisa Disterheft
Anthony Mattke
Drew Guikema
Caitlin Krueger
Daniel Dahan
Tristan Giese
Claire Roberts
Alexandra Siticov
Jane Del Favero
Kevin Shen
David Tew
Jordana LaChance
Shaan Batra
Christopher Aronson
Cody Murphy
Al King
Armondo Mendez
Alexander Weiss
Susan Stevens
Justin McQuaig
Ben Paynter
Liam Williams
Christopher Hoeh
Barnaby Anderson
Renzo Fanchini
D. Ferrara
Jeanne Cadoret
Viktor Moyseyenko
Micah Crowsey
Shaun Read
Alexander Schäuble
Kathleen Mcgaw
Joshua Jordan

Daniel Sutherland
Elias Mastoras
Mark Brawley
Stef Van Rossem
Scott Lesser
Jared Roe
Gunnar Pálsson
Christopher Chiu
Brian Jost
Chad Schneider
Madelen Zackrisson
Jean-Paul Rohan
Marijn Hubert
Alessandro Bottin
Bradley Mclain
Harald Scheirich
Kevin Cheung
J Thorpe
Britta Olofsson
Craig Kimerer
Jack Harwood
Philippe gilbert
Ciaran Morris
Robin Kageyama
Sambo Virak Touch
John Nienart
Todd Knealing
Paul Rabin
Ibrahim Ali
Ted Snowdon
Jacob D. McAlpin
Cody Wright
Alek Bruckman
Boriss Potasevs
Sharon Fetter
Ken Kastel
Nicholas Lui Ming Yang
John A. Freeman
Tahj Merriman
Eric Greve
David Card
Ron Isdale
Joshua wang
Allen Arnold
Miguel Garcia
William Ritchie
Josh Dechant
Heather Worker
Eugene Leung
Tim Bland
Raymond Fu
David Goodwin
Dr Daniel König
Andreas Asselman
Rachit Modi
Nathan Peterson
Duncan Robsinon
Michael Page
Carsten Prag
Oliver Hoelzl
Andrea Barbarano
Pierre Zarebski
Judith Blanc
Knut Bjørnar Wålberg
Alex Hese
Ed Kowalczewski
Jonathan Hall
Jeffrey Chau
Matthew Morgan
Bernd Grobauer
Alexis Leto
Charles Clarke
Amy Oliver
Sebastian Vela
Alex Manzanares
Mark Dodwell
Pablo Collazo
Scavee Stephane
Tyler Smith
Michael Angarone
Karol Stola
Costa Nikou
Mariya Olshevska
Nate Oesch
Jason Green
Ty Hudecki
A Almeida
Sylvain Herlédan
Gregory Warren
Tony Hsieh
Denise Voskuil-Marre
Anne-Marie Held
Cameron Dow
Jens Cramer
David Figueroa
Ang Wei Jun
Andrew Liquigan
Seung Lee
Jennifer Macdonald
Caleb Barefoot
Jett Atwood
Brendan
William Fong
Vlad Spears
Erica Smith
Terkel Gjervig
Xavier Hicks
Michail Bobkov

Alvin Kiew
Joshua Copus
Lars Possberg
Elaine Amrein
Matthijs Schaap
Debra Keller
Jackson Chao
John Loner
Christopher Cordell
Raissa Shafer
Peter Ng
Hana Kucharová
Joao Gastao
Lewis Martin
George MacDonald
Mark Paul Corcoran
Drew Kochanowski
Michael Villarreal
Andrea Franceschini
Brian Behrman
Rusty McLellan
Jesse D Merriam
Andreas Hamm
Alex Greenwood
Erik Sommer
Brad Dancer
Edward Rivis
Collin Tullius
Lee Kenning
John Palmer
Albert van Breemen
Metro Sauper
Alun Davies-Baker
Benjamin San Souci
Remi Fayomi
Umberto Lenzi
John Domer
PR Taylor
Alec Yzaguirre Williams
Todd Smith
Matt Kuhn
Saw Kyaw Lwin
Jon Garner
Rainer Jenning
Elizabeth and Lauren Shoemaker
Jack D Johnson
Stephen Archibald
Fabrice Vicente
Marlon Rodrigues
Rex Dylan van Coller
Robert J McElfresh
David J Guttridge
Bill S. Johnson
Jeff Renfer
Wong Chun Yu
Brian Davidson
Alan Batson
Dr John Urquhart Ferguson
Lita Wilch
Omar Kooheji
Christina Huynh
Terje Hammer Meling
Samantha Netzley
Geeyung Li
Russell Corless
Michael Bagdasarian
Michelle Acosta
Steve Smith
Björn Lindholm
Alexandra Schmid
Jascha Buder
Kirsten Wilson
Jacob England
Tiphaine Surygala
Jonathan Cohen
Edward B Norris
Charles Sousa
Winston Berty
Stijn Christiaens
Stephen Vernor
Kira Parker
Carlos Costa
Kyle Clifton
Brian Dooley
Cezar Chan
Melissa frey
Simon Lam
Ralph Röschlaub
Luke Crook
Steve VanSickle
Brett Garner
Trey McLemore
Pernet Thibaut
Roland J. Veen
Daniel Martinez
Johan Ollars
Zachary Jesko
Jerry Matsko
Simon Frydrych
Alex Assouline
Kim Schumacher
Fiona Fallows
Gerardo Vázquez Rodriguez
Jorden Varjassy
Dirk Mahabir
Damon Kasberg
David Mills
Daniel Glymond

Johannes Dobler
Christian Muck
Jose Luis Saldana
Dejan Mauzer
Ryan Ludington
Jessica Melville
Jason Forbes
Jeremy Gaul
Adam Gibson
Nataya Castillo
Gary Stahlberg
Leon Higley
Patrick Heintschel
Joe Westrich
Justin Loudermilk
Anael Verdier
Sean Owen
Marc-André Laurence
Artana Decarlo
Iván Rodríguez Dorantes
Darren Cilia
Kelly McFadzen
Andrew Orford
Michael Stevens
Allen Murray
Catrin Hartleif
Teodorescu Simona
Conor Dalgarno
Andrew Negus
Matt Ellis
Kevin Connelly
Fiona McCarthy
Erik Tesson
Jalea Ward
Jeffrey Parkinson
K Shaw
Troy Peterson
Jill M Sheehan
Lucy Brown
Tamaryn Gallagher
Jing Danforth
Kathy Stewart
Jake Clark
Trevor Moffat
Christopher Northern
Martin Szalowski
Brad Elsmore
Jamie Thompson
Anthony Bamber
Kevan Chapman
Jaime Wojick
Matthew Flick
Mara Lonner
Melinda Stanley
Ryan Clark
John Redhead
Michael Beeson
Garry Fisher
John F Falconio
Renzo Castro Jurado
Brett Morrison
Rachel Quinney
Des Embrey
Garrett Lee Smith
Evan Chambers
Mitchell Yang
DH Vanderlaan
James Chaddick
Daniel Britt
Igor Fridland
Gary Nicol
Anton Abela
Karole Rispoli
David Magson
Douglas Patac
Gregory Freeman
Sacha Hussmann-Lapierre
Matthew DeHaan
Youri Vandevelde
John Wagenman
Ruben Valdez
David Masterson
Adrian Langford
Mike Lin
Brittany Sparks
Andrew Taylor
Takuma Kudo
Alexander Schöffmann
Rachel McCalpin
Sean Clark
David Quinn
Fabian Lempke
Otter Morryn
Joao Andrade Nascimento Vieira
Imago Edizioni De Lorenzo
Charles Swift
Chris McCall
Jimmy Vetayases
James Edward Johnson
Dominic Danson
Hugo Wetterberg
Jonathan Fabris
Philip Watson
Manfred Menhart
Shelby Goicochea
Alan Cohen
Mike Cadogan
Ralph Caspers
Brandon Draheim
Andrew Bingham

Joel Tan
Peter Rowley
Nicholas Hendley
Hoang D Nguyen
Luke Ahrndt
Debra Wilcox
Espen Flatmo
Bob Pinaha
Jonathan Tran
Alexandra Langthaler
Kelly Zhang
David Ruiz Mateo
Wendy L Schultz
Popko Nieboer
Christopher Golden
Stephen Morey
Elizabeth Freise
Rory McCabe
Dustin Manning
Christopher Shelley
Martin Crimes
Ian Graves
Matthew Yeary
Dennis Hughes
Jeffrey Rae
Gilles Bone
Kyla Palin
Joakim Mäkipää
Constanza Olmedo
Michael Rotbøll Sjøgreen
Travis Andrew Moore
Christoffer Danielsen Dyrøy
Tyler Beal
Michael K. Eagar
Larry Gilman
Judy Durkin
Richard Palmer
Daniel Perez
John Busby
Jerry Tan
Melinda Gramnaes
Kimberly O'Reilly
Paul Nash
Wiebe Walstra
Jonathan Hall
Sean McCallum
Tianchan Wang
Susy Hendy
Kai Laschki
Richard L Purvis
James Sims
Nadine Zacek
Anna Bataeva
Luca Galli
Bernd Amann
Chung Ting Wang
Lizzy Munday
David Evans
Peter Köhler
Chu Kin Fai
David Thomas
Abhilash Sarhadi
Bernard Nathalie
Franklin Onyekwum
Trond Davidsen
Michael Philo
Ben Villoresi
David Barker
Adam Cecchetti
Richard Halton
Joshua Corbin
Chris Armstrong
Søren Niedziella
Thomas Baul
Ralf Hilgenstock
Yuliya Artyukh
Timothy Batchelder
James Morrissey
C. Joshua Villines
Helen H Harrison
Andy Wood
Monica Lang
Zac
Mitul Thobhani
Mark Walker
René Schultz
Joern Welle
Tobias M. Christensen
Daniel Cao
Lorenz Aebi
Michael Sonson
Mathew Brown
Ron Wood
William Switzer
Marc Baruth
Sabrina Mueller
Troy Teague
Kalan C Dawson
Christopher Stevens
Samuel Clem
Steven Wotzka
Kristin Nybrott
Edwin Casey
Fedor Nikolett
Nicholas Stair
Stig Jørund B Arnesen
Eva Rothwangl
Martin Kuhn

Pietro Sala
Herbert Yun
Cindy Wong
Justin Allison
Rousseau
Lena-Marie Jakobsen
M. Dzaky Alfajr Dirantona
Alejandro Pueyo García
Colin J Corgan
Philip Sawdon
Matthew Vella
Bhavanjot Kang
Brett Reynolds
Jon Chui
Arturo Bejar
Hayder Al-Bayaty
Aaron Kim
Vivian Haviland
Nikita Burachenko
Dag Risnes
Brittany Wilbert
Randy Romero
Fredrik Barkels
Carlos Galindo Moya
Guy Farrow
Delphine Desrosiers
Anthony Messier
Shawn Fleming
Michael Mihalecz
Tim Jones
Gabriel Ruiu
Simone Birks
Paul Cervenka
Kevin Mitts
Nathan Pavey
Dennis Edward Fitzgerald
Dawn Oshima
Anders Thorvik
Dean McDonald
Roman Habrat
David Clapham
Paul Smith
RJ Brudenell
Rukesh Patel
Steven Fukuhara S
Jean-Luc Reyes
Tim Voves
Ana Fernandes
Wally
Käser Robin
Shivani Grover
Martin Spenner
Cang Ling Yee
Ben Watson
Brynne Williamson-Lawson
Maik Schulz
Hannah Brown
Josh Engwer
Robert S. Randolph
Harald Kirschner
Jenyi Wu
Richard Thorp
Brian Kang
Chi-Yeung Li
ICS Information Systems
Timo Savolainen
Matt Shores
Huezin Lim
Terry Jendersee
Jamie Harries
Justin Schield
Casey
Jere Aunola
Chad Eatman
Sameul Oosthuizen
Ralph Rutter
Louise Wilson
Richard Szeto
Tom Weir
Kareem Matariyeh
Alec Guilleminot
Mark Drespling
Marko Tatge
Kayur Patel
Marc Goldner
Morgan Stacy
Gert Thijs
Juhan Sonin
Stephen Dahlin
Scott Kelly
D.Walraad
Cullin Lassiter
Matt Higgins
Max Hime
Dr. Prach Kamlangsinserm
Billy Mizrahi
Ben Hogan
Trevor Rand
Dan Pusceddu
Kelly Van Campen
Danette Akiyama
Jessica K. Wong
Karuna Møller

Wiebke Walbaum
Joshua Tan Chee Yong
Alex Allievi
Colin Patrick Cross
Ryan Farmer
Malcolm Farm
Dean Klemick
Jason Waggoner
Melissa Brennan
Rainer Meissner
Marvin Clifford Haibach
Ivar Troost
Eusella Hodson-Whittle
David Klatte
Julian Horne
Marion Dengler
Adrian Matusek
Martin Maltzahn
Karl Werner Belowodski
Damiano Luciani
Cindy Déjardin
Theresa Bucsics
Graeme Monk
Peter Barrass
Tucker B Costello
Bernat Ferraguad Sanchis
Simon Moore
Sanford White
Francis Urszinger-Woon
Luke Potter
Joshua Coulter
Chang Su Ling
Valentin Torres
Michael Maurer
Michael Negron
Edwin Tse
Haya Al-Thani
Erik Olson
Jimmy Law
Olivier Martin
AJ Andino
Ashley Reeves
Christiaan Bouwman
Christian Widmer
Michal Szostak
Indijas Subasic
Danny
JD Stiebel
Joel D. Roettger
Sarah Hardie
Rodrigo Lamas
Christina Zimmerman
Daryl Bamforth
Calvin Winner Liemena
Sara K Tays
Ben Whately
Jerry Harris
Jay Lester
K S Robeson
Linda
7XMen & Company Ltd.
Todd Solberg
Armando
Anthony Butler
Myla Cyrino
Marksou
Thomas Kleinberger
Dre
Gagan Bhele
Dilara
Derek Watson
Jakyru
Ben
Frank Pizzuta
Marion Pellerin
Ben Smith
Pete Gutierrez
XIIINationGaming
Thomas Treptow
Lukasz Wieloch
June Wu
Snorre Nilssen Vestli
Richard Tawn
Craig Lawrie
S J Bennett
L Bulters
Max Eichman
Branton Davis
Sal Vador
Kerry Vaughan
Patrick Emling
Kim McAuliffe
Sean Clancy
Alex Graham
Russell Belfer
Thanit Thamsukati
Andy Dufresne